SENECA'S CHARAC'

Seneca's Characters addresses one of the most enduring and least theorised elements of literature: fictional character and its relationship to actual, human selfhood. Where does the boundary between character and person lie? While the characters we encounter in texts are obviously not 'real' people, they still possess person-like qualities that stimulate our attention and engagement. How is this relationship formulated in contexts of theatrical performance, where characters are set in motion by actual people, actual bodies and voices? This book addresses such questions by focusing on issues of coherence, imitation, appearance, and autonomous action. It argues for the plays' sophisticated treatment of character, their acknowledgement of its purely fictional ontology alongside deep – and often dark – appreciation of its quasi-human qualities. *Seneca's Characters* offers a fresh perspective on the playwright's powerful tragic aesthetics that will stimulate scholars and students alike.

ERICA M. BEXLEY is an Associate Professor of Classics at Durham University. She has published in *Classical Philology*, *The Classical Journal*, *Trends in Classics*, the *Cambridge Classical Journal*, and *Mnemosyne*. This is her first book.

CAMBRIDGE CLASSICAL STUDIES

General editors
J. P. T. CLACKSON, W. M. BEARD, G. BETEGH,
R. L. HUNTER, M. J. MILLETT, S. P. OAKLEY, R. G. OSBORNE,
C. VOUT, T. J. G. WHITMARSH

SENECA'S CHARACTERS

Fictional Identities and Implied Human Selves

ERICA M. BEXLEY
University of Durham

CAMBRIDGE
UNIVERSITY PRESS

University Printing House, Cambridge CB2 8BS, United Kingdom

One Liberty Plaza, 20th Floor, New York, NY 10006, USA

477 Williamstown Road, Port Melbourne, VIC 3207, Australia

314–321, 3rd Floor, Plot 3, Splendor Forum, Jasola District Centre, New Delhi – 110025, India

103 Penang Road, #05-06/07, Visioncrest Commercial, Singapore 238467

Cambridge University Press is part of the University of Cambridge.

It furthers the University's mission by disseminating knowledge in the pursuit of education, learning, and research at the highest international levels of excellence.

www.cambridge.org
Information on this title: www.cambridge.org/9781108477604
DOI: 10.1017/9781108770040

© Faculty of Classics, University of Cambridge 2022

This work is in copyright. It is subject to statutory exceptions and to the provisions of relevant licensing agreements; with the exception of the Creative Commons version the link for which is provided below, no reproduction of any part of this work may take place without the written permission of Cambridge University Press.

An online version of this work is published at doi.org/10.1017/9781108770040 under a Creative Commons Open Access license CC-BY-NC-ND 4.0 which permits re-use, distribution and reproduction in any medium for non-commercial purposes providing appropriate credit to the original work is given. You may not distribute derivative works without permission. To view a copy of this license, visit https://creativecommons.org/licenses/by-nc-nd/4.0

All versions of this work may contain content reproduced under license from third parties.

Permission to reproduce this third-party content must be obtained from these third-parties directly.

When citing this work, please include a reference to the DOI 10.1017/9781108770040

First published 2022

A catalogue record for this publication is available from the British Library.

Library of Congress Cataloging-in-Publication Data
NAMES: Bexley, Erica M., 1982– author.
TITLE: Seneca's characters : fictional identities and implied human selves / Erica M. Bexley.
DESCRIPTION: Cambridge, United Kingdom ; New York, NY : Cambridge University Press, 2022. | Series: Cambridge classical studies | Includes bibliographical references and index.
IDENTIFIERS: LCCN 2021037868 (print) | LCCN 2021037869 (ebook) | ISBN 9781108477604 (hardback) | ISBN 9781108725774 (paperback) | ISBN 9781108770040 (ebook)
SUBJECTS: LCSH: Seneca, Lucius Annaeus, approximately 4 B.C.-65 A.D. – Tragedies. | Seneca, Lucius Annaeus, approximately 4 B.C.-65 A.D. – Characters. | Characters and characteristics in literature. | Human behavior in literature. | BISAC: HISTORY / Ancient / General | LCGFT: Literary criticism.
CLASSIFICATION: LCC PA6686 .B49 2022 (print) | LCC PA6686 (ebook) | DDC 872/.01–dc23/eng/20211027
LC record available at https://lccn.loc.gov/2021037868
LC ebook record available at https://lccn.loc.gov/2021037869

ISBN 978-1-108-47760-4 Hardback
ISBN 978-1-108-72577-4 Paperback

Cambridge University Press has no responsibility for the persistence or accuracy of URLs for external or third-party internet websites referred to in this publication and does not guarantee that any content on such websites is, or will remain, accurate or appropriate.

For I., D., and M.

Because without the three of you, I would be so much less than myself

Je est un autre

(Arthur Rimbaud, *Lettres du Voyant*)

Father: I'm surprised at your incredulity. Perhaps you gentlemen are not used to seeing characters created by an author spring to life up here one after another. Perhaps because there is [*he points to the* Prompter's *box*] no script that contains us?

(Luigi Pirandello, *Six Characters in Search of an Author*)

CONTENTS

Acknowledgements		*page* viii
Introduction		1
1	Coherence	23
	1.1 *Medea*	28
	1.2 *Thyestes*	60
2	Exemplarity	99
	2.1 *Troades*	117
	Bridge: Seneca	144
	2.2 *Hercules*	153
3	Appearance	181
	3.1 *Phaedra*	183
	Bridge: Character Portraits	235
	3.2 *Oedipus*	243
4	Autonomy	263
	4.1 Freedom	265
	4.2 Revenge	292
	4.3 Suicide	329
	Afterword	347
Bibliography		350
Index of Passages Discussed		374
General Index		381

ACKNOWLEDGEMENTS

Writing this book has been a lesson in the value of getting things done earlier and faster, a lesson I have learned the hard way. Unlike many first monographs, mine did not begin life as a doctoral dissertation, but emerged gradually, as a shadowy prospect, during the time I spent at the Australian National University immediately post-PhD. There ensued a change of hemispheres and several institutions before I arrived and settled in Durham's Department of Classics and Ancient History. Before I could complete the typescript to my satisfaction, however, there also ensued a child (a most welcome joy) and a pandemic (not so welcome). Throughout all of this, my book project remained a constant, sometimes nagging, companion: when would it be finished? When could I remove it from my list of responsibilities and hand it over to the academic community at large? That I have, now, achieved this goal is an immeasurable relief.

Understandably, an enterprise as long-lived and much-travailed as this one accrues a lot of debts. The ideas contained within these pages have been aired, in various forms, to audiences at: Melbourne and Sydney Universities, the Australian National University, Cornell, Oxford, Edinburgh, Swansea, UWTSD Lampeter, the Cambridge Philological Society, the Cambridge A Caucus seminars, the University of Belgrade, St Andrews, and Durham. In every case I am grateful for having had the opportunity to present my research to such appreciative and helpful colleagues; I have benefitted from each and every one of these events. Special thanks are also due to three departments in particular: to the Cambridge Classics Faculty, for believing in me to the extent of giving me a job when I badly needed one (and for letting me sneak my monograph into their 'Classical Studies' series); to Swansea's Department of Classics, Ancient History and Egyptology for giving me my first ongoing position and for its warm, friendly

Acknowledgements

atmosphere in which my research flourished; and finally, to Durham's Department of Classics and Ancient History, for granting me, alongside stable employment, the stability of a home.

I have profited from conversations with colleagues and students at all levels, both formally and informally. Teaching the *Thyestes* at Cambridge and again at Swansea sharpened my insight into this tightest and darkest of Senecan dramas. Similarly, though perhaps less expected, my Advanced Latin classes at Durham, on Plautus and Terence, got me thinking about the quasi-comic aspects of Seneca's tragedies. Equally helpful were the conversations I enjoyed, and remarks, criticism, and encouragement I received from the following colleagues: George Boys-Stones, Barbara Graziosi, Kathryn Stevens, Ioannis Ziogas, Richard Hunter, Stephen Oakley, Emily Gowers, Fritz-Gregor Herrmann, Helen Slaney, Matthew Leigh, and Peter Davis. And, although it is not my doctoral dissertation, this book still bears the imprint of my formative years at Cornell; many and sincere thanks are due to the Cornell Classics department for accepting me, long ago, into its remarkable graduate programme, and to my supervisory committee – Mike Fontaine, Jeff Rusten, Charles Brittain, Fred Ahl – for pushing me to question the scholarly status quo and to think about Seneca in new ways. Fred Ahl and Mike Fontaine in particular have provided unstinting support in the form of academic insight, publishing opportunities, and career advice. Ample thanks must also be given to the two anonymous Cambridge University Press readers, whose suggestions greatly improved the book's argument and my sense of the project overall. I am grateful, too, to my CUP production team: my content manager, Nicola Maclean; production manager, Jayavel Radhakrishnan; and copy editor, Maria Whelan. Their help and care with the typescript has been immeasurable. Lastly, I must thank both Cambridge University Press and DeGruyter for permission to republish some material: parts of Chapter 1 have been adapted from my *CCJ* article, 'Recognition and the Character of Seneca's Medea'[1], while the last section of Chapter 3 has been

---

[1] Bexley, E. M. (2016) 'Recognition and the Character of Seneca's Medea' *CCJ* 62: 31–51.

Acknowledgements

adapted from my 'Doubtful Certainties: The Politics of Reading in Seneca's *Oedipus*'[2]. Reprinted with permission.

At the end of this long catalogue come my deepest, most personal expressions of gratitude. To Emily Gowers for supporting my research and my career before I was even aware of it, for calming my anxieties and providing kind advice, for being so reliable and so generous with her time. To my parents, who taught me the value of hard work and persistence, and who continued to believe in me even – especially! – when I was floundering. Finally, to my beautiful family: my husband, Ioannis, who encouraged this project from its slender beginnings all the way through to my final flurry of work under quarantine conditions, who listened patiently to my ideas, pushed me to argue them with more force, and put up with me on the many occasions when the project stalled or hit dead ends. He has been living with this book for as long as I have; I'm sure his relief at its publication equals if not exceeds my own. And to my little daughter, Daphne, who arrived during my drafting of the final chapter, and to Marcus, my even littler son, who burst onto the scene in time for copy editing and indices. Both have helped, in their own ways, with smiles that are utter sunshine.

---

[2] Bexley, E. M. (2016) 'Doubtful Certainties: The Politics of Reading in Seneca's *Oedipus*' in P. Mitsis and I. Ziogas (eds.) *Wordplay and Powerplay in Latin Poetry*. Berlin: 355–76.

INTRODUCTION

What is fictional character? Despite appearances, the question is not straightforward, and the longer one contemplates it, the more troublesome it becomes. Some answers provide superficial satisfaction: we may say that characters are 'beings in fictional worlds', or, 'representations of human agents'. But such explanations do little more than open windows onto a vast and enduring paradox, because actual human selfhood is not a fiction, while a character's approximation of it is not, strictly speaking, human. 'Fiction' and 'being' preclude each other, or at best, mingle like oil and water, because human lives are contingent and variable, while characters' lives are circumscribed by, and devised for, the plot and duration of the work to which they belong. However much they may seem to develop, they are never imbricated in a process of 'becoming'; they are always already absolute, perfected. A human may 'be', but a character simply 'is'.[1]

The core issue is ontology. While humans are mortal and have consciousness, are capable of self-directed action, corporeally real, and possess private intentional and emotional states – to name just a few features – characters are deathless, infinitely repeatable, ultimately incapable of self-determination, physically insubstantial, and lacking a conscious interior. Yet even these seemingly obvious distinctions become unsteady when subjected to further interrogation, because, in practice, actual human autonomy is not much less circumscribed than a character's;[2] because

---

[1] States (1985a) 87 describes characters as people 'with the slack of indeterminate being taken up'.
[2] Smith (2010) 238 cautions against too strict a division between characters' agency and people's, because while characters are bound by larger dramatic structures, 'persons possess (more or less) circumscribed autonomy, agency within limits. We are never wholly autonomous, and we tend to overrate the degree of our autonomy, and especially the autonomy of others.'

Introduction

our knowledge of each other's private consciousness and intentions is limited to their external manifestation; because characters in movies and plays *do* enjoy a degree of corporeal realness; and because many characters transcend their original fictional contexts to feature in subsequent, supplemental works, and to persist as powerful, changeable presences in their audiences' imaginations. Characters are not people, but their precise degree of non-humanness is difficult to ascertain.[3]

This book argues for a dual treatment of fictional characters, as imaginative fabrications and as human analogues.[4] While my immediate focus is Senecan tragedy (on which more anon), my approach to this material rests on the broader belief that all fictional beings comprise both textual and quasi-human aspects. They are formal products of language and structure and, simultaneously, person-like in their modes of existence; this binary is the source of their complexity and fascination, and disregarding half of it means failing to capture the full significance of characters as the most pervasive and enduring of fictional phenomena. Of course, they are at base textual entities, mirages fashioned entirely from language, marks on the page (χαρακτῆρες) that convey the impression of a personality.[5] Our knowledge of any given character is limited to what the author chooses to tell us. To lift a phrase from T. S. Eliot, it is not only Seneca's *dramatis personae* that have 'no "private life"',[6] but all fictional beings: they can never be extracted fully from their textual milieu; they lay no claim to an independent, personal mindset; they have no real psychological interior; we cannot follow them home, or backstage, or pursue them beyond the public boundaries of their narratives. In these terms, characters' humanness is an illusion that springs from the coincidence of language, plot structure, and repeated themes. They can be disassembled into these component parts, though most readers and viewers will resist doing so because of the powerful

---

[3] See Eder, Jannidis, and Schneider (2010) 6–17 for the major scholarly views of fictional ontology.
[4] The term 'human analogue' comes from Smith (1995).
[5] On χαρακτήρ's original meaning of 'stamp' or 'engraving', see Worman (2002) 17. On its evolution into contemporary English usage, Williams (2014) [1976] 230 provides a brief but erudite account.
[6] Eliot (1999) [1927] 70.

illusionary impulses governing their sympathetic enjoyment of the story.

But there is nothing trivial about this sympathetic involvement, for this is where the pendulum of fictional character swings towards the opposite pole, away from pure form and in the direction of mimesis. After all, most fictional people embody human capacities and attitudes to a greater or lesser degree. They speak, act, move, and think in identifiably human ways, albeit ensnared in the skein of representation. Characters are implied people; they are 'an intensified simplification of human nature',[7] and as such, they invite precisely the kinds of inferences that their fictional existence precludes. The illusion of their autonomy, say, or their emotional depth comes not just from the author's clever manipulation of literary conventions, but also from readers' willingness to imagine and engage with fictive *personae* as though they were real people. Characters are not independent beings, but they frequently take on 'lives of their own' in spin-off works, fan fiction, adaptations, impersonations, and even Wikipedia entries. They have no real psychological interior, but audiences will nevertheless form judgements – quite often conflicting judgements – about their implied personalities. We cannot follow them home, but we may be tempted to supplement their stories by extending them beyond the temporal or spatial bounds imposed by the work in question.[8] In extreme cases, characters may even become extensions of their authors: Jane Eyre blends into Charlotte Brontë, or, in the eyes of one Flavian playwright, Thyestes blends into Seneca.[9] An audience's sense of personal connection is a large part of what activates characters, what makes them memorable, potent, and at the same time, so challenging for literary critics to pin down.

---

[7] States (1985a) 91.
[8] Typically, this takes the form of unwarranted speculation about a character's motives, or equally unwarranted enquiry into the details of his or her 'life story'. Vermeule (2010) explores the phenomenon in broad terms. Garton (1972) 6 flags its occurrence in ancient thought, with reference to the kind of naïve speculation satirised in Juvenal *Sat.* 7.233–6.
[9] The playwright in question is the anonymous author of the *Octavia*, who clearly saw in Seneca's Thyestes (*Thy.* 421–90) a reflection of Seneca's own, ill-fated return from exile (*Oct.* 377–436). On the frequent conflation of Jane Eyre with her creator, Charlotte Brontë, see Hughes (2018).

Introduction

How Senecan drama negotiates this balance between characters as textual constructs and as implied humans is the subject of my present study. Primarily, I have formulated my arguments in response to the intertextual and metapoetic analysis that has dominated anglophone scholarship on Senecan tragedy for decades (and to a great extent, the entire field of Latin literature).[10] To be sure, this approach has produced many valuable insights and deserves praise for deepening our knowledge of Seneca's poetic texture, but its implicitly reflexive view of art does not do justice to the mimetic aspect of Senecan tragedy, its representation of extreme emotional states and formidable expressions of individual will. Granted, figures like Medea and Atreus are the compound products of earlier poetic traditions, and awareness of this background enhances their intellectual and aesthetic appeal, but their most immediate and – arguably – powerful effects stem from their monstrous embodiment of destructive human appetites, that is, from their mimesis of actual human traits, distilled to almost painful intensity and explored within the analogous landscape of fiction. Studying characters – as one of the most 'human' elements of this humanistic discipline – seemed to me the best way to supplement intertextual trends and, at the same time, to open new avenues of scholarly discussion.[11]

One could of course demur that Senecan scholarship also abounds in moral/psychological treatment of the tragedies' *dramatis personae*, chiefly as Stoic-inflected representations of the

---

[10] Major intertextual studies of Senecan tragedy include Schiesaro (2003) esp. 70–138; Littlewood (2004) 259–301; Seo (2013) 94–121; and Trinacty (2014), as well as (2016) and (2018). The collection of essays in Stöckinger, Winter, and Zanker (2017) relies on predominantly intertextual approaches. Senecan metapoetics and self-reflexivity are often construed more narrowly as metatheatre, which is likewise a major trend in scholarship on the plays. Principal studies include Boyle (1997) 112–37; Schiesaro (2003); Erasmo (2004) 122–39; Littlewood (2004) 172–285; Kirichenko (2013) 17–165.

[11] Avenues that have existed for some time in scholarship on Greek tragedy, as witnessed by the debate over formalist/structuralist versus humanist treatments of character, the former side championed by Gould (1978) and Goldhill (1990), and the latter by Easterling (1973) and (1977), though her later work (1990) is more sympathetic to the anti-humanist standpoint. This particular manifestation of a long-standing issue originates with Jones (1962) 11–62, who cautions against applying anachronistic notions of individuality and inwardly realised consciousness to the *dramatis personae* of the classical Athenian stage. See Seidensticker (2008) 333–45 for a summary of both sides.

passions.[12] This is absolutely true, and for such studies, the characters' quasi-humanity is a pre-requisite assumption for their conduct being measured against Stoic ethics. But this approach is likewise limited, in some instances because it does not sufficiently accommodate characters' fictional qualities[13] and in others, simply because it does not acknowledge its fundamental view of characters as human analogues. The result is a lopsided assessment of Senecan drama and the erection of a hermeneutical hierarchy in which Seneca's prose works (non-fictional and therefore belonging to the 'real world') must be used to elucidate his dramatic compositions (fictional and therefore parasitic upon the 'real world').[14] My investigation, by contrast, envisages a dialogue between the literary and philosophical components of Seneca's oeuvre, a dialogue in which the tragedies highlight ideas and problems latent in the Stoic writings, not just vice versa.[15] A crucial, albeit secondary, consequence of my combining characters' fictional and quasi-human aspects is a contribution to the ongoing project of 'seeing Seneca whole': this approach is a vital means of bridging the moral and poetic works, of uncovering and testing their points of intersection.[16]

Given the nature of my aims, I do not pursue a purely formal study of characterisation in Senecan tragedy. This is not about Seneca's 'poetics' or 'rhetoric' of character, although I do consider his techniques of construction when and as the occasion demands. Instead, I focus on how Seneca's characters define themselves (and less often, each other), and how Seneca invites audiences to perceive his *dramatis personae* either as fictional constructs or as implied human personalities or, most often, both at once.

[12] An approach with a long history, and more enduringly popular than intertextual analysis. For anglophone scholarship, see in particular Marti (1945); Poe (1969); Pratt (1983); Gill (1987) and (2006) 421–34; Nussbaum (1994) 439–83. German scholarly treatment of this issue is by far the most prolific; a representative sample includes Gigon (1938); Egermann (1972) [1940]; Knoche (1972) [1941]; Lefèvre (1972) [1969] and (1985).
[13] Thus, for instance, the work of Marti (1945) and Pratt (1983).
[14] Schiesaro (2009) 222 frames this hierarchy in terms of 'rational' versus 'irrational', but the effect is the same.
[15] An approach pioneered by Braden (1985) 5–62 and elaborated more recently by Bartsch (2006) 255–81 and Star (2012) 23–83.
[16] The main volume is Volk and Williams (2006), though monographs such as Littlewood (2004) and Staley (2010) also make considerable efforts to combine Seneca's tragic and philosophical material.

Introduction

I concentrate on those elements of identity that permit maximum contact between the categories of 'character' and 'person', which in the case of Senecan tragedy are: behavioural coherence and self-sameness (Chapter 1); role models and imitative selfhood (Chapter 2); physical appearance (Chapter 3); and the pursuit of autonomy (Chapter 4). Discussion pivots around the term 'identity', as a neutral word indicative of human traits but equally applicable to fictional figures, and largely unencumbered by the semantic baggage of terms such as 'personality' and 'selfhood',[17] though I do use these throughout, as rough synonyms rather than distinct categories, whenever variation is required.

This issue of terminology and its attendant intellectual categories raises additional questions of how, or even whether, Seneca himself defines 'character', and whether he distinguishes between its human and fictional manifestations. The latter question is, I hope, answered over the course of this study, as I demonstrate how Seneca judges and fashions characters on the model of human beings and – crucially – vice versa, how he defines human selfhood in aesthetic and representational terms. The former question also receives some treatment, chiefly in Chapter 1, where I explore Stoic theories of *persona* and their bearing on normative behaviour versus individuality, subsidiary to my main point about coherence and self-sameness. Usefully, this Stoic concept of *persona* also encompasses issues of essential versus constructed/acquired character traits, for it undertakes to match innate, largely typified, personal qualities with their appropriate social expression; ideally, one builds upon what one is born with. I hasten to add, though, that this dynamic of individuality and normativity, essentialism and constructedness, is not solely the province of Stoic *persona* theory; rather, it underpins Roman thinking about exemplarity, which I chart in Chapter 2, and Seneca's quasi-physiognomic, quasi-Stoic treatment of body language, addressed in Chapter 3. In

---

[17] For definitions of 'personality', 'self', and 'personhood', and their relative applicability to ancient literature, Gill (1996) 1–18 is indispensable. Although I do not fully concur with his 'object-participant' model, at least not for Seneca, I do take his views on board, implicitly, in trying not to impose anachronistic concepts on Seneca's notion of human identity. The topic of selfhood in Seneca came to prominence with Foucault (1986) 39–68 and is now the subject of a major collection of essays in Bartsch and Wray (2009).

sum, this study of Senecan tragedy is not about deriving strict classifications of 'character' and 'person' from his philosophical works and applying them to the plays (aside from the hermeneutical problems flagged above, such explicit classifications are thin on the ground, which could lead to the erroneous conclusion that Seneca simply wasn't interested in such topics). Instead, I have set out to uncover where and with what effect Seneca allows these qualities to blend, and how their definition emerges from the evidence rather than being imposed upon it.

This approach has necessitated my focusing on certain Senecan plays at the expense of others. While I cover in depth *Medea*, *Thyestes*, *Troades*, *Hercules*, *Phaedra* and *Oedipus*, I leave *Phoenissae* and *Agamemnon* relatively untouched. My reason for doing so is not their lack of fit with the project. Quite the opposite: both plays' family entanglements can be approached in terms of genealogical exemplarity (Chapter 2), while the *Agamemnon* also fits within Chapter 4's discussion of revenge. Their omission from this study is meant purely to avoid unnecessary repetition, but I also hope that they will prove fruitful ground for other scholars. Another – perhaps less fortunate – result of my approach to Senecan tragedy is its minimisation of the plays' choral passages. Despite the odes' undeniable relevance to the tragedies' thematic texture,[18] they elucidate character only in peripheral ways, while the chorus itself claims – at best – a highly circumscribed identity, hence its attendant relegation to the margins of my discussion. As with *Phoenissae* and *Agamemnon*, this omission will, I hope, be supplemented by future scholarship.

A final caveat about the aims of this book: it does not set out to rehabilitate Seneca's characters as complex or 'rounded' representations of human uniqueness.[19] The figures in these tragedies have often been dismissed as one-dimensional, rhetorical, or unrealistic – in sum, the stunted creations of Seneca's own, presumably, stunted talent for drama. August Wilhelm von Schlegel famously called them 'neither ideal nor real people, rather gigantic, shapeless marionettes, set in motion now on the

---

[18] Amply demonstrated by Davis (1989) and (1993).
[19] The concept of the 'rounded' character comes from Forster (1927) 43–64. Seo (2013) 5–6 critiques and cautions against its application to fictional beings in Latin literature.

string of unnatural heroism, now on one of equally unnatural passion'.[20] T. S. Eliot remarked, 'Seneca's characters all seem to speak with the same voice, and at the top of it; they recite in turn.'[21] More sympathetic critics likewise acknowledge that mannerism hampers these characters' emotional or personal depth: they 'bounce off each other like billiard balls', declares Gordon Braden; Charles Segal asserts 'Seneca's artificial style makes the problem of the credibility and intelligibility of his characters particularly acute.'[22] All of these scholars make a valid point: Seneca's *dramatis personae* do not exhibit the *vraisemblance* prized by writers of the nineteenth and early-twentieth centuries, nor do they share the relative complexity, sophistication, and sensitivity displayed by figures in Greek tragedy. A few critics, with Anthony Boyle in the vanguard, have set out to refute, or at very least readjust, these propositions by claiming that Seneca's characters do in fact possess psychologies of remarkable depth and intricacy.[23] Such refutation is, however, unwarranted, not just because the psychology of Seneca's characters is more stylised than individual, but also because this kind of argument tries to rectify a defect by denying it altogether rather than claiming it as a virtue. Yes, Seneca's characters have a somewhat monodimensional timbre, but that is part of their compelling dramatic power. An emotionally sophisticated Atreus would not be half as absorbing as the single-minded, morally myopic tyrant whom Seneca brings to the stage. If anything, this study celebrates rather than relegates the monotonous intensity of Seneca's tragic characters.

---

[20] Schlegel (1809) reprinted in Lefèvre 1972, 14: 'Ihre Personen sind weder Ideale noch wirkliche Menschen, sondern riesenhafte unförmliche Marionetten, die bald am Draht eines unnatürlichen Heroismus, bald an dem einer ebenso unnatürlichen ... Leidenschaft in Bewegung gesetzt werden.'
[21] Eliot (1999) [1927] 68.
[22] Braden (1970) 19, and Segal (1986) 14. Though dated, Garton (1959) 1–3 remains a useful account of the critical vicissitudes that have beset Seneca's *dramatis personae* as the result of evolving scholarly paradigms.
[23] See in particular Boyle (1997) 15–31. Segal (1986) similarly perceives great psychological depth emerging from Seneca's rhetorical style. Arguments about the characters' psychological *vraisemblance* surface every now and again in Senecan scholarship: their first major articulation in the twentieth century is Herrmann (1924) 488–92.

Introduction

Theories of Character

The division I have outlined between character as a textual construct and as an implied human is replicated in the scholarship on character as well, most of which divides into two camps: those who treat character as a product of language and structure, and those who view fictional people as mimetic of actual ones.[24] Brief review of these theoretical approaches is necessary here, partly in order to situate my own undertaking within this scholarly landscape and to bring more of this particular theoretical discussion into the field of Classics (where it has been largely overlooked), and partly to highlight character's remarkable neglect in twentieth- and early twenty-first-century literary theory. That character is at once the most prominent and the least theorised element of literature is a well-acknowledged fact. Writing in 1978, Seymour Chatman noted with dismay 'how little has been said about the theory of character in literary history and criticism'.[25] The situation has hardly changed in the intervening forty years. In 2003, Alex Woloch called character 'so important to narrative praxis but ever more imperilled within literary theory'[26] and in 2014, John Frow described it as 'this most inadequately theorised of literary concepts'.[27] Such a glaring gap in scholarship lends particular urgency to my present project.

The main reason for this neglect has been the dominance of formalist, structuralist, and post-structuralist views, all of which share in a broad ideology of 'decentring' the individual.[28] Adherents of these schools eschew notions of the discrete, bounded, autonomous *ego* in favour of inter- or impersonal forces such as

---

[24] Woloch (2003) 14–18.
[25] Chatman (1978) 107.
[26] Woloch (2003) 14.
[27] Frow (2014) vi, written in echo of Frow (1986) 227: 'the concept of character is perhaps the most problematic and the most undertheorised of the basic categories of narrative theory'. Similar protests have been voiced by Culler (1975) 230, 'character is the major aspect of the novel to which structuralism has paid least attention and been least successful in treating'; Hochman (1985) 13, 'Character has not fared well in our century'; and Rimmon-Kenan (2002) 31, 'the elaboration of a systematic, non-reductive, but also non-impressionistic theory of character remains one of the challenges poetics has not yet met'. Fowler (2003) 3, and Eder, Jannidis, and Schneider (2010) 3–4 similarly acknowledge character's neglect in twentieth-century literary theory.
[28] Culler (1975) 230; Rimmon-Kenan (2002) 31–3.

language, discourse, power, and cultural codes. Identity, on this model, comes to be seen as fluid or fragmented, always incomplete and always eluding final definition. Concepts of stable or unified personality, on the other hand, are treated as the illusory, sometimes even regrettable, outcomes of oppressive cultural norms and dominant knowledge systems. While it is understandable and even laudable that such a view dismisses the nineteenth-century ideal of realist, individualised characters capable of transcending their given narratives, still its fondness for abstract models of identity and for downplaying human agency has stark consequences for the discussion and appreciation of fictional character.[29] When people themselves are regarded as constantly shifting products of cultural codes, character, too, loses its singularity and becomes merely another interchangeable element of literary (or dramatic/cinematic) conventions. The fragmented person is reflected in fragmented fictional beings. Thus, Hélène Cixous protests that, 'the ideology underlying [the] fetishisation of 'character' is that of an 'I' who is a *whole* subject ... conscious, knowable', whereas the actual individual is 'always more than one, diverse, capable of being all those it will at one time be, a group acting together'.[30]

Consequent to their vision of dispersed subjectivity, twentieth-century theorists concentrate on the technical and compositional elements of fictional character: lexis, signification, action, plot structure. Such components have the attraction of seeming objectively quantifiable,[31] and also of subsuming characters' supposedly personal attributes into the practical service of narrative. The character, like the individual, dissolves into systems of signification and spheres of action, and as such, has no more claim on the critic's, or audience's attention than any other conventional element of fiction; hence its critical neglect. The most extreme versions

---

[29] Consequences outlined convincingly by Smith (1995) 17–35.
[30] Cixous (1974) 385 and 387.
[31] Besides being a central – albeit often unstated – aim of formalist, structuralist, and post-structuralist schools, the desire to discuss literature in objective, 'scientific' terms also motivated adherents of New Criticism, who similarly preferred studying form over character. States (1992) 4 sums up the problem in general: 'Clearly it is difficult to be scientific, or even analytical, about character, and one suspects that the interest in plot and narrative over character in recent theory has arisen because events are more or less hard and indisputable 'facts'. It is impossible to say exactly why Hamlet slays Polonius, but no one doubts that he did.'

Introduction

of this reaction against character's implied individualism go as far as dispensing with personal pronouns on the basis that they ascribe an erroneous impression of human coherence; characters are 'it'.[32]

This broad trend towards abstraction originates with the Russian formalists, and in particular, with the work of Boris Tomashevsky and of Vladimir Propp. For Tomashevsky, fictional characters were 'sorts of living supports for the text's various motifs'.[33] A story's protagonist, Tomashevsky maintained, was necessary to the tale only as a compositional means of unifying the work's central themes and of providing 'personified motivation' for the connections between them.[34] Propp, too, subordinated characters to the demands of narrative in his taxonomic study of Russian folklore, which classified these traditional stories according to thirty-one categories of plot structure and seven standard roles.[35] Though Propp's 1928 monograph, *Morphology of the Russian Folktale*, was more a work of cultural anthropology than a literary manifesto, it went on to exert tremendous influence over critical theories of literature in the mid-twentieth century, in France above all.

The intellectual offspring of Russian formalism was French structuralism. Algirdas Greimas adopted Propp's taxonomy of roles as a universal model for fictional character and used it to develop his own 'actantial' theory of narrative, which correlated plot structure to the grammatical rules governing sentences.[36] Greimas was more extreme than either Propp or Tomashevsky in bleaching all the personal colour from fictional *personae*: characters, on his model, were *actants* and *acteurs* that occupied narrative positions equivalent to syntactic elements such as 'subject'

[32] To highlight the depersonalising effect of structuralist criticism on literary character, Weisenheimer (1979) 187 attempts just such an analysis of Jane Austen's Emma: 'Emma Woodhouse is not a woman nor need be described as if it were.'
[33] Tomashevsky in Todorov (1966) 293: 'sortes de supports vivants pour les différents motifs'. On the formalist origins of twentieth-century character criticism, see Woloch (2003) 15–16.
[34] Tomashevsky in Todorov (1966) 293.
[35] Propp's seven roles are as follows: the hero; the false hero; the villain; the helper; the donor; the dispatcher; the sought-for person and her father. Culler (1975) 232–3 provides a succinct explanation of Propp's theory and influence.
[36] On Greimas, see Culler (1975) 233–5; Hochman (1985) 23–4; Rimmon-Kenan (2002) 36–7.

Introduction

and 'object'. These positions were not the exclusive preserve of characters, either: inanimate objects and abstract concepts could fulfil them equally well. Thus, the fictional *persona* became a noun of which something could be predicated.[37]

Classifying characters according to narrative function, or grouping them into typologies, is by no means a mistaken enterprise, and depending on the literary genre involved, this model may actually be the most effective. A telling example is Northrop Frye's codification of comic characters, which remains even now a valuable framework for analysing the stock roles and stock scenarios of *comoedia palliata*.[38] But if we apply this theory to, say, the psychologically intricate characters that populate the Victorian novel, then we will inevitably be left with a lot of residue, with details that seem superfluous to the plot and to the character's immediate function within it. Faced with this obvious gap in structuralist theory, Roland Barthes proposed a more nuanced, semiotic approach to character, which argued for the reader's role in employing established cultural and literary codes to decipher the connotations of a given character's traits and from there, to assemble them into the mirage of a personality.[39] Essentially thematic in outlook, this theory defines character as the meeting point of normative, culturally embedded assumptions about behaviour and appearance, stabilised by the application of a proper name.[40] These connotations are never absolute, either, and their shifting, open-ended nature means that readers must engage constantly in the process of formulating characters from the text's many signifiers. Thus, while Barthes allows for some discussion of characters' implied human traits, he still presents those traits – and the individuality and agency they imply – as

---

[37] Especially in the work of Todorov, who follows Greimas' model.
[38] Frye (1990) [1957] esp. 43–51. Segal (1987) applies Frye's framework to Plautine comedy with excellent results. This kind of typological approach to character functions most effectively in the genres of comedy and romance, where characters, in the words of Hochman (1985) 77, 'are often more coherent, monolithic and stable ... than the more self-contained and less stylised characters of the novel and of tragedy'.
[39] Barthes (1974). Goldhill (1990) 111–14 stresses the benefits of Barthes' theory in contrast to purely formalist analyses of character.
[40] Barthes (1974) 67. On the proper name's pivotal ability to generate the illusion of fictional personhood, see also Docherty (1983) 43–86.

Introduction

incidental outcomes of supra-personal forces. Here, too, both character and person remain decentred.

These modernist and postmodernist approaches to character have undeniable strengths. They are entirely justified, for instance, in their desire to avoid subjective, impressionistic evaluations of fictional beings, and in their eschewal of abstract psychologising. However, they also exhibit two major weaknesses. First, in their push to reject character's referential qualities (that is, its potential, analogic relationship to something outside the text), many of these theories merely reframe rather than eradicate the role of mimesis, thus unwittingly confirming its importance.[41] If – to furnish a reductive example – characters reflect the disintegration of the human subject, then their dissolution into textual components remains a mimetic event, a mirroring of the world as writers, audience, and critics are presumed to experience it. Such logical inconsistency passes largely unrecognised by many postmodern theorists and cautions against their wholesale renunciation of older, humanist analyses of character, which, despite their many faults (explored below), were at least right in assuming a basic level of analogy between the character and the actual human agent.[42]

The second weakness is the modernist/postmodernist rejection of character's saliency. If characters are merely plot devices, or configurations of language, or the meeting points of connotative descriptions, then they cannot, at base, be said to differ from the fictional representation of other objects and actions. An approach that treats characters as systems of signification puts them on practically the same symbolic level as anything else – a car, a street, a tree. In the words of Joel Weisenheimer: 'Under the aegis of semiotic criticism, characters lose their privilege, their central status, and their definition.'[43] This is a critical problem that

---

[41] As Smith (1995) 31–5 rightly observes.
[42] Thus Smith (1995) 35: 'The challenge would be to devise a concept of character which is not an analogue to the person; then we might have a truly non-mimetic theory of character. But to do so would so strongly violate our most basic assumptions about what the notion of character is, and what critical function it performs, that it would not be recognisable as a concept of character.'
[43] Weisenheimer (1979) 195. Barthes (1974) 178 warns against this scholarly dissolution of character: 'from a critical point of view ... it is as wrong to suppress character as it is to take him off the page and turn him into a psychological character (endowed with possible motives): *the character and the discourse are each other's accomplices*'. But

13

Introduction

Murray Smith tackles and, to my mind, resolves in a particularly convincing manner, by proposing that characters constitute audiences' major point of entry into fictional worlds, and that what audiences recognise in characters, at the barest level, is an analogue of human agency.[44] Thus, narrative actions gain meaning *because* we imbue them with intent, and events or bodily states are significant *for* the emotions assumed to underpin them. Fictional works cannot seem to avoid stimulating such inferences, even when they portray characters as constellations of semiotic data.[45] Of course, one does not have to accept Smith's view, but any treatment of character should accommodate its ongoing and pervasive presence in fiction, a presence that would, surely, be much less enduring if it claimed no more significance than any other fictional component.

Any attempt to resurrect scholarly inquiry into literary character is therefore faced with a need to reformulate or to break away from the critical paradigms that have endured for most of the twentieth century. Since prevailing approaches have, by and large, impoverished academic debates about literary character, they really should be placed aside in favour of new methods. At the same time, such an inquiry must also avoid the ludicrous excesses indulged by earlier eras of character criticism and against which twentieth-century theorists reacted. For if it is insufficient to regard character merely as a textual 'space where forces and events meet',[46] it is equally insufficient to treat fictional beings independently of their narratives, as though they possess a personal past and a private

---

Barthes himself engages in at least a mild form of such suppression by making character the product of discourse.

[44] Smith (1995) 17–20.
[45] Nabokov's *Real Life of Sebastian Knight* is a good example. Though Sebastian is explicitly presented as a (re)construction of textual information, V.'s – and by extension, the reader's – interest in reconstructing him is powered by the assumption that Sebastian must have had some identifiable wholeness and agency even if it cannot, now, be recovered. Nabokov's Sebastian is striking and unsettling precisely *because* the character upsets assumed categories of behavioural integrity and knowability; if these categories were only a mirage – as some post-structuralist arguments imply – then there would be nothing particularly unusual about Sebastian's portrayal. Smith (1995) 26–7 makes a similar point about the defamiliarising use of two actors in Buñuel's *That Obscure Object of Desire*.
[46] Culler (1975) 230.

Introduction

psychology. Characters are not just text, but they are not real people, either. This deeply mistaken inclination to treat characters as independent entities wholly extractable from their texts informed almost all literary criticism prior to the twentieth century. It peaked in the eighteenth and nineteenth centuries, when critics undertook with great enthusiasm to assemble moral portraits of fictional figures, assessing them in the same way one might inquire into the behaviour of a friend or acquaintance. Maurice Morgann's 1777 *Essay on the Dramatic Character of Falstaff*, for example, contemplates how this character's personal history contributes to his morality; a century later, Mary Cowden Clark produced a book devoted to speculating about the childhoods of Shakespeare's heroines. The chief weaknesses of such enquiries are their over-reliance on subjective judgements and unquantifiable material; their unwillingness to acknowledge the cultural specificity of both identity and characterisation; and their all-too-easy movement beyond the information provided by the text. While none of these critics ever actually argued for characters' *reality*, their approach over-emphasised the character–person analogy, to the point where it disregarded or minimised the role played in character formation by formal and structural requirements, by language and culture, genre, and convention. Such faults have, understandably, received a lot of criticism – perhaps most famously in Lionel Knights' 1933 polemic, 'How Many Children Had Lady Macbeth?' – and no serious literary scholar would now presume to make unsubstantiated personal inferences about fictional beings. But the fact that many *consumers* of fiction still make such inferences, and that fiction itself invites them, means that the critic must account for their possibility, namely by acknowledging that characters are constructed according to a human model, albeit one subject to change and revision depending on culture and era.

We have come a long way from Seneca, but this overview forms a crucial background to my methodological aims. My approach in this study proposes to bridge, by combining, the 'antinomies of theory' outlined above.[47] In other words I recognise fictional figures

---

[47] The phrase comes from Woloch (2003) 14.

Introduction

both as textual entities *and* as implied human beings. This practice concurs with a modest yet growing trend in character criticism, which identifies fictional beings as human analogues shaped, confined, and made intelligible by the conventions of narrative and genre: Baruch Hochman (1985), James Phelan (1989), Murray Smith (1995), Alex Woloch (2003) and John Frow (2014) have all, in their various ways, contributed to my developing a satisfactory theoretical framework for discussion of Seneca's *dramatis personae*. I follow Woloch particularly, in maintaining that fictional characters exist in two simultaneous modes, the representational/mimetic and the structural/textual, and that the chief issue in their analysis is not 'either/or' but how to capture the dialogue between them.[48] How does characters' fictionality give way to humanness and vice versa? Moreover, as intimated above, I make this choice not for the bland purpose of selecting a third way between two polarities, but because I feel it corresponds to a balance (and tension) within fictional character itself.

For Seneca's *dramatis personae*, this means that their embeddedness within poetic and dramatic traditions, their metatheatrical self-consciousness, the semiology of their bodies, their (openly acknowledged) subordination to the demands of narrative and genre are all, always in dialogue with their implied possession of behaviour traits and intentional states, their implied capacity for perceptual activity and self-impelled action. When Medea proclaims, 'now I am Medea' (*Medea nunc sum*, *Med.* 910), she identifies not only her fulfilment of a pre-scripted dramatic role and attainment of an anticipated fictional ontology, but also her quasi-human ability to fashion her own identity, make and implement decisions about her future, and render herself recognisable to others. The proclamation celebrates her fictional agency as much as it denies it.

If there is an elephant in this room it is the question of what actually constitutes a human. If characters are, as I argue, analogues of human agency, how exactly can this sense of a 'person' be defined without recourse to untenable claims about 'universal human nature'?[49] One

---

[48] Woloch (2003) 17.
[49] Thus Phelan (1989) 11: 'talk about characters as plausible and possible persons presupposes that we know what a person is. But the nature of the human subject is of course

Introduction

solution is Smith's 'person schema', a heuristic set of characteristics derived from anthropology and open to culturally specific accretions when/as needed; the schema comprises seven components: a discrete human body; perceptual activity; intentional states; emotions; the ability to use/understand natural language; the capacity for self-directed action and self-interpretation; the potential for traits.[50] Smith stresses that these basic requirements are merely a conceptual framework employed to interpret fictional situations by audiences and critics alike; they are by no means a totality, but a foundation that can be adjusted to meet the specific demands of any given context. To some extent, my study of Seneca employs these characteristics as a measure of 'humanness', but in fuller attempt to avoid unwarranted generalisations, I relate the 'humanness' of Seneca's characters primarily to the models of behaviour found in Seneca's own work, and in his contemporary Roman culture. At base, I assess Seneca as much as possible on his own terms.

Identities on Stage

Although in almost all respects diverse and conflicting, the theories discussed in the preceding section have one thing in common: they were developed for and pertain to narrative literature, principally the novel. The question of character has received more attention in this field than in any other, and with good reason, because the novel's form combined with the relative intimacy of its delivery grants authors more scope in the creation of implied human complexity. Even in Classics, where narrative literature is less prevalent than its modern counterpart, the recent (and exciting) upsurge of interest in literary character clusters around either the ancient novel (e.g. De Temmerman 2014) or Homeric epic (e.g. Kozak 2016), a genre that has long proved itself amenable to narratological analysis.[51]

---

a highly contested issue among contemporary thinkers.' See also Goldhill (1990) 100–5 on the dangers of character criticism disregarding cultural embeddedness.
[50] Smith (1995) 21.
[51] De Temmerman (2014) employs an explicitly narratological approach. Kozak (2016) is more implicit, examining the *Iliad* as a 'serial narrative' that comprises episodes, arcs, and development on the analogy of TV serials.

Introduction

Drama, on the other hand, is a different beast and requires a slightly different approach. Notably, the character–person dynamic assumes new urgency when transferred to the stage, where the fictional presence of *dramatis personae* is also a tangible presence, generated by the real voices, bodies, and *being* of actors. If a character in a novel or a long narrative poem demonstrates mimetic affinities with human behaviour, or thoughts, or appearance, those affinities only grow tighter and more complex in the context of the theatre. Naturally, most audience members receive plays with the same kind of 'double vision' they exercise for all works of fiction; they accept the illusion without surrendering to it entirely. Medea is not *really* killing her children; a person embodying Iago is only *pretending* to plot Othello's downfall. But stories of mistaken audience responses always circulate – from the anecdote about pregnant women suffering miscarriages at the sight of Aeschylus' Furies (*Vita* 9) to the tale of a Canadian prairie farmer shooting Iago at the tragedy's climax[52] – and they raise a wry smile not just at individual gullibility, but at the ontological confusion underpinning all theatrical events. Theatre is both real and not real; the actor both is and is not who he/she purports to be.[53] Michael Goldman sums up the problem in particularly perceptive terms:[54]

> The type of self to which we pay most attention in the theatre – the 'character' presented by the actor – could be said to have unique ontological status. It is not the personal self of the actor, but the self he creates by acting. And in that creation the gap between self and deed seems curiously to vanish. A character in the theatre, the created self, is identical with the actor's deed.

A dramatic character's whole existence depends upon action, not only in the sense that an unfolding of events reveals a character's nature (which happens in novels as well) but also in the more fundamental sense that drama implies praxis. Stage characters owe their being to the performance of deeds, whether substantial, as in a sword fight, or unobtrusive, even static, as in sitting on a chair.

---

[52] Reported in Garton (1972) 27.
[53] For further discussion of this phenomenon, see Worthen (1984) 3 and Bexley (2017) 173.
[54] Goldman (1985) 10.

Introduction

The performer's movement, gestures, expressions, and voice are the chief means by which audiences translate him or her into a *dramatis persona*, mainly by inferring an underlying identity that unifies and gives meaning to these snapshots of behaviour. Thus, a lot of activity pursued on stage is simultaneously the character's and the actor's. Although there is an obvious gulf between killing and pretending to kill, in the case of simpler actions such as standing, walking, talking, these lines converge entirely: the character and the person behind the character are doing exactly the same thing. Hence character assumes an additional layer of human resemblance.[55]

It could be argued that this performative aspect of drama is difficult to measure and consequently too speculative to warrant inclusion in my study of dramatic character. Certainly, we cannot ascertain how specific audiences feel or felt about the 'reality' of the *personae* enacted before them, nor should we assume that an audience reacts as a coherent unit. The problem grows particularly acute in the case of Senecan tragedy, because there is no firm evidence that these plays were ever staged during Seneca's lifetime, and because scholars disagree over whether he intended them for performance, recitation, excerpting, or any combination of the three.[56] If Seneca only ever meant his tragedies to be read, then why concern ourselves with performance criticism as opposed to literary interpretation? I do not wish to revisit this longstanding debate here, and I am, in any case, agnostic on the question of staging: Seneca's plays *can* be performed (and are,

---

[55] Storm (2016) 2. Similarly, Bordwell, cited in Eder, Jannidis, and Schneider (2010) 23: 'It is particularly in the cinema that a character has 'a palpable autonomy, that seems to make action subordinate to his/her prior existence', and a similar statement can of course be made for theatre.'

[56] Such a long-lived debate has spawned many variations, of which I summarise merely the main, most influential examples. In favour of recitation: Boissier (1861); Eliot (1999) [1927]; Beare (1945); Zwierlein (1966); Fantham (1982); Goldberg (1996) and (2000); Mayer (2002). In favour of performance: Herrmann (1924); Bieber (1954); Fortey and Glucker (1975); Braun (1982); Sutton (1986); Boyle (1997); Davis (2003); Kohn (2013). A significant subdivision of the 'performance' approach is the idea that Seneca's plays were designed to fit – or to be adapted to – the genre of pantomime dance: see Zimmerman (1990); Zanobi (2008) and (2014); and Slaney (2013). On scholars' tendency to overestimate the dichotomy between categories of 'performance' and 'recitation', see Harrison (2000) 138, and Bexley (2015).

Introduction

frequently),[57] and there is nothing in them that irremediably contravenes the conventions and technical capacities of the early imperial Roman theatre. While valuable up to a point, the debate too often diverts attention away from the plays themselves. It also creates too stark a choice between theatrical and poetic techniques or effects, as though an unperformed play could be treated only as poetry and not as drama. This is where scholarly appreciation of Seneca most often stumbles. For even if we take the minimalist position that these dramas were neither performed in ancient Rome nor intended for performance, we still cannot deny that they were written *as dramas*, that they belong to the genre of tragedy and hence, that they deserve to be discussed in theatrical as well as literary terms. In other words, a certain theoretical appreciation of the dramatic event, like the notion of enacted character that I have sketched above, may profitably be applied to Seneca's work, not just for the purpose of enriching scholarly knowledge, but also to pay Seneca his dues as a playwright. Regardless of their actual staging, these tragedies – and Seneca's writing in general – demonstrate keen awareness of the actor's art, its ambiguities and its power. Seneca perceives theatre as a vital model for thinking through issues of identity, selfhood, and action.[58] It stands to reason, therefore, that theories of dramatic enactment can be used in return to elucidate Seneca's work, so long as they are used with an adequate degree of caution.

Throughout this book, therefore, I take it as axiomatic that Seneca in his tragedies is alert to the possible meanings and effects of theatrical performance, even if he does not have a specific form of staging in mind. When, for instance, he has the recently blinded Oedipus declare, 'this face befits Oedipus' (*vultus Oedipodam hic decet, Oed.* 1003), he activates an obvious reference to the mask,

---

[57] The APGRD database lists a substantial number of such performances (www.apgrd.ox.ac.uk/research-collections/performance-database/productions). Slaney (2016) is invaluable on the performance history both of Senecan drama and, more broadly, of the 'Senecan aesthetic' that permeates multiple Western theatre traditions.

[58] A point well made, in varying forms, by Hijmans (1966); Rosenmeyer (1989) 37–62; and Bartsch (2006) 208–29.

Introduction

the dramatic *vultus* that designates Oedipus as a specific *persona* and signals that *persona* to the audience.[59] At an intradramatic level, however, in the imaginary world of the play, Oedipus' statement refers to the *face* as an index of identity. Specifically, the protagonist implies that his present appearance correlates with his moral and social state as the punished perpetrator of parricide and incest. The act of self-blinding is, for Seneca's Oedipus, a desperate effort to match punishment with crime: he seeks a form of retribution that isolates him from his deceased father and still (at this moment) living mother (*Oed.* 949–51); he aims to occupy an indeterminate space between life and death in echo of his confused familial status as son, father, brother, and husband; he associates blindness with the darkness of his wedding night (*Oed.* 977).[60] Hence, his mutilated face is a physically realised metaphor for his life, and evidence of his newfound congruence with himself. It is proof of *who* Oedipus is – his particularity as an individual – and this is where Seneca's cleverness becomes truly apparent, because as a mark of such identity, the face performs the same job as a mask. Drama allows for this degree of confluence in a way that most other fictional media do not. Seneca's audience is not faced with a strict choice between seeing a character's purely textual manifestation and seeing his/her quasi-human aspects. Rather, the two categories are shown to overlap, as the mask becomes a face and the face a mask, and audience members engage in the same process of decoding its symbolism regardless of whether they view the scene in a detached manner, as self-conscious metatheatre, or in a fully involved one.

Such overlap of blatantly fictional and quasi-human qualities is, I argue throughout, a distinctive feature of Seneca's *dramatis personae*. When Medea and Atreus seek recognition from their victims, they do so not just as self-aware performers, but also as moral agents seeking to confirm their behavioural consistency. When Pyrrhus and Astyanax are judged on the model of their heroic fathers, the comparison invokes both a personal, biological connection and

---

[59] Boyle (2011) *ad Oed.* 1003.
[60] Busch (2007) 254–60; Braund (2016) 60–1. In a related vein, Poe (1983) 155 argues that Oedipus' self-punishment is figured as an act of retribution, which implies its mirroring of his crime.

the abstract repeatability of a copy. The bodily descriptions so prominent in *Phaedra* and *Oedipus* configure characters, simultaneously, as human analogues in possession of (illusory) minds and consciousness, and as purely textual surfaces offered up for interpretation. Finally, acts of revenge and suicide accentuate the characters' agency and autonomy at an intradramatic level while foreclosing it at an extradramatic one. Every manifestation of conscious fictionality in the tragedies is accompanied by an equivalent – mostly commensurate, sometimes conflicting – manifestation of implied humanness. The dynamic is compelling; it highlights Seneca's considerable power as poet and dramatist. And failing to acknowledge it means seeing only half of the story.

CHAPTER I

COHERENCE

Identity is predicated largely upon coherence. The quality of being *idem*, to use the term's etymological root, or 'the sameness of a person ... at all times in all circumstances', to use the *Oxford English Dictionary* (2nd ed.) definition (entry 2a), is what allows any given individual to be recognised as such. Behavioural continuity ranks alongside bodily continuity as one of the most crucial markers of selfhood, underpinned by the myriad habits and repetitive actions that comprise the fabric of a person's daily life. To simplify a point made by Plato (*Laws* 792a) and Aristotle (*NE* 1103a17), ἦθος – character or disposition – emerges from ἔθος – habit; identity implies that one does the same or similar things, and believes and professes and aims to achieve the same or similar things *identidem*.[1] Such repetition, and the links it creates between past and present conduct, forms a gauge to future actions, too. Conversely, we are labelled as behaving 'out of character' whenever we break this mould and deviate from the expected. Though it sounds tautological, there is a lot of truth in the claim that you have to keep being you in order to be you. Identity is not achieved in an instant, nor presented at birth as a given, but built and judged over time. One's own and others' sense of one's self unrolls and evolves from the memory and maintenance of specific behavioural choices. What makes the amnesiac or the schizophrenic, for example, so troubling as identities is precisely this lack of continuity, predictability, and finally, knowability.

This chapter employs the concept of moral and dispositional coherence to explore the identity of the two most impressive and emblematic characters of Senecan tragedy: Medea and Atreus.[2]

---

[1] *Identidem* obviously contributes to the evolution of the modern English term 'identity'. On ἦθος, De Temmerman (2014) 5 remarks: 'the term's original meaning ... foregrounds habituation as a factor involved in *shaping* it'.

[2] Braden (1985) 42 declares them 'Seneca's strongest dramatic creations' and remarks in an earlier publication – Braden (1970) 28 – that the plays in which they feature are Seneca's 'best realised works'. Dingel (1974) 88–9 regards them as parallel creations.

23

Coherence

Although, on first glance, these two *dramatis personae* may not seem particularly promising candidates for qualities such as constancy and uniformity, having often been cited as paradigms of uncontrolled passions and consequently fractured selfhood,[3] they actually display acute concern for presenting themselves as integrated and continuously unified individuals.[4] Single-minded in their pursuit of evil, Atreus and Medea resort repeatedly to measuring their current behaviour against deeds performed in the past and those they intend to perform in the future. They interrogate the extent to which their present selfhood matches their projected ideal, and how well their present performance fits the literary and theatrical expectations attendant upon their inherited roles. Shortfalls are met with bitter self-reproach. Not only are Atreus and Medea aware of their own *personae*, but they are also aware of how to fashion and maintain those *personae* in ways that render them recognisable to others.

Recognition and recognisability are likewise key elements in the assessment of identity, and they form a recurrent thread of discussion throughout this chapter. Because Seneca conceives of identity as end-directed, as the outcome of persistent, congruent, self-fashioning, it stands to reason that he anticipates its confirmation in summative moments of acknowledgement. Recognition is a natural complement to this teleological concept of selfhood, and the urgent repetition evinced by Seneca's *dramatis personae*, while it may seem endless, always looks towards its final, terrible realisation in ultimate wickedness. Coherence in Senecan tragedy is best understood through the prism of recognition scenes, for it is here that questions of identity are posed with particular urgency. Are characters really who they claim to be? Have they revealed or

---

Consciously or not, scholars of Senecan tragedy tend to analyse Atreus and Medea side by side: see, for example, Boyle (1997) 116–33 and Littlewood (2004) 180–240. Casual remarks by Gill (2006) 424 show just how instinctive this comparison has become.

[3] Prominent examples from anglophone scholarship: Marti (1945) 229–33; Poe (1969); Pratt (1983) 81–91 and 103–7; Nussbaum (1994) 439–83, with some important caveats; Gill (1987) and (2006) 421–34.

[4] Thus, Schiesaro (2003) 208: 'Medea, although we might want to see her portrayed as an unruly, furious, and uncontrollable maenad, in fact consistently evaluates her predicament and displays dogged determination to achieve her goals.' Gill (2006) 424 voices a similar opinion, though he ends up arguing against it: 'Seneca's Medea ... is a highly integrated and consistent character.'

concealed aspects of themselves? Have they changed in any fundamental way since they first stepped onto the stage? Senecan *anagnorisis* ('recognition') builds on a venerable Greco-Roman tradition of dramatic recognition scenes and adapts it to a new purpose, namely demonstrating that consistent performance of one's role leads to confirmatory acknowledgement of the identity one seeks. For Atreus and Medea, recognition marks not a moment of unmasking or the revelation of a previously dissembled identity, but rather proof of just how consistently they have played their assigned parts. And just how comprehensively they have achieved their feats of horror.

Recognition

As a necessary prelude to the topic of self-coherence, I consider first the close conceptual relationship that binds recognition to identity on the one hand, and to dramatic performance on the other. In the theatre (and in literature more broadly)[5] *anagnorisis* draws attention to characterisation, motivation, psychology, and typology; it prompts audiences to contemplate how *dramatis personae* construct their own and others' sense of self. Yet scenes of *anagnorisis* on stage also raise questions about identity that extend beyond the immediate, imaginary world of the play to encompass human action, self-presentation, and the role of performance in everyday life. Dramatic recognition gestures to the potential gap between who people are and who they appear to be. In doing so, it threads the character, the actor, and the moral agent onto the same continuum.

This connection between *anagnorisis* and selfhood is part of recognition's status as 'a peculiarly dramatic device'.[6] Recognition belongs to drama more than to any other literary genre, the reason being that it implicates a character's identity in precisely the same way that theatrical performance implicates an actor's. When performers assume a role, they not only destabilise their own identity – at least in the eyes of others – but they also raise the far more troubling possibility that all human selfhood is precariously fluid.

---

[5] Cave (1988) studies recognition as a literary, not exclusively dramatic device.
[6] Goldman (2000) 8.

This possibility arises from the actor's skill in editing, rehearsing, and developing behaviour so that it appears seamless and convincing.[7] Such self-fashioning belies to some extent the idea of naturally unified identity, and when skilled theatrical performers portray an image of unified selfhood, they paradoxically reveal that selfhood to be a construct and its image an illusion. The issue, therefore, is not merely that actors engage in contrived conduct, but that their professional activity blends the categories of 'natural' and 'contrived', preventing any simple distinction between 'reality' and 'fiction', 'person' and 'character'.

It follows that the anxiety attendant upon *anagnorisis* in ancient drama reflects the ontological anxiety surrounding actors themselves. Recognition in dramatic performance typically attempts to dispel the threat of problematic selfhood by generating a sense of resolution and declaring the newly revealed or more fully apprehended identity to be true and correct. Ion is restored to himself when Creusa recognises his birth tokens; Oedipus is likewise restored to himself, albeit unhappily, when he uncovers the truth about Laius' killer; Sophocles' Orestes reveals himself to Electra at the conclusion of an elaborate performance in which he goes as far as announcing his own death.[8] In every case, the formerly deceptive or mistaken identity is pronounced a momentary aberration rejected in favour of a more fundamental, and presumably natural, kind of selfhood. Against the actor's protean qualities, recognition scenes champion the claims of birth, family ties, and inherent characteristics. Even when they occur in the middle of a play's action, such scenes constitute moments of resolution and stability,[9] so much so that they feature increasingly as a denouement in ancient drama; it is no coincidence that all of Seneca's recognition scenes take place at the ends of his plays.[10]

---

[7] For the notion of seamless performance or 'flow', on stage and in life: Goldman (2000) 63–73 and Turner (1982) 55–6.

[8] This final example, the recognition scene in Sophocles' *Electra*, achieves resolution not just by stabilising identity and re-establishing a family relationship, but also by likening Orestes to a tragic messenger (*El.* 1098–1114), thus evoking the penultimate scene of a tragedy, and by association, the concluding function of *anagnorisis*. On Orestes as a messenger, see Ringer (1998) 185–6.

[9] Thus Cave (2008) 122: 'The typical recognition plot deals in closure.'

[10] Besides this chapter's treatment of *Med.* 978–1027 and *Thy.* 970–1112, see: *Her.* 1138–1344; *Phaed.* 1159–1280, discussed from another perspective in Chapter 3; and *Oed.* 998–1061.

Coherence

Thus, the traditional recognition scene in Greek and Roman drama is a moment that pivots upon revelation, as characters either uncover a previously misapprehended identity, or realise more fully the capacities of an individual they have hitherto underestimated. As Aristotle defines it, the central principle of recognition scenes is change (μεταβολή, *Poetics* 1542a), whether that change applies to largely external circumstances, like social status and family relationships, or internal ones, such as a character's *ethos* and sense of self. The act of *anagnorisis* is, typically, a turning point that resolves uncertainties, reveals secrets, and clarifies misunderstandings.[11] Seneca, however, handles the recognitions scene of *Medea* and *Thyestes* in a unique way, treating them as moments in which identity, far from being altered or rediscovered, is instead amplified and thereby validated. Genuine and constructed selfhood are not incompatible in Seneca's view, with the result that his characters engage in performance as a means of self-realisation.[12] They approach recognition as the final stage in a steady and inherently theatrical process of moral and psychological development, which they pursue over the course of an entire play. In the words of Brian Hook: 'Senecan self-presentation does not operate as self-revelation as much as self-confirmation.'[13]

Consequent to its focus on identity, *anagnorisis* may also be said to delineate character both as an implied human personality and as a fictional construct. The duality is confirmed by the act of recognition itself, which draws attention on the one hand to a character's selfhood, and to the confluence of actor and character (as we have seen), and on the other hand, emphasises a character's status as a fabricated dramatic entity. While the mimetic or representational aspect of recognition deals with a character's 'human' traits – and behind it, a performer's human traits – the semiotics of recognition treat those traits as an assemblage of textual information. In semiotic terms, the act of recognising means interpreting

---

[11] Clarification may, however, be only temporary. Duckworth (1952) 151–60 discusses examples from *palliata* in which recognition complicates later action. On recognition and disclosure, see Kennedy and Lawrence (2008) 2.
[12] Edwards (2002), on the coincidence of acting and self-actualisation in Seneca's work.
[13] Hook (2000) 58.

correctly the signs that indicate a given character's identity: the marks on Oedipus' body; the tokens kept in Ion's box. Terence Cave notes that scenes of recognition become 'a focus for reflection on the way fictions as such are constituted'.[14] They can resemble processes of reading and writing, as characters and audience alike are called upon to analyse the symbols displayed before them and to organise those symbols into some kind of coherent whole. Such 'textual recognition' (as I shall call it) often occurs at the expense of 'ethical recognition' and vice versa, since highlighting one requires us to dismiss or minimise the other. We may read a character either as a quasi-human or as a literary entity; the two rarely coincide. But Seneca's recognition scenes *are* one example of this rare coincidence: the figures involved in them construct their identities in terms that are simultaneously metapoetic and moral, literary and personal.

1.1 *Medea*

Recognising Seneca's Medea

The final exchange between Jason and Medea begins with Medea standing on the roof of her house accompanied by one child and carrying the body of the other in her arms. In defiance of Jason's pleas, she kills the second son, climbs into an airborne chariot, and throws the children's bodies down to their father, declaring, 'do you recognise your wife? This is how I usually escape' (*coniugem agnoscis tuam? / sic fugere soleo*, *Med.* 1021–2). At first glance, the request seems metatheatrical, and this is how it has most often been interpreted.[15] By asking Jason whether he recognises her, Seneca's Medea highlights her status as a dramatic

---

[14] Cave (1988) 46. Likewise, Kennedy and Lawrence (2008) 2: 'recognition becomes key to the way we make meaning and the way we read'.
[15] Boyle (1997) 132 and (2014) cxv–cxvii and *ad Med.* 1019–22; Littlewood (2004) 192; Trinacty (2014) 125–6. Winterbottom (1976) 39, in his review of Costa's commentary, takes this metatheatrical interpretation for granted. For metatheatre in the *Medea* more generally, see also Mowbray (2012) 399–407; Kirichenko (2013) 101–18 and Michelon (2015) 46–54. Despite the reservations of Rosenmeyer (2002), I use the term 'metatheatre' advisedly, to refer to all instances of theatrical self-reference, and especially to those that highlight the conventions of theatre qua conventions. All translations are my own unless otherwise stated.

1.1 *Medea*

character that has previously performed the same story in Euripides' and Ennius' dramas, and probably in Ovid's lost tragedy as well.[16] If she uses *sic* to mean specifically her airborne flight from Corinth,[17] then yes, we have witnessed this scene before at the close of Euripides' version. Seneca's audience would also doubtless have been familiar with Ovid's *Metamorphoses*, in which Medea departs the scene in a flying chariot drawn by serpents on no fewer than three separate occasions (*Met.* 7.220–3; 350–1; 398). Her exit has become a demonstrable cliché, and Seneca invites the audience to recognise it as such.

Medea's *agnoscis*, too, may be construed as encouraging a metatheatrical interpretation, not only because of its self-reflexive presence in a recognition scene, but also because, as Stephen Hinds has shown, Latin poets often use the verb to signify their allusions to earlier writers.[18] *agnoscere* denotes an open practice of poetic appropriation, as in Seneca the Elder's remark that Ovid lifted phrases from Vergil *non subripiendi causa, sed palam mutuandi, hoc animo ut vellet agnosci* ('not for the sake of stealing, but of borrowing openly, with the intent that it be recognised' *Suas.* 3.7).[19] With this meaning activated, recognition of Medea's character deepens and broadens to encompass recognition of Seneca's place within the Greco-Roman literary tradition. Metatheatrical connotations are further compounded by *soleo*, which, like *agnoscis*, can function as an 'Alexandrian footnote', signalling the poetic past that informs Medea's current behaviour;

---

[16] On the traceable parallels between Euripides' and Seneca's Medeas, see Costa (1973) 8; Gill (1987); and Lefèvre (1997a). Arcellaschi (1990) examines Medea's role in Roman drama, and Manuwald (2013) presents a deft survey of the heroine's changing representation in Latin literature. Too little of Ovid's *Medea* survives for scholars to gauge its influence on Seneca's version. There are, however, demonstrable links between Ovid's depiction of Medea in *Heroides* 12 and *Metamorphoses* 7, and the figure portrayed in Seneca's tragedy: see Leo (1878) 166–70, and for more recent discussion, Hinds (1993) 34–43 and (2011) 22–8; Trinacty (2007) and (2014) 93–126; and Boyle (2014) lxxiii–lxxvi.

[17] Both Costa (1973) *ad Med.* 1022 and Boyle (2014) *ad Med.* 1019–22 take *sic* as referring to the chariot. Hine (2000) *ad Med.* 1022 notes more cautiously that *sic* could also refer to Medea's habit of inflicting death before departure, and that the line is probably meant to convey both meanings simultaneously.

[18] Hinds (1998) 9.

[19] Bartsch (2006) 262.

both the audience and Medea herself have grown *accustomed* to her leaving the stage in this manner.[20] The overall effect of Medea's question, on this reading, is to widen as much as possible the gap between intra- and extra-dramatic levels of recognition: the audience comprehends who Medea is because the audience has read Euripides, Ennius, and Ovid, while Jason, presumably, has not.

It is also tempting to infer from Medea's combination of *soleo* and *agnoscis* a reference to the visual dimension of theatre, whereby any given scene may reproduce aspects of other, preceding performances. This argument must remain speculative, given the lack of evidence for Seneca's plays ever being staged during his lifetime. Yet, even if Seneca's *Medea* was not performed in front of a first-century AD Roman audience, the visual qualities of its final scene – Medea above in a chariot; Jason below on the ground – could still be understood as replicating the visual qualities of Euripides' version. And, in the unknowable event that Seneca's tragedy was actually performed during his lifetime, Medea's *agnoscis* would surely encourage the audience to recognise this visual parallel.[21] Such 'optical allusion' – as Robert Cowan has dubbed the technique – is not uncommon in ancient drama, a famous example being Aristophanes' use of the *mechane* in the *Peace* (80–179) to parody Euripides' *Bellerophon* (306–8 Kannicht).[22] It would, of course, be even more metatheatrical to evoke such visual recollection in the context of an actual recognition scene.[23]

The Medea that emerges from this reading of the final exchange is a self-consciously theatrical construct, a fictional entity

---

[20] The term 'Alexandrian footnote' derives from Ross (1975) 78, where it describes Roman writers' methods of appealing to literary tradition. On Seneca's *soleo* as an Alexandrian footnote, see Boyle (1997) 132 and Cowan (2011) 363.
[21] As Boyle (2014) cxvi points out, there is also the opportunity for Jason (and the audience) to recognise, visually, the correspondence between Medea's character and her mask.
[22] Cowan (2013).
[23] Thus, Easterling (1997) 168–9 argues for visual similarity between the Aeschylean, Sophoclean, and Euripidean versions of Electra's reunion with Orestes: in Aeschylus, Electra carries an urn of funeral offerings (*Ch.* 84–151); in Sophocles, Orestes presents Electra with an empty urn (*El.* 1113–1219); in Euripides, Electra carries a water jar (*El.* 54–149). The latter two versions evoke aspects of the Aeschylean 'stage picture' partly in order to summon recognition from the audience.

1.1 *Medea*

assembled from earlier texts and a dramatic role embodied by earlier performers.[24] She is also, crucially, slotted into a literary tradition in a way that contributes to the perceived stability and coherence of her character. This Medea is the product of multiple iterations of the same behaviour maintained and revisited across a number of separate instantiations in poetry and drama. She fulfils her *dramatis persona* in a way the audience has come to expect from its previous encounters with her textual self. She is recognisable because she sticks to the established script.

Besides confirming Medea's textual identity, however, the exchange and its explicit stress on recognition also confirm her ethical identity as an implied human personality, and this is an aspect of the scene that has received far less scholarly attention. When Medea cites prior dramatic versions of herself, she invites the audience to see in her current behaviour the degree of self-coherence necessary for creating not just a recognisable theatrical role but also a stable, recognisable personality. *anagnorisis* of Medea qua fictional construct coincides with acknowledgement of her personal qualities as a moral agent.[25] Medea is who she is because she behaves in keeping with the requirements of her *persona*, which enables others to perceive a link between her deeds and her nature.[26]

Medea's use of *soleo* is a case in point, because as well as being a potential marker of intertext, it also – quite simply – indicates customary activity: what a person tends to do, what he or she is therefore likely to do, and as a result, who he or she is likely to be. Seneca's Phaedra uses it in this way to describe Theseus' philandering habits, and her sarcastic remark, *praestat . . . nuptae quam solet Theseus fidem* ('Theseus displays to his wife his usual

---

[24] A point made long ago by Wilamowitz-Moellendorf (1919 III) 62, whose quip, 'diese Medea hat Euripides gelesen' ('this Medea has read Euripides'), has become one of the mainstays of scholarship on Senecan tragedy.

[25] Bartsch (2006) 261 makes a similar observation: 'The result of the drama's attention to the question of recognition is that *personal* self-recognition and *literary* recognition necessarily coalesce here.' See also Boyle (2014) cxvi.

[26] A point raised by Sissa (2006) 41–2, in relation to tragic *anagnorisis*: 'Tell me how you act and I will tell you what kind of person you are . . . recognition of agency implies recognition of moral identity, because the nature of an act . . . exposes the character of the agent.' See also Aristotle *Poetics* 1452a35. On the confluence of *being* and *doing* in Seneca's characterisation of Medea, see Campbell (2019).

faithfulness' *Phaed.* 92) does not appear to activate any specific allusion. David Armstrong notes similar occurrences of the term in Seneca's *Troades*, where it refers more to the Greeks' practice of sacrificing a virgin prior to long sea voyages than to the iteration of a specific poetic text: Pyrrhus demands from Agamemnon permission to sacrifice Polyxena on the basis that these are *solita* ('customary', *Tro.* 249), and Calchas concedes that permission with the wry comment, *dant fata Danais quo solent pretio viam* ('fate grants passage to the Danaeans at the usual price', 360).[27] The term also features in *Hercules*, where it denotes the hero's past undertaking of Atlas's task: *mundum solitos ferre lacertos* ('shoulders accustomed to holding up the sky', *Her.* 1101). In these passages, characters cite each other's habitual behaviour as a way of passing judgement on personal qualities. Who you were in the past dictates who you should be in the future.

Hence, Medea's triumphant *soleo* at 1022 signifies not only her meta-literary habits, but also the behaviour she has repeated across the course of her life as a quasi-human within the drama, specifically, her tendency to commit brutal murders immediately prior to or during her flight.[28] Slaughter and escape are two events that recur, paired, throughout Medea's story: she dismembers her brother, Absyrtos, as she sails from Colchis; she destroys Pelias before leaving Thessaly; she leaves behind in Corinth the bodies of Creon, Creusa, and her own two children. Seneca stresses throughout the play this repetition inherent in Medea's story, and he draws particular attention to the killing of Absyrtos because this act provides a precedent for Medea's impending infanticide. Just as Medea will kill the second child in Jason's presence, so she recalls Absyrtos' death being 'thrust in his father's face' (*funus ingestum patri*, 132); similarly, she treats the slaughter of her own children as a warped form of payment for her brother's murder (956–7; 969–71; 982). Imagery of dismemberment is also used to connect the two events: when Medea in her final monologue urges her own children to embrace her – *et infusos mihi / coniungite artus* ('and join with me your poured out limbs', 946–7) – her

---

[27] Armstrong (1982) 240.
[28] A meaning championed by Armstrong (1982) 240 and upheld by Hine (2000) *ad Med.* 1022.

1.1 *Medea*

stilted and sinister language[29] evokes the several references she has already made to Absyrtos' limbs (47–8; 912), while *infusos* recalls the blood she has shed elsewhere (134–5: *funestum impie / quam saepe fudi sanguinem*, 'how often I have spilled blood, murderously'; 452–3: *quaeque fraternus cruor / perfudit arva*, 'the fields drenched in my brother's blood'). Pelias' death, too, involves dismemberment and so forms part of this nexus (133–4; 475–6). The overall effect of these associations is to demonstrate that Medea has always performed the kinds of actions she will perform again by the end of this play. Not just the external audience, but Jason too, as Medea's internal audience, is called upon to recognise the uniformity of her behaviour.

Medea alludes to that uniformity even in Jason's presence: the first words she speaks to him in the entire play are, 'I have fled, Jason, I am fleeing. Changing abodes is nothing new, but the reason for flight is new: I used to flee on your behalf' (*fugimus, Iason, fugimus. hoc non est novum, / mutare sedes; causa fugiendi nova est: / pro te solebam fugere*, 447–9). Her language here is almost identical to her statement in the recognition scene – *sic fugere soleo* – which, notably, comprises her final speech to Jason. Close correspondence between the two passages hints at an equivalent correspondence between Medea's past and present action, and also between her individual actions and declarations over the course of the play. Once again, Medea prompts Jason to acknowledge the behavioural patterns that have long since defined her character. In fact, this is a notable instance of her quasi-human and fictional identities converging, because when she announces that her action is not new – *hoc non est novum* (447) – the phrase's meta-literary resonance is just as irresistible as its claims about personal coherence. Medea and Jason (*fugimus*: I/we) have escaped before in Euripides, in Apollonius, in Ovid, to name but a few prominent examples. The habitual nature of this activity, its repetition across literary texts and within these characters' 'lives', is a core constituent of their identity and a means by which they

---

[29] Segal (1986) 9 remarks that the 'depersonalised and abstract vocabulary' used by Seneca to describe Medea's embrace of her children (946–7) not only gives the passage a 'self-consciously artificial' quality, but also sounds ominous in the context of the protagonist's impending crime.

33

may be judged. Poetic iteration coincides with, and bolsters, personal continuity.

It follows that *anagnorisis*, too, may be used to affirm coherence in a personal as well as literary sense. Seneca certainly deploys the concept in this way at the end of *Epistle* 120, in terms that cannot fail to evoke the dramatic tradition of recognition scenes:

> Magnam rem puta unum hominem agere. Praeter sapientem autem nemo unum agit, ceteri multiformes sumus. Modo frugi tibi videbimur et graves, modo prodigi et vani; mutamus subinde personam et contrariam ei sumimus quam exuimus. Hoc ergo a te exige, ut qualem institueris praestare te, talem usque ad exitum serves; effice ut possis laudari, si minus, ut adgnosci.
>
> Consider it a great thing to play the part of one man. Besides the sage, however, no one plays the part of one man; the rest of us are multiform. Now we seem to you sober and serious, now wasteful and vain; we keep changing our mask and we put on the opposite of what we have taken off. Therefore, demand this of yourself: that you maintain right to the end the character you have resolved to present. Bring it about that you may be praised, or if not, at least recognised. (*Ep.* 120.22)

This passage harnesses a theatrical analogy to illustrate the Stoic principle of *constantia*: Lucilius is advised to continue behaving 'in character', as it were, to cleave to the role he has adopted and to perform it in a consistent manner because only then will he render himself recognisable to others.[30] Coming at the end of this extended theatrical parallel, *adgnosci* suggests the concluding and validating function typically ascribed to dramatic recognition scenes: people's habit of switching between roles creates the kind of ontological instability that *anagnorisis* aims to resolve. The twist here is that, contrary to standard Greco-Roman dramatic practice, *anagnorisis* establishes Lucilius' identity not through revelation, but through steady confirmation. The recognition that Seneca envisages in *Epistle* 120 involves no unveiling of a previously unsuspected identity, for that would imply *inconstantia*; rather, Lucilius is understood and acknowledged as the person

---

[30] On self-coherence and consistency in Sen *Ep.* 120.22, see Edwards (2002) 382; Inwood (2005) 288–93; Bartsch (2006) 262; Star (2012) 65–9; Aygon (2016) 61. Also useful are the comments of Brunt (1975) 13–14 on the Stoics' tendency to think about *constantia* in terms of theatrical roles.

1.1 *Medea*

he has always, consistently, been. Likewise, when Seneca declares at the beginning of *Epistle* 31, *agnosco Lucilium meum* ('I recognise my Lucilius'), he means that Lucilius is now fulfilling the promise – and even more literally, the *person* – he had previously displayed (*incipit, quem promiserat, exhibere, Ep.* 31.1). Lucilius has not suddenly altered his character but has simply come closer to perfecting a disposition to which he aspires.[31]

The same may be said of Seneca's Medea, who, in her final showdown with Jason, seeks recognition for an identity she has been developing over the entire course of her play. Medea has not changed her personality in the tragedy's final few lines, nor has she revealed a new aspect of herself: she has merely amplified and perfected a role she has long desired to enact. How Seneca depicts and explores this process of self-development is the subject of the next two sections.

Appropriate Behaviour

The heroine's self-fashioning is most apparent in the way she cites her own name at critical points in the tragedy. Although her illeism has already attracted considerable scholarly attention,[32] it is worth reviewing briefly here, in order to show how Medea uses it to ensure her self-coherence and *constantia*. Compared to Euripides' heroine, who utters her own name on only one occasion (Eur. *Med.* 402), Seneca's does so a remarkable seven times: 'Medea remains' (*Medea superest*, 166); 'Medea is a greater fear' (*est ... maior metus / Medea*, 516–17); 'Medea does not compel you' (*nec ... te ... / Medea cogit*, 523–4); 'undertake whatever Medea can do' (*incipe / quidquid Medea potest*, 566–7); 'now I am Medea' (*Medea nunc sum*, 910). She begins the play by invoking deities *quosque Medeae magis / fas est precari* ('whom it is more right for Medea to call upon', 8–9); later, she rationalises that her children's crime is having Medea for a mother (*et maius scelus / Medea mater*, 933–4). When the Nurse uses Medea's name to command

---

[31] Bartsch (2006) 260–2.
[32] Traina (1979) 273–5; Segal (1982) 241–2; Petrone (1988) 61–2. Fitch and McElduff (2002) 24–7 make some pertinent, general comments on self-naming in Senecan tragedy.

35

Coherence

her attention, the heroine famously replies, 'I shall become her' (Nut: *Medea*— Med: *Fiam*, 171). The cumulative effect of all this self-naming is that Medea's conduct becomes a process of self-construction in which the protagonist knows her role and strives to live up to it.[33] Like Lucilius in *Epistle* 120, Seneca's Medea tries as much as possible to remain 'in character'. She performs herself both in the literal sense of acting a dramatic part and in the figurative sense of developing a stable, recognisable identity. Her behaviour throughout the play is simultaneously metatheatrical and quasi-Stoic; her self-citation alludes to her previous appearances in drama, and in literature more generally, at the same time as it emphasises continuity between her past, present, and future actions.

Medea's *fiam* at line 171 is a particularly telling example of this overlap between metatheatrical and Stoic versions of her identity. On the one hand, the word conveys Medea's awareness of her own literary past, and presents her behaviour as a model derived from earlier poetry. In fact, it confirms Medea's already paradigmatic status via allusion to Hypsipyle's remark in *Heroides* 6.151, *Medeae Medea forem* ('I would have been a Medea to Medea').[34] On the other hand, *fiam* evokes not just textual identity, but a slow and deliberate process of ethical self-construction. Medea will 'become' Medea because she will 'be made' into Medea: the verb's passive force connotes a quintessentially Senecan Stoic project of self-reform, one that splits the individual into moral agent and malleable object. Seneca uses the verb in a similar manner at *de Ira* 2.10.6, when he declares, *neminem nasci sapientem sed fieri* ('the wise man is not born but made'). Interpreted alongside such evidence, Medea's promise to work upon and thereby achieve an ideal version of herself begins to sound like a distinctly Stoic goal. Her implied human identity is no less consciously constructed, and no less paradigmatic than her fictional one.

---

[33] Fitch and McElduff (2002) 25: 'self-naming is often a way of defining who one *should* be, an index of the gap between one's present performance and one's ideal role'. See also Braden (1985) 42 and Rosenmeyer (1989) 52.

[34] Trinacty (2007) 71–2.

1.1 *Medea*

Medea's self-citation is also quasi-Stoic in the way it leads her to resemble an actor. Just as a theatrical performer adopts a part and endeavours subsequently to maintain it, so Medea strives to bridge the distance between her current and ideal self. In this regard, too, her behaviour relates to Seneca's advice in *Epistle* 120, where the main point of the theatrical analogy is to associate people with stage performers.[35] According to Seneca, most individuals change their masks frequently (*mutamus subinde personam*), but the wise man plays just a single role, that of himself (*unum hominem agere*). Thus, far from claiming that all acting is inherently deceptive, Seneca allows the possibility that consistent performance will in fact establish and enhance genuine selfhood. Playing one role is the same thing as being one person: Seneca exploits the semantic range of *agere* that 'subsumes within it both the act that is in earnest as well as the act that is just an act'.[36] Whenever Seneca's Medea resorts to the talismanic power of speaking her own name, whenever she projects her actions onto the silhouette of her pre-established role, whenever she seeks an audience for her atrocities (e.g. *Med.* 992–4), she points up the presence of the actor behind the theatrical event. In doing so, moreover, she overturns the insincerity typically associated with dramatic performance, because her self-aware enactment enables her to pursue and achieve unity; it closes rather than opens the gap between the performer as person and as role.

The theatrical analogy Seneca employs in *Epistle* 120.22, and which I regard as central to understanding Medea's bid for recognition, most likely derives from Stoic *persona* theory, in which individuals are understood to perform roles that merge with and thereby display normative aspects of their identity.[37] The main proponents of this theory, Panaetius and Cicero (*Off.*

---

[35] Frede (2007) 160 discusses the ways in which Stoic theatrical metaphors establish a link between actors and human beings; see also Gibson (2007) 125. Sources – mostly philosophical – that use the 'dramatic simile of life' have been collected by Kokolakis (1969).
[36] Gunderson (2015) 19.
[37] On the relationship between performance and identity in Stoic *persona* theory, see Burchell (1998) and Bartsch (2006) 220–9. Gill (1988) explores how the theory engages with concepts of personhood and personality. Nédoncelle (1948) provides useful background on the semantic range of the term *persona*.

1.107–115),[38] hold that human selfhood comprises four distinct facets or *personae*, each of which must be observed according to what befits it. The first of these *personae* is universal, pertaining to humans' shared condition as rational beings. The second *persona* rests upon individual attributes and aptitudes that are nonetheless conventional rather than radically unique (a good example might be someone with a talent for public speaking devoting themselves to oratory).[39] The third *persona* is imposed by circumstances, such as being born into wealth or poverty, and the fourth derives from choices individuals make over the course of their lives. Under this schema, tailoring one's conduct to one's *persona* is the ethical equivalent of achieving a seamless performance: both activities require an outwardly directed display of self-coherence intended to guarantee recognisable identity; actor and role are assumed ultimately to coalesce. Of course, Seneca's Medea is not strutting around on stage proclaiming the value of this particular Stoic theory, but her methods of self-assessment display deep affinities with it. Acute consciousness of the demands placed upon her by her dramatic *persona* recalls the Stoic injunction that people should not deviate from their assigned parts in life. In both cases, decisions about future behaviour are made according to their degree of fit with: a) the capacities one has displayed to date and the circumstances in which they have been exercised, and b) the expectations incumbent upon a given role. Like Medea, Stoic *persona* theory celebrates personal coherence and continuity achieved via sincere, self-actualising performance.

One does not have to look far in Seneca's tragedy to find evidence of Medea's consummate ability to 'play one person' (*unum hominem agere*). So unvarying are the traits she exhibits throughout the play that many of her final deeds are alluded to as

---

[38] Although Panaetius' work has been lost, it is widely regarded as the basis for Cicero's account of *persona* theory in *Off.* 1.107–21. Cicero himself (*Att.* 16.11.4) acknowledges Panaetius as his source. For more detail on Cicero's Panaetian background, see Dyck (1996) 17–29, and fuller treatments in Pohlenz (1934), and Gärtner (1974). De Lacy (1977) 169 demurs – against Cicero's own statement – that nothing specifically identifies Panaetius as the author of Cicero's fourfold *persona* theory but admits that there are very few alternatives.

[39] Further discussion in Gill (1994) 4607.

1.1 *Medea*

early as her opening monologue. To some extent, this is a standard Senecan technique, whereby the tragedies' initial scenes hint obliquely and ironically at events the audience knows will occur by the plays' end.[40] Yet the parallels between Medea's first speech and final actions are so close that they suggest a greater than usual effort on Seneca's part to link the two scenes. For example, Medea proclaims darkly that she has given birth to her revenge though she is not yet conscious of its precise form (*parta iam, parta ultio est: / peperi*, 'now it is born, my revenge is born: I have given birth' 25–6).[41] The metaphor resumes when she remarks, 'a home born through crime must be abandoned through crime' (*quae scelere parta est, scelere linquenda est domus*, 55). Further hints of her future infanticide lurk in Medea's exhortation to 'seek a path to revenge through the vitals themselves' (*per viscera ipsa quaere supplicio viam*, 40), referring in this instance to the entrails of a sacrificial animal, but also anticipating the murder of her offspring, and perhaps even evoking her later claim to extract with a sword any foetus recently implanted within her womb (*in matre si quo pignus etiamnunc latet / scrutabor ense viscera et ferro extraham*; 'if there is any love pledge hiding even now within this mother, I shall search my innards with the sword and drag it out', 1012–13).[42]

In her search for an appropriate course of action, one that will grant her the most successful form of revenge, Seneca's Medea acknowledges both implicitly and explicitly the contours of her destined role. Parity is all: future violence must develop from the models of the past; she vies to equal and to exceed the acknowledged potential of her earlier self. 'Whatever wickedness Phasis and Pontus witnessed, the Isthmus will witness ... wounds and slaughter and death spreading through the limbs' (*quodcumque*

---

[40] Pratt (1983) 34.
[41] Hinds (2011) 24 notes that this line most likely alludes to Ovid *Her.* 12.208: *ingentes parturit ira minas*.
[42] Medea's reference to sacrifice in lines 38–40 is, in the words of Costa (1973) *ad loc.*, 'enigmatic and sinister': besides indicating actual, sacrificial animals, the *victimae* Medea mentions may be variously interpreted as Jason and Creusa or Medea's children, while, as Zwierlein (1986b) proposes, the *viscera* could be regarded as belonging to Medea herself. On the language of pregnancy and birth in Medea's opening monologue, see Rimell (2012) 227–8, and McAuley (2016) 219–20.

39

vidit Phasis aut Pontus nefas, / videbit Isthmos ... / ... / ... vulnera et caedam et vagum / funus per artus, 44–5; 47–8): the rough fates of Pelias and Absyrtus set the stage for the murders to come. Medea envisages for herself a *persona* in keeping with her past conduct and also with the established constraints of her dramatic part. The young Medea is asked to step aside in favour of the fully matured, fully murderous mother: *gravior exurgat dolor: / maiora iam me scelera post partus decent* ('a heavier grief swells up: greater crimes befit me now that I have given birth' 49–50). Once again, the remark foreshadows her infanticide and hence, the source of her perfected identity: *scelera* and *partus* jostle uncomfortably close together, as though Medea's mind was making connections it could not yet admit to itself, and in this context, *gravior* inevitably conjures the shadow of its cognate, *gravidus*.[43] Medea's thought processes in this scene are geared towards not just the right or the most effective act of vengeance, but the one that most suits her nature. The question lingering behind her opening monologue, and breaking through to the surface in line 50, is *quid deceat*? How should Medea respond to the situation in which she has been placed? What is the 'right' thing to do?[44]

This concept of *decorum*, of appropriateness, unites *persona* theory to its desired outcome of *constantia*: one achieves moral coherence by fulfilling one's allotted role in a way that 'fits' its requirements.[45] If one happens to be lame, for example, one should not attempt to become an athlete, for that would not be fitting or seemly. Significantly for Seneca's Medea, *decorum* is also closely connected to notions of self-performance, as the following passage from Cicero's *de Officiis* demonstrates:

expendere oportebit quid quisque habeat sui eaque moderari, nec velle experiri quam se aliena deceant; id enim maxime quemque decet quod est cuiusque maxime. Suum quisque igitur noscat ingenium, acremque se et bonorum et

---

[43] The *gravior/gravidus* link has also been spotted by Boyle (2014) *ad Med.* 48–50, and McAuley (2016) 220.
[44] Bartsch (2006) 264–5.
[45] The role of 'fitting behaviour' (τὸ πρέπον, *decorum*) in Stoic *persona* theory is discussed by Brunt (1975) 13–16; Gill (1988); Dyck (1996) *ad Cic. Off.* 1.93–9; Gibson (2007) 122–6.

1.1 *Medea*

vitiorum suorum iudicem praebeat, ne scaenici plus quam nos videantur habere prudentiae. Illi enim non optimas sed sibi accommodatissimas fabulas eligunt

> Each person ought to consider what characteristics belong to him, and to manage them, without wishing to test how someone else's characteristics might suit him; for what suits each person most of all is that which is most his own. Let each man therefore know his own natural disposition and show himself a sharp judge of his good morals and vices, so that actors may not seem to have more wisdom than us. For they select not the best plays, but the ones most appropriate for them (*Off.* 1.113–14)

Cicero's advice has much in common with the end of Seneca's *Epistle* 120: both texts compare people to actors; both stress the need for individuals to remain consistent within their chosen roles. Where Seneca warns against changing masks, Cicero cautions people not to exchange their characteristics for others' that may not suit them (*nec velle experiri quam se aliena deceant; id enim maxime quemque decet quod est cuiusque maxime*). On this analysis, achieving *decorum* is the equivalent of 'playing one person'. Naturally, this is only a metaphor in Stoic theory, a way of articulating specific ethical precepts; people are not really actors. But the theory undeniably promotes a view of the self as conscious performance, and when this view is transmitted into theatre proper, as is the case in Seneca's *Medea*, then stage acting undergoes a substantial metamorphosis and becomes less about pretence than about candour. What may seem the ultimate example of *inconstantia* – actors assuming someone else's characteristics – becomes instead the epitome of constant, unfeigned selfhood.

Whether Seneca's Medea actually draws on Cicero *Off.* 1.113–14 cannot be known for certain, but in addition to her use of *decent* in line 50, there is another tempting parallel towards the end of the play, when the heroine declares, *Medea nunc sum; crevit ingenium malis* ('now I am Medea; my character has grown through evils' 910). Medea's avowed knowledge of her *ingenium* resembles Cicero's injunction for each man to know his own natural disposition (*suum quisque ... noscat ingenium*); in each case, self-awareness is the key to achieving an appropriate identity.[46] For

---

[46] Gibson (2007) 121–2 and Dyck (1996) *ad Off.* 114 both see in Cicero's *suum quisque ... noscat ingenium* a submerged reference to Delphi's γνῶθι σεαυτόν. Seneca's Medea, likewise, seems to know herself very well, and this possible link to Delphi's motto is

41

Medea, moreover, *ingenium*'s semantic association with birth (*gigno; genus; genius*) allows even tighter links to be drawn between her given disposition and her fully realised self: the protagonist's inborn nature is confirmed by her killing what she has borne.[47] This is a deeply disturbing form of *decorum*, but it is *decorum* all the same.

Finally, it is worth pointing out that Medea's *decorum* is fictional as well as quasi-human, because the term denotes not just appropriate behaviour, but also literary appropriateness.[48] Horace in the *Ars Poetica*, for instance, uses *decet* to describe the fit between style and genre (*singula quaeque locum teneant sortita decentem*; 'let each individual thing, allotted, keep to its appropriate place' *Ars* 92), or the way a character's words harmonise with his or her emotions (*tristia maestum / voltum verba decent, iratum plena minarum*; 'sad words suit a sorrowful face, threating words an angry one' *Ars* 105–6). Viewed against this background, Medea's aspiration to commit suitable crimes becomes a meta-literary and, more narrowly, metatheatrical statement that draws attention to her conduct as a fabricated dramatic character. In fact, her fictional and implied human identities overlap, because metatheatricality helps the audience comprehend Medea's self-consistency: only if we know Medea's story in advance can we truly appreciate the uniformity of her conduct.[49] Like performance, *decorum* is a concept that straddles the spheres of ethics and aesthetics, thereby ensuring that Medea accomplishes *constantia* in that most inconstant of mediums: fiction.

Past Continuous

As I have noted already in the introduction to this chapter, coherence can only ever be judged over stretches of time, when habits

---

reinforced by Medea's ancestry: she is the daughter of the Sun, and Apollo is the Sun god.

[47] McAuley (2016) 224 on Medea's *ingenium*: 'Medea has given birth *to* – and crucially *for* – herself.'

[48] The overlap between aesthetic/literary and ethical appropriateness is discussed by Gibson (2007) 115–47. Seo (2013) 13–15 and 94–123 asserts *deocrum*'s importance as a guiding principle for characterisation in Latin literature.

[49] Similarly, Gill (1987) 32 remarks of Medea's final monologue: 'Medea's self-reinforcement by her image of herself gains force by allusion to the literary tradition in which that image has come to be shaped.'

1.1 *Medea*

are acquired and individual actions crystallise into patterns. For Seneca's Medea, this kind of *constantia* manifests itself in her obsessive concern for continuity with the past. What has happened before must happen again, over and over, because this is what it means for Medea to be 'Medea'.

Scholars have rightly recognised that return is a major motif in this tragedy, as Medea desires simultaneously to retrace her steps (*redire*) and to recuperate what she has lost (*reddere*).[50] In response to Creon's order that she leave his kingdom and 'go and complain to the Colchians' (*i, querere Colchis*, 197), Medea agrees on one condition: 'I'm going back, but he who brought me should take me' (*redeo. Qui avexit, ferat*, 197). As Lisl Walsh observes, Seneca's Medea 'views the present as a logical repetition of past events'; she has fled with Jason several times before so it is only to be expected that the same should happen now.[51] 'Give me back my crime', she demands of Creon (*redde crimen*, 246) – by which she means Jason – and later in the same exchange, 'give the fugitive back her ship, or give back her companion' (*redde fugienti ratem / vel redde comitem*, 272–3). She repeats the request to Jason himself in Act 3 in a move that corroborates her coherence at an intratextual level as well as demonstrating the two scenes' repetitious similarity: 'repay this suppliant' (*redde supplici … vicem*, 482); 'give back to the exile what's hers' (*redde fugienti sua*, 489). Medea envisages departure from Corinth only in terms of revisiting a familiar set of locations rather than setting out for somewhere new: 'To whom,' she asks Jason, 'are you sending me back?' (*ad quos remittis?* 451, repeated almost verbatim at 459: *quo me remittis?*) She argues that she cannot possibly return to Phasis or Colchis, the Symplegades, Iolcus, Tempe (451–7). Contrary to the Argo's daring outward exploration of new territory (301–79),[52] Medea, its most famous cargo, continually expresses her wish to retrace old steps.

---

[50] The foundational study is Schiesaro (2003) 209–13, followed by Walsh (2012) 77–80, and Slaney (2019) 62–70. Guastella (2001) 200–3 discusses more broadly the role of past, present, and concepts of repayment in Medea's logic. On general motifs of repetition in Senecan tragedy: Boyle (1983), and Gunderson (2017).
[51] Walsh (2012) 79.
[52] On the Argo's programmatic importance within Seneca's *Medea*, see Slaney (2019) 70–9.

Coherence

Hers is not purely an impulse towards regression, however, since Medea's statements look forwards to the future just as much as they look backwards to her undeniably chequered past.[53] In wanting to flee *with Jason* (she even invites him to join her at 525: *innocens mecum fuge*; 'flee with me, guiltless'), Medea hopes not only to reinstate a (presumably) happier period of her life, but also to begin again, if not precisely a*new*. When she ponders how Jason ought to have reacted to the marriage foisted upon him by Creon, she argues first for suicide (138–9), but retracts the idea immediately in favour of his continued life: *si potest, vivat meus, / ut fuit, Iason* ('if possible, let Jason live, as he was – mine' 140–1). Her ideal is for Jason to remain the same, a hope that seems to encapsulate a certain wistful affection on Medea's part, but also hints at the story's grim end. For Medea's hope will be fulfilled: Jason will never really belong to nor be seen as belonging to anyone else; he will remain hers and that is the core of her revenge. Her sweet sentiment turns sour, but still, the two meanings occupy the same continuum. Essentially, Medea resurrects the past in order to move on: *scelera te hortentur tua / et cuncta redeant* ('let your crimes encourage you, and let them return – all of them' 129–30). What she has previously committed for Jason, she will now commit against him.

To attain coherence, one's endings need to reflect one's beginnings, which is a fitting aim for the protagonist of a play that commences and concludes with the same word (*di*, 1; *deos*, 1027). Medea seeks balance as she orchestrates her tragic performance:

> paria narrentur tua
> repudia thalamis: quo virum linques modo?
> hoc quo secuta es. rumpe iam segnes moras:
> quae scelere parta est, scelere linquenda est domus.

> May the stories of your divorce
> equal those of your marriage: how should you leave your husband?
> The same way you followed him. Now break through these torpid delays:
> a home born through crime must be abandoned through crime.
>
> (*Med.* 52–5)

---

[53] Here I diverge slightly from Schiesaro (2003) 209–13, who emphasises the retrogressive aspect of Seneca's Medea, and from Guastella (2001) 199, who argues that Medea's impending 'divorce' from Jason represents an irreparable break between her past and her present.

1.1 *Medea*

In Medea's eyes, *repudium* brings her marriage full circle and is less a new event than the recasting of an old one.[54] It both builds upon and outstrips its earlier model, which is what Medea also hopes for her identity throughout the drama. Rhetorical antithesis reinforces at the level of composition the equilibrium she attributes to her actions: *quo ... linques ... / ... quo secuta es; quae scelere parta est, scelere linquenda est domus*. Once again, the implicit logic of Medea's reasoning is that she will dissolve her relationship with Jason via infanticide, just as she initiated it, long ago, through fratricide: although she does not yet realise it at this early point in the drama, her children's deaths will replicate and pay for that of Absyrtus. More generally, she looks to her formerly wild passion for Jason, to its stimulus that drove her to dare the unthinkable, as a model for her future revenge: *si quaeris odio, misera, quem statuas modum / imitare amorem* ('if you wonder what limit, wretch, to put on your hate, copy your love' 397–8).

It is of course possible to take *narrentur* in line 52 as a metapoetic marker that activates memories of Medea's past appearances in literature. Though a fairly generic allusion, the most likely text this word calls to mind is *Heroides* 12, where Medea narrates the circumstances of her marriage to Jason and its blood-soaked dowry in terms similar to, albeit far more muted than, Seneca's (*Her.* 12.113–6; 199–203). Yet a direct intertext is not absolutely necessary here, because even without one Medea's exhortation still functions as a meta-literary promise to cohere with preceding representations of her character. Not only does her personal past duplicate her poetic past, but her personal future duplicates it as well: the tale of her *repudium* has likewise already been told, many times over, and this Medea aspires to match it (*paria*) by reiterating her actions in a context simultaneously personal, mythic, and poetic. Hence, in terms of her fictional as well as her quasi-human identity, Seneca's Medea vows to unite her past, present, and future into one seamless whole.

This obsession with temporal continuity also emerges at the micro level of Medea's grammar, specifically in her preference for

---

[54] On the Roman quality of Medea's *repudium* and its relationship to actual Roman legal procedures, see Abrahamsen (1999); Guastella (2001); McAuley (2016) 211–13.

Coherence

reiterating in quick succession the same verb in two different tenses:

> quodcumque vidit Phasis aut Pontus nefas
> videbit Isthmos
>
> whatever wickedness Phasis and Pontus witnessed
> the Isthmos will witness
>
> (*Med.* 44–5)
>
> fugimus, Iason, fugimus
>
> We have fled, Jason, we are fleeing
>
> (*Med.* 447)
>
> excidimus tibi?
> numquam excidemus
>
> Have you forgotten me?
> You will never forget me[55]
>
> (*Med.* 561–2)

Medea's iterative language forges links from past to present, past to future, in a bid to ensure parity between her deeds and their deserts, her former and current self, her suffering and Jason's. Very occasionally, these verbal doublets signify how Medea's life in Corinth differs from her former good fortune, as when the heroine remarks to Creon that she was a more than eligible match as a young Colchian virgin: *petebant tunc meos thalamos proci, / qui nunc petuntur* ('back then princes were seeking my hand in marriage, princes who now are sought' 218–19). But, most of the time, Medea's *geminatio* constitutes an acknowledgement of patterns of behaviour in her life, and of the symbolic similarity that couples Jason's losses to her own. 'May the children be lost to their father's kisses; they have been lost to their mother's', she avers towards the end of her last monologue (*osculis pereant patris, / periere matris*, 950–1). Payback, like self-formation, is all about balance, which Medea achieves right down to the level of syntax.

---

[55] More precisely, 'have I slipped from you[r memory]? I shall never slip [from your memory]', but the translation I give above captures the punch of Medea's (and Seneca's) Latin.

1.1 *Medea*

I have examined already how Medea's opening monologue gestures towards the play's culminating events, but there is one example still outstanding that deserves consideration here, namely, the heroine's flight from the stage in an airborne chariot. In her initial complaint over Jason's betrayal, Medea appeals to her ancestor, the Sun, for rescue:

> da, da per auras curribus patriis vehi,
> committe habenas, genitor, et flagrantibus
> ignifera loris tribue moderari iuga
>
> Let, let me ride through the air in my ancestral chariot.
> Entrust me with the reins, father, give me leave
> to guide the fiery steeds with blazing straps
>
> (*Med.* 32–4)

The image conjured in these lines is reified by the play's end, and lexical echoes further confirm the link: Medea's final line to Jason is, 'I shall ride through the air in a winged chariot' (*ego inter auras aliti curru vehar* 1025, cf. *per auras … vehi*, 32).[56] It is precisely these kinds of parallels that establish Medea's identity as a coherent individual. The woman the audience sees at the tragedy's outset is the same one Jason sees at its end, in her famous assertion of *anagnorisis*. To some extent, of course, this is not surprising, because moments of recognition are predicated upon connecting the past to the present and in Greek tragedy, *anagnorisis* typically recalls events that have happened offstage in a time prior to the drama's beginning.[57] For example, Aeschylus' Electra recognises the cloth she wove for baby Orestes; Sophocles' Oedipus discovers himself by tracing his origins back to the moment his parents exposed him, and to his quarrel at the crossroads. But Seneca's *Medea* differs from this trend because the past recalled most powerfully in its recognition scene is the protagonist's initial monologue, and this compositional choice, in turn, allows Seneca to shift his emphasis from revelation to confirmation. By calibrating a careful set of parallels between the play's first and final scenes, Seneca calls attention to the heroine's self-conscious continuity rather than, as

---

[56] Boyle (2014) *ad Med.* 32–6.
[57] Zeitlin (2012).

happens in most recognition scenes, the recovery of a seemingly lost identity that has been distorted or mistaken over time.

Medea and the sapiens

It may seem odd, at first, to attribute quasi-Stoic or Stoic-inflected *constantia* to Seneca's Medea, a woman in the grip of passion and plotting a terrible revenge. It can and has been argued that Medea's identity actually disintegrates over the course of the play.[58] If one takes the Stoic position, broadly stated, that virtue means following nature, which in turn means exercising one's *ratio*, then Medea cannot be said to attain even remotely Stoic status. If, as Seneca asserts, nobody except the *sapiens* (i.e. the ideal Stoic wise man) can succeed in 'playing the role of one man', doesn't Medea's submission to *ira* and *furor* mean that she fluctuates and must, by definition, be inconsistent?

There is no easy answer to this question. True, Medea's final monologue (893–977) presents a self divided and indecisive, very much on the Euripidean model.[59] Seneca's heroine wavers between successive swellings of spousal anger (916–25; 950–7) and maternal pity (926–47); she addresses her *furor* (930), *dolor* (914; 944), and *ira* (916; 953) as though they were independent entities battling for control of her soul; she justifies infanticide via the wild logic that her children stand in for those Creusa never had (921–2) and that their deaths will be payment for her betrayal of Aeetes and Absyrtus (957; 970–1); she even hallucinates that her brother is present, accompanied by a crowd of Furies (958–68) and committing retributive murder through her unwilling hand (969–70). Reinforcing these impressions of wild fluctuation is Medea's description, at several points in the tragedy, as *incerta* – 'unstable', 'indecisive'. The Nurse calls her such at 382 and Medea twice applies the adjective to herself, first when she admits to being 'carried along in all directions, unsteady, frenzied, mad' (*incerta*

---

[58] Henry and Walker (1967) 175–9 and (1985) 113–14; Gill (2006) 421–35. Tietze Larson (1994) 140–5 argues for precisely the opposite course from what I'm pursuing here, namely that Seneca's Medea is a prime example of *inconstantia*.

[59] The two monologues' parallels and differences are the subject of careful study by Gill (1987). On Medea's psychological instability, see also Gill (2009) 66–76.

1.1 *Medea*

vecors mente non sana feror / partes in omnes, 123–4) and later, in her final monologue, when she is tossed by competing surges of love and hate: 'a rip-tide sweeps me along, uncertain' (*anceps aestus incertam rapit*, 939). The terminology is significant because Seneca elsewhere envisages the Stoic sage possessing psychological stability to such an extreme extent that it sometimes verges on immobility (e.g. *Clem.* 2.5.5; *Ep.* 59.14; *Const.* 2–3).[60] If the *sapiens* will not be moved, where does that leave Seneca's Medea?

Clearly, there is *some* element of constancy in her *persona*, despite the evidence I have cited to the contrary. This coherence is highlighted not just by my preceding discussion, but also by a particular trend in Senecan scholarship that has been gaining momentum over the last few decades. Recent work by Shadi Bartsch and Christopher Star has demonstrated how deeply Stoic notions of selfhood permeate Seneca's tragedies, to the extent that Seneca's *dramatis personae* employ Stoic methods of self-construction to vastly un-Stoic ends.[61] Shakespearian scholars likewise have detected in Seneca's tragic *corpus* a distinct inclination towards 'amoral constancy', whereby characters cleave to their wickedness and so exhibit a disturbing similarity to the *sapiens*.[62] In a related vein, Roy Gibson has shown how Ovid spots and playfully slips through loopholes in Cicero's theory of appropriate behaviour.[63] The conduct of Seneca's Medea could likewise be regarded as illustrating potential contradictions at the heart of Cicero's and Seneca's ethical theory, since emphasis on self-consistency leaves open the slim possibility of people persevering in wickedness, and emphasis laid upon fitting behaviour – *quid decet* – can surely lead to individuals perpetrating further crimes on the basis that such action suits their moral makeup.[64]

---

[60] Miles (1996) 40–51, and further discussion below, 85–6.
[61] Bartsch (2006) 255–81; Star (2006) and (2012) 62–83. Johnson (1988) 93–7 also sees in Seneca's Medea a perverted image of the Stoic *proficiens*.
[62] Brower (1971) 164, and Miles (1996) 57–62. More broadly, Braden (1985) 28–62.
[63] Gibson (2007) 117–29.
[64] Gill (2006) 431–2 argues that if a decision is made in favour of the passions according to what is mistakenly perceived as appropriate, this will not result in true, Stoic *decorum*. Cicero, too, circumvents the possibility of 'bad' *decorum* by declaring *admodum autem tenenda sunt sua cuique, non vitiosa, sed tamen propria, quo facilius decorum illud,*

Such cracks in the logic of *decorum* are sometimes visible in Seneca's prose works, as in the assertion at *de Vita Beata* 3.3 that, 'the happy life is one in harmony with its own nature' (*beata est ... vita conveniens naturae suae*) and similarly, *Epistle* 41.8, where humans are said to achieve moral perfection by 'living in accordance with their own natures' (*secundum naturam suam vivere*). Admittedly, both passages situate self-coherence squarely in the context of *ratio*, which should make such harmony the preserve of virtue alone. But Seneca's self-reflexive formulation, bereft of qualifiers, remains troubling. As Elizabeth Asmis notes, 'one's own nature is ... an ambiguous expression. It can denote human nature in general, as characterised by rationality, and it can also denote each human being's individual nature.'[65] By exalting the life lived ὡμολογουμένως ('in agreement') but omitting τῇ φύσει ('with nature'), Seneca opens the door, just slightly, to a- or immoral constancy, where individuals perfect their own natures regardless of virtue's normative demands.[66] Medea coheres with herself even if she doesn't cohere with *ratio*.

The theatrical metaphor of Stoic *persona* theory is likewise problematic, because it leaves little if any room between the role and the performer: if you are your *persona*, what happens when the most appropriate *persona* for you is Medea, or Atreus?[67] An approach to selfhood that relies so much on dramatic analogies inevitably runs into problems when placed in actual drama. Seneca's Medea does exhibit the irrational, passionate behaviour

---

quod quaerimus, retineatur (*Off.* 1.110) The difficulty in Senecan drama, however, is that a character's *decorum* is primarily literary – for example Medea cannot *not* commit infanticide – and therefore tends to warp the parameters of ethical self-development. Since Medea's dramatic *persona* is such that she must engage in criminal acts, pursuing ethical *decorum* requires her to decide in favour of destructive, irrational behaviour.

[65] Asmis (1990) 226.

[66] Evidence for the Stoic principle of 'living in accordance with nature' is conflicting, with some of its formulations indicating, at best, a strand of individualism in Stoic thought, at worst, solipsism. Stobaeus (*SVF* III 12) says that Cleanthes added τῇ φύσει ('with nature') to Zeno's τὸ ὁμολογουμένως ζῆν ('to live in agreement'). Diogenes Laertius 7.87 attributes τῇ φύσει to Zeno. Chrysippus glossed 'nature' as τήν τε κοινὴν καὶ ἰδίως τὴν ἀνθρωπίνην ('both common nature and private human nature' *SVF* III 4; Diog. Laer. 7.89). For further discussion of the phrase's individualistic/solipsistic implications, see Braden (1985) 19–20, Asmis (1990) 225–6.

[67] As Gibson (2007) 122–6 demonstrates, this issue troubles Cicero's treatment of *decorum* and *persona* theory throughout *Off.* 1.92–151.

1.1 *Medea*

that brands her the antithesis of the *sapiens*, yet she also displays a remarkable ability to monitor and fashion her conduct along Stoic lines.

Such an impasse need not imply that Seneca intended to criticise in his tragedies principles he had preached elsewhere;[68] the cause is subtler than that, and may well lie not (or not only) in the potential conflicts of philosophy, but in Seneca's vocabulary. Because Seneca conceives of identity and morality in Stoic terms, he uses his arsenal of distinctly Stoic language to describe people and their morals, regardless of whether those people are real or fictive.[69] In the case of his Medea, acts of self-exhortation and her desire to arrive at an ideal version of herself must be conveyed in broadly Stoic vocabulary because this, for Seneca, is the definitive way of portraying moral identity, judgement, and action. The uniformity of Seneca's style across his philosophical and dramatic oeuvre leads to friction between artistry and ethics, but that friction may not be entirely intentional on Seneca's part.

A clear example of this stylistic overlap is Seneca's Cato who, in the *de Providentia*, behaves in almost exactly the same manner as Seneca's Medea.[70] The Cato portrayed in this text cites his own name as a means of ensuring that his impending suicide fits the reputation he has so far assumed: 'Cato has a way out' (*Cato qua exeat habet, Prov.* 2.10); 'this sword will grant Cato the freedom it was not able to grant the fatherland' (*ferrum istud ... libertatem, quam patriae non potuit, Catoni dabit, Prov.* 2.10); 'for Cato, seeking death at another's hands is as disgraceful as seeking life'

---

[68] Cf. Dingel (1974) 118, who argues that Seneca's tragedies contradict his philosophy at the most fundamental level. The majority of scholars dealing with this issue pursue a more moderate approach, asserting that Seneca's plays engage with his philosophy chiefly by providing negative *exempla* of the passions; a representative sample of such scholarship includes: Knoche 1972 [1941]; Marti (1945); Lefèvre 1972 [1969]; Pratt (1983) 73–131; Henry and Walker (1985); Davis (2003) 69–74. Star (2012) 83 comes to one of the subtlest possible conclusions: 'In his tragedies, Seneca is neither negating, inverting, nor denying his philosophical ideals; rather, he is expanding them.'

[69] Shelton (1978) 70–1 proffers a similar explanation for the quasi-Stoic characterisation of Seneca's Hercules: 'he has the qualities admired in a Stoic sage, but he abuses them. Is Seneca trying to demonstrate the dangerous potential of the Stoic sage? I think, rather, that he characterises people in Stoic terms because these are the most common to him ... Stoic terms may simply reflect Seneca's manner of expression.'

[70] Johnson (1988) 88 notes a broad correspondence between these two figures. Star (2006) 218–21 sees in the Cato of *Prov.* 2.10 a model of Stoic self-command that is replicated in the tragedies.

(*tam turpe est Catoni mortem ab ullo petere quam vitam*, *Prov.* 2.10). Like Medea, Cato envisages his self as a role from which he should not deviate; he treats his past identity as a paradigm for future conduct. He even refers explicitly to the concept of *decorum* when he defines death by another's hand as 'a compact with fate that does not suit [his] greatness' (*fati conventio ... quae non deceat magnitudinem nostram, Prov.* 2.10).[71] The evident parallels between Cato and Medea generate difficulties for Seneca's ethical theory: while Cato puts his precepts to a relatively innocuous purpose and ends up being applauded for his *constantia*, Medea adopts the same attitudes as a means of accomplishing bloody revenge. The outcome depends upon which character one chooses to maintain.

Another crucial point to emerge from Medea and Cato's resemblance is that invoking one's own name does not have to be metatheatrical. Although Seneca sketches Cato's death in undeniably dramatic terms and frames the episode as a 'spectacle worthy for a god to gaze upon' (*spectaculum dignum ad quod respiciat ... deus, Prov.* 2.9),[72] Cato is not performing himself as an intrinsically theatrical role; he is a person, not a character. Further, the episode's dramatic colouring, combined with its emphasis on *constantia* and *decorum*, suggests the underlying influence of Stoic *persona* theory. Cato's performance is intended to validate his identity via sincere enactment of a pre-existing role. Like Medea's reasoning throughout her tragedy, Cato's relies on the memory of who he was and the expectations that he and others have developed from observing patterns in his behaviour.[73]

---

[71] In a similar manner, Cicero in *Off.* 1.112 argues that suicide was an act suited to Cato's *persona*: *atque haec differentia naturarum tantam habet vim, ut non numquam mortem sibi ipse consciscere alius debeat, alius in eadem causa non debeat. Num enim alia in causa M. Cato fuit, alia ceteri, qui se in Africa Caesari tradiderunt? ... Catoni cum incredibilem tribuisset natura gravitatem, eamque ipse perpetua constantia roboravisset semperque in proposito susceptoque consilio permansisset, moriendum potius quam tyranni vultus aspiciendus fuit.*

[72] On Cato's death as spectacle and Cato as actor, see Edwards (2002) 390–1; Solimano (1991) 70–1; Hijmans (1966) 237–8.

[73] Walsh (2012) 80 argues that the major difference between Medea and Cato in the *de Providentia* is Medea's reliance on past versions of herself, as opposed to Cato's reliance on abstract principles, but I disagree: although Seneca's Cato has not been subject to the same literary repetition as his Medea, he still conceives of his past self as a model for his current conduct.

1.1 *Medea*

Similar to Medea asking for recognition at the end of her play, Cato seeks self-confirmation during and through the last moments of his life, his suicide; a coherent performance, like a coherent identity, is best judged at the end.

There are other ways, too, in which Medea resembles a Stoic *sapiens*, even in her seemingly irrational final monologue. Star points out that Medea's last big speech in the drama exhibits numerous examples of Stoic-style self-exhortation via which the protagonist attempts to recover a state of *constantia*.[74] Utterances such as *nunc hoc age, anime* ('do it now, soul' 976) and *quaerere materiam, dolor* ('seek your material, o my pain' 914) recall the self-command Seneca advocates elsewhere as a means of ensuring coherent conduct: 'demand it of yourself', he tells Lucilius in *Epistle* 120.22 (*a te exige*).[75] The Cato of *de Providentia* likewise uses self-directed imperatives to guarantee the continuity of his actions: *aggredere, anime, diu meditatum opus, eripe te a rebus humanis* ('embark on this long-contemplated task, my soul: rip yourself away from human affairs' 2.10). Admittedly, Cato's route to *constantia* is smoother than Medea's, but, even though she undergoes an intense struggle with opposing desires, she nonetheless reasserts her recognisably vengeful *persona* by the tragedy's end. Moments before plunging her sword into her second son, she has regained enough confidence to command not just execution of the task, but active enjoyment of it: *perfruere lento scelere, ne propera, dolor* ('take pleasure in this gradual crime, my pain, don't rush' 1016).[76]

As an epilogue to this section, I wish to consider briefly one more, potential barrier to Medea's attaining *constantia*: trickery. Deceit is an undeniable motif in this play. Characters fear Medea as an architect of *fraus* (e.g. 181; 290–1), and their fear is not without reason, for she has plotted it in the past (475) and plots it again in the present (564; 693; 881). *dolus* likewise figures as a prominent term in the tragedy (e.g. 496; 882). This vocabulary of deception is sometimes treated as having metatheatrical currency because it implies pretence, which is assumed in turn to imply

---

[74] Star (2012) 77–82.
[75] Star (2012) 23–69.
[76] The similarities I examine here rest primarily on Medea's *manner* of speech, but there are also examples of her *content* reflecting Stoic precepts; see Chapter 4, 289–91.

dramatic performance.[77] Stage actors can be said to deceive the audience inasmuch as they don a *persona* other than their own and lead us to believe, however superficially and momentarily, in the fictions they create.[78] Playwrights achieve the same kind of effect, albeit through less immediately devious means. On this basis, Medea's skill in trickery could be said to enlarge her characterisation as a self-conscious performer and even as a quasi-dramaturg, or poet. However, while Seneca's Medea undoubtedly occupies these roles, she does so via sincere rather than deceptive conduct. Not once in her interaction with other characters does she fabricate what she feels or intends. While she may tell the occasional half-truth, she never really dissembles, and in the face of so much self-conscious illeism, she cannot seriously be thought of as playing any role other than her own. Instead, the deception taking place in this tragedy happens because of misinterpretation, because, for example, Jason believes Medea values her sons more than her marriage (442–3), or because Creon wants to be viewed as a fair ruler and thus grants her an extra day, despite his deep mistrust (285–99). Just as Medea enacts a genuine *persona*, so, paradoxically, she achieves *fraus* without being *falsa* herself.

Recognition without Revelation

I have argued so far that Medea's recognition comes as no real surprise, that the play's audience, at least, ends up recognising a figure it has known all along and of whose capacities it has been forewarned throughout the drama. Jason, one could argue, is in a slightly different position, because his *anagnorisis* of Medea involves painful realisation of his own errors. What Jason experiences in the tragedy's final scene is a moment of re-appraising and re-knowing (hence: ἀνα-γνωρίζω) a person he knew before, but whom he had seriously underestimated.[79] Forcing Jason to this

---

[77] See in particular Michelon (2015) 46–54.
[78] Thus, Michelon (2015) 17 calls deception the 'meccanismo fondamentale dell'azione teatrale' ('essential mechanism of theatrical action'). For my caveats on this approach, though, see Chapter 3, 212–13.
[79] Thus, Cave (1988) 33: "Ana-gnorisis', like 're-cognition' ... implies a recovery of something once known rather than merely a shift from ignorance to knowledge.'

1.1 *Medea*

new level of comprehension is certainly one of Medea's aims, but it is overshadowed by her need for Jason to validate her self-construction and acknowledge its coherence. Significantly, she phrases her final question to him in terms that call attention to her normative identity: not, 'do you recognise me?' but 'do you recognise your wife?' The third-personal formulation invites Jason to acknowledge an essential congruence between Medea's individual behaviour and the role it has been designed to fulfil. Further, it invites Jason to recognise in Medea precisely the woman he once married, the woman whose conduct has never really changed in spite of her wildly fluctuating temper. In the words of Alessandro Schiesaro:[80]

> To be able to 'recognise' Medea as 'Medea', or Atreus as 'Atreus', is predicated on the immutability of fundamental characteristics which define them as what they are ... They both guarantee that past patterns will prevail: they rise from the certainty of a model which their antagonists need to learn. Once they do, once they 'recognise', they admit the fallibility of their desire, or hope, for change.

This Medea is the same as she always was, and Jason's primary purpose in the final scene is to corroborate her *constantia*.

Another crucial way in which Jason validates Medea's identity is through his role as spectator.[81] When he arrives on the scene, Medea calls him *spectator iste* (993) and declares, *quidquid sine isto fecimus sceleris perit* ('whatever crime I committed outside his presence has been wasted', 994). Besides being metatheatrical and deeply sadistic,[82] this desire for an audience is a symptom of Medea's careful self-fashioning, since, as Seneca and Cicero both imply, verification of consistent conduct depends on its being seen. One's personal coherence is, in the end, discerned and judged by others, and the normative nature of Stoic *personae* implies outward evaluation as opposed to private, individual fulfilment. Even in the case of people evaluating *constantia* for and within themselves, the activity requires one to develop a self-critical gaze that performs the function of an external assessor: Lucilius must

---

[80] Schiesaro (2003) 213.
[81] Dupont (1995) 185. Braden (1985) 61 remarks that Seneca's tragic protagonists often desire validation from their victims.
[82] On sadistic spectatorship in Senecan tragedy, see Littlewood (2004) 215-39.

monitor himself as 'Lucilius', Cato as 'Cato', Medea as 'Medea'.[83] This is exactly what the heroine of Seneca's *Medea* has been doing over the course of her tragedy, and in the play's last few moments, she hands that responsibility over to Jason. He is there not just to be an internal, metatheatrical audience for Medea's spectacular performance, but also to provide acknowledgement of her identity. Once again, the final exchange in this drama hinges on the authorising rather than revelatory function of recognition. *anagnorisis* in this instance does not involve unmasking or disclosure, but continuity and validation.

Recognition without Reunion

So, Medea achieves coherent selfhood in the end, but it comes at the expense of everything else. Whereas conventional recognition scenes tend to involve a renewal of family relationships,[84] Seneca's Medea realises the opposite, namely acknowledgement of her ability to destroy interpersonal ties. Her request that Jason recognise her as his wife plays ironically on the ideas of reunion and legitimacy germane to *anagnorisis* in both tragic and comic plotlines. Such recognitions typically reassert and also authorise relationships between people: Electra regains her brother; Ion reclaims his status as Creusa's child; Oedipus learns simultaneously his true parentage and the socio-sexual boundaries he has unwittingly crossed.[85] The results are even more pronounced in New Comedy and *palliata*, where long-lost children are recovered and status issues resolved so that long-term lovers are finally able to unite; *anagnorisis* brings with it the prospect of restoring order to previously incomplete, incorrect, or unbalanced collectivities.[86] Seneca's Medea, however, longs to cut all social ties, and the profusion of family terms used by Seneca throughout the tragedy

---

[83] This 'internalisation' of social judgement is a marked trait of Seneca's philosophy: see Roller (2001) 77–88 and Bartsch (2006) 183–229.
[84] On the key role of family relationships in *anagnorisis* see Aristotle *Poetics* 1452b, as well as the structural study by Sissa (2006).
[85] Goldhill (1986) 84.
[86] Konstan (1983).

1.1 *Medea*

only serves to emphasise his heroine's ruinous pursuit of isolation and autonomy.

One example is Medea's obsessive desire to be acknowledged as Jason's wife.[87] She begins her tragedy by invoking 'the gods of marriage and Lucina guardian of the marriage-bed' (*di coniugales tuque genialis tori, / Lucina, custos* 1–2), and refers to herself as *coniunx* far more frequently than other characters in the play refer to her as such.[88] Like the Medea of Ovid's *Heroides*, she focuses on her dowry and on the impossible process of restitution she feels that Jason ought to perform as a consequence of their 'divorce': *tibi patria cessit, tibi pater frater pudor / hac dote nupsi; redde fugienti sua* ('my fatherland fell to you, my brother, father, modesty. I married you with this dowry; give the fugitive back what is hers' 487–8). Her opening speech even includes the bitter wish that Jason's future sufferings will make his marriage to her seem a blessing in retrospect: *me coniugem optet* ('let him long for me as his wife' 22).[89] In fact, the wish verges on paradox, because having Jason long for her as his wife is precisely what Medea wants at this early point in the drama. Yet she also wants to achieve her identity by destroying family ties so that Jason no longer has any wife at all.

The same paradoxical tension underlies her final request for Jason's recognition, for Medea wants Jason to claim her and no other in the role of his wife, but she also wants to confirm that she has abolished all of that role's actual, social requirements. This conflict is heightened by her use of the verb *agnoscere*, which can refer specifically to legitimisation and family reunion, as is often the case in descriptions of parents legally recognising their offspring: *quem ille natum non <u>agnoverat</u>, eundem moriens suum esse dixerat* ('he had not <u>acknowledged</u> him as a son, but declared him so on his deathbed' Nep. *Ag.* 1.4); *expositum qui <u>agnoverit</u>, solutis alimentis recipiat* ('a father who <u>recognises</u> a son exposed in infancy should take him back only after having paid for his

---

[87] See in particular Abrahamsen (1999); Guastella (2001); Walsh (2012), and McAuley (2016) 201–28. Frank (1995) also makes some pertinent observations about the rhetorical effects of kinship terms in Senecan tragedy.
[88] A tendency noted by Abrahamsen (1999) 110–13.
[89] Although Zwierlein (1986a) follows Axelson in emending *optet* to *opto*, I agree with Hine (2000) *ad loc.* that the MSS reading should be retained because the contradictory sentiment seems typically Senecan.

upbringing' Quint. *Inst.* 7.1.14). Placed alongside these examples, Medea's request for recognition evokes familial restoration and the resumption of social duties: Jason is called upon to recognise Medea's spousal status in a legal as well as emotional sense, even while Medea's vengeful acts have precluded the possibility of reunion.[90] Thus, Seneca's recognition scene hints at only to deny the renewal that *anagnorisis* typically brings. Confirmation of Medea's identity prevents rather than generates social reintegration.

Such allusions to reunification haunt the final exchange between Jason and Medea as if to remind the audience of other, happier versions of dramatic recognition. For example, when Jason arrives on stage, Medea describes the culmination of her revenge as a moment that reverses time and reinstates her as a virginal Colchian princess:[91]

> iam iam recepi sceptra germanum patrem,
> spoliumque Colchi pecudis auratae tenent;
> rediere regna, rapta virginitas redit.
> o placida tandem numina, o festum diem,
> o nuptialem!

> Now, now I have regained sceptre, brother, father,
> and the Colchians keep the spoils of the golden fleece;
> the kingdom has been restored, my plundered virginity restored.
> O divine powers, finally favourable, O festive day,
> O wedding day!
>
> (*Med.* 982–6)

Medea's assertion is a hyperbolic reflection of the customary events of recognition scenes, in which brothers really are united with sisters, and fathers with children. Even Medea's perversely gleeful reminder that this is Jason's wedding day (*o nuptialem!*) conjures, obliquely, the love matches that tend to conclude New Comic and *palliata* plots.[92] Moreover, with Creusa now dead by

---

[90] The legality – or otherwise – of Medea's marriage to Jason is treated by Abrahamsen (1999) and McAuley (2016) 205–6.

[91] Medea's claims make no sense if taken literally, but Schiesaro (2009) 228–34 is right to suggest that they are symptomatic of Medea's obsession with the past and with her past self. As Kerrigan (1996) 277 points out, undoing the past is one of the avenger's main aspirations.

[92] Despite pioneering work by Tarrant (1978) and Grant (1999), Seneca's debt to New Comedy/*comoedia palliata* remains a relatively unexplored and potentially very rich topic.

1.1 *Medea*

Medea's hand, the heroine's exultant *o nuptialem* articulates her own, sole claim to be Jason's wife; it hints, bitterly, at the resumption of social relationships so often dependent on acts of *anagnorisis*.

In like manner, Jason's acceptance of his sons' bodies seems to build upon, almost to parody, the convention of parent–child recognition that pervades earlier drama. The event is facilitated by Medea herself, who differs from Euripides' heroine in her lack of concern for her children's burial (cf. Eur. *Med.* 1378–83).[93] Rather than carry the corpses with her, Seneca's Medea leaves them for Jason, declaring sarcastically, 'now take back your sons, as their parent' (*recipe iam natos parens*, 1024). Comparable language of restitution and recovery is used to describe family reunions in *comoedia palliata*, as in Plautus' *Captivi*, when Hegio thanks the gods for 'giving back and restoring' his son (*quom te reducem tuo patri reddiderunt*, 923),[94] or in Terence's *Hecyra*, when the courtesan Bacchis reveals Myrrina's background story and, as a direct consequence, restores to Pamphilus both his son and his spouse (*gnatum ei restituo . . . /uxorem . . . reddo*; 'I return his son to him . . . / I give back his wife' 818–19). The parallels in vocabulary suggest a further, structural similarity: like the fathers of Roman comedy, Jason takes part in a recognition scene in which he is granted the opportunity to acknowledge and reclaim his children. The verb *recipere* may even suggest the legitimising function of *anagnorisis* since it, along with *agnoscere*, features in the legal maxim reported by Quintilian (*Inst.* 7.1.14: *expositum qui agnoverit, solutis alimentis recipiat*; 'a father who recognises a son exposed in infancy should take him back only after having paid for his upbringing'). Thus, Medea's language in this final exchange pushes Jason, however ironically, to assume an authorising, paternal role in relation to the family he has disrupted. Seneca's handling of the scene draws attention to the reintegration and social harmony so often consequent upon acts of recognition, making their absence from his tragedy all the more acute. The paradox for Seneca's Medea is that self-coherence and consequent

---

[93] Hine (2000) *ad Med.* 1024
[94] It must, however, be noted, with Lacey (1978–79) 132, that Plautus rarely uses the father–son reconciliation motif to conclude his plays.

recognisability entail the kind of crimes that will destroy any chance of a family reunion. Acting in the role of Jason's wife leads Medea, ultimately, to be a wife in name only. Likewise, she leaves Jason in the purely nominal position of *parens*.

So, Medea's pursuit of ideal selfhood happens at the expense of the self-in-relationship, and her solipsism stands in stark contrast to the conventionally social consequences of recognition. Like the Stoic sage, of whom she is a dark mirror image, Seneca's Medea achieves a radical form of independence – a kind of *autarkeia* – as a result of her conscious, careful self-realisation.[95] What we see, what we in fact *recognise* in Seneca's Medea are the aims of self-coherence and self-perfection taken to an extreme where being true to oneself all but means producing and upholding one's own definition of virtue. Geoffrey Miles remarks that Stoic doctrine contains within it the potential for this sort of amoral constancy, in which 'authenticity of the self becomes an end in itself'.[96] Such potential only increases in the context of Senecan drama, where the performance of dramatic roles bleeds into the performance of implied human ones. It is Medea's combined sense of herself as both a dramatic character and a quasi-human personality that leads her to pursue an unwavering course of wickedness and, by the tragedy's end, to expect audience acknowledgement for the consistent playing of her destructive, selfish, violent role.

1.2 *Thyestes*

Recognition in the Thyestes

It is not only in the *Medea* that Seneca uses a recognition scene to explore questions of identity and self-coherence; the *Thyestes*, too, addresses such topics in its final Act, albeit with a shift in focus that incorporates two characters, and two perspectives, in contrast to Medea's monolithic vision. The exchange begins with Thyestes sated to the point of discomfort by a meal whose grisly provenance is still unknown to him; upon Atreus' entrance, Thyestes greets his

---

[95] Both Braden (1985) 34 and 57, and Johnson (1988) 87 and 93–7 perceive traces of Stoic *autarkeia* in Medea's conduct. Fuller discussion in Chapter 4.
[96] Miles (1996) 61.

1.2 *Thyestes*

brother and asks to see his children. Atreus responds by unveiling the boys' heads and hands,[97] and inquiring with characteristic black humour, *natos ecquid agnoscis tuos?* ('do you recognise your sons at all?' 1005). Thyestes replies, *agnosco fratrem* ('I recognise my brother' 1006).

At first glance, Atreus and Thyestes' interaction appears to fit a standard pattern of recognition, in which one or more characters acquire new and typically unexpected information, which then leads to a change in their circumstances. It is in fact possible to interpret the scene according to Aristotle's definition of *anagnorisis* as, 'a change from ignorance to knowledge, generating either love or hate between characters marked for either good or bad fortune' (ἐξ ἀγνοίας εἰς γνῶσιν μεταβολή, ἢ εἰς φιλίαν ἢ εἰς ἔχθραν, τῶν πρὸς εὐτυχίαν ἢ δυστυχίαν ὡρισμένων, *Poetics* 1452a30-2). Thus, the brothers' final confrontation is the moment at which Thyestes realises that he has been led into a trap (ἐξ ἀγνοίας εἰς γνῶσιν μεταβολή), and that instead of being co-regent, he is the victim of brutal revenge (πρὸς εὐτυχίαν ἢ δυστυχίαν); it is also the moment at which Atreus drops his pretence of reconciliation (ἢ εἰς φιλίαν ἢ εἰς ἔχθραν).

But Thyestes' reply, *agnosco fratrem*, suggests that the true focus of this scene lies elsewhere, that it is not only about disclosure and newly acquired knowledge, but also about recognisability. In declaring that he recognises Atreus, Thyestes implies that his brother's identity is closely bound up with, even dependent upon, the process of *anagnorisis*. Like Seneca's Medea, Atreus seems to use recognition as a means of confirming his self-coherence and asserting the character traits that Thyestes has already acknowledged earlier in the play. Also like Medea, Atreus achieves recognition primarily through understanding his *persona* and the patterns of behaviour incumbent upon it, while Thyestes embodies the opposite: an inconsistent individual fundamentally lacking in self-awareness. Questions about Thyestes' identity, and *his* recognisability, suffuse this final

---

[97] Despite the lack of implicit stage directions, it is reasonable to assume that Atreus presents Thyestes with his children's remains, whether on a platter, in a casket, or in the hands of servants. Braun (1982) 45–6 argues that this exchange requires performance in order to be understood and regards it as definitive proof that Seneca wrote for the stage. Further discussion of the scene's dramaturgy can be found in Calder (1983) 187, and Kohn (2013) 130–1.

exchange as well, even though neither character addresses them openly. To what extent does Thyestes know himself? And does his changeable behaviour have any bearing on the painful revelation he undergoes in the tragedy's final Act? The recognition scene that concludes Seneca's *Thyestes* expands upon many of the key features present already in the *Medea*.[98]

Recognition and Role-Play

One of these features is the self-conscious theatricality that colours Atreus and Thyestes' conversation. As in the *Medea*, the characters' prominent use of *agnoscere* points up the conventional form and purpose of recognition scenes, thereby inviting the audience to construe Atreus and Thyestes as essentially theatrical figures whose roles have been enacted before. Although neither of the brothers makes any reference to 'customary' behaviour (there is no *sic fugere soleo* here), the scene's insistent repetition of *agnoscere* nonetheless reminds us that this is not the first time Atreus and Thyestes have staged their fraternal conflict. Indeed, their story was popular subject matter for ancient dramatists, and for Roman playwrights especially,[99] while one of the most famous pre-Senecan versions of the play, Accius' *Atreus*, appears to have concluded with a similarly gruesome scene of unveiling (226–32 Ribbeck, *TRF²*).[100] Even if precise allusions slip our grasp, owing

---

[98] In making this claim, I do not mean to suggest a particular sequence for the tragedies' composition, though the *Thyestes* is generally thought to have been one of the last plays Seneca wrote. Fitch (1981) remains the standard authority on the play's dating.

[99] From the Greek versions, it appears that Sophocles' *Atreus* and Euripides' *Thyestes* were both known to Roman readers. Fragments survive from at least three Roman versions: Ennius' *Thyestes*; Accius' *Atreus*; and Varius' *Thyestes*. In addition, we hear of numerous plays being composed on the topic throughout the late republic and early empire: by Cassius of Parma (Pseudo-Acro *ad* Hor. *Epist.* 1.4.3); by Sempronius Gracchus (Ov. *Pont.* 4.16.31); by Mamercus Scaurus (Dio 58.24.3–4); by Pomponius Secundus (Nonn. 144.24); by the (fictive?) Maternus in Tac. *Dial.* 3.3. Goldberg (1996) 277 remarks that Thyestes' story became a 'rhetorical cliché' in first-century AD Rome. Caution must be exercised, though, because not all versions can be assumed to have dealt with precisely the same parts of the Atreus-Thyestes myth, for example Jocelyn (1967) 413 argues that the events of Ennius' *Thyestes* take place at Thesprotus' court in Epirus, following Atreus' revenge, and Warmington (1988) 346 regards this play's action as occurring in two localities: Mycenae, then Epirus.

[100] For Accius' likely influence on Seneca, see Zwierlein (1983) 123–4; Tarrant (1985) 42–3; and Boyle (2006) 127–33. Careful work by Leigh (1997) demonstrates that

1.2 *Thyestes*

to the fact that Seneca's is the only complete surviving tragedy on this topic, it is still possible to detect subtle irony in Atreus asking Thyestes whether he recognises his children (*Thy.* 1005): Thyestes has, presumably, performed this scene before, and he should know by now what to expect.

The potential metatheatricality of this final exchange becomes more prominent when viewed against the backdrop of the tragedy overall, where Thyestes in particular is often portrayed as playing a role. The reunion in Act 3, for example, begins with Atreus inviting the audience to see Thyestes through his eyes, as some sort of distasteful spectacle: *aspice, ut multo gravis / squalore vultus obruat maestos coma / quam foeda iaceat barba* ('look at how his dirty, matted hair envelops his gloomy face, how his foul beard droops' 505–7).[101] Thyestes himself continues the metaphor when he casts Atreus as a spectator to his grovelling apology: *lacrimis agendum est. supplicem primus vides* ('I must plead my case with tears. You are the first to see me beg' 517). By asking his brother to assume the pose of an internal audience member – something Atreus is only too happy to do – Thyestes activates a self-consciously dramatic scenario in which the histrionics of an orator (*lacrimis agendum est*) merge with those of an actor, and we are left querying the sincerity of Thyestes' teary performance. The move also places Atreus in a position of power, which he consolidates by designing further roles for Thyestes. 'Remove your hands from my knees' he chides the grovelling figure, 'and seek my embraces instead ... Put aside your filthy clothing ... and take up richly adorned garments like my own' (*a genibus manum / aufer meosque potius amplexus pete. / ... / ... squalidam vestem exue, / ... et ornatus cape / pares meis*, *Thy.* 521–6). Via this false promise of reconciliation and its implicit lure of luxury,[102] Atreus compels Thyestes to perform the role that has been devised for him. The

---

Varius' tragedy is also likely to have featured Thyestes' cannibal feast, though the exiguous nature of that play's remains makes measuring Seneca's debt impossible.

[101] Thus Boyle (2017) *ad Thy.* 504–7: 'Part of the extraordinary dramatic power of this play is Atreus' ability to control the audience and to shape the play in conjunction with them.'

[102] Thyestes' appetitive weakness is noted by Boyle (1983) 216–17, Tarrant (1985) *ad Thy.* 524–6, and Meltzer (1988) 320. It is analysed at greater length by Davis (2003) 43–52.

summons to change clothing is not just an index of (feigned) hospitality, but also a metatheatrical gesture of the sort more commonly found in Plautine comedy (e.g. *Pseud.* 735; 751–5).[103] Thyestes the actor must remove his old costume (*exuo* can be used as a technical term in the theatre) and assume along with his new robes his fully tragic role; he must undergo a transformation from shabby sylvan hermit into the royal personage required by tragic convention.[104] Concomitantly, Atreus confirms for himself the part of dramaturg, dictating his brother's gesture, outfit, and general comportment in the manner of a playwright or director.[105]

Self-conscious allusions to theatrical performance ripple through the *Thyestes*' final Act as well, with Atreus treating his brother more and more as a spectatorial object. Following an initial gloat of triumph, he commands his servants to 'unbar the palace doors and throw the festal house open to view' (*fores / temple relaxa, festa patefiat domus*, 901–2), a move that enables him to accompany the play's external audience in watching Thyestes at the banquet.[106] The ensuing scene, in which Thyestes sings to himself a fifty-line song, is framed not just as Atreus eavesdropping on his brother's private thoughts, but also as Thyestes, unwittingly, giving a very public and stage-managed performance. Once again, Thyestes is playing precisely the role Atreus has designed for him, and Atreus stands back to admire the results:

> libet videre, capita natorum intuens
> quos det colores, verba quae primus dolor
> effundat aut spiritu expulso stupens
> corpus rigescat. fructus hic operis mei est.
> miserum videre nolo, sed dum fit miser.

---

[103] Elements of *comoedia palliata* in Seneca's *Thyestes* have been explored by Meltzer (1988) 314–15.
[104] See, for example, Mercury's definition of the tragic genre at *Amphitruo* 61 as plays in which 'kings and gods walk the stage'.
[105] Thus, Littlewood (2008) 254: 'Atreus expresses his domination of Thyestes by making him perform as an actor who cannot resist his script or more simply as a visual object.' For Atreus as dramaturg, see Tarrant (1985), Boyle (1997) 117–18, the much broader study by Schiesaro (2003) 45–61, and Mowbray (2012) 401–2. Mader (2010) shows how Atreus assimilates cruelty to processes of artistic creation.
[106] Schiesaro (2003) 60; Boyle (2017) *ad Thy.* 903–7.

1.2 *Thyestes*

> I want to see how his face changes colour as he gazes
> on his sons' heads, what words his initial grief pours forth,
> or how his body stiffens, dumbfounded, breathless.
> This is the fruit of my labour.
> I don't want to see him wretched, but to see him *becoming* so.
>
> (*Thy.* 903–7)

By focusing closely upon individual physical details, Atreus imagines Thyestes as a consummate actor, someone so skilful he can represent not just an emotional state, but also the entire process involved in reaching that state.[107] Under Atreus' equally skilful direction, Thyestes' face and body are imagined as achieving the kind of expressive faculty his role requires of them. Further, as a proleptic description of the impending recognition scene, Atreus' words lead the audience to evaluate Thyestes' subsequent reaction in terms of his imputed thespian competence: *we* watch while he gazes at his sons' remains, and *we* are curious to see how his response registers in his visage, his body, and his language.[108] While Thyestes embarks, unhappily, on the process of recognising his sons, so the tragedy's audience begins to recognise, even to acknowledge, correspondences between Atreus' description and Thyestes' enactment. Such metatheatricality gains an added dimension when the scene is staged, because the actor playing Thyestes may choose to perform his recognition precisely in accord with Atreus' preceding sketch.

A final, clinching detail of Thyestes' actor status is the festival setting of the banquet that seals his fate. Atreus calls the occasion a 'festal day' (*festum diem*, 970) and Thyestes employs the same phrase when drunkenly urging himself to be happy: 'why do you forbid me', he asks his long-accustomed wretchedness, 'from celebrating this festal day?' (*quid ... festum ... vetas / celebrare diem?* 942–3). Gary Meltzer notes that such vocabulary 'evokes the conventions of comedy' where 'drunken celebration, singing and feasting' are typical features, especially as markers of the

---

[107] Similarly, Mowbray (2012) 402 notes that Atreus' words 'emphasise that it is the process rather than the result that matters ... he would like to experience the action-over-time phenomenon inherent in being a spectator at a play'. Mader (2010) interprets the passage according to the tragedy's broader themes of punishment-as-process and violence-as-artistry.

[108] Littlewood (2008) 259.

drama's happy ending.[109] I would take Meltzer's idea one step further here, and suggest that *festus dies* is also meant to evoke the context of the *ludi* that typically hosted performances of Roman drama.[110] If Seneca's *Thyestes* was indeed staged on just such a festival occasion, then the phrase's metatheatrical connotations would be virtually impossible to ignore: Thyestes, like an actor, participates in the Saturnalian hedonism of Atreus' *ludi*, albeit with less than comic results. The phrase retains much of its force even when removed from this immediately ludic context and, in conjunction with Atreus' repeated use of *videre*, encourages the audience to regard Thyestes as a performer both in Seneca's and in Atreus' play.

When Thyestes performs these roles within the tragedy, moreover, he draws attention to himself as a *dramatis persona* that may be assumed and put aside at will; the part of 'Thyestes' is embodied and played in accordance with Atreus' – and Seneca's – script. To the extent that Atreus represents a playwright, Thyestes can also be said to represent a constructed literary character, a purely textual entity animated and controlled by someone else. Thyestes the actor alters his costume and gesture at another's bidding; Thyestes the character alters his circumstances and eventual fate. Viewed within the play's broader context, then, the recognition scene acquires a metatheatrical quality in which Thyestes – qua character and actor – performs a part that somebody else has orchestrated and is now sitting down to observe.

But what of Atreus? To a lesser extent, the recognition scene casts him, too, as an actor, in addition to his more conspicuous roles as dramatist and director. When Thyestes states, *agnosco fratrem* ('I recognise my brother' *Thy.* 1006), he acknowledges both Atreus' essential moral qualities – their true ugliness now fully apparent – and the well-known parameters of Atreus' dramatic part: this conduct, in this scene, is how we expect Thyestes' brother to behave.

Unlike Thyestes, however, who assumes the roles he is given, Atreus does not seem inclined to play any part other than his own. Admittedly, he deviates from his usual disposition at the beginning

---

[109] Meltzer (1988) 315.
[110] A suggestion I have since found, as well, in Boyle (2017) *ad Thy.* 942–6.

1.2 *Thyestes*

of Act 3, when he reins in his anger temporarily in order to stage a scene of reconciliation: *cum sperat ira sanguinem, nescit tegi—/ tamen tegatur* ('when anger hopes for blood, it does not know how to be hidden— but let it be hidden', *Thy.* 504–5). This momentary aim of covering up his true feelings resembles an actor's ability to assume identities other than his or her own. Atreus prepares for his reunion with Thyestes in a manner akin to an actor rehearsing a part, and his complicit aside to the audience confirms this association even in the absence of any explicitly metatheatrical language.[111] With Thyestes almost within earshot, Atreus adds, *praestetur fides* (507), a slippery declaration that can mean either 'let me fulfil my promise / keep my word', or, 'let me display my trustworthiness / let a believable performance be given'.[112] Of course, the *fides* that requires a performance in order to seem so is not really *fides* at all; once again, a gap appears to open between who Atreus is and who he professes to be. But the very ambiguity of his rhetoric ensures, paradoxically, that Atreus can play a part and remain true to himself, since the false *fides* he enacts before Thyestes is, at the same time, Atreus' being faithful to his own intentions. He has resolved to greet his brother and to entice him back to royal power, which is exactly what he proceeds to do, albeit with a purpose that Thyestes cannot yet divine. Hence Atreus' role-play may be seen as articulating a genuine facet of his identity, a characteristic he shares with Seneca's Medea, and which will occupy the bulk of my discussion in the chapter sections to come. Before plunging back into this topic of sincere performance, however, I would like to consider one more example of Atreus' theatricality, namely, his famous opening monologue.

Atreus enters the stage in Act 2 upbraiding himself for tardiness in the matter of revenge:

> ignave, iners, enervis et, quod maximum
> probrum tyranno rebus in summis reor,
> inulte: post tot scelera, post fratris dolos
> fasque omne ruptum questibus vanis agis
> iratus Atreus?

---

[111] Moore (1998) examines the metatheatrical effects of asides in Plautus.
[112] Further discussion of the line's meaning can be found in Tarrant (1985) *ad Thy.* 507, Schiesaro (2003) 55, and Boyle (2017) *ad Thy.* 504–7.

> Useless, feckless, impotent, and what I regard
> the greatest source of shame for a tyrant in high power,
> unavenged: after so many crimes, a brother's betrayal,
> all moral codes broken, do you act as angered Atreus
> by means of empty complaint?
>
> (*Thy.* 176–80)

Critics have often commented upon the speech's metatheatrical quality.[113] Because *agere* means both 'performing a deed' and 'performing a stage role', Atreus' language draws attention to the fact that he is currently acting in front of an audience, and that his character, like Medea's, has been played before. By citing his own name, Seneca's Atreus measures himself against a prior dramatic tradition only to find that his present conduct falls far below the expected mark: *questibus vanis agis / iratus Atreus?* As Gordon Braden notes, the participle-noun combination *iratus Atreus* is reminiscent of a play title, such as *Hercules Furens*, or of the excerpted roles that, according to Suetonius, Nero liked to perform on stage: *inter cetera cantavit Canacem parturientem, Oresten matricidam, Oedipodem excaecatum, Herculem insanum* ('he sang, among other parts, Canace in labour, Orestes the matricide, Oedipus blinded, Hercules insane' *Ner.* 21.3).[114] Horace, too, uses this kind of phrasing to denote the principal characteristics of individual tragic roles – *sit Medea ferox invictaque, flebilis Ino, / perfidus Ixion, Io vaga, tristis Orestes* ('Medea should be fierce and unbowed, Ino teary, Ixion treacherous, Io wandering, Orestes morose' *Ars* 123–4.) – as does Quintilian: *ut sit Aerope in tragoedia tristis, atrox Medea, attonitus Aiax, truculentus Hercules* ('So, in tragedy, Aerope is morose, Medea fierce, Ajax mad, Hercules aggressive' *Inst.* 11.3.73). In fact, for Horace and Quintilian as well as for Seneca's Atreus, these formulaic classifications may well be designed to evoke stage characters' masks, in which case Atreus once again asserts himself as a role, implying that his present 'empty complaints' do not suit the dictates of his costume.

---

[113] Braden (1970) 17, and (1985) 42; Boyle (1997) 117 and (2006) 211; Fitch and McElduff (2002) 25; Erasmo (2004) 124.

[114] Braden (1985) 42. *Hercules Furens* is in fact the title of the Senecan play given by the 'A' branch of MSS, while the 'E' branch gives simply *Hercules*.

1.2 *Thyestes*

Thus, Atreus' speech identifies him from the outset as a well-known *dramatis persona*, classifiable not just by his name, but also by his appearance, and by the emotion he is typically assumed to exhibit. The near-anagram of *iRATUS* and *ATReUS* further suggests that rage is embedded within Atreus' dramatic part and essential to its realisation.[115] Like Medea, this Atreus can be seen to construct himself as a fundamentally literary (and more specifically, theatrical) entity. Consequently, the recognition he receives may be interpreted as an acknowledgement of his textual identity, that is, of his existence as an assemblage of earlier texts and performances. Atreus is recognisable – to Thyestes, to the audience – because he has performed his part in accordance with its pre-established parameters. Although the lack of surviving precedents renders dramatic allusions far less apparent in Seneca's *Thyestes* than in his *Medea*, there is still little doubt that a metatheatrical atmosphere suffuses the final scene.

Performing the Self

Atreus' opening speech deserves further consideration, however, because it establishes his quasi-human identity just as much as his fictional one. Significantly, Atreus' language describes no division between himself and the part he plays: he both *is* and *acts* Atreus, and does not pretend to be another person in the manner of a professional stage artist. Whereas the notion of acting, singing, or dancing a role is typically expressed by a verb plus accusative– as in the phrase *agere partes* ('to play a part')[116] – Atreus employs instead a nominative in apposition (*agis / iratus Atreus*) and this subtle syntactical shift conveys the equivalence of his *dramatis persona* and his self. Senecan scholars tend to overlook this small but crucial point. When Seneca, elsewhere, describes people pretending to be angry, or enacting the roles of angry men, he uses the

---

[115] Burnett (1998) 12; Fitch and McElduff (2002) 25 n.22
[116] *OLD s.v.* 'pars' entry 9. Cf. Sen. *Contr.* 2.6.4: *nec amantem agis, sed amas*; Sen. *Ep.* 120.22: *unum hominem agere*. The same construction is used to describe singing a role – as in the passage from Suetonius *Nero* 21.3, cited above – and dancing one, for example *Latin Anthology* R. 310: *Andromacham atque Helenam saltat*, and further discussion in Kokolakis (1976) 217–29.

69

standard accusative construction: *nam et histriones in pronuntiando non irati populum movent, sed iratum bene agentes* ('for actors also move their audience with their delivery, not by being angry, but by acting well the part of an angry man' *Ira* 2.17.1). Similarly, *Epistle* 80.7 uses the phrase *agere felicem* to refer to someone pretending to be happy. The accusative is such a natural, instinctive companion of *agere* that it may even be ventured as the reason for the variant, and ultimately unsustainable, reading found in the A manuscripts of Seneca *Thyestes* 179–80: *questibus vanis agis / iras?*[117] The reader who altered this line presumably expected Atreus to perform his anger rather than, as the more difficult and accepted phrasing implies, to perform *as himself*, as 'Atreus enraged'.

While it may seem pedantic, this grammatical point is actually vital, because it implies that Atreus envisages his role as a genuine expression of his identity. There is no difference, for Atreus, between being true to his dramatic part and being true to his self. In addition, the semantic range of *agere* allows the theatrical metaphor to be combined with the simpler meaning of 'behave' or 'perform an action', a combination that once more suggests the equivalence of acting a part and being a person.[118] These two facets of Atreus' identity overlap, since in attempting to meet the qualities and requirements of his dramatic role he also strengthens his status as an implied human personality.

This link between actor and role, character and person, is drawn tighter still when Atreus alludes to the Stoic concept of *decorum*, specifically in regard to his position as tyrant, which he feels he has so far failed to fulfil: *quod maximum / probrum tyranno rebus in summis reor / inulte* ('what I regard the greatest source of shame for a tyrant in high power: unavenged' 176–8). Atreus knows that

---

[117] Tarrant (1985) *ad Thy.* 179–83 notes that the difficult expression, *agis* minus an object, is almost certainly authentic.
[118] Roach (1996) 3 describes a similar semantic range for 'performance' in English. In both cases, the term's variety of meanings suggests a theoretically crucial and enduring confluence of theatre and 'real life'. See also Aygon (2016) 222: 'Il arrive aussi que Sénèque associe les deux sens du verbe *agere* (se comporter/jouer un rôle), notamment lorsqu'un personnage s'interpelle lui-même' ('Seneca happens to link the two meanings of the verb *agere* (to behave/play a role) especially when a character is addressing himself').

1.2 *Thyestes*

in order to achieve this title he must set aside his present grumbling in favour of setting fire to the world around him: *iam flammis agros / lucere et urbes decuit* ('it has already been fitting for fields and cities to flash with fire' 182–3); the rules of *decorum* demand he engage in actions appropriate to his particular status. Moreover, the part of tyrant that Atreus cites in this passage is not just a dramatic role, a prior instantiation either of Atreus himself or of any other violent autocrat known to stalk the ancient stage, but also a social role, an occasional and acknowledged – if not exactly welcome – aspect of ancient politics. Thus, when Atreus evaluates his (currently insufficient) tyrannical *persona*, he behaves much like an aspiring Stoic who has been enjoined to weigh his actions according to what befits (*decet*) his status, abilities, and circumstances.

This need to align one's actions with one's given social role is a recurring theme in Stoic accounts of *decorum*/τὸ πρέπον. For instance, Epictetus advises individuals to 'preserve appropriate behaviour as men, as sons, as parents, and so forth according to other terms for relationships' (τὸ πρέπον σώζουσιν ὡς ἄνδρες, ὡς υἱοί, ὡς γονεῖς, εἶθ᾿ ἑξῆς κατὰ τὰ ἄλλα τῶν σχέσεων ὀνόματα, *Diss.* 4.6.26). In the *Enchiridion*, Epictetus describes the form and content of life's duties as dependent upon each person's particular social position, with the result that a poor man cannot hold office or display his munificence in acts of euergetism, while a wealthy man is clearly free to do so (*Ench.* 24).[119] In a similar manner, Cicero discusses *decorum* in terms of social status at *Off.* 1.122–4, and besides addressing the broad categories of old and young men, and private individuals, he glances at the obligations incumbent upon specific public posts.[120] Thus, he pronounces that it is the proper function (*proprium munus*) of magistrates 'to maintain the laws, to dispense justice, and to keep in mind the things entrusted to their good faith' (*servare leges, iura describere, ea fidei suae*

---

[119] Such focus on social roles is central to Epictetus' notion of a person, on which, see Frede (2007) 154–7.

[120] More than any other Stoic writer, Cicero elides the concept of a person's 'proper function' with his or her social role, as can be seen from his decision to translate Panaetius' τὰ καθήκοντα ('appropriate acts') as *officia* ('duties' but also 'public offices'). For fuller discussion of this overlap, see Brunt (1975) 15; Miles (1996) 26; Roller (2001) 91.

commissa meminisse, Off. 1.124). Seneca's Atreus likewise acknowledges the exigencies and expectations involved in being a tyrant, even though his role, unlike that of Cicero's magistrate, is not a particularly admirable one.

In general, Seneca takes a dimmer view of such precepts, and discourages people from following them too closely (*Ep.* 94.1). Yet he does resort to Cicero's and Epictetus' ideas when explaining why a Cynic philosopher should not ask for money: *indixisti pecuniae odium; hoc professus es, hanc personam induisti: agenda est* ('you have proclaimed your hatred of money; this has been avowed, you have adopted this role: you must play it' *Ben.* 2.17.2).[121] Once again, the similarity to Atreus should be clear, since Seneca, like his fictional tragic protagonist, plays on a double meaning of *agere* as 'to act a role' and 'to behave', and treats *persona* in the similarly dual sense of 'dramatic role' and 'station in life'. It is this slippage between the theatrical metaphor and the human reality it has been designed to represent that allows us to view Atreus' self-construction in quasi-human as well as fictional terms. At the same time as being a metatheatrical trope, understanding and evaluating one's role is an activity germane to Stoic ethical theory. Leaving aside, for the moment, all questions about Atreus' morality, we can see that his methods of self-assessment are equally relevant to the fictional world portrayed on stage and to the non-fictional world beyond it; this way of thinking about the self applies to people as much as it applies to dramatic characters, with the result that Atreus treats himself simultaneously as a literary construct and an implied human personality.

Decorum, *Text, and Ethics*

This potential blurring of fiction with life derives not just from the Stoics' use of *decorum*/τὸ πρέπον, but from the very terms themselves, which conveyed an aesthetic meaning long before they were endowed with an ethical one.[122] In fact, the Stoics'

---

[121] Further discussion of this passage can be found in Aygon (2016) 49–50.
[122] Pohlenz (1965) 100–4, surveys the aesthetic connotations of τὸ πρέπον in fifth and fourth century BC Greek texts. Gibson (2007) 124–5, discusses the aesthetic origins of

1.2 *Thyestes*

interest in suitability and seemliness speaks to their view of personal conduct as an artistic project. In the words of Christopher Gill, Stoic ethical theory 'invites each person to adopt ... a quasi-aesthetic attitude towards himself and his life';[123] good behaviour, like good art, is imagined to be the appealing outcome of conscious and skilful (self-)fashioning. *decorum*'s connotations are such that the term assimilates rules for human conduct with principles of literary style, and in particular, of characterisation, so that the aspiring Stoic is urged to compose his identity in the manner of a poet composing a text:

> Haec ita intellegi, possumus existimare ex eo decoro, quod poetae sequuntur ... Sed ut tum servare illud poetas, quod deceat, dicimus, cum id quod quaque persona dignum est, et fit et dicitur, ut si Aeacus aut Minos diceret 'oderint dum metuant' aut 'natis sepulchro ipse est parens' indecorum videretur, quod eos fuisse iustos accepimus; at Atreo dicente plausus excitantur, est enim digna persona oratio; sed poetae quid quemque deceat, ex persona iudicabunt; nobis autem personam imposuit ipsa natura magna cum excellentia praestantiaque animantium reliquarum. Quocirca poetae in magna varietate personarum etiam vitiosis quid conveniat et quid deceat videbunt.

> We can infer that these things [moral *decorum*] are understood in this way from that seemliness which poets maintain ... We say that poets observe what is fitting when actions and words are worthy of each individual role, with the result that if Aeacus or Minos were to utter the lines 'let them hate as long as they fear', or, 'the parent himself is a tomb for his sons', it would not seem fitting, because we agree that these men were just; but Atreus provokes applause when he says these lines, because the manner of speech is worthy of his role. Poets, however, will judge what befits each individual according to his role, while nature herself has imposed on us a role greatly superior to and excelling all other creatures. Consequently, poets will see what is suitable and appropriate for a great variety of characters, even for wicked ones. (*Off.* 1.97)

Here Cicero explains *decorum* in terms of artistic congruence. Developing the analogy of moral agent as poet,[124] he recommends that individuals engage in actions most appropriate to their rational

---

the term *decorum*. On the difficulties raised by translating τὸ πρέπον as *decorum*, see Dyck (1996) *ad Off.* 1.93–9.

[123] Gill (1994) 4606–7. Renaissance writers, such as Castiglione in his *Il cortegiano*, likewise recognised this aesthetic approach to selfhood as a major theme in Cicero's *de Officiis*.

[124] Thus Dyck (1996) *ad Off.* 1.126–49: 'the simile of the playwright (§97–98) really controls the whole presentation of *decorum*'.

73

nature, and to their specific, personal qualities; he cites, by way of illustration, the dramatist's need to correlate a character's dialogue with his or her given *persona*. Just as the sentiment *oderint dum metuant* ('let them hate as long as they fear' Accius 203–4 Ribbeck *TRF*²) suits Atreus on stage, so are goodness, constancy, and restraint presumed to suit human beings.

By eliding the two meanings of *decorum*, however, Cicero risks derailing his own argument, because no matter how much Atreus' 'seemliness' meets aesthetic requirements, it can hardly be deemed an example of morality. As Gibson remarks, 'if ethically dubious sentiments are appropriate on the dramatic stage, then might not dubious actions – by an obvious if irresponsible logic – be appropriate to certain characters on the stage of life?'[125] Although Cicero attempts to circumvent such 'irresponsible logic' – by claiming that only the poet will consider what befits <u>bad</u> characters (*etiam vitiosis quid conveniat*, *Off.* 1.97) – he fails because of the slipperiness of his analogy in this passage, which links moral agents not just to poets, but also to actors and characters.[126] Atreus as a stage *persona* is used to illustrate how individuals should manage their *personae* in day-to-day life. Cicero brings the fictive tyrant and the aspiring Stoic into uncomfortable proximity when he declares that Atreus earns applause by speaking in character (*Atreo dicente plausus excitantur, est enim digna persona oratio*) and that the moral agent who achieves *decorum* 'provokes the approval of those around him' (*movet adprobationem eorum, quibuscum vivitur*, *Off.* 1.98). In both instances, *decorum* is presented as a somewhat visual quality that demands an appreciative audience.[127] Performing one's

---

[125] Gibson (2007) 125. Edwards (2007) 159 makes a similar observation: 'the metaphor of acting also allows scope for moves which could be seen as undermining orthodox Stoicism. The fascination of the stage is hard to resist. The most compelling characters are not always the most virtuous.'

[126] This link between moral agents and actors, which I have explored briefly above in relation to Seneca's Medea, is actually a very common feature of Stoic ethics: see, for example, Cic. *Fin.* 3.24 or Ariston of Chios in Diogenes Laertius 7.160 / *SVF* I 351, who states that the sage is a good actor, capable of playing Thersites or Agamemnon as fate requires.

[127] The visual aspect of *decorum* in Stoic texts derives from the root meaning of πρέπω as 'to be conspicuous / to shine forth'; see Dyck (1996) *ad Off.* 1.93–9 for further discussion.

1.2 *Thyestes*

persona correctly means engaging in actions appropriate to it: Atreus, in this passage, does precisely that. Thus, by merging *decorum*'s ethical and aesthetic connotations, Cicero leaves open the possibility of amoral constancy, of individuals pursuing morally reprehensible ends yet still achieving *decorum*.[128]

This reasoning applies to Seneca's Atreus even if we loosen the connection between moral agents on the one hand and stage characters on the other. Cicero in the theatrical analogies of *de Officiis* Book 1 is above all interested in associating the *proficiens* with the actor or poet, both of whom seek congruence in the compositions they present to an admiring public. But Atreus, too, behaves and evaluates his actions *as an actor*, particularly in his opening monologue, and his main purpose in doing so is to ensure appropriate conduct, coherence at once moral and aesthetic. Hence, there remains a potential and troubling parallel between Seneca's Atreus and the aspiring Stoic. Atreus may claim *decorum* chiefly as an actor and as a character, but that brings him perilously close to achieving it as an (im)moral agent, too, especially given that his performance is such as fundamental source of his self-realisation. Like Medea, Atreus knows, studies, and plays his assigned dramatic role in a way that recalls the injunctions of Stoic *persona* theory.

The unsettling blend of ethics and aesthetics also features in Atreus' plan for revenge: *dignum est Thyeste facinus et dignum Atreo* ('the crime is worthy of Thyestes and worthy of Atreus' 271). As a cognate of *decorum*, *dignus* conflates Atreus' dramatic (and more broadly literary) identity with the behavioural standards of his implied human personality. On the one hand, his intended crime is worthy of him because it adheres to paradigms established in earlier literature: it fits the pattern of revenge in Accius' *Atreus*, and more explicitly, it follows the story of Tereus, Procne, and Philomela, which Seneca's Atreus nominates as his model (*Thy.* 272–3; 275–7). Just as Procne slaughtered and served up her son to her husband, so Seneca's protagonist will slaughter and serve up

---

[128] Another potential source of amoral constancy in the *de Officiis* is the emphasis Cicero places on personal characteristics (the Panaetian second *persona*), which, as Gibson (2007) 123–4 points out, might lead individuals to cultivate vicious rather than virtuous behaviour on the basis that it suits their natural attributes.

his brother's children to his brother. In doing so, he will fulfil a poetic identity that derives from Ovid *Metamorphoses* 6.424–673, and behind this Latin precedent, from Sophocles' (now lost) *Tereus*.[129] So, Seneca's Atreus attains *decorum* by following the parameters of a pre-established, specifically literary *persona*. Like the Atreus in *de Officiis* 1.97, who speaks in a manner worthy of his character (*digna persona oratio*), Seneca's Atreus behaves appropriately by pursuing what is *dignum* for his textual, theatrical self.

On the other hand, though, *dignum* also has ethical connotations, so that Atreus' statement at 271 reflects upon his quasi-human *persona*. In effect, Atreus implies that he will realise his selfhood by exacting vengeance upon Thyestes: his chosen deed (*facinus*) is the kind of crime (*facinus*) that will enable him to be truly, properly 'Atreus', and to acquire *dignitas* as an individual.[130] By declaring the appropriateness of his revenge, Seneca's Atreus encourages his audience not only to look back to prior literary realisations of his role, but also to anticipate, on the basis of his present self-projection, the identity he will display by the drama's end. Like Medea, like a Stoic *proficiens* who understands what is appropriate for him, Atreus works towards perfecting his *persona*.

Thus, when Seneca's Atreus employs principles of *decorum* to fuel his own, vicious self-construction, he capitalises on the concept's innate weakness and vulnerability to misappropriation. It is not as if Atreus has taken a pristine Stoic idea and warped it out of shape by applying it to the dark world of his tragedy; the idea itself was problematic long before it reached Senecan drama. By combining ethics with aesthetics, and by developing an implicit connection between moral agents, poets, literary characters, and actors, Cicero's account of *decorum* lays itself open to precisely the kind of self-justification practised by Seneca's Atreus.

---

[129] Schiesaro (2003) 70–99 provides a full and fascinating discussion of the Ovidian intertext.

[130] As Tarrant (1985) *ad Thy.* 271 points out, 'Seneca's characters have an acute, if twisted, sense of their *dignitas* and insist on committing only those crimes appropriate to it.' Braden (1970) 23, similarly remarks that *dignum* 'is not altogether ironic, at least to Atreus'.

1.2 *Thyestes*

Nor is Cicero the only author to give an ambiguous account of *decorum*. Owing to the *de Officiis*' popularity, the concept of 'seemliness' pervades a lot of late republican and early imperial Latin literature, where its function as a moral principle overlaps frequently with principles of artistic composition.[131] A particularly relevant example for Seneca's Atreus comes from the *Ars Poetica*, where Horace advises poets that the rules for appropriate conduct in life correspond to appropriate characterisation in literature:

> qui didicit, patriae quid debeat et quid amicis,
> quo sit amore parens, quo frater amandus et hospes,
> quod sit conscripti, quod iudicis officium, quae
> partes in bellum missi ducis, ille profecto
> reddere personae scit convenientia cuique.
>
> He who has learnt what is owed to one's country, and to one's friends,
> how a parent, a brother, and a guest should be loved,
> the duty required of a councillor and a judge, the role
> of a leader sent into war, that man assuredly
> knows how to render things befitting each character.
>
> (*Ars* 312–16)

Via the terms *officium* (314), *persona* and *conveniens* (316), Horace makes it clear that he is alluding to Cicero's *de Officiis*.[132] He adopts Cicero's main analogy as well, only in reverse: the good poet is the equivalent of a moral agent who knows what befits each person according to his or her station in life. But lurking beneath this analogy is the riskier comparison between suitable public behaviour and suitable behaviour in literature. The *persona* in life becomes the *persona* in text, with the result that amoral *decorum* seems both viable and justifiable. It is easy to translate Horace's advice into Atreus' self-construction: Seneca's protagonist must be bloodthirsty and violent because

---

[131] Approaches to the topic of *decorum* in late republican / early imperial Latin literature include: Labate (1984) 121–74; Gibson (2007) 115–47; and to a lesser extent, Oliensis (1998) 198–223.

[132] For the *de Officiis*'s influence on Horace's *Ars Poetica*, see Oliensis (1998) 200–6 and Gibson (2007) 133–42. Rudd (1989) 35–6 argues for *decorum*'s overall importance as a major theme in the *Ars Poetica*. Brink (1971) *ad Ars* 316 remarks the plausible allusion to Cicero's *persona*-theory (*Off.* 1.107–21) but cautions against regarding the passage as doctrinally Stoic.

such characteristics are part of his *officium* as a tyrant, and of his inherited dramatic *persona*. Atreus must commit crimes just as a magistrate must uphold the law and a child obey its parent. The ethics of *decorum* all but encourage unethical conduct.

To Thine Own Role Be True

I return from this lengthy but necessary digression to the topics of *anagnorisis* and self-coherence. If Seneca's Atreus actually pursues the *decorum* he envisages, it follows that his behaviour will be consistent and consequently, recognisable. Like Medea, Atreus can realise his ideal selfhood only via seamless and steadfast enactment of his allotted role. On top of his efforts to harmonise his actions with his given identity, he must display the kind of constancy that will enable both Thyestes and the play's audience to acknowledge his ethical *persona*.

Initial survey of the tragedy suggests that Atreus fails in this regard, because his successful revenge depends upon his faking affection for Thyestes that he does not really feel. Atreus plays a role in order to lure his brother back to Argos, and to the extent that it conceals or glosses his intentions, that role is not entirely genuine. But neither is it entirely false, because one of Atreus' most prominent traits is his ability to manipulate language, and to exploit its ambiguities so that he lies and tells the truth concurrently.[133] Take, for example, the words with which he greets Thyestes:

> fratrem iuvat videre. complexus mihi
> redde expetitos. quidquid irarum fuit
> transierit; ex hoc sanguis ac pietas die
> colantur, animis odia damnata excidant.
>
> It is a pleasure to see my brother. Return my embrace
> so eagerly sought, all anger has passed;
> from this day forward, may blood and family ties be cherished,
> may hatred be renounced and vanish from our hearts.
>
> (*Thy.* 508–11)

---

[133] Atreus' linguistic cleverness is remarked on by Meltzer (1988), and Schiesaro (2003) 111–13.

1.2 *Thyestes*

This declaration of good faith seems, superficially, very inviting, and Thyestes is so convinced by it that he apologises immediately for ever having harmed his brother: *diluere possem cuncta, nisi talis fores. / sed fateor, Atreu, fateor, admisi omnia / quae credidisti* ('Were you not like this, I could explain everything away, but I confess, Atreus, I confess, I perpetrated all the things you thought I did', 512–14). Thyestes is thoroughly taken in. He is persuaded of his brother's goodness, but Atreus' speech is laced with double meanings that his victim cannot detect. Thus: Atreus *is* delighted to see his brother, not because he desires reconciliation, but because the prospect of revenge instils in him a perverse sense of pleasure. The participle *expetitus* is similarly ambiguous, since it can denote something desired and something sought with hostile intent.[134] When Atreus declares, *quidquid irarum fuit / transierit*, Thyestes interprets this to mean that his brother no longer feels anger, whereas Atreus' real feelings are so extreme that they have surpassed (*transierit*) such paltry classification. As the minister remarks in Act 2, Atreus' revenge is worse than mere anger (*maius hoc ira malum*, 259). Atreus has not dropped his indignation but gone beyond it.

Even the most reverent sections of Atreus' greeting can be seen to represent his true attitude. In his exhortation to 'cherish blood and family ties' (*sanguis ac pietas ... / colantur*) the verb's sacral overtones hint at his plan to kill Thyestes' children in a travesty of religious ritual, while *sanguis* also recalls his preceding admission of bloodlust (*cum sperat ira sanguinem, nescit tegi*; 'when anger hopes for blood, it does not know how to be hidden' 504).[135] Equally implicit in this phrase is the memory of Thyestes' adultery as an act that transgressed both *sanguis* and *pietas*, and that will lead to Atreus' transgression of the same. The greeting's final line is ominously vague: it could mean that Atreus promises to cease his hostilities, but it could just as easily be an exhortation for Thyestes to lay aside the *odium* he previously felt for his brother. Rightly or not, Atreus regards Thyestes as a threat, and his desire for 'hearts to be free from anger' (*animis odia ... excidant*) can be

---

[134] Tarrant (1985) *ad. Thy.* 509.
[135] Tarrant (1985) *ad. Thy.* 510.

read as his attempting to allay Thyestes' potential aggression. The entire speech is a masterpiece of subtly sinister intent that enables Atreus to act in character at the same time as appearing not to.

It is testament to Atreus' self-coherence that he manages to maintain this performance for the full duration of the play; rarely does he utter a sentence that is not riddled with double meanings. For instance, he boasts of having returned Thyestes to his birthright: *maior haec laus est mea / fratri paternum reddere incolumi decus* ('Mine is the greater praise, restoring to my brother, safe, his ancestral glory' 527–8). While not the conciliatory gesture that Thyestes takes it for, neither is this claim pure falsehood. The truth is that Thyestes will remain *incolumis* (in the strict sense that he will not suffer irreparable bodily damage), and that Atreus will treat his revenge as cause for acclaim (*nunc meas laudo manus*; 'now I praise my handiwork' 1096). Besides denoting the Pelopid diadem, moreover, the expression *paternum decus* can also denote Thyestes' children, who are 'the glory of their father' on the model of such phrases as *decus innuptarum* ('the most prominent of the unmarried women' Cat. 64.78) and *o decus Argolicum ... Ulixes* ('O Ulysses, glory of the Argives' Cic. *poet.* 29.1). Seneca, too, employs the phrase when he has Eurybates describe Agamemnon as *telluris ... Argolicae decus* ('the glory of the Argive land' *Ag.* 395). If this sense is accommodated, then Atreus' ostensible promise of returning power to Thyestes becomes instead a much more ominous promise to return Thyestes' sons to their father, which the audience already knows will happen in a savagely literal way. Finally, the semantic link between *decus* and *decorum* suggests, albeit in fainter tones, both the personal appropriateness of Atreus' conduct and the aesthetic appropriateness of the tragedy's eventual outcome. Revenge, the act of returning Thyestes to his birthright, is the primary means by which Atreus achieves his identity. Far from being false performances, therefore, Atreus' ostensible displays of goodwill repeatedly enact his *persona*'s most genuine aspects.

Atreus' word games have long been recognised as major sources of black humour and dramatic irony in this play, where the distance separating Thyestes' perspective from the audience's is also the distance between the superficial and hidden meanings of

1.2 *Thyestes*

Atreus' statements.[136] When, at the end of Act 3, Atreus leaves the stage promising to 'give the gods their designated offerings' (*ego destinatas victimas superis dabo*, 545), only the audience can see the darker nuance lurking under his seemingly pious sentiment: Atreus will perform a sacrifice, but Thyestes' children will be the victims, and the recipient his own prospective godhead (712–14).

Deceptive language permeates Act 5 as well, because Atreus exploits the coincidence of literal and figurative registers to round off his revenge with a series of jokes at his brother's expense.[137] In response to Thyestes' sudden discomfort following the banquet, Atreus (ostensibly) reassures him: 'believe that your children are in their father's embrace' (*esse natos crede in amplexu patris*, 976); 'no part of your offspring will be taken from you' (*nulla pars prolis tuae / tibi subtrahetur*, 977–8); 'I shall present the faces you long for' (*ora quae exoptas dabo*, 978). When he urges Thyestes to 'take up the ancestral cup, with wine poured in' (*poculum infuso cape / gentile Baccho*, 982–3), the suggestively transferrable epithet, *gentile*, alludes to his earlier act of mixing wine with the blood of Thyestes' offspring (917).[138] Blinded by the conventional sense of Atreus' words, Thyestes cannot see the cruel reality of taking them at face value.[139]

While Atreus evidently manages to deceive Thyestes, his success does not have to mean that he himself behaves in a deceptive manner. Alessandro Schiesaro describes Atreus' linguistic prowess as 'sophisticated dissemblance'[140] but the label is inappropriate because Atreus never really dissembles; he never plays a role

---

[136] The main studies are Meltzer (1988) and Schiesaro (2003) 111–13. Earlier scholarship acknowledges Atreus' wit, and the more general presence of humour in Senecan tragedy but tends to regard such moments as bad taste: see comments by Duff (1964) 209; Baade (1969) xvii; and an uncharacteristically dismissive remark by Tarrant (1985) *ad Thy.* 1046–7, to the effect that Thyestes' reluctance to beat his breast is 'a dreadful specimen of misplaced cleverness'.

[137] Meltzer (1988) 314 remarks upon Atreus' tendency to combine the symbolic with the literal meaning of words and images, especially during this final exchange.

[138] Tarrant (1985) *ad Thy.* 982–3; Meltzer (1988) 316.

[139] Here I disagree with Schiesaro (2003) 111, who claims that Thyestes is 'literal-minded'. Certainly, Thyestes is presented as less clever than Atreus, but it is precisely his failure to take Atreus' statements literally that generates such dramatic irony in the tragedy's final Act.

[140] Schiesaro (2003) 111. Michelon (2015) 36–45 similarly argues that *dolus* and *fraus* are core elements of Atreus' characterisation.

81

other than his own, and although sometimes economical with the truth, he neither distorts nor misrepresents his intentions, merely grants Thyestes the liberty of interpreting them in a positive light. Atreus remains true to his word, just in a way that Thyestes does not expect. The real cleverness of Atreus' performance lies in his enticing Thyestes to deceive himself and knowing that his brother is willing to do so.[141]

Thus, a large part of Atreus' *constantia* comes from his ability to 'play one role' (*unum hominem agere, Ep.* 120.22). While he does not share Medea's obsessive need to derive coherence from repetition of the personal past,[142] nonetheless he exhibits and exhorts himself to uniformity over the course of the play. Seneca reinforces this uniformity, moreover, via numerous lexical correspondences that link Acts 3 and 5, to show that the Atreus who greets his brother so warmly is precisely the same man who subsequently slaughters, cooks, and dishes up his brother's children. Atreus has not changed, not in any essential way, even if Thyestes' perception of him has. For example, Atreus speaks of *complexus expetitos* ('eagerly sought embraces' 508–9) when greeting his newly returned brother in Act 3, and resorts to the same vocabulary in the final Act, when revealing the children's grisly remains: *iam accipe hos potius libens / diu expetitos ... / fruere, osculare, divide amplexus tribus* ('now, rather, greet gladly these [children] you have sought for so long ... enjoy them, kiss them, divide your embraces by three' 1021–3). The latter scene mirrors the former because it, too, is a warped moment of reunion in which Thyestes 'welcomes' his sons just as Atreus has earlier welcomed Thyestes. Another notable correspondence is the verb *reddere*, which Atreus uses when promising to reinstate Thyestes in his royal birthright (*fratri paternum reddere incolumi decus*, 528), and again when he gloats over having united Thyestes and his children forever: *reddam, et tibi illos nullus eripiet dies* ('I shall return them, and no day will take them from you' 998).

---

[141] Thus, Harrison (2014a) 600–1: 'Atreus makes the single correct assumption that Thyestes will deceive himself at the prospect of a return to luxury.'
[142] The ancestral past does, however, loom large in Atreus' sense of himself and his action within the tragedy: see Boyle (1983) 220–2, and Fitch and McElduff (2002) 27–8.

1.2 *Thyestes*

Divinity is also a theme that binds the latter half of the play, first with Atreus declaring his intent to perform a sacrifice (*ego destinatas victimas superis dabo*; 'I shall give the gods their designated offerings', 545), then with the messenger's report that Atreus has sacrificed Thyestes' children as offerings to himself (*mactet sibi*, 713),[143] and finally with Atreus likening his own success to deification (*aequalis astris gradior*; 'I stride equal to the stars' 885) and claiming that he is 'the highest of heavenly beings' (*o me caelitum excelsissimum*, 911).[144] Such connections demonstrate the evenness and coherence of Atreus' character, and the undeviating manner in which he performs his part. The only difference between the Atreus Thyestes encounters in Act 3 and the one he encounters in Act 5 is Thyestes' own clarity of perception.

The recognition scene in the *Thyestes*, therefore, pivots upon Atreus seeking acknowledgement for his consistent self-presentation. When the protagonist asks Thyestes, 'do you recognise your sons at all?' (*natos ecquid agnoscis tuos*, 1005), not only does he invite the father to identify the body parts placed before him, but also, at a more abstract level, to validate the fact of Atreus' revenge. This moment is the final goal at which all of Atreus' actions have been aimed; in acknowledging the deed, Thyestes acknowledges the person behind it as well. By killing, cooking, and serving Thyestes' sons, Atreus has fulfilled the requirements of both his fictional and his quasi-human identity. Thyestes certainly thinks so: *agnosco fratrem* ('I recognise my brother' 1006).

Atreus sapiens

Atreus' uniform conduct equates him, in a warped and paradoxical way, with Cicero's and Seneca's images of the Stoic sage. A handful of scholars note this connection and tend to regard it

---

[143] Traina (1981) 151–3 argues on the basis of Latin religious terminology that *sibi* goes with *mactet* (rather than with the other option, *dubitat*), with the result that Atreus here occupies the dual role of the priest conducting and the god receiving a sacrifice.
[144] On themes of divinity in the *Thyestes*, see in particular Boyle (1983) 218–20 and (1997) 51–2. Seneca's text also hints that, in claiming divine status for himself, Atreus draws upon the widespread trope of poetic immortality, for example Ov. *Met.* 15.875–6: *parte tamen meliore mei super alta perennis / astra ferar*.

as a case of antithesis rather than resemblance, of Atreus as anti- rather than quasi-*sapiens*.[145] But Atreus' qualities are modelled so closely on Stoic principles of 'appropriateness' that, I would argue, he represents their extension, not their negation.[146] By remaining within his own role and giving a faithful, unvarying performance, Atreus may be said to achieve the *decorum* that Cicero defines in minimal terms as 'nothing more than evenness in the overall course of life and of each individual action' (*decorum nihil est profecto magis quam aequabilitas universae vitae, tum singularum actionum, Off.* 1.111). Atreus maintains *aequabilitas* throughout the course of the play's events, in each of the deeds he perpetrates. His command of language also ensures harmony between what he says and what he does, with the result that his behaviour matches the core qualities that Seneca attributes to the *sapiens: maximum hoc est et officium sapientiae et indicium, ut verbis opera concordent, ut ipse ubique par sibi idemque sit* ('this is the greatest duty and proof of wisdom, that deeds should be in accord with words, that [the wise man] should, everywhere, be the same and equal to himself' *Ep.* 20.2). Like the Senecan wise man, Atreus is *unus idemque inter diversa* ('one and the same in varying circumstances' *Const.* 6.3), displaying an identical *persona* when he welcomes Thyestes and when he exults in the macabre fact of his revenge.

Such ethical and figurative constancy crystalises into a literal event when Atreus proceeds to kill Thyestes' sons. The messenger who reports this crime describes a kind of earthquake – 'the whole palace trembled as the ground shook' (*tota succusso solo / nutavit aula*, 696–7) – and adds that Atreus remains unaffected by the surrounding physical tumult: *movere cunctos monstra, sed solus sibi / immotus Atreus constat* ('the portents moved everyone, but Atreus alone, unmoved, stands his ground' 703–4). Here Seneca combines literal and metaphorical registers, so that the ground's physical movement, its jolting of palace and attendants alike, becomes an emotional or

---

[145] Seidensticker (1985) 131 calls Atreus, an anti-*sapiens*, 'der stoische Weise auf den Kopf gestellt' ('who turns the wise man upside-down'); Tarrant (1985) 24 calls Medea and Atreus 'perverted mirror images of the *sapiens*'.

[146] An idea floated by Miles (1996) 51–9.

1.2 *Thyestes*

psychological *motus*, to which everyone except Atreus succumbs.[147] A similar blend of meaning occurs in Seneca's philosophical works, where strength of character is illustrated, again and again, via images of physical endurance.[148] Seneca's *sapiens* is *inconcussus* (*Ep.* 45.9 and 59.14); he will not, in the psychological sense, be moved (*ille ne commovetur quidem*, *Ep.* 35.4). As Miles observes, Seneca envisages *constantia* in terms of 'motionlessness of immovable objects triumphantly withstanding irresistible forces'.[149] In this regard, as in so many others, Atreus resembles a Stoic hero who remains true to his purpose and true to his self despite all opposition.

Immovability is, in Senecan Stoicism, the companion of self-coherence, because being shaken implies changing the course of one's action and consequently, changing one's identity. In the same letter that Seneca praises the *sapiens* for his steadfastness, he also advises Lucilius, *profice et ante omnia hoc cura, ut constes tibi* ('make progress and endeavour above all else to be consistent with yourself' *Ep.* 35.4). The phrase is similarly used to describe psychological tranquility and wholeness at *Ep.* 66.45, *animus constat sibi et placidus est* ('the soul is consistent and calm'), and at *Consolatio ad Polybium* 8.4, where Seneca counsels the addressee not to undertake light literary pursuits until his mind 'is wholly self-consistent' (*nisi cum iam sibi ab omni parte constiterit,*). In all cases, *constantia*, the attainment or recovery of it, is envisaged as the state of being at one with oneself, of being congruent as opposed to changeable or unsettled. Atreus, too, appears to possess this quality of self-coherence, because the messenger in the *Thyestes* employs exactly the same expression – *sibi ... / ... constat* (703–4) – to describe Atreus' firmness of purpose. There are undeniable Stoic overtones here: Richard Tarrant deems Atreus' pose 'a travesty of *constantia*', while Anthony Boyle calls it 'an ironic exemplification of ... Stoic

---

[147] The interrelationship of moral/psychological and physical universes is a recurrent theme in Seneca's tragedies, and one with roots in Stoic philosophy: see Herington (1966) 433 on the *Thyestes* in particular; Rosenmeyer (1989) 113–203; and Williams (2012) *passim*, but especially 17–92.

[148] On images of physical endurance in Seneca's prose works, see Lavery (1980) 147–51; Miles (1996) 38–57; and Wilson (1997) 63–7.

[149] Miles (1996) 45.

virtue'.[150] But I am inclined to view Atreus' self-coherence as more than a passing parody, because he displays throughout the tragedy substantial if warped associations with Stoic *persona* theory, with the principles of *decorum*, with Stoic ideals of moral constancy in the face of enormous opposition. Although Atreus is not interested in pursuing virtue, although he is in fact intent upon committing a particularly heinous set of crimes, nonetheless his behaviour recalls Seneca's vision of *constantia sapientis* in numerous fundamental respects. In doing so, it lays bare the theory's potential perils, showing consistent selfhood to be a largely solipsistic enterprise in Seneca, something that tilts dangerously towards becoming an end in itself.[151] Most critics would argue that Seneca's Atreus cannot claim *constantia* because he is not virtuous. I see the equation in reverse: Atreus demonstrates a high degree of coherence, and that makes *constantia* a problematic virtue.

In this regard, it is also worth noting that the expression *sibi constat* can imply not just moral/personal coherence but also coherence of literary characterisation. Horace uses it in this latter sense when giving advice to playwrights in his *Ars Poetica*:

> aut famam sequere aut sibi convenientia finge
> scriptor. honoratum si forte reponis Achillem,
> inpiger, iracundus, inexorabilis, acer
> iura neget sibi nata, nihil non adroget armis.
> sit Medea ferox invictaque, flebilis Ino,
> perfidus Ixion, Io vaga, tristis Orestes.
> siquid inexpertum scaenae conmittis et audes
> personam formare novam, servetur ad imum,
> qualis ab incepto processerit, et <u>sibi constet</u>.

> Either follow tradition or invent what is self-consistent.
> If, by chance, you bring Achilles back on stage to be honoured,
> make him impatient, irascible, relentless, fierce,
> he should say laws don't apply to him, always reach for the sword.
> Medea should be fierce and unbowed, Ino teary,

---

[150] Tarrant (1985) *ad Thy.* 703–4; Boyle (2017) *ad Thy.* 703–6. Agapitos (1998) 238 likewise treats the passage as a mockery of Stoic values. Davis (1989) 428 notes the phrase's Stoic colouring.

[151] Thus Miles (1996) 61: 'Seneca's is essentially an individualistic philosophy: the Senecan Stoic's aim is self-consistency and self-perfection, the fact that this is ultimately 'for the good of all men' being only an added justification.'

1.2 *Thyestes*

Ixion treacherous, Io wandering, Orestes morose.
But if you bring to the stage something untried, and dare
to fashion a new character, make sure it maintains to the end
the nature it had from the beginning, and that it is self-coherent.

(*Ars* 119–27)

The passage combines ethics with aesthetics in a way that resembles, and thus sheds light on, Seneca's own work. Like Atreus' self-affirming exhortation to act *iratus* (*Thy.* 180), Horace advises playwrights to align characters with the emotions most appropriate to them: Achilles must be *iracundus* in order to be properly Achilles. It is not hard to detect shadows of moral *decorum* lurking behind such poetic *decorum*, and Horace, like Cicero before him and Seneca after him, allows the possibility of its justifying bad behaviour on the sole plea of suitability: a patient, even-tempered, gentle Achilles may be morally preferable, but aesthetically unrecognisable. Horace's notion of preserving a consistent character from beginning to end likewise finds echo in Seneca's instruction to Lucilius at *Ep.* 120.22: *qualem institueris praestare te talem usque ad exitum serves* ('maintain right to the end the character you have resolved to present' cf. *Ars* 126–7: *servetur ad imum / qualis ab incepto processerit.*) One can *constat sibi* as a character and as a person, and the overlap of these two realms allows Seneca's audience to see Atreus' fictional identity concurrently with his quasi-humanness. Atreus pursues coherence both as an implied person and as a *dramatis persona*.

Furthermore, the blending of these two realms warns against overhasty dismissal of Atreus' *constantia*, for although Seneca's *Thyestes* is a work of fiction, fiction itself plays a prominent role in the formation and articulation of these particular Stoic precepts. It is clear that Seneca understands coherence as a literary as well as a philosophical concept, and this coincidence not only precludes rigid separation of his tragedies from his prose works but could even be said to render Atreus' *decorum* more, not less, real. Rather than an imitation or a parody of the principle, Atreus' *constantia* is a valid instantiation of a virtue destabilised by its own wayward logic. *decorum*'s patently aesthetic qualities all but encourage Atreus' being brought in as an example of the self that Stoic self-coherence can create. Of course, Seneca's project in the tragedies does not have to be so blatantly didactic, and I would definitely guard against interpreting it as such. But it is equally true that the philosophical material present in Seneca's dramas is not so much a reflection of what he has written elsewhere, as an extension of the same mirror, with a slightly darker tint. Consciously or not, Seneca encourages his readers to put Atreus and Lucilius side by side.

As in the case of Seneca's Medea, the argument I advance here is a minority view. Most critics of Senecan tragedy prefer to see Atreus as a fluctuating, changeable figure completely at the mercy of his own destructive *furor* and *ira*.[152] By giving in to his passion, Atreus should – according to strict Stoic reasoning – exhibit a fragmented *persona*, fickle, unreliable, inconstant in purpose.[153] Seneca himself suggests as much in the *de Ira*, when his fictional interlocutor protests, 'some angry people behave consistently and control themselves' (*at irati quidem constant sibi et se continent, Ira* 1.8.6), but Seneca responds in the negative: 'only when anger is receding and yielding on its own accord, not when it is boiling' (*cum iam ira evanescit et sua sponte decedit, non cum in ipso fervore est, Ira* 1.8.6). According to this view, Atreus, who revels in *ira* as his defining quality, should be either an incoherent individual, or a calm one. This is not the case, however: Atreus manages to be both angry and stable, and his accomplishment speaks to the ambiguities latent in Stoic *decorum*. It also speaks to Seneca's immersion in the Stoic vocabulary of identity, to the extent that any kind of self-construction pursued by the characters in these tragedies becomes a quasi-Stoic act, even if it is far from virtuous. Atreus succeeds not because he is 'good', but because he knows himself, understands his capacities, and follows the established parameters of his role.

---

[152] A broad yet representative sample of this view: Knoche (1972) [1941]; Herington (1966) 453–4; Poe (1969); Staley (1981); Pratt (1983) 103–7; Lefèvre (1997b) 60–8.
[153] It could be argued that Atreus' insatiable appetite for revenge is likewise a symptom of inconstancy, which Poe (1969) and Littlewood (2008) certainly suggest. But Atreus' revenge is also a kind of self-fulfilment, so that he may be interpreted as hungering after both. Moreover, he does appear to achieve satisfaction, and hence, recognisability, by the end of the play (e.g. 1096ff).

1.2 *Thyestes*

Inconstant Thyestes

Atreus' selfhood is so firm that Thyestes, too, recognises his brother's essential qualities long before the final moment of *anagnorisis*. While en route to Argos, Thyestes disputes with his eldest son the extent of Atreus' good intentions, and whenever the young man voices his optimism, Thyestes responds with deep misgivings. He fears – rightly as it happens – that Atreus poses a threat to his children: *vos facitis mihi / Atrea timendum* ('you render Atreus a source of fear for me' 485–6). He also doubts whether any love is possible between himself and his brother:

> amat Thyesten frater? aetherias prius
> perfundet Arctos pontus et Siculi rapax
> consistet aestus unda et Ionio seges
> matura pelago surget et lucem dabit
> nox atra terris, ante cum flammis aquae,
> cum morte vita, cum mari ventus fidem
> foedusque iungent.

> Does Thyestes' brother love him? Sooner will the sea
> drench the heavenly Bear, and the snatching wave
> of the Sicilian tide cease flowing, and ripe crops
> rise from the Ionian deep, and black night bring light
> to the earth, sooner will water make an alliance
> with fire, life with death, the wind with the sea.
>
> (*Thy.* 476–82)

The irony of Thyestes' *adynata* is that several of them await him. Atreus' sacrifice and Thyestes' unwitting cannibalism will cause night to overtake day (776–8; 789–93; 990–5) and death to be joined with life (1035–51).[154] Although not fully aware of it, Thyestes has anticipated the arc of his own story. He has also painted an unnervingly accurate portrait of his brother, which only confirms Atreus' undeviating conduct and consequent recognisability. This begs a question: if Thyestes has such insight into his brother's character, why does he accept Atreus' invitation?[155]

---

[154] See Boyle (2017) *ad Thy.* 476–82.
[155] Senecan scholarship has never really succeeded in resolving this issue, although the question about Thyestes' motives is posed with particular urgency by Boyle (1983) 213–18.

Coherence

The simple answer is that Thyestes is fickle. In contrast to Atreus, Thyestes does not match his words to his deeds, and seems to possess little comprehension of his own *persona*.[156] Whereas Atreus stands *immotus* and thereby displays his self-coherence, Thyestes' initial appearance is marked by physical faltering.[157] He declares that he 'moves forward an unwilling step' (*moveo nolentem gradum*, 420), while his son Tantalus describes him as 'caught in uncertainty' (*se ... in incerto tenet*, 422) and 'stepping back from the sight of his homeland' (*a patria gradum / referre visa*, 429–30). He accepts the crown from Atreus a mere two lines after asserting his 'definite plan' to refuse it (*respuere certum est regna consilium mihi*, 540). Later, in Act 5, he cries while celebrating his good fortune (938–44), and spurns the past poverty (920–37) to which he has previously devoted such praise (446–70).[158] Seneca's Thyestes is a figure riddled with contradictions.

Thyestes' inconsistency is the opposite of Atreus' quasi-Stoic self-coherence. When discussing the need for harmony between a man's beliefs and his deeds, Seneca defines *sapientia* as the act of 'always feeling willingness for the same thing, and always feeling unwillingness for the same thing' (*semper idem velle atque idem nolle*, *Ep.* 20.5). Thyestes clearly subverts the precept, not only by continuing to move when his foot is *nolentem* (420), but also by desiring a feast that he will not, ultimately, want to have consumed. If the highest expression of Atreus' power is to make people 'want what they do not want' (*quod nolunt velint*, 212), then Thyestes' fate is the ultimate example of that power: he consumes his own flesh and blood even though his 'hands are unwilling to obey' (*nolunt manus / parere*, 985–6), and orders himself to be of good cheer even as 'tears fall from his unwilling face' (*imber vultu nolente cadit*, 950).[159] Thyestes, it seems, falls

---

[156] The contrary argument pursued by Curley (1986) 148–51, namely that Atreus misunderstands Thyestes and Thyestes comprehends his brother only too well, is not particularly convincing.
[157] Miles (1996) 58.
[158] On Thyestes' contrasting attitudes towards his exile, see Lefèvre (1985) 1274–8, and Rose (1986–7) 121–5.
[159] Lexical connections noted by Tarrant (1985) 47, and Rose (1986–7) 123 and 127.

1.2 *Thyestes*

victim to Atreus not because he fails to understand his brother, but because he fails to understand his own wishes.

Unsurprisingly, Seneca's *Thyestes* also differs from Atreus in displaying two *personae* rather than a single distinct one over the course of the tragedy. Scholars have often remarked that Thyestes grows steadily to resemble Atreus the more time he spends in his brother's presence: having once decried the treacherous pleasures of royal luxury (453; 455–8), he ends up reclining upon purple and gold (909), drinking from a silver cup (913), wearing Tyrian purple (955–6), and dwelling within precisely the kind of 'towering house' he had denounced at the outset (*domum / ... imminentem*, 455–6 cf. the description of the Pelopid palace at 641–56).[160] The Thyestes of Act 5 mimics Atreus' speech patterns, too, when he commands himself to forget 'grim poverty, the companion of fearful exile' (*trepidi comes exilii / tristis egestas*, 923–4). Atreus speaks of exile in identical terms, calling himself a *trepidus exul* ('frightened fugitive', 237) during Thyestes' former rule in Argos, and characterising Thyestes' experience as 'grim poverty' (*tristis egestas*, 303).[161] The Thyestes of Act 3, in contrast, praises exilic poverty for keeping him safe (449–52). This split *persona*, this metamorphosis from humble forest-dweller to gluttonous aristocrat, becomes especially prominent when Thyestes, surprised by his sudden sadness in the middle of the banquet, commands himself to 'banish old Thyestes from [his] mind' (*veterem ex animo mitte Thyesten*, 937). Self-naming, as we have seen, is usually a method of achieving *constantia* in Seneca tragedy, but in this case, it points towards the major fault line in Thyestes' character, the fact that he vacillates between two irreconcilable modes of behaviour.

This lack of self-coherence is accompanied by an equal lack of self-knowledge.[162] Of course, it is central to the play's plot that Thyestes does not know until too late what his meal contained, but such ignorance in Seneca's version is not ancillary; it is, rather, a defining aspect of Thyestes' character. The messenger portrays

---

[160] Rose (1986–7) 124 is a particularly acute study of this metamorphosis. See also the comments by Tarrant (1985) *ad Thy.* 453 and Boyle (2017) *ad Thy.* 908–12.
[161] Parallels discussed by Rose (1986–7) 123.
[162] On Thyestes' lack of self-awareness, see Davis (1989) 429.

Coherence

it, ironically, as the only benefit of Thyestes' situation: 'the one good thing in your troubles, Thyestes, is that you do not know your troubles' (*in malis unum hoc tuis / bonum est, Thyesta, quod mala ignoras tua*, 782–3). Atreus adopts a harsher view, and complains that his revenge fell short because Thyestes 'with his wicked mouth tore his sons apart, but he did so unaware, and they were unaware' (*scidit ore natos impio, sed nesciens, / sed nescientes*, 1067–8).[163] More than mere sadism, Atreus' remark recalls a key point about the construction of identity in Senecan drama: one must understand one's capacities in order to attain the appearance – which is also the reality – of coherent selfhood. We have seen that Cicero in the *de Officiis* counsels each man to 'know his own natural disposition' (*suum quisque ... noscat ingenium, Off.* 1.114); Medea and Atreus both adhere to this advice, but Thyestes evidently does not. The portrait he paints of himself in Act 3 no longer applies by Act 5. Although Thyestes enters the stage declaring that, for him, 'daytime is not devoted to sleep and night joined to sleepless revelry' (*nec somno dies / Bacchoque nox iugenda pervigili datur*, 466–7), these are precisely the kinds of activities he is engaged in by the tragedy's end.[164] Both as a quasi-human and as a fictional identity, Thyestes seems unaware of how he is going to behave.

Thyestes' cannibalism, too, functions as a symbol of his ignorance, because when he consumes his own children, he literally does not know what is inside him. The boundaries of his identity blur: his chest 'groans with a groan that is not [his]' (*meum ... gemitu non meo pectus gemit*, 1001), and his body becomes composite: 'as a father, I crush my sons, and I am crushed by my sons' (*genitor ... natos premo / premorque natis*, 1050–1), with the phrase's chiastic structure reinforcing its sense of interchangeability. Physical confusion mirrors Thyestes' behavioural

---

[163] Crucially, this scenario would negate any need for recognition qua revelation, because Thyestes, although powerless, would already be fully aware of his deeds. That Atreus desires such a possibility shows, once again, his interest in using *anagnorisis* for validation rather than disclosure.

[164] Notably, Seneca uses the metonymic *Bacchus* to connect Thyestes' image of the drunken ruler (*nec somno dies / Bacchoque nox iugenda pervigili datur, Thy.* 466–7) with a later image of Thyestes himself (*satis mensis datum est / satisque Baccho, Thy.* 899–900).

1.2 *Thyestes*

confusion: his *persona* is just as incoherent as his body, and vice versa. When the play's second chorus describes 'death weighing heavily' (*illi mors gravis incubat*, 401) on the ambitious king, who ends his days 'unknown to himself' (*ignotus... sibi*, 403), it anticipates the image of Thyestes in the final Act, burdened by his children's death and unaware of what his body contains.[165]

What Seneca says of the fallible human multitude applies particularly well to his Thyestes: *mutamus subinde personam et contrariam ei sumimus quam exuimus* ('we keep changing our masks and we put on the opposite of what we have taken off' *Ep.* 120.22).[166] Although an older trend in Senecan scholarship interprets Thyestes in partially positive terms, as a Stoic *proficiens* who fails to uphold his principles,[167] this character is, instead, problematic and divided from the moment he steps onto the stage. His fickleness has obvious implications for the recognition scene, too, namely that Thyestes is slow to recognise his own situation even though he acknowledges Atreus' selfhood with ease. The process of *anagnorisis* in the *Thyestes* is drawn out not just for dramatic effect, but also to emphasise the extent of the victim's ignorance. Thyestes' first assumption upon being presented with his sons' heads is that the boys have been murdered and their remains left lying on the ground as fodder for birds and beasts (1032–3). That he is still at this moment unaware of his own cannibalism points to a broader lack of self-knowledge: Thyestes has acted without full understanding of his deeds, and he remains unaware of what is – literally and figuratively – going on inside him, until Atreus announces the entirety of his and his brother's crime. Whereas Atreus is recognisable, Thyestes, it seems, cannot manage to play just one, consistent part.

---

[165] Davis (1989) 429 remarks that *ignotus sibi* applies to Thyestes.
[166] Cicero's definition of vice at *Tusc.* 4.29 also seems eminently applicable to Seneca's Thyestes: *habitus aud adfectio in tota vita inconstans et a se ipsa dissentiens*. Notably, Thyestes' change of clothing can also be read as symbolic of his changeable nature.
[167] A representative sample: Gigon (1938) and Knoche 1972 [1941], and in anglophone scholarship, Poe (1969) 360–1, Hine (1981) 272–3, Pratt (1983) 103–7.

Recognition and Isolation

Constancy in Senecan tragedy is not just amoral; it is also destructive. Like Medea, who pursues her ideal selfhood by removing or rendering void all interpersonal ties, Atreus tears apart his own family not just in the name of revenge, but also for the purpose of self-realisation. Earlier, I discussed how *anagnorisis* in the *Medea* subverts traditional relationships between recognition and reunion; the same thing happens in the *Thyestes*, with the protagonist seeking acknowledgement for the deeds he has perpetrated against his own relatives. The final Act of this play sees Atreus triumphant, and totally isolated.

The vocabulary of reunion is even more prevalent in *Thyestes'* recognition scene than it is in *Medea*'s. Thyestes demands that Atreus 'return [his] sons to [him]' (*redde iam natos mihi*, 997), and Atreus responds by assuring his brother, darkly, of eternal union: 'I shall return them, and no day will take them from you' (*reddam, et tibi illos nullus eripiet dies*, 998). Seneca expands upon this (warped) motif of parent–child recognition by having Atreus refer repeatedly to physical acts of welcome: 'believe that your children are here, in their father's embrace' (*hic esse natos crede in amplexu patris*, 976); 'open your embrace, father, they have come' (*expedi amplexus, pater; / venere*, 1004–5); 'enjoy them, kiss them, divide your embraces by three' (*fruere, osculare, divide amplexus tribus*, 1023). With such statements, Seneca adapts a traditional feature of *anagnorisis* in Greco-Roman drama, where characters' first impulse following a happy moment of recognition is, typically, to embrace. Thus, when Sosicles realises the identity of his twin brother, Menaechmus, he exclaims that he 'cannot refrain from hugging [him]' (*contineri quin complectar non queo*, *Men.* 1124); Daemones, in the *Rudens*, takes his long-lost daughter, Palaestra, in his arms (*ut te amplector lubens!* 'how gladly I embrace you!' *Rud.* 1175). Similar scenes are also found in tragedy, as when Sophocles' Electra realises that Orestes is not dead, but standing right beside her: Ἔχω σε χερσίν; ('do I hold you in my arms?' *El.*1225).[168] Seneca's

---

[168] There is also an ironic quality to Electra's question, because prior to embracing the body of the real Orestes, she has been holding in her hands the urn assumed to contain her brother's ashes – 'Orestes' in another, far less substantial form.

1.2 *Thyestes*

Atreus, by contrast, draws attention to the futility and impossibility of such positive emotional displays. Whereas traditional recognition scenes tend to reassert an individual's legitimate identity, and thereby reintegrate that individual with a collectivity such as the family, Atreus overturns the process: he destroys and dis-unites individuals as a way of asserting his own identity.

In fact, legitimacy is a major theme both in the *Thyestes*'s recognition scene, and in the play overall.[169] Because of Thyestes' adultery with Aerope, Atreus worries about his own sons' parentage (240; 327–30), which he plans either to confirm or to deny categorically via his revenge. When Thyestes displays grief upon learning of his cannibalism, Atreus takes this to mean that his brother's children were legitimate (*certos*, 1102) and that his own sons, Agamemnon and Menelaus, are also legitimate by association. Although Atreus' logic is far from secure, his preoccupations have significant bearing on the moment of *anagnorisis*, where the verb *agnoscere* evokes the legal recognition of children, just as it does in the *Medea*. By asking Thyestes whether he recognises his sons – *natos ecquid agnoscis tuos?* 1005 – Atreus also demands that his brother acknowledge and validate the children's parentage (cf. Nep. *Ag.* 1.4 and Quint. *Inst.* 7.1.14, above). Ironically, the assertion of legitimacy that Atreus orchestrates in this scene happens at the expense of the family, not to its benefit.

This legal sense of *agnoscere* also links back to the play's first Act, in which the Fury, while enumerating events to come, poses an elusively ambiguous question: *ecquando tollet?* ('will he ever lift it/them up?' 59). Most editors assume that the line refers to Atreus picking up a weapon, especially in the context of the Fury's prior, impatient demand, *dextra cur patrui vacat?* ('why is the uncle's right hand empty?' 57). However, *tollere* can also refer to a father picking up a newborn child in a formal gesture of recognition.[170] Plautus' *Amphitruo* provides an apt, if irreverent, parallel in a plot that likewise deals with issues of paternity and

---

[169] Fuller discussion in Chapter 4, 309–20.
[170] Interpretation of these lines is problematic. Line 57 refers to Thyestes – *nondum Thyestes liberos deflet suos* – but Tarrant (1985) and Zwierlein (1986a) bracket it as spurious because it disrupts the Fury's otherwise chronological description of events. If

legitimacy: Jupiter, as the real father and counterfeit Amphitruo, commands Alcmena to 'lift the child up, when it's born' (*quod erit natum tollito*, *Amph.* 501). Seneca's text is less explicit, but even if we accept this meaning as a mere shadow in the Fury's speech, it still seems to anticipate Atreus' concerns over parentage and Thyestes' eventual, ill-fated *anagnorisis*.

Just as Medea does with Jason, so Atreus puts Thyestes in the position of authorising and admitting responsibility for a family he has previously disrupted. Atreus demands from his brother validation both of the children's parentage, and of his own power to make Thyestes suffer. His self-construction is bound so inseparably to the act of revenge that any acknowledgement of the deed itself becomes, by extension, acknowledgement of Atreus' identity (as Thyestes quickly realises). Practising constancy sets Atreus on a path of conflict with the entire world around him, and his self-realisation prevents rather than generates social harmony. *anagnorisis* in Seneca's *Thyestes* perverts some of the most standard connotations of recognition in Greco-Roman drama: instead of uncovering an unexpected identity, it confirms an extant one; instead of reasserting relationships between previously estranged individuals, it destroys interpersonal ties precisely in order to declare their legitimacy.

Motifs of isolation in this final Act pertain not only to Thyestes' gruesome (re)union with his offspring, but also to Atreus' sense of self-deification, which approximates to Stoic *autarkeia*. Seneca's philosophical writings often equate the *sapiens* with a god: he is likened to Jupiter (*Ep.* 9.16); his soul 'ought to be such as befits a god' (*talis animus esse sapientis viri debet qualis deum deceat*, *Ep.* 92.3); Lucilius 'will rise as the equal of god' if only he takes nature for his guide (*par deo surges*, *Ep.* 31.9). Atreus envisages for himself a similar degree of divine equality when he boasts of walking 'level with the stars' (*aequalis astris gradior*, 885). An image that, in Senecan Stoicism, is meant to articulate the wise man's perfect

---

57 is removed, then *tollet* most likely refers to Atreus' sword. If, on the other hand, it is kept – and Tarrant (1985) *ad Thy.* 58–9 is not beyond entertaining this possibility – then *tollet* may evoke Thyestes' later act of lifting the children's flesh to his lips or, as I propose, may create a broader, thematic link with the Roman custom of fathers acknowledging paternity by lifting children up from the ground.

1.2 *Thyestes*

union with nature becomes in the *Thyestes* an index of Atreus' self-motivated removal from the bounds of human society. Like Medea, Atreus uses his vengeance and attendant self-construction to achieve a radical form of independence: he attains a unified and fully realised identity by cutting familial and social ties; his self-sufficiency is innately destructive. Even Thyestes' acknowledgement of fraternity – *agnosco fratrem* (1006) – indicates, ironically, that Atreus has sabotaged all blood relationships just in order to arrive at this moment of recognition. He fulfils his allotted *persona* at the expense of everything else.

Conclusion

Erik Gunderson describes the Stoic *proficiens* as 'someone looking back at himself *as if* from the terminus of the journey as he advances along the road to the same end'.[171] Medea and Atreus also behave this way: they project idealised identities and proceed to evaluate their current selves from that future perspective. The activity is typical of Seneca's *dramatis personae*, who engage in it not only for metatheatrical effect, but also to monitor their selfhood and thereby ensure its constancy. Medea and Atreus want to match their behaviour to their roles, and their words to their deeds; they endeavour to achieve *aequabilitas* across sequences of dramatic action, and in Medea's case, across the entire arc of her literary and mythological life. Constancy in Senecan tragedy is sought with great effort and won at great cost.

It is also a principle that requires evaluation over time. Logically enough, constancy is not an instant character trait, but one that may be discerned only towards a story's end. It is when Medea requests recognition from Jason that she proves the full extent of her self-coherence. When Thyestes recognises Atreus, he draws attention to the end-directed self-construction his brother has pursued with such vehemence. Scenes of *anagnorisis* in these tragedies are designed to validate, often via the agency of an unfortunate spectator, the identities that protagonists have crafted and perfected through their crimes.

---

[171] Gunderson (2015) 9.

Recognition is a point at which multiple topics from Senecan philosophy and Senecan drama intersect. As the conclusion of a constant performance (*Ep.* 120.22), *anagnorisis* combines implied human *personae* with dramatic ones, renders *constantia* dependent upon external acknowledgement, and comes perilously close to divorcing self-coherence from virtue. Exhortations to behave in a morally upright manner hold less sway when seemliness (*decorum*) is envisaged primarily in terms of a seamless performance. Medea and Atreus both capitalise on the moral ambiguity of this principle, and invoke *decorum* as a means of persevering in the fundamentally wicked activities for which their roles befit them. Thus, the recognition scenes in each of these tragedies emphasise the complex interplay between literary character and actual, human selfhood. In doing so, they open up the possibility for *constantia* to become an im- or amoral quality.

CHAPTER 2

EXEMPLARITY

No matter how much identity relies on an individual's own memory and habits, it also relies on community, on the social relationships that stimulate people continually to define and adjust their sense of self. The previous chapter examined how identity derives from 'sameness', from the quality of being *idem*. This chapter discusses identity as the outcome of *identification*, that is, of people observing and appropriating each other's characteristics in order to define their own.[1] Self-development is a fundamentally mimetic project to which the selection and emulation of role models is essential. When people identify with others, or identify themselves *in* others, they gain a sense of their own being, its capacities and its boundaries. Negative identification achieves the same result from the opposite direction, as the self takes shape in contrast to or reaction against qualities it perceives as wrong. The entire process is so commonplace that it is easy to lose sight of its central paradox: we copy each other in order to achieve distinctiveness; our being unique is predicated largely upon our being similar. This aspect of personal identity entails perennial negotiation between the individual and the group, between the particular and the general – categories at once co-dependent and deeply antagonistic. We are *like* but not *identical* to our parents, friends, colleagues, and peers: it is from this intersection of singularity and absolute correspondence that the human self emerges.

For the Romans, this process takes the form of emulation and exemplarity, and its chief domain is the elite family. Offspring, especially but not exclusively male, are regarded as moral and physical replicas of their forebears, whose models they are encouraged to imitate in order to assert themselves. Being a Scipio, or a Cato, or a Piso – to name just a few – comes with the expectation that one will exhibit the talents, attitudes, and conduct typically

---

[1] On identification as an element of identity formation, see Wilshire (1982).

associated with one's family. It also comes with the expectation that one will employ these generic, replicable characteristics to achieve outstanding, individual greatness. As Catherine Baroin remarks, 'a young man belonging to a famous family has to make a first name for himself ... and achieve distinctiveness' but, paradoxically, 'he only does so by being similar (*similis*) even identical to someone else'.[2] The exemplary individual is at once a copy and a singular instance of exceptional behaviour. The *exemplum*, as an intellectual tool, likewise mediates between the categories of particular and general: as a model, it must, by definition, be absolutely typical and imitable; but its being a model also means that it is set apart, excerpted, special.[3] Discourses of exemplarity function as a kind of social glue, granting individuals prominence and the opportunity for self-definition while at the same time confirming their ties to a specific community and set of traditions. In Roman culture, *exempla* constitute a cornerstone of pedagogy; a source of collective memory; a stimulus for elite competition; a mark of genealogical prestige – above all, they are a wellspring of familial and social continuity, of self-perpetuation and replication. Like the broader human activity of identifying the self in and through others, Roman exemplarity encourages self-development via assimilation and mimetic identification. A Scipio, or a Cato, or a Piso can be defined as such only in relation to the lineage from which he springs.

exempla pervade Senecan tragedy as well, where they likewise tend to be associated with ingrained patterns of family conduct. For instance: Phaedra interprets her errant passion for Hippolytus on the model of her mother's bovine lust (*fatale miserae matris agnosco malum: / peccare noster novit in silvis amor*; 'I recognise my wretched mother's fateful evil: our love knows how to sin in the woods' *Phaed.* 113–14); Atreus, too, cites familial precedent when contemplating revenge (*Tantalum et Pelopem aspice; / ad*

---

[2] Baroin (2010) 28.
[3] On the *exemplum*'s contradictory position both as an exception and a rule, see Lowrie (2007) esp. 97, and Agamben (1998) 22: 'What the example shows is its belonging to a class, but for this very reason the example steps out of its class in the very moment in which it exhibits and delimits it.' For the *exemplum*'s mediation between the particular and the general, Lowrie and Lüdemann (2015) is an invaluable resource.

haec manus exempla poscuuntur meae; 'look to Tantalus and Pelops; my hands are called to these examples' *Thy.* 242–3).[4] Here the pressure of exemplary emulation joins forces with biological inheritance to produce unavoidable, all but imperative templates for behaviour: Atreus' wickedness must live up to, by imitating, that of his predecessors; Phaedra's experience conforms, unwittingly, to the contours of her mother's. Biological and genealogical repetition combine with the *exemplum*'s innate capacity for replication. The consequences for identity are stark: Seneca's characters not only model themselves on their forebears, but even end up following them, on many occasions, against their better judgement. *exempla*, like blood, will out.

Following initial consideration of *exempla* in Roman culture, this chapter examines the interlinked themes of exemplarity and family relationships in two tragedies, *Troades* and *Hercules*. In the former play, the past maintains such an oppressive grip on the present that Pyrrhus can barely be dissociated from Achilles and Astyanax from Hector. The identity of the son is bound up with that of the father, whether through opposition or similarity. In his portraits of these two young men, Seneca explores the tensions underlying human, and specifically Roman, practices of mimetic and sympathetic identification. Where exactly does a person begin and end? Where do the boundaries of his or her attributes lie? And does the social pressure of *exempla* encourage self-improvement or foreclose it? *Troades* depicts a world dominated by paradigmatic precedents, a world in which the individual struggles to gain clear purchase and a clear outline. *Hercules*, by contrast, presents a hero so exceptional he follows no model but his own. Seneca's Hercules is detached from his family emotionally, morally, and physically. He displays commensurate detachment from any need to emulate his forebears and thereby integrate himself within a community. Having no-one to compete with, and no-one to copy, Hercules engages in the vertiginous pursuit of self-*aemulatio*, an activity that overrides the bonds of biology,

---

[4] Segal (1986) 115–29 and Kirichenko (2013) 44–59 examine the ominous presence of parental models in the *Phaedra*. Boyle (1983) argues for intergenerational repetition as a structuring motif in the *Thyestes* and the *Agamemnon*. For the broader use of precedents by Seneca's characters, see Garton (1972) 200–1, and Fitch and McElduff (2002).

genealogy, and eventually, society. Rather than ensure continuity and connectedness, Hercules' exemplarity leads only to alienation; his self-*aemulatio* both adopts and warps the *exemplum*'s standard purpose.

Inherited Models

Similitude and imitation are principles at the heart of Roman – indeed, of all – exemplary discourse.[5] By providing people with models to emulate or to avoid, *exempla* function analogically, so that their goal of moral transformation is achieved by duplicating and reproducing prototypical behaviour. In the words of Alexander Gelley, the *exemplum*'s purpose 'becomes that of propagating itself, creating multiples'; it perpetuates attitudes, values, and patterns of conduct in a manner reminiscent of artistic mimesis.[6] The Romans themselves were fully aware of the imitative impulses governing acts of exemplarity. To cite two disparate but representative instances: Horace, in the *Sermones*, has his father caution him against disgraceful love affairs by uttering the injunction, *Scetani dissimilis sis* ('don't be like Scetanus' *Ser.* 1.4.12); in an entirely different genre and tone, but nevertheless expressing the same sentiment, Livy introduces his historical work as a memorial source of examples *inde tibi tuaeque rei publicae quod imitere capias* ('from which you may choose what to imitate for yourself and for your state', *praef.* 1.10). Both authors acknowledge that the *exemplum*'s moral-didactic efficacy[7] – not to mention its potentially wayward influence – stems from its innate

---

[5] Langlands (2018) 86–111 is an acute study of imitation and replication in Roman exemplarity. Roller (2018) 1–31 is a similarly insightful overview, especially of the *exemplum*'s role in setting norms (and thus, inviting repetition). Other scholarly treatments of the issue include Lyons (1989) 26–8; Mayer (1991) 141–76 on Seneca; Hölkeskamp (1996) 312–15 on collective memory in ancient Rome; Feldherr (1998) on Livy; Chaplin (2000) on Livy; Roller (2004) 23–8 on Horatius Cocles; Barchiesi (2009) on the overlap between literary and cultural imitation in Roman exemplarity; Van Der Blom (2010) on Cicero; Goldschmidt (2013) 149–92 on Ennius.

[6] Gelley (1995) 3. On the topic of mimesis, Langlands (2018) 99 notes the Romans' tendency to conflate ethical with aesthetic forms of imitation.

[7] On the moral-didactic function of Roman *exempla*, useful studies include: Bloomer (1992); Skidmore (1996) esp. 13–82; Chaplin (2000); Wilcox (2006) and (2008); Morgan (2007) 122–57; Turpin (2008); Langlands (2008), (2011), (2015), (2018); and Van Der Blom (2010).

capacity for iteration. The example, by definition, demands to be copied.[8]

A conspicuous consequence of this iteration, in Roman culture at least, is the tendency for exemplary narratives to cluster around family groups, as though on the assumption that genetic inheritance and the bestowal of a family name bring with them a predisposition for specific activities, attitudes, and forms of behaviour. The phenomenon is particularly marked in the case of 'structurally' similar *exempla*, namely, deeds that reproduce in full the individual features and narrative contours of earlier models.[9] Matthew Roller remarks that this kind of exemplarity is apt to be associated with particular *gentes*: 'the idea that certain patterns of behaviour do or should run in families ... is widespread in Roman culture'.[10] The habit develops not only because intra-familial models provide a convenient rubric for categorising exemplarity, but also because of a deep-seated conceptual link: the *exemplum*, like the parent, is an authoritative model that calls for imitation, and successful imitation, in turn, furnishes outward proof of hereditary character. Exemplary lineage and genealogical lineage function in equivalent ways, and frequently overlap.

To illustrate this point, we may review one of Rome's most celebrated *exempla*: the Decii Mures.[11] The sequence begins with the elder Publius Decius Mus sacrificing himself in an act of *devotio* against the Latins at Veseris in 340 BC (Livy 8.9); his son, also named Publius Decius Mus, follows suit with his own act of *devotio* at the battle of Sentinum in 295 BC (Livy 10.28.6–18); there is even a tradition – most likely spurious – that the third Publius Decius Mus, grandson of the first, dies by *devotio* at Ausculum in 279 BC (Dio fr. 43; Cic. *Fin.* 2.61; *Tusc.* 1.89;

---

[8] Thus, Lyons (1989) 26: 'Both in the form it takes in texts and in the view of the world it projects, the example depends upon repetition.'
[9] As opposed to 'categorically' similar *exempla*, which tend merely to be grouped under the same rubric, for example as instances of *virtus* or *fides*. The terminology comes from Roller (2004) 23–4.
[10] Roller (2004) 24–5, and n.54. See also Mayer (1991) 144.
[11] Fuller treatments of the Decii Mures can be found in Litchfield (1914) 46–8; Oakley (1998) *ad* Livy 8.9–11; Edwards (2007) 25–6; Goldschmidt (2013) 156–8. Quintilian *Inst.* 12.2.30 implies that the Decii Mures were some of the most well-known and frequently cited Roman *exempla*.

Ennius *Ann.* 6.191–4).[12] Repetition across generations creates and at the same time authorises the act's symbolic value: for the latter two Decii Mures, *devotio* is assumed to represent a key means of living up to one's name and of affirming one's lineage.[13] Tradition renders the name and the deed all but interchangeable, as illustrated most clearly by the last of these three *exempla*, where Roman authors are less concerned with the event's historicity than with its adherence to an established family model: Decius Mus the grandson is thought to have committed *devotio* because that is what Decii Mures typically do.

Thus, in Roman discourses of exemplarity, moral resemblance confirms genetics. Cicero (*Brut.* 133) declares that the oratorical talents of Catulus senior (consul 102) may be inferred from those of Catulus junior (Q. Lutatius Catulus Capitolinus). Ovid states the idea more openly still when he wishes of his anonymous, elite addressee, *sic iuvenis similisque tibi sit natus et illum / moribus agnoscat quilibet esse tuum!* ('may your son resemble you thus and may everyone recognise him as yours because of his conduct' *Trist.* 4.5.31–2). To underscore the hereditary nature of the son's *mores*, Ovid evokes in these lines the Roman ritual of a father acknowledging his paternity. In the same way that a Roman father would accept the child as his own (*agnoscere* cf. Chapter 1, 57–8 and 95.) and thereby facilitate its inclusion within the family unit, so, in Ovid's couplet, the son's behaviour is hoped to substantiate his biological origins (*illum* ... / *agnoscat* ... *esse tuum*) and guarantee his position within elite society. Naturally, the quality of such replication depends upon the *mores* themselves; it is

---

[12] Although certainty is beyond our grasp, suggestions that the third Decius Mus died in an act of *devotio* at Ausculum appear to hold little historical weight: the evidence of Cic. *Fin.* 2.61 and *Tusc.* 1.89 is inconclusive, while Dio fr. 43 states that Decius, after contemplating *devotio* at Ausculum, eventually decided against it. The passage from Ennius – *Ann.* 6.191–4 – while undoubtedly referring to a *devotio*, remains a matter of debate, with Cornell (1986) 248–9 and (1987) 514–16 asserting that it most likely refers to the second Decius Mus consecrating himself at Sentinum in 295 BC, while Skutsch (1987) 512–14 opts instead for the third Decius Mus, at Ausculum.

[13] Instructive in this regard is the speech Livy puts into the mouth of the second Decius Mus (10.28.13): *'quid ultra moror' inquit 'familiare fatum? datum hoc nostro generi est ut luendis periculis publicis piacula simus. iam ego mecum hostium legiones mactandas Telluri ac Dis Manibus dabo.'* Besides being the defining feature of the Decii as a *gens* (*familiare fatum*), the act of *devotio* also verges on being a genetic imperative (*datum hoc nostro generi est*), something imposed by nature as well as culture.

Exemplarity

possible to reproduce bad examples as well as good ones. Of Verres' father, for instance, Cicero remarks tartly to the jury, *qualis fuerit ... ex eo quem sui simillimum produxit recognoscere potestis* ('what he was like you can infer from the faithful copy of himself that he has brought into the world' *Verr.* 2.1.32 trans. Greenwood).[14] Moral resemblance, like physical, can have its ugly side.

The pursuit of exemplary behaviour can also be seen to strengthen distant family ties or to formulate family connections where none may in fact exist. While the Decii Mures all belong to the one, immediate bloodline, adoptive relationships are likewise capable of fostering imitative conduct, as in the case of Scipio Aemilianus, whose decisive role in the Third Punic War mirrors that of his adoptive grandfather, Scipio Africanus, in the First.[15] The most telling example, though, is Marcus Junius Brutus, whose nominal (if not actual) relationship to the man responsible for ending Tarquin's tyranny is depicted as influencing – perhaps even providing crucial impetus for – his role in Caesar's assassination. Dio's account stresses this demand for continuity and duplication:

γράμματά τε γάρ, τῇ ὁμωνυμίᾳ αὐτοῦ τῇ πρὸς τὸν πάνυ Βροῦτον τὸν τοὺς Ταρκυνίους καταλύσαντα καταχρώμενοι, πολλὰ ἐξετίθεσαν, φημίζοντες αὐτὸν ψευδῶς ἀπόγονον ἐκείνου εἶναι· ἀμφοτέρους γὰρ τοὺς παῖδας, τοὺς μόνους οἱ γενομένους, μειράκια ἔτι ὄντας ἀπέκτεινε, καὶ οὐδὲ ἔγγονον ὑπελίπετο. οὐ μὴν ἀλλὰ τοῦτό τε οἱ πολλοί, ὅπως ὡς καὶ γένει προσήκων αὐτῷ ἐς ὁμοιότροπα ἔργα προαχθείη, ἐπλάττοντο, καὶ συνεχῶς ἀνεκάλουν αὐτόν, 'ὦ Βροῦτε Βροῦτε' ἐκβοῶντες, καὶ προσεπιλέγοντες ὅτι 'Βρούτου χρῄζομεν.' καὶ τέλος τῇ τε τοῦ παλαιοῦ Βρούτου εἰκόνι ἐπέγραψαν 'εἴθε ἔζης,' καὶ τῷ τούτου βήματι, ἐστρατήγει γὰρ καὶ βῆμα καὶ τὸ τοιοῦτο ὀνομάζεται ἐφ' οὗ τις ἱζόμενος δικάζει, ὅτι 'καθεύδεις, ὦ Βροῦτε' καὶ 'Βροῦτος οὐκ εἶ.'

Making the most of his having the same name as the great Brutus who overthrew the Tarquins, they distributed many pamphlets, declaring that he was not truly that man's descendant; for the older Brutus had put to death both his sons, the only ones he had, when they were mere lads, and left no offspring whatever.

---

[14] Further discussion of these three examples – Cic. *Brut.* 133 and *Verr.* 2.1.32, and Ov. *Trist.* 4.5.31–2 – can be found in Baroin (2010) 37–41.
[15] Family ties are still relevant in Scipio Aemilianus' case, since he is the cousin of the man who adopts him. But, in contrast to the Decii Mures, no direct line of biological descent links the exemplary grandfather to the exemplary grandson. On exemplarity as a trope in Scipio Aemilianus' life story, see Polybius 31.24.5, with Habinek (1998) 50–1; on his use as an *exemplum* for later Romans, see Van Der Blom (2010) 108, especially n.118.

Nevertheless, the majority pretended to accept such a relationship, in order that Brutus, as a relative of that famous man, might be induced to perform equivalent deeds. They kept continually calling upon him, shouting out 'Brutus, Brutus!' and adding further 'We need Brutus.' Finally on the statue of the early Brutus they wrote 'We wish you were alive!' and upon the tribunal of the living Brutus (for he was praetor at the time and this is the name given to the seat on which the praetor sits in judgment) 'Brutus, you're asleep,' and 'You are not Brutus.' (Dio Cassius 44.12 trans. Cary, lightly modified)[16]

As Dio presents it, the issue is not whether Brutus can claim a genuine family connection to his illustrious predecessor (and the Romans themselves may not have known either way); rather, the mere possibility of this relationship imposes upon Marcus Junius Brutus the need to replicate certain patterns of conduct (ὅπως ὡς καὶ γένει προσήκων αὐτῷ ἐς ὁμοιότροπα ἔργα προαχθείη).[17] In effect, it is the process of exemplarity that renders Brutus kinsman to his early republican counterpart. The *exemplum* is treated much like a set of inherited characteristics; it is both a source and confirmation of identity in ways similar to a parent. Brutus must live up to the promise implicit in this name because that name represents, simultaneously, a potential genealogical connection and a laudable instance of anti-tyrannical resistance. To be fully himself, he must adopt the normative actions of another; in order to be *a* Brutus, he must copy *the* Brutus.

So Roman discourses of exemplarity occupy a point of intersection between genetic replication and behavioural imitation.[18] Not only does the idea of family resemblance encompass a standard expectation that children will inherit their parents' features and bearing, but it also extends into full arcs of narrative action, where offspring reproduce their ancestors' deeds, and those deeds come to substantiate parentage. Understandably, this sort of cultural practice has a deep effect on how individuals shape and perceive their identities, and on how they evaluate the identities of others. In its most extreme form, Roman exemplarity demands that the

---

[16] A similar version of the story is reported by Plutarch *Brutus* 9.3–4.
[17] Thus Edwards (2007) 150 extrapolates from Marcus Brutus's story, 'in Roman political life, one could not escape the destiny of one's own name. A particular name might in itself provoke desire for external fame.'
[18] Wilcox (2006) 80–1 detects a similar play of literal versus metaphorical reproduction in Seneca's portrayal of female exemplarity.

Exemplarity

individual subordinate his or her sense of personal discreteness to broader matrices of tradition and ancestry. Self-development, on this model, amounts to little more than selecting and recycling the activities of those who have gone before; Marcus Junius Brutus, for one, appears to exercise little choice in matters of self-determination.

Yet herein lies the complexity and richness of Rome's rubric of *exempla*, because selecting and recycling other people's activities is a fundamental means of human self-formation, no matter what its specific cultural grounding. To cite Bruce Wilshire:[19]

mimesis of others must occur in that typification of the world essential to the emergence of any coherent experience of it. I become *a* human being only by learning to do the sorts of things *other* human beings do ... I must mime what others do and say about thing, and so I must mime the others. I continually return to *myself* via the others, conditioned by the others.

Roman exemplarity is, among many other things, a culturally embedded expression of this basic human need, a need to imitate not just for the sake of learning, but also, more deeply, for the sake of formulating oneself via subjunctive possibilities of being. For instance: I see a man fighting with a sword and I decide to copy or abstain from this action only after engaging in a rapid process of imaginative substitution whereby I take this man's place ('is this the sort of thing I, too, should / could do?'). My identity, that is, my sense of myself-in-the-world, 'is structured and polarized by possibilities of kinds of existence largely set by others'.[20] Viewed from this angle, Marcus Brutus' imitation of Lucius falls fully within the bounds of regular human self-development: it is an action (like all actions) arrived at via the subjunctive substitution of oneself for another.

Hence, exemplary imitation does not so much preclude individualism as it highlights the fact that all individuals are assembled from pre-existing components. Brutus qua singular person is also, simultaneously, Brutus qua type; he is at once a unique instance of being and a version of things that have gone before him. Brutus' identity, like the *exemplum* itself, mediates between

---

[19] Wilshire (1977) 199.
[20] Wilshire (1977) 200.

the categories of particular and general. Popular identification of Marcus with Lucius Junius Brutus illustrates in condensed form a tug-of-war between two inseparable and conflicting forces: on the one side, individualism, ambition, and the sense of oneself as a discrete, autonomous unit; on the other, biological and genealogical ties coupled with the pressures of tradition and exemplarity. Similitude leads paradoxically to uniqueness, and vice versa.

The Art of Exemplarity

Besides balancing the rival demands of uniqueness and typification, individuality and social relationships, Roman discourses of exemplarity also mediate between categories of actual and fictional selfhood. On the one hand, *exempla* are meant to guide and transform personal traits; they are supposed to orchestrate changes in the way people behave and think of themselves qua living beings. At a basic level, as we have seen, exemplary practice encapsulates the crucial mechanism of human self-formation and self-comprehension that is one's mimetic identification with others. It also performs the even more basic function of confirming genealogies and situating people within their specific biological lineages. Although it often blurs or exceeds the strict boundaries of the individual, Roman exemplarity nonetheless operates in the essentially human, personal, 'real' sphere of identity.

On the other hand, though, the *exemplum*'s iterative and imitative nature can also conjure a process of artistic representation, in which statues replicate their referents and images are reflected in mirrors. The person qua *exemplar* represents a timeless, replicable symbol, an identity template, as it were, capable of being transferred to other individuals in other eras.[21] Via its memorialising and paradigmatic functions, exemplarity narrows personal identity from an endless range of contingent, indeterminate possibilities to a static, complete, and relatively limited set of characteristics. Being a role model entails also being a role. In this sense, an exemplary person approximates to a statue, a painted image, or even a fictional character; he or she moves into the realm of

---

[21] Roller (2018) 71–6 explores timelessness as a characteristic of Roman exemplarity.

representation, becomes a surrogate self.²² The connection is closest in the case of deceased individuals whose identity necessarily endures in a fixed state, but neither did Roman culture shy away from associating living individuals with aesthetic objects.

To illustrate this idea, I return to Dio's account of Marcus Junius Brutus (cited in the preceding section). Here, anonymous protestors use the elder Brutus' statues as a means of urging the living Brutus to act: τῇ τε τοῦ παλαιοῦ Βρούτου εἰκόνι ἐπέγραψαν 'εἴθε ἔζης,' ('on the statue of the early Brutus they wrote 'We wish you were alive!'', 44.12). The exchange envisaged is one of man and monument.²³ Should the living Brutus opt to participate in Caesar's assassination, he will effectively reanimate his predecessor's statue by copying the deeds it represents and embodying all that it stands for. At the same time, he will liken himself to the statue by partaking in the memorialisation of his great predecessor and the symbolic replication of his qualities. Marcus Junius Brutus is at once his own fully realised self and the replication of another; the exchange goes both ways.²⁴

Dio's anecdote is far from a lone instance of such exemplary exchange between person and effigy. Statues of exceptional historical figures were a common topographical feature in the city of Rome, their main purpose being to commemorate and perpetuate particularly laudable forms of behaviour. Augustus, notably, harnessed this custom to his own ends when he erected in the two colonnades of his forum sculptures of *summi viri* from Rome's past, dressed in triumphal regalia (Suet. *Aug.* 31.5).²⁵ Besides memorialising these individuals and their achievements, Augustus drew an explicit comparison with himself: he 'proclaimed by edict that this

---

[22] Nappa (2018) 82 formulates a similar concept in reference to *imagines* in Juv. *Sat.* 8: 'Surrogate bodies are representations of the individual [i.e. statues, paintings] and as such they bring the individual into the realm of the textual. Thus, once the body is given a surrogate, the individual becomes subject not only to those things that can be done to his actual body but to the way he can be coopted and manipulated in the sphere of representation.'

[23] Hölkeskamp (1996) 302–6 and Roller (2004) 10–23 discuss the close connection between monuments and *exempla*.

[24] On the frequent equivalence between imitator and imitated in Roman exemplarity, see Langlands (2018) 99–100.

[25] The *Forum Augustum*'s content and its commemoration of the exemplary past have been treated in detail by Flower (1996) 224–36, and Gowing (2005) 138–45.

[statue group] had been devised for citizens to demand that both he, while he lived, and his successors, matched the example set by those men' (*professus et edicto commentum id se ut ad illorum velut exemplar et ipse dum viveret et insequentium aetatium principes exigerentur a civibus*, Suet. *Aug.* 31.5). Veiled in this ostentatious display of false modesty is the claim that Augustus himself embodies a living *exemplum*;[26] he is the inevitable next figure in this procession of *summi viri*, simultaneously a live version of them and a statue of himself.[27] Such was the culture of exemplarity in ancient Rome that it envisaged a fluid relationship between reality and representation, human beings and reproducible symbols.

This fluid relationship is also articulated by metaphors of reflection, which Roman writers often employ to describe emulative aims and conduct.[28] Thus: Demea in Terence's *Adelphoe* counsels his son, Ctesipho, to 'look into others' lives as though into a mirror' (*introspicere, tamquam in speculum, in vitas omnium*, 415), which implies that the young man, beyond simply being guided by good models, will reproduce them *in extenso*.[29] Seneca, too, draws on this metaphor when he calls Cato a 'living image of virtue' (*virtutum viva imago*, *Tranq.* 16.1) and summarises a list of exemplary deeds from Roman history as 'offering to us the image of virtue' (*imaginem nobis ostendere virtutis*, *Ep.* 120.8). The idea, once again, is that exemplarity demands imitation and thereby generates copies in a manner analogous to artistic mimesis. Cato is both an embodiment of virtue and a symbolic instantiation of himself; being an *exemplar* fixes him in the perpetual, reproducible state of an image (*imago*) and more specifically, given the Roman context, of an ancestral wax mask (*imago*).[30] Like the

---

[26] On Augustus' self-exemplarity, see Lowrie (2007) 102–12.

[27] This statue group also evokes the genealogical aspect of exemplarity since, as Zanker (1990) 213–14 and Flower (1996) 224–36 both observe, the *summi viri* claim affinity with the *imagines* typically displayed in aristocratic *atria*. Augustus used this statue group to appropriate the *summi viri* of the Roman past as if they were his own family, in addition to the *imagines* he inherited upon his adoption into the Julii.

[28] See Gelley (1995) 3 on exemplarity's connection to pictorial realisation. Bartsch (2006) 125–7 and Baroin (2010) 37–47 discuss the term *imago* as a metaphor for exemplarity in Roman culture.

[29] Mayer (1991) 144–5 argues for the essentially Roman nature of this advice.

[30] Seneca plays with the idea more explicitly in *Ep.* 84.8: *etiam si cuius in te comparebit similtudo, quem admiratio tibi altius fixerit, similem esse te volo quomodo filium, non quomodo imaginem; imago res mortua est*. Here, the son is presented as the living (and

Exemplarity

ancestral portraits that line elite *atria*, Cato's *imago* memorialises his deeds and functions as a spur to future emulation, effectively, to generating yet more copies.

A particularly rich instance of the *exemplum*'s mimetic impulses is Livy's story of the elder Publius Licinius Calvus, who persuades voters to elect his son to the tribunate in his stead, on the basis that the young man has been fashioned into 'the image and likeness' of his father (*effigiem atque imaginem*, 5.18.5). The story's events articulate issues of inheritance and family resemblance: Calvus is depicted as the physical reflection of his progenitor – a statue or portrait (*effigiem*) – and this bodily similarity is meant to corroborate a further moral and dispositional likeness.[31] Transfer of political office from father to son encapsulates processes of biological descent and genealogical preservation. The younger Calvus is at once a flesh-and-blood version of his father and an artificial replica of him. Biology, exemplarity, and artistic representation converge in this anecdote, with each engaging in an equivalent act of reproductive repetition.[32]

Crucially for Seneca, this nexus between art, *exempla*, and family traits claims a long history of association with theatrical performance, as the phrase 'role model' suggests even now.[33] Anyone who trains him- or herself to imitate another person's actions and qualities pursues an enterprise equivalent to that of the stage artist, who both copies and – so to speak – 'revivifies' the identities of dramatic characters.[34] Theatrical performance shares with exemplarity an impulse to re-embody established *personae*: there are deep and cogent similarities between reproducing Cato's conduct in life and Medea's conduct on stage. Like the individual

---

presumably, developing, changing) alternative to the changeless death-mask/mirror image. Affinity between ancestral *imagines* and exemplarity is explored by Baroin (2010) 23–5, and Uden (2010) 121–2.

[31] O'Sullivan (2009) 468 explains how this episode combines notions of patrilineal succession with the mimetic repetition of art objects.

[32] Bexley (2017) 167–70 explores the parallel qualities of biological reproduction and artistic production, both of which rely on generating copies.

[33] The caveats of Bell (2008) 2–6 notwithstanding, the modern term 'role model' seems to me entirely suitable for describing Roman exemplarity, especially given the latter's theatricalised qualities.

[34] The symbolic link between acting and resurrection has been theorised by Blau (1982/3); Rayner (2006) ix–xxxv; and Bassi (2017). See also Bexley (2017) 172–80 on death's association with performance in the pseudo-Senecan *Octavia*.

aspiring to embody a past *exemplum*, the actor's art requires him or her to identify with another self, to inhabit that self and assume its characteristics. The exemplary individual, in turn, resembles a fictional character, a *dramatis persona* that may be adopted, adapted, and reperformed endlessly.

Roman practice brings the two realms of exemplarity and theatre into particularly close conjunction. The principal context for their meeting was the aristocratic funeral, at which professional performers were hired to don the wax masks (*imagines*) of the dead man's ancestors and to accompany the procession in a visually powerful display of upper-class lineage. The reanimation of past *exempla* becomes, on this model, an inherently dramatic activity, while the ancestors themselves become analogous to dramatic characters: they are identity templates, their selfhood already fully defined, unconditional, and capable of being transferred from person to person.

The Roman aristocratic funeral was designed chiefly to enact social and familial continuity. It bolstered collective memory and preserved the cultural values epitomised by Rome's *maiores*.[35] Once the cortège had reached the Rostra, a son or close male relative would deliver a eulogy celebrating the deceased's achievements, listing alongside those of his ancestors, the official posts he had held; the ancestors themselves, re-incarnated by actors, sat behind the speaker on the platform, and listened.[36] The custom was intended to spur emulative behaviour among the family's younger generations, and more generally, among the attending Roman populace.[37] As the representative of his family's future, the eulogist also aspired to be the physical and moral embodiment of its exemplary past. His need to imitate and thereby preserve dynastic traditions was symbolically and visually equivalent to the actors' assumption of ancestral forms: like a living monument, or the latest performer of a long-standing role, the deceased's heir was called upon to uphold the *exempla* of his progenitors. These converging lines of impersonation and

---

[35] Flower (1996) 91–127; Hölkeskamp (1996) 320–3; Dufallo (2007) 4–6.
[36] The principle ancient source for this information is Polybius 6.53–4.
[37] As implied by Polybius 6.54. Sallust *Iug.* 4.5–6 invests the *imagines* with an equivalent role in spurring emulative exemplarity.

Exemplarity

inheritance articulated with striking economy the theatrical (and frequently biological) replication inherent in all acts of exemplarity.

Re-embodiment of exemplary individuals even occurred on the stage itself, via the Roman tradition of *fabulae praetextae*. Although it seems unlikely that these plays ever took place during actual funeral ceremonies,[38] they nonetheless developed from much the same constellation of moral and cultural attitudes: like the actors wearing *imagines* at an aristocratic funeral, the characters in an historical drama epitomised the ancestral ties that bound the exemplary past to its re-enactment, and therefore to its perpetuation, in the present. *Praetextae* such as Accius' *Decius* and *Brutus* may well have been commissioned to celebrate contemporary patrons through praise of their exceptional predecessors.[39] In this context, too, the discourse of exemplarity effects a fluid transition between the singular, self-contained person and the general, reproducible art object: the figure on stage is a real flesh-and-blood human impersonating and thereby becoming a copy of an historical *exemplar*. The *exemplar*, likewise, is reanimated as a living being *and* confirmed as a mimetic object. In the likely case that patrons attended the performances of such *praetextae*,[40] comparisons could easily be drawn between the actual descendant sitting in the audience and the representation of his ancestor on stage. Doubtless this was one of the reasons for Marcus Junius Brutus wanting to re-stage Accius' *Brutus* at the *Ludi Apollinares* of 44 BC, in the aftermath of Caesar's assassination: as the current liberator of the Republic, he would be visibly mirrored by the character embodied in the play; Marcus Brutus himself, and the actor playing Lucius Brutus would both be

---

[38] Flower (1995) 177–9, refuting claims by Dupont (1985) 218–24.
[39] Who commissioned *fabulae praetextae* and to what purpose, are questions addressed by Flower (1995); Manuwald (2001) 119–21; and Kragelund (2002) 25–7. Fuller assessment of Accius' *Decius* and *Brutus* is in Kragelund (2016) 46–57.
[40] It would certainly make sense for patrons to attend performances of the *praetextae* they had commissioned, especially if – as is thought – the plays took place at *ludi votivi* or to mark the dedications of temples: see Flower (1995) and Kragelund (2002). Cornelius Balbus is reported to have attended the performance of his *Iter* at the *ludi* he hosted in Gades in 43 BC – see Pollio's letter to Cicero, *Fam.* 10.32 – but this evidence should not be taken as representative, since Balbus is the only Roman aristocrat known to have penned his own *praetexta* featuring himself as the heroic protagonist.

exemplary copies of the actual, historical individual on whom the *praetexta* centred.[41] The imitation that underpins all acts of exemplarity would ensure Marcus Brutus' personal, biological identity at the same time as rendering him an artificial duplicate of an earlier model.

My reason for dwelling at such length on this issue is to show how easily the discourse and praxis of Roman exemplarity binds actual people to their fictional or plastic counterparts. Roman *exempla* cross and re-cross the boundary between person and character, especially in their more theatrical manifestations. By likening individuals to art objects and dramatic roles, exemplarity bestows an identity that is circumscribed, reproducible, and timeless, in comparison to the contingent, time-bound singularity that characterises human lives. Such circumscribed identity, admitting of minimal (if any) variation and capable of being repeated *ad infinitum*, a stable and complete set of traits, is precisely what characters possess. To a lesser degree, this is also true of statues, so that the relationship of person to effigy approaches even if it does not quite reach the character–person binary. Given the prevalence of such practices in ancient Rome, it is unsurprising to find in Senecan tragedy a similarly permeable boundary between fictional and actual modes of being.

Metapoetic Families

Before turning to Seneca, though, I consider one more matter: the relationship of exemplarity to literary allusion. In a wide-ranging 2009 article on the topic, Alessandro Barchiesi draws attention to 'the link in Roman letters between repetition of past *exempla* and textual self-reference'.[42] The *exemplum*, like the quotation to which it is closely related,[43] prompts intertextual associations,

---

[41] Brutus never realised these aims: he fled Italy prior to the *ludi Apollinares* taking place, and Gaius Antonius (brother of Marc Antony) in his role as the acting *praetor urbanus*, had Accius' *Tereus* staged instead of the *Brutus*, doubtless to avoid inspiring popular support for Caesar's assassin; see Cicero *Att.* 16.2.3; 16.5.1; *Phil* 1.36. Erasmo (2004) 96–9 explores this putative re-performance as a culminating example of metatheatre that blends historical with dramatised events.

[42] Barchiesi (2009) 59.

[43] As Lowrie (2007) 97 remarks, '*exempla* by definition occur in contexts of citation'. On the relationship between *exempla* and quotation, see also Agamben (1998) 21–2; Goldschmidt (2013) 152–3; and Waldenfels (2015) 37.

Exemplarity

and opens a window onto the shadows and outlines of a given work's literary genealogy. Through the *exemplum*, the author can show, and the reader see, which texts are being imitated and enshrined as paradigms.

Instances of such self-reflexive literary exemplarity are not far to seek; certainly, they saturate Seneca's drama, but first it will be profitable to examine one example so apt and so popular that it could be said to occupy its own exemplary status within the scholarly literature on Roman exemplarity, namely, Aeneas' address to Ascanius at *Aeneid* 12.435–40:[44]

> disce, puer, virtutem ex me verumque laborem,
> fortunam ex aliis. nunc te mea dextera bello
> defensum dabit et magna inter praemia ducet.
> tu facito, mox cum matura adoleverit aetas,
> sis memor et te animo repetentem exempla tuorum
> et pater Aeneas et avunculus excitet Hector.
>
> Learn courage from me, boy, and true toil;
> learn fortune from others. Now my right hand
> will protect you in war and lead you to great prizes.
> When, in the near future, you reach maturity, make sure
> you remember, and as you recall the examples of your family
> may your father Aeneas, and uncle Hector inspire you.

As Goldschmidt remarks, the *exemplum* fulfils its moral-didactic function at both an intra- and extra-textual level in this passage: Ascanius must learn from Aeneas and Hector just as the generic Roman *puer* whom Ascanius represents, 'the boy reader of epic in future Rome', must learn from the models he encounters in the text itself.[45] Aeneas is a model for his son and for the audience of Vergil's epic. This double layer of exemplarity renders Aeneas at once a quasi-human and a fictional identity. Within the fictive world enclosed by the epic's narrative, Aeneas figures as an implied human personality, a father delivering precepts to his son, and a man whose valorous deeds (*virtutem ... verumque*

---

[44] Analysis of the passage can be found in Barchiesi (2009) 43, and Goldschmidt (2013) 149–50.
[45] Goldschmidt (2013) 149. Tarrant (2012) *ad Aen.* 12.435 notes the generalising force of *puer*: 'the individual addressee stands for the wider audience that is meant to hear and respond to the speaker's message'.

laborem, 435) will be emulated by and reproduced in future generations. Like countless other instances of exemplary discourse in Roman culture, this passage from the *Aeneid* connects moral paradigms with genealogical lineage, so that Ascanius' need to satisfy the demands of his parental model becomes, at the same time, his means of securing a place within an ancestral group (*exempla tuorum*, 439). *Pater Aeneas* likewise combines literal fatherhood with the fatherly authority of the *exemplum*.

At the extra-textual level, however, Aeneas' instruction signifies in a self-reflexive manner the poetic tradition of which he is a part. By citing himself and Hector as models, Aeneas – and Vergil behind him – looks forward to the work's reception by future Roman audiences, and at the same time, glances back to a long-established practice of readers extracting exemplary lessons from Homeric epic.[46] Ascanius is encouraged to treat his father as a textual construct from which he may learn the lessons customarily proffered by epic poetry. This discourse of exemplarity, in turn, draws attention to the *Iliad*'s pervasive presence as an intertext throughout the *Aeneid* – a presence that grows particularly acute in Book 12 – and to Hector's role as one of many literary models for the character of Aeneas himself.[47]

The passage's metapoetic connotations extend further still, because when Aeneas acknowledges his paternal status (*pater Aeneas*), he not only evokes his dynastic and didactic duties, but also alludes to Vergil's position as a literary son to Homer's towering father figure.[48] Vergil the poetic offspring hopes he can live up to the standards set by his great poetic progenitor. Paradigms pervade the passage at all levels, and, just as is the

---

[46] On Homer's role as a pedagogical text and source of moral guidance, see Skidmore (1996) 3–7, with references. For exemplarity within the *Iliad* itself: Willcock (1964) and Goldhill (1994) 60–6.

[47] In fact, Hector is a model for both Aeneas and Turnus in Book 12, as is Achilles: see West (1974) and Quint (1993) 65–83 for detailed discussion of these Iliadic intertexts. Barchiesi (2009) 43 notes that Aeneas' advice to Ascanius at *Aen.* 12.435–40 also draws on Sophocles' *Ajax* 548–51, and Tarrant (2012) *ad Aen.* 435–6 detects a further allusion to Accius' reworking of Sophocles (156 Ribbeck *TRF*²).

[48] Thus Hardie (1993) 102: 'Scenes of instruction and transmission feature prominently in the *Aeneid*, and in many cases a metapoetical symbolism lies close to the surface.' For the metapoetic function of parent–child relationships in the *Aeneid*, see also O'Sullivan (2009) and Rogerson (2017).

2.1 *Troades*

case in Roman society, the *exemplum* here combines moral with artistic *aemulatio*, biological inheritance with acts of imitative duplication, and textual with human (or, for Aeneas, implied human) identity. Exemplarity's imitative impulse enables both characters and people to be interpreted as actual individuals on the one hand, and on the other, as literary or plastic artefacts. As the preceding surveys demonstrate, these two categories often converge.

2.1 *Troades*

Achilles' Shadow

Imitative exemplarity is likewise a major theme in Seneca's *Troades*, where it acts as a spur to future accomplishments, and delineates characters' identities via a combination of ancestral and literary inheritance. The *exemplum*'s iterative qualities are matched, in this tragedy, by iteration at the level of dramatic action and mythological events: just as the past replays – or must be prevented from replaying – in the present, so characters must formulate their current selves by reproducing and referring to earlier behavioural models. As a result, identity is envisaged primarily in terms of copies, whether biological, moral, poetic, or artistic – and frequently several of those categories at once. In the *Troades* as in Roman culture more generally, exemplarity stands at the intersection of text and humanness, shaping individuals' conduct at the same time as – even by means of – compelling people to become duplicates.

Scholars of Senecan tragedy have, for a long time now, acknowledged and discussed the various motifs of repetition that form a crucial part of the *Troades*' thematic texture.[49] The mythological past furnishes paradigms for current events, and the *dramatis personae* invoke precedents at every turn: Agamemnon has previously sacrificed a virgin to the Trojan cause, so there is the expectation that he will do so again (246–9; 360–1); Hector once

---

[49] Schetter (1965); Owen (1970); Lawall (1982) 250–2; Wilson (1983); Colakis (1985); Boyle (1994) 23–6 and (1997) 59 and 70–3; Raby (2000); Volk (2000); Schiesaro (2003) 190–202; McAuley (2016) 282–94.

defended Troy, so both Andromache and Ulysses assume that Astyanax will do the same (469–74; 529–33; 550–1); just as Helen's marriage once brought grief to the Trojans, so – on a smaller scale – her announcement of Polyxena's 'marriage' will be greeted with mourning (861–3). The dead hand of the past maintains an iron grip over the present in this tragedy, with successive characters compelled to relive earlier occurrences or to re-embody earlier figures.

The play's action, too, is structured around duplicate scenes and duplicate *personae*: the *agon* between Andromache and Ulysses in Act 3 reprises that between Agamemnon and Pyrrhus in Act 2, with the former figure of each pair attempting to preserve the life of a Trojan child; Ulysses and Helen also perform parallel roles as the characters sent to find Astyanax and Polyxena, and to ensure preparations for their respective sacrifices; two ghosts appear; two children die; events centre upon two tombs, of Achilles and of Hector.[50] This pervasive doubling – at the level of the play's content and of its form – lends a paradigmatic quality to characters and their conduct, as if everything that someone does, and all that someone is, may be adopted and repeated by other people at other times. Virtually every deed and every person in this tragedy is ghosted by the memory of former events, and by the further possibility of those events re-occurring in the future.

Exemplarity looms large in such circumstances. Action in the *Troades* tends to be framed by the presence of parental models,[51] and especially by the father–son relationship that features so prominently in the literary and cultural discourses of Roman *exempla*. A clear instance of this dynamic is the protracted exchange between Pyrrhus and Agamemnon that occupies almost the whole of Act 2. Ostensibly a debate over whether the Greeks are justified in their plan to sacrifice Polyxena as an offering to Achilles' shade, the dialogue rapidly dissolves into an *altercatio* focused on Agamemnon's past and Pyrrhus' current

---

[50] Lawall (1982) 250 provides a comprehensive list of the *Troades*' doublets. Other studies of the play's parallel and/or cyclical sequences include: Schetter (1965); Owen (1970); Wilson (1983) 43; and Boyle (1997) 72–3. See Marshall (2000) on the prominence of the play's two tombs.
[51] Colakis (1985); Volk (2000); McAuley (2016) 257–94.

2.1 *Troades*

behaviour.[52] Both characters have recourse to Achilles as a moral-didactic and genealogical paradigm for Pyrrhus, whose identity is governed almost entirely by 'the implications of heredity'.[53] Achilles in this exchange is held up as a model for Pyrrhus to follow, and at the same time, portrayed as the wellspring of Pyrrhus' present actions, reactions, and attitudes.

Pyrrhus himself is keen to forge strong links with his father, which he does first of all by listing Achilles' achievements and declaring that he 'enjoys tracing the celebrated deeds and great praise of [his] glorious parent' (*inclitas laudes iuvat / et clara magni facta genitoris sequi*, 236–7). Punctuating as it does two catalogues of Achilles' feats – his victories in Troy (238–43) and elsewhere (215–28) – the statement implies primarily that Pyrrhus takes pride in reciting his father's attainments. But beneath the immediate, rhetorical connotations of *sequi* ('to list', 237) is the suggestion that Pyrrhus will also follow and conform to (*sequi*) his illustrious parent's example.[54] The two catalogues are intended not only to exalt Achilles and thereby defend his ghost's request,[55] but also to stress continuity between father and son: Pyrrhus has inherited this record of achievement and hopes to be able to match it.

---

[52] Schiesaro (2003) 190–4 stresses the central role that precedents (and arguments from precedent) claim in this scene.

[53] Fantham (1982) *ad Tro.* 203–49.

[54] Translations in Fantham (1982) 142 and Fitch (2004) 193 give only the rhetorical sense of *sequi*, but Wilson (2010) 111 captures the ambiguity: 'I am happy to follow / my great father's glorious honours and his famous deeds.' Seneca also uses *sequor* to mean 'follow an example' at *Phoen.* 331–2, where Oedipus declares of his sons: *meorum facinorum exempla appetunt / me nunc secuntur.* On *sequor* as a key term in Roman exemplary discourse, see Baroin (2010) 32–6 and Langlands (2018) 95.

[55] It is not entirely clear whether Agamemnon and Pyrrhus know about the preceding appearance of Achilles' ghost, especially since neither character mentions the apparition, and since Agamemnon appeals to Calchas' authority – not the ghost's – as the only way of resolving the deadlock. Given these considerations, Owen (1970) 122, and Fantham (1982) 83, regard Agamemnon and Pyrrhus' debate as a discrete scene, unconnected to Talthybius' report (*Tro.* 164–202). However, I concur with Colakis (1985) 150, that Seneca's text assumes a connection between the two scenes because 'in the context of the play the ghost has supplied the motive for Agamemnon and Pyrrhus' dispute'. Seidensticker (1969) 164 n. 27 arrives at much the same conclusion: 'Der Agon setz Achilleus' Forderungen, die der Bote in direkter Rede wiedergibt (191–96), voraus' ('the confrontation presupposes Achilles' demands, which the messenger reports in direct speech (191–96)').

Exemplarity

Achilles' status as a moral-didactic *exemplum* is further confirmed by the resemblance this speech bears to a *laudatio funebris*. Like the male scion of a prominent Roman family delivering a public eulogy in praise of his deceased (most likely male)[56] relative's accomplishments, Pyrrhus recites, commemorates, and celebrates his father's deeds in the context of a discussion about the rites owed to his shade; though not identical, the two scenarios are certainly analogous. And that analogy extends to the content and structure of the speeches themselves, because Roman funeral orations appear – from the minimal fragments that remain – to have included detailed accounts of the dead man's career accompanied by references to the careers of his most conspicuous ancestors. *Laudationes* typically took the form of catalogues that proceeded in chronological order from the recipient's initial accomplishments to his latest: Q. Caecilius Metellus' *laudatio* for his father, delivered in 221 BC and thus the oldest recorded specimen of that genre, seems to have listed in ascending sequence the posts of *pontifex maximus*, two consulships, and the dictatorship (*patris sui L. Metellis pontificis, bis consulis, dictatoris*, Pliny *Nat.* 7.130).[57] Epitaphic inscriptions, which exhibit many characteristics of the *laudatio* genre, also tend to catalogue achievements chronologically, either from first to last or vice versa: Cn. Cornelius Scipio Hispanus is commemorated for having filled the roles of praetor, curule aedile, quaestor, and military tribune (*ILS* 6), and L. Munatius Plancus for having held the consulship and censorship, in addition to having been hailed twice as *imperator* (*ILS* 886).[58] In a similar manner, the Pyrrhus of Seneca's *Troades* enumerates his father's youthful victories over Telephus (215); Cilician Thebes (219); Lyrnessos (221); Pedasus (222); Chryse (223); Tenedos (224); Lesbos (226); and Cilla (227),

---

[56] Although the exemplarity of Roman aristocratic funerals concentrated above all on the male line, there are recorded instances of *laudationes* being delivered in memory of prominent women, for example Caesar's eulogy for his aunt Julia in 69 BC (Suet. *Jul.* 6.1) and Augustus' for Caesar's sister in 51 BC (Suet. *Aug.* 8.1; Quint. *Inst.* 12.6.1).

[57] According to Flower (1996) 138–9, this summary of L. Metellus' career, reported by Pliny and preceding an actual fragment from the *laudatio* at *Nat.* 7.139, 'probably reflects the shape of ... material in the oration'.

[58] Texts of these and other, similar inscriptions have been collected by Flower (1996) 326–30.

followed by his Trojan victories: Hector (238); Memnon (239); and Penthesilea (243).⁵⁹ When he sums up his father's youthful feats as a 'journey' (*iter est Achillis*, 232), the metaphor of the road all but evokes the *cursus honorum* around which so much of Roman elite life, and the funeral speech itself, was structured.⁶⁰ By celebrating Achilles' exemplarity, Pyrrhus implies that his own identity stems from the model of his father; this foremost Trojan hero will 'live on' through his son in much the same way that descendants at a Roman funeral were assumed to perpetuate a family line via the dual ties of biology and *exempla*.

Pyrrhus' desire to emulate his father is not just empty rhetoric, either. Seneca draws an implicit comparison between the young warrior's first martial feat, the slaughter of King Priam (*caede ... regia*, 309) and Achilles' first, the wounding of King Telephus (*cruore regio*, 217), where similar phrasing suggests the deeds' equivalence.⁶¹ Pyrrhus also reproduces Achilles' paradigm in Act 2 simply by engaging in a quarrel with Agamemnon, an episode that will be discussed in detail below. Such imitation of Achilles' *exemplum* transforms Pyrrhus into a virtual *Achilles redivivus* who has already begun to be responsible for visiting a second round of grief upon the Trojans. Andromache acknowledges as much when, near the close of Act 3, she tasks Astyanax with delivering a reproachful message to Hector in Hades: *lentus et segnis iaces? / redit Achilles* ('do you lie there slow and sluggish? Achilles has returned' *Tro.* 805–6). In one regard, Andromache refers to Achilles' literal if insubstantial return in the form of a ghost, a spectral offstage presence reported by Talthybius in Act 2 (168–202); viewed from another angle, however, her phrase suggests Achilles' symbolic resurrection in the person of his son, Pyrrhus, who even now perpetuates his father's hostility towards the Trojans. Besides living in Achilles' shadow, Pyrrhus *becomes*

---

⁵⁹ As noted by Fantham (1982) *ad Tro.* 215ff, Seneca's catalogue bears close resemblance to Odysseus' list of Achilles' deeds in Ovid *Met.* 13.171–8, though Seneca's version, partly by virtue of being put into Pyrrhus' mouth, is far more evocative of a *laudatio*. On the *laudatio*'s presence in Latin literature more generally, see Dufallo (2007) 53–73 (Cicero *Philippic* 2) and 84–6 (Propertius 4.11), and Flower (1996) 110–12 (the parade of heroes at *Aeneid* 6.756–886).
⁶⁰ A metaphorical connection noted by Baroin (2010) 36.
⁶¹ Fantham (1982) *ad Tro.* 217 calls it 'a cross-reference to Pyrrhus' own deeds'.

Exemplarity

Achilles' shadow, imagined by himself and by others in the play as the living *exemplum* of his great progenitor.

Agamemnon likewise cites Achilles as both a source of and a paradigm for Pyrrhus' current behaviour. Emphasising the Iliadic hero's capacity for clemency over his capacity for violence, Agamemnon confronts Pyrrhus with his killing of Priam, the very man Achilles once chose to spare:

> haud equidem nego
> hoc esse Pyrrhi maximum in bello decus
> saevo peremptus ense quod Priamus iacet,
> supplex paternus
>
> I do not at all deny
> that this is Pyrrhus' most glorious deed in war:
> Priam, his father's suppliant, lies dead
> by his brutal sword
>
> (*Tro.* 310–13)

The sarcastic vocabulary of praise in this passage echoes only to refute Pyrrhus' preceding attempt to assume the mantle of his father's glorious deeds. Agamemnon both acknowledges and reinterprets the notion of 'incomparability' present in Pyrrhus' earlier *laudatio*: whereas Achilles' martial exploits surpass the title of *summum decus* (231), Pyrrhus' fall far below the level of *maximum* (311); the father's exceptional status has not been conferred on the son.[62] For Agamemnon, Priam's death, the old man's literal severance from life, symbolises Pyrrhus' severance from his father's model. This discontinuity comes through especially clearly in lines 312–13, where *iacet* is all but pressed into double service and prompts us to imagine Priam lying down in supplication (*iacet / supplex*) as well as lying down dead (*peremptus ... iacet*); what Achilles has done, Pyrrhus has undone.[63] Agamemnon reiterates the idea when he declares, a few lines further on, 'among those Thessalian vessels, there was deep peace for Hector's father' (*in istis Thessalis navalibus / pax alta*

---

[62] Flower (1996) 139 remarks that tropes of 'incomparability' typically featured at the climax of *laudationes*.
[63] Fantham (1982) *ad Tro.* 313 observes in addition that Pyrrhus violates an inherited obligation by killing his father's suppliant.

2.1 *Troades*

rursus Hectoris patris fuit, 325–6). Here the phrase *Hectoris patris* draws attention to the significance of father–son relationships and implies once again that Pyrrhus has not maintained his predecessor's *exemplum* because he has offered Priam only the *pax* of death whereas Achilles once offered the *pax* of clemency.

Agamemnon's criticism owes an oblique debt to the confrontation between Priam and Pyrrhus in *Aeneid* 2.526–58, where the Trojan king himself, having just witnessed Polites' death, accuses Pyrrhus of failing to follow Achilles' model:[64]

> at non ille, satum quo te mentiris, Achilles
> talis in hoste fuit Priamo; sed iura fidemque
> supplicis erubuit corpusque exsangue sepulcro
> reddidit Hectoreum meque in mea regna remisit

> But Achilles, from whom you falsely claim to descend, did not behave in this way towards Priam, his enemy; he respected the
> rights and immunity
> of a supplicant, and gave back Hector's bloodless body
> for burial, and let me return to my kingdom
>
> (*Aen.* 2.540–3)

O'Sullivan observes of this passage: 'Priam refers to his Iliadic persona in the third person, thereby emphasising that we are in a post-Iliadic world, and highlighting how far removed Pyrrhus' blasphemy is from Achilles' behaviour.'[65] As happens frequently in Roman discourses of exemplarity, imitative conduct is imagined as a facet of biology, so that Pyrrhus' failure to uphold Achilles' *exemplum* also casts doubt on his parentage (*satum quo te mentiris, Achilles*, 2.540). Vergil's Pyrrhus draws on the same set of

---

[64] Although *Tro.* 310–13 and 325–6 exhibit only minimal verbal correspondence to *Aen.* 2.540–3, the passages are united by their articulation of the same broad idea – namely that Achilles' merciful treatment of Priam reproaches Pyrrhus' brutality – and by the simple fact that the *Aeneid* exercises such a pervasive influence over Seneca's *Troades*. As noted by Ahl (1986) 36–7, investigated more fully by Zissos (2009), and to a lesser extent, Putnam (1995) 258–61, Aeneas and his Roman future constitute a jarringly 'present absence' in this play. Other connections between Seneca's *Troades* and Vergil's epic are addressed by: Steele (1922) 15–18; Fantham (1982) *passim*, but especially 21–4; Lawall (1985) 245; Boyle (1994) *passim*; Schiesaro (2003) 195–9; Trinacty (2014) 40–3 and 168–9; Ker (2015) 116–17; McAuley (2016) 282–3.

[65] O'Sullivan (2009) 459, with the accompanying caveat that Priam's recollection is skewed: 'after all, Achilles *killed* Hector, and did even worse things to the body than Pyrrhus has done to Polites, and Priam witnessed it all'.

associations when, unperturbed by Priam's reproach, he vaunts, *referes ergo haec et nuntius ibis / Pelidae genitori. illi mea tristia facta / degeneremque Neoptolemum narrare memento* ('all right, you will go as a messenger and report these things to my father, Peleus' son. Remember to recount these savage deeds of mine, and to say that Neoptolemus is degenerate' *Aen.* 2.547–9). In this context of fathers and patronymics, *degener* implies both Pyrrhus' moral unworthiness and his descent from Achilles, that is, his weakened embodiment of a once noble bloodline.[66] As in Seneca's *Troades*, the character and conduct of Vergil's Pyrrhus are judged according to the standards set by his famous forebear; Achilles qua parent merges with Achilles qua *exemplum*.

Achilles' paradigm, moreover, maintains concurrent influence over both the fictional and quasi-human aspects of Pyrrhus' identity. In *Aeneid* 2.526–58, Achilles represents a moral-didactic model for Pyrrhus' implied human personality, and, at the same time, symbolises the literary past of Vergil's epic.[67] His parental model is at once deeply personal – a father embodying moral guidance for his son – and essentially abstract: a character whose parent text, the *Iliad*, epitomises the aesthetic benchmark for Vergil and his readers.

The same applies to Agamemnon and Pyrrhus' dialogue in the *Troades*, where Achilles' exemplarity symbolises first of all the facts of biological inheritance, the behavioural characteristics that have or have not been passed down from Achilles to his son. Secondly, this paternal paradigm is meant to influence that conduct, while at the same time representing a literary model for Pyrrhus' characterisation. Agamemnon recalls Achilles' deeds primarily in the hope that Pyrrhus will learn from them, just as Agamemnon himself claims to have acquired greater wisdom from witnessing Troy's fall (*magna momento obrui / vincendo didici*; 'I have learnt by conquering that greatness can be crushed

---

[66] Cf. the title of Val. Max. 3.5, *Qui a parentibus claris degeneraverunt*, and Tac. *Ann.* 1.53.8, where the verb is used of Sempronius Gracchus, with the same implication of genetic descent combined with moral degradation. Goldschmidt (2013) 158 remarks that narratives of exemplarity can be used to illustrate de- rather than (or as well as) regeneration.

[67] As explored by O'Sullivan (2009) 459–62.

2.1 *Troades*

in an instant', 263–4. Cf. *disce* at *Aen.* 12.435, above), and just as Troy, too, in this pervasive atmosphere of moral-didactic exemplarity, becomes a *documentum* (5) of power's ultimate fragility. How one approaches the past and which lessons one chooses to learn from it are major themes in this play; Achilles' *exemplum* adheres within this wider matrix, and Agamemnon wields it like a pedagogical tool intended to alter Pyrrhus's identity for the better.

In making the comparison, though, Seneca also implies that Achilles is a meta-literary symbol and Pyrrhus the poetic replica of his Iliadic forebear.[68] Recalling the quarrel from *Iliad* Book 1, Seneca's Agamemnon admits to a sense of déjà-vu that inevitably colours his impression of the young man's temperament:

> iuuenile uitium est regere non posse impetum;
> aetatis alios feruor hic primus rapit,
> Pyrrhum paternus. spiritus quondam truces
> minasque tumidi lentus Aeacidae tuli
>
> Being unable to govern one's anger is a young man's fault;
> for others, it is due to the first heat of youth,
> for Pyrrhus it is paternal. I once endured patiently
> the harsh arrogance and threats of raging Aeacides
>
> (*Tro.* 250–3)

Here, Agamemnon blends literal with literary genealogies, parent with parent text, so that Pyrrhus is seen not only to exhibit character traits inherited from his father, but also to fulfil – by replaying it – a role established in and via an earlier poetic work. The *paternus feruor* displayed by Pyrrhus (251–2) recalls the μῆνιν ... Πηληϊάδεω Ἀχιλῆος ('the wrath of Achilles, Peleus' son' *Il.* 1.1) that drives the action of the *Iliad* and, more specifically, suffuses that epic's opening dispute: what Agamemnon has encountered before with Achilles (*quondam*), he now encounters all over again in the hero's son; the same goes for Seneca's readers. The *exemplum* that Agamemnon cites in this passage proves an occasion for literary self-reflexivity, and Pyrrhus' identity is

---

[68] This change of tack is indicative of broader inconsistencies in Agamemnon's argument, where Achilles is deployed alternately as a positive paradigm, and as a negative one. Yet such inconsistencies are characteristic of the *exemplum*'s openness to appropriation: see in particular Lowrie (2007).

Exemplarity

treated as something that derives as much from a textual as from a biological source. Exemplary imitation, which elsewhere in the exchange functions as a means of moral and personal self-fashioning, becomes in this instance an act of literary mimesis, with Pyrrhus reproducing his Iliadic father's paradigm, and Seneca, as we shall see, copying parts of Homer's paradigmatic text.

Parent and Parent Text

As Seidensticker recognises in his careful, pioneering study of the scene, Pyrrhus and Agamemnon's quarrel in *Troades* Act 2 recapitulates in a minor key the confrontation between Agamemnon and Achilles in *Iliad* 1.[69] Seneca's Agamemnon openly acknowledges the Homeric intertext at 252-3 (above), and Pyrrhus foreshadows its appearance when he describes Chryse – Chryseis' homeland, and one of the many locales conquered by Achilles – as 'the cause of strife for kings' (*causa litis regibus Chryse*, 223).[70] But most of the Homeric allusions in this scene comprise excerpts from Achilles' speeches in *Iliadi* 1, adapted and echoed by Seneca's Pyrrhus.

Thus: when Pyrrhus accuses Agamemnon of cowardice – *timide, cum increpuit metus* ('you are fearful when danger roars', 302) – he repeats in condensed form the same complaint voiced by Homer's Achilles: οὔτέ ποτ' ἐς πόλεμον ἅμα λαῷ θωρηχθῆναι /οὔτε λόχονδ' ἰέναι σὺν ἀριστήεσσιν Ἀχαιῶν / τέτληκας θυμῷ· τὸ δέ τοι κὴρ εἴδεται εἶναι ('Never / once have you taken courage in your heart to arm with your people / for battle, or to go into ambuscade with the best of the Achaians. / No, for in such things you see death.' *Il.* 1.226-8 trans. Lattimore). When Pyrrhus sneers at Agamemnon's power, the phrase *regum tyranne* ('tyrant over kings' 303) not only distorts the Homeric formula ἄναξ ἀνδρῶν, but also recalls Achilles' insinuations at *Iliad* 1.287-8: ἀλλ' ὅδ'ἀνὴρ ἐθέλει περὶ πάντων ἔμμεναι ἄλλων, / πάντων μὲν κρατέειν ἐθέλει, πάντεσσι δ'ἀνάσσειν ('Yet here is a man who wishes to be above all others, / who wishes to hold power

---

[69] Seidensticker (1969) 170. The Iliadic echoes of *Troades* 203-370 have been explored more fully by Fantham (1982) *ad loc*. See also Wilson (1983) 34-8.
[70] Seidensticker (1969) 166, and Fantham (1982) *ad Tro.* 220.

2.1 *Troades*

over all, and to be lord of / all' trans. Lattimore).[71] Both the Homeric father and the Senecan son make threats against Agamemnon's life: Pyrrhus declares *nimium diu / a caede nostra regia cessat manus / paremque poscit Priamus* ('for too long now has my hand refrained from slaughtering kings, and Priam demands his equal' 308–10), while Achilles remarks darkly, ἧς ὑπεροπλίῃσι τάχ᾽ ἄν ποτε θυμὸν ὀλέσσῃ ('By such acts of arrogance he may even lose his own life' *Il.* 1.205 trans. Lattimore). When, in the *Troades*, Pyrrhus demands to know whether Agamemnon will continue depriving warriors of their prizes – *solusne totiens spolia de nobis feres?* ('will you alone, so often, bear away spoils at our expense?' 305) – he not only alludes to Agamemnon's forcible appropriation of Briseis in the *Iliad*, but also conjures Achilles' comments about Agamemnon receiving an unequal share of the plunder: ἀλλὰ τὸ μὲν πλεῖον πολυάϊκος πολέμοιο / χεῖρες ἐμαὶ διέπουσ᾽· ἀτὰρ ἤν ποτε δασμὸς ἵκηται, / σοὶ τὸ γέρας πολὺ μεῖζον ('Always the greater part of the painful fighting is the work of / my hands; but when the time comes to distribute the booty / yours is the far greater reward' *Il.* 1.165–7 trans. Lattimore). Although relatively broad and loose, the allusions are also inescapable, clustered together in such a way as to make the Homeric intertext instantly apparent: Pyrrhus steps into his father's role and repeats his father's words.

This convergence of textual reiteration and reiterated behaviour points once again to the presence of exemplarity. The analogical force of the *exemplum* defines Pyrrhus' identity in terms of his biological, personal, and literary resemblance to his father: Pyrrhus adopts Achilles' model to the extent that he becomes a copy of it, a figure whose disposition and patterns of conduct appear to have been predetermined by a combination of genealogical and poetic fiat. Achilles' authority as a parent merges with Homer's authority as the wellspring of the debate with Agamemnon: both dictate how Seneca's Pyrrhus is meant to behave, and ultimately, who he is meant to be. Thus, Pyrrhus in the *Troades* is at once a quasi-human figure who has inherited his father's traits, and a textual construct whose inherited traits

[71] Fantham (1982) *ad loc.*

amount to little more than a pastiche of quotations. If exemplarity may be defined as a form of citation, that is, of referring to and reproducing extant paradigms in the field of human activity, then Seneca's Pyrrhus reinforces this definition literally, by citing Homer's *Iliad*; his personal emulation is mirrored in acts of literary allusion.

As a specific consequence of Seneca's dramatic medium, Pyrrhus' exemplarity also evinces links to performance, both in a theatrical and in a more generic sense. The son's biological re-embodiment of his father is accompanied by performative re-embodiment, as Pyrrhus breathes new life into Achilles' words, and re-enacts Achilles' quarrel in updated form. Like an actor assuming a part, or the scion of an aristocratic family at a Roman funeral, Pyrrhus revivifies in his own flesh-and-blood presence the skeletal template of somebody else's identity. His status as a substitute equates to his status as a performer. And the performative qualities of exemplarity become all the more apparent if the scene is staged, because then Pyrrhus' assumption of his father's traits finds a parallel in the actor's assumption of Pyrrhus' character. In both instances, successful emulation reifies what would otherwise remain an abstract and largely textual model, and at the same time entails a diminution or even denial of the performer's individuality: exemplarity renders Pyrrhus, like the actor, a version, a copy, a type.[72]

Hector's Son

If there is one character in the *Troades* subject to greater exemplary pressure than Pyrrhus, that character is Astyanax, who can barely be said to exist beyond symbolising his father Hector's heroism. More so than Pyrrhus, Astyanax is defined exclusively via his patrimony: Calchas refers to him as *Priami nepos Hectoreus* ('Priam's grandson via Hector', 369), and Ulysses, in the space of just one Act, calls him *Hectorea suboles* ('Hector's scion', 528), *futurus Hector* ('a future Hector', 551), *Hectoris natum* ('Hector's son', 554), and *stirps Hectoris* ('Hector's

---

[72] On the similarity of *exempla* to typologies, see Kraus (2005) esp. 187 and 193.

2.1 *Troades*

stock', 605). Even Andromache, whose motherhood might otherwise be expected to endow her with a more nuanced perspective, struggles to see her son in any terms other than his illustrious parentage.[73] She refers to the child as *Hectoris proles* ('Hector's offspring', 597), and later apostrophises her absent husband: 'there is nothing in my son that pleases me apart from you' (*non aliud, Hector, in meo nato mihi / placere quam te*, 646–7). When faced with the choice of surrendering Astyanax or enduring the destruction of Hector's tomb, she rapidly concludes that this is a false dichotomy: both of them belong to and represent Hector; both preserve his memory (*utrimque est Hector*; 'Hector is on both sides', 559). From the Trojan viewpoint as much as from the Greek, Astyanax claims little or no identity independent of his father's.

Caution must be exercised here: Astyanax's name, which is solidly dactylic, cannot be accommodated within the iambic trimeter that forms the bulk of Seneca's tragic dialogues (in fact, the name appears only once in Senecan drama, at *Agamemnon* 639, a section of choral lyric). So there are practical, metrical reasons for the playwright of the *Troades* choosing to describe this boy in periphrastic ways.[74] Yet Seneca's interest in Astyanax's genealogy far exceeds the basic constraints of scansion: he is, rather, at pains to illustrate a relationship of exemplarity between father and son, hence the obsessive focus on Hector (as opposed to any other family member) and on the distant, yet constant possibility that Astyanax will resurrect Troy. It is by emphasising Astyanax's status as a copy that Seneca makes both Astyanax and Hector into *exempla*.

At the most literal level, Astyanax represents a version of Hector simply because he resembles him. Andromache sees in her son a direct reflection of her husband's face – *hos vultus meus / habebat Hector* ('my Hector used to have those features' 464–5) – and, in the description that follows, she portrays the boy as Hector's bodily copy: *talis incessu fuit / habituque talis, sic tulit*

---

[73] Andromache's obsession with Hector has been well noted by Fantham (1986) 275–8; Volk (2000); Raby (2000) 179–82; and McAuley (2016) 266–72 and 280–94.
[74] Something neither Wilson (1983) 45 nor Colakis (1985) 152 takes into account when stressing the significance of Astyanax's namelessness.

Exemplarity

fortes manus, / sic celsus umeris, fronte sic torva minax / cervice fusam dissipans iacta comam ('he was like this in his gait, like this in his posture, thus he carried his brave hands, thus were his shoulders held high, thus he looked threatening with his grim brow, tossing back his neck and shaking his flowing hair' 465–8). In a move characteristic of exemplary narratives, Andromache conflates past and present in Astyanax's person: he *is* what Hector *was*.[75] The terms *talis* and *sic* function as implicit stage directions in this passage, with the performer of Andromache's role presumably gesturing towards her son, or even guiding him to adopt Hector's posture.[76] Attention is thereby focused upon Astyanax's immediate, tangible, bodily presence, which is subsequently elided with an absent, imagined body from the past (*fuit*; *tulit*). Of course, this resemblance may be partially a figment of Andromache's imagination, a delusory outcome of her obsessive love for Hector, especially since the Astyanax we meet elsewhere in Act 3 appears not *celsus* (467) but small (e.g. *parvulam stirpem*; 'tiniest offspring', 456, and *parvus comes*; 'little companion', 537). Essentially, what Andromache does at *Troades* 465–8 is envisage her son as a grown man, describing not (quite) the individual stood before her, but his anticipated resemblance to his now deceased father. This comparison is prompted by exemplarity as much as by nostalgia, since, besides being the physical embodiment of the past, Astyanax also represents the future of his *gens*; he is expected, simultaneously, to perpetuate his father's memory and to surpass it.

This motif of bodily resemblance recurs at 647–8 when Andromache, apostrophising Hector, utters a distraught prayer for their son's life: *vivat ut possit tuos / referre vultus* ('let him live so that he can revive your face'). From Andromache's perspective, this is Astyanax's sole purpose in living: his memorialisation of her deceased husband. The boy reiterates the past (*referre*) by calling Hector's lost visage to mind (*referre*); his

---

[75] Negotiating between past and present, and in many instances conflating the two, is a typical feature of exemplarity: see in particular Hölkeskamp (1996); Chaplin (2000) 198–202; and Roller (2004) 31–8.

[76] Boyle (1994) *ad Tro.* 466 notes that *talis* and *sic* could be stage directions. Another instance of *sic* potentially referring to stage action is *Med.* 1022, <u>*sic fugere soleo*</u>.

2.1 *Troades*

identity stretches beyond the present time and beyond the bounds of his own body.[77] Physical similarity indicates that Hector can be copied in precisely the same manner as an *exemplum*, so that his position as Astyanax's father also renders him Astyanax's prototype.

Yet Hector's *exemplum* goes beyond mere matters of bodily resemblance. When Andromache regrets that her son is 'too similar to his father' (*nimium ... similis patri*, 464) she implies both that Astyanax reflects Hector's appearance and, by extension, that he will match Hector's achievements. Each of these propositions worries her (hence: *nimium*) because, on the one hand, Astyanax's presence reminds her constantly of Hector's loss, and on the other, because the likelihood of his inherited prowess in battle makes him a conspicuous target for the conquerors' pre-emptive killings. In Andromache's mind, physical mimesis cannot be uncoupled from behavioural mimesis, as indicated by her rapid transition from describing Astyanax's physique (464–8) to imagining his deeds:

> eritne tempus illud ac felix dies
> quo Troici defensor et vindex soli
> recidiva ponas Pergama et sparsos fuga
> cives reducas, nomen et patriae suum
> Phrygibusque reddas?

> Will it come, that time and fortunate day
> when, as defender and avenger of Trojan earth,
> you may establish renascent Pergamum, and lead back
> the citizens dispersed in flight, and restore their name
> to the Phrygians and to the fatherland?
>
> (*Tro.* 470–4)

Any reader with even a passing knowledge of Vergil will be alert to Seneca's trademark irony in this passage. The playwright undercuts Andromache's hopes via a 'future reflexive' evocation of the *Aeneid*: we know that Troy's future lies elsewhere, in Italy, and that it will be secured not by repeating the past, but by patiently, sometimes painfully renouncing it.[78] Yet the futility of

---

[77] Thus Hardie (1993) 89 on Roman discourses of intergenerational continuity: 'Identity is not limited to the present time or to the living body.'
[78] On repeating versus renouncing the past in the *Aeneid*, see in particular the masterful study by Quint (1993) 50–96. The term 'future reflexive' was coined by Barchiesi

Andromache's aspirations does not make them purely irrational.[79] Her reasoning, in fact, adheres closely to Roman discourses of exemplarity, employing as it does two core principles of iteration and resurrection. Like Astyanax's body, this vision of his achievements amalgamates several timeframes to the effect that the young boy's future consists in bringing back the past. Each individual act of repetition and return (*recidiva*; *reducas*; *reddas*) points to Astyanax's overall mimicry of his father's model, by which he restores Hector in all but the most literal sense. Heroic deeds, like Hector's body, can be copied, and Astyanax is assumed to arrogate his father's *exemplum* almost by virtue of his being 'the true offspring of a mighty sire' (*magni certa progenies patris*, 461). Ethical resemblance presupposes biological similitude.

Ulysses, too, regards Astyanax as a version of his father, and conversely, Hector as an *exemplum* for the boy. When he confesses that the Danaans fear a *futurus Hector* (551) not only does Ulysses conflate temporalities in the same way as Andromache, but he also assigns Hector to the category of repeatable paradigms. Like, for instance, the word *Caesar*, *Hector* moves from designating a unique, specific individual to signifying a title, a part (and in this case, a set of traits that others may adopt as required).[80] As discussed earlier in this chapter, exemplarity naturally produces such typologies, because commemoration of exceptional deeds/people leads to their being enshrined not as isolated events, but as readily available templates.[81] The exemplarity of Lucius Junius Brutus transforms him from person into statue, from Brutus-as-individual to what that individual represents, in effect, to Brutus-as-symbol. Hector's *exemplum* has for Astyanax the same effect as Lucius Brutus' does on the late republican Marcus: to become fully himself, to grow into his heritage, Astyanax must adopt the

---

(1993) to define how later texts allude to preceding ones via visions of the future. Zissos (2009) 193–8 discusses in depth the 'intertextual irony' of 'Andromache's 'epic ambitions' in the *Troades*.

[79] Responding to the condemnatory judgements of, for example, Volk (2000) and Fantham (1986), McAuley (2016) 280–94 argues that Andromache's motivation actually obeys an inner logic.

[80] The analogy comes from Kraus (2005) 186 n.11: 'The shift from Caesar-as-person to Caesar-as-type is greatly facilitated by the development of *Caesar* as a title.'

[81] As discussed by Kraus (2005) 187, Barchiesi (2009) 46–7, and Roller (2015).

2.1 *Troades*

identity of another. Such exemplarity transforms Astyanax, too, into a symbol, as what would otherwise be an intimate, flesh-and-blood connection to his father becomes instead a relationship based on standardised, analogical qualities. The personal has become impersonal, or even supra-personal.

The Ghosts of Fathers Past

The motif of death and resurrection furnishes yet another point of contact between Astyanax and Hector's (or Pyrrhus and Achilles') relationship and Roman discourses of exemplarity. Despite the play's notoriously contradictory stance on the afterlife,[82] it is still the case that, in Mairéad McAuley's words, 'some of the dead ... have real and *material* power over the living' in the *Troades*.[83] The appearance of Achilles' and then Hector's ghosts, whatever their respective levels of reality,[84] is responsible for setting in motion the majority of the tragedy's events. In addition, these ghosts have an equally substantial impact on the identities of their descendants, particularly on how those identities are perceived. Thus, as the moral and physical embodiment of his father, Astyanax is seen to continue his deceased parent's lineage in a manner analogous to resurrection, preserving Hector and, in a sense, returning him to life.[85] Like a Roman son or grandson delivering a funeral eulogy, Astyanax is his forebear's ghost at the same time as being his successor.

Astyanax acquires ghostlike qualities primarily through his role as Hector's replacement: the shadow of his father's features can be discerned in his face, and the purpose of his future is to take up

---

[82] A topic examined by: Cattin (1956); Owen (1970); Bishop (1972); Fantham (1982); Lawall (1982); and Colakis (1985).
[83] McAuley (2016) 281, emphasis original.
[84] Andromache certainly appears to hallucinate Hector's presence at *Troades* 683–5, while her earlier account of Hector's appearance in a dream (443–60) can be substantiated only through the subsequent accuracy of the ghost's warning. Owen (1970) 126 regards the tragedy's ghosts as symbolic manifestations of other characters' psychological states, and questions the reality not only of Hector's shade, but of Achilles' as well: 'Our ghosts manifest ourselves ... Talthybius swears to an otherwise unverifiable supernatural event; Pyrrhus ignores it, Agamemnon discounts it, Andromache experiences a vain approximation to it.'
[85] Colakis (1985) makes this argument about the *Troades* as a whole: life after death is ensured through children.

133

Exemplarity

Hector's past.[86] When Astyanax cringes at the prospect of entering Hector's tomb, Andromache chooses to interpret this reaction as evidence of the young boy's parentage: *turpesne latebras spernis? agnosco indolem: / pudet timere* ('do you scorn repulsive hiding places? I recognise your in-born nature: feeling fear is shameful' 504–5).[87] The child's ghostliness is further compounded by Andromache's desire to 'close [his] living eyes with her hand' (*ut mea condam manu / viventis oculos*, 788–9), and also by her recital of a formal, funereal lament for Astyanax while the boy is still standing beside her (766–85).[88]

Astyanax resembles a shadow even in terms of his literary character, because the future that Andromache had planned for her son – re-establishing Troy (470–4); ruling over the Trojans (771–3); avenging the Greek conquest (660, 774); and leading the *lusus Troiae* (777–9) – has already been claimed by Aeneas, Ascanius, and the *Aeneid*.[89] Seneca ensures that his audience is well aware of this last, cruel fact, for when Andromache enumerates her child's physical features at 467–8 (*sic tulit fortes manus, / sic celsus umeris, fronte sic torva minax*; 'thus he carried his brave hands, thus were his shoulders held high, thus he looked threatening with his grim brow'), she echoes her Vergilian counterpart in *Aeneid* 3, who sees in the young Ascanius a shadow of her own lost son: *o mihi sola super Astyanactis imago. / sic oculos, sic ille manus, sic ora ferebat* ('O the only image of Astyanax left to me. Thus were his eyes, thus his hands, thus his face' *Aen.* 3.489–90).[90] Astyanax's raw biological identification with his father is overlaid by the repetition of one poetic work within another. The effect of this clever intertext is to render Astyanax in the *Troades* not just the reflection of a past individual (his own father), but also the dim outline of a future figure (Aeneas' son), whose survival has

---

[86] Thus McAuley (2016) 284: 'For both Greeks and Trojans, he is – and is not quite – the living incarnation of his father. Neither just image nor just body, living or dead, original or copy, who is the real ghost here, Hector or his son?' See also Erasmo (2008) 44.
[87] Fantham (1986) 275; Volk (2000) 201.
[88] Fantham (1982) *ad Tro.* 766 and Wilson (1983) 42 identify the passage as a formal lament.
[89] Zissos (2009) examines how this Vergilian future supplants Seneca's Astyanax.
[90] A connection first noted by Steele (1922) 16.

2.1 *Troades*

already been confirmed in an earlier text. Caught between Hector and Ascanius, Andromache's son seems doubly a phantom.

The foremost focus of these spectral themes is Hector's tomb, which occupies the centre of the stage, and concomitantly, the centre of several characters' thoughts for most of Act 3. More than just a convenient hiding place for Astyanax, it symbolises the ghostly aspects of the boy's identity, and the exemplarity underpinning his relationship with his father. By disappearing into and later emerging from the tomb, Astyanax all but undergoes a process of death and rebirth, which corroborates at a visual level his perpetuation of Hector's *exemplum*. Astyanax is his father, resurrected, reinstated, recovered from the dead. Andromache alludes to precisely this duality when she declares of the child hidden inside the monument both that 'he lies among the dead' (*inter extinctos iacet*, 603) and that he will survive if only Hector protects him: *Hector ... / ... fideli cinere victurum excipe* ('Hector ... receive with your faithful ashes one who is going to live' 501–2). The two states turn out to be symbolically equivalent, because Hector's *exemplum* makes Astyanax into a living image *and* a ghost, simultaneously the fleshly embodiment of his father and a mere trace of the deceased man's past existence. When Andromache calls upon Hector's shade to 'break fate's barrier' (*rumpe fatorum moras*, 681) and come to his family's rescue, it is the son, not the father, who actually emerges from the tomb (705). Thus Seneca's dramaturgy demonstrates for the audience what Andromache must learn the hard way: these two men are interchangeable.

Further highlighting this connection between exemplarity and death is the tight network of lexical correspondences that Seneca constructs throughout the play. Just as Astyanax experiences the 'vast weight of the tomb' (*immane busti pondus*, 689), so, likewise, the boy's 'great nobility presses upon him as a heavy weight' (*grave pondus illum magna nobilitas premit*, 491), and relatedly, 'Achilles' axle trembles under Hector's weight' (*Peliacus axis pondere Hectoreo tremens*, 415).[91] Literal pressure from the father's body, or from its resting place, is accompanied by the figurative pressure of an *exemplum* and the need to live up to one's

---

[91] McAuley (2016) 284 notes the first of these two parallels.

genealogy.[92] This metaphorical burden weighs down Astyanax (*premit*, 491) in the same way that Hector and his offspring are feared to crush each other should the tomb be razed: *ne pater natum obruat / prematque patrem natus* ('so that the father does not overwhelm the son nor the son press down on the father' 690–1). Like a similarly phrased statement at *Thyestes* 1050–1 (*genitor en natos premo / premorque natis*; 'look, I, the father, weigh down my sons and am weighed down by my sons'), the chiastic arrangement of *Troades* 690–1 implies a reciprocal relationship between *pater* and *natus*, in this case, an elision of identity brought about by Hector's *exemplum*.

Another thematic word is *iacere*, which refers, in turn, to Hector prostrated in death (*iacuit peremptus Hector*, 238); Astyanax lying hidden in the tomb (*inter extinctos iacet*, 603); Hector lying inactive in Hades (*lentus et segnis iaces?* 805); and finally, to Astyanax lying at the base of Troy's walls, 'a shapeless corpse' (*iacet / deforme corpus*, 1116–17). This sequence of lexical correspondences demonstrates just how closely Astyanax follows his father's model – sometimes willingly, sometimes under compulsion – and how the *exemplum*'s imitative impulse leads Astyanax from being his father's ghost to dying, like Hector, beneath the walls of Troy.

When Andromache hears that her son's body lies broken and disfigured, she concludes, *sic quoque est similis patri* ('in this way, too, he resembles his father' 1117). An expression of 'perverse satisfaction' and a notable instance of Seneca's grim humour,[93] Andromache's remark also encapsulates the analogical force of exemplarity that has oppressed Astyanax throughout his brief existence. Alive or dead, the son resembles the father physically, and that bodily likeness has been accompanied by moral emulation – or expectations of moral emulation – to the extent that his identity cannot be separated from Hector's. Andromache taps into a fundamental truth here, a truth no less significant for being wryly expressed: Hector's *exemplum* and Astyanax's need to duplicate it (hence: *similis patri*) are exactly what has led to the boy's death at

---

[92] A common metaphor of hereditary, according to Baroin (2010) 26.
[93] The quotation comes from Volk (2000) 200.

2.1 *Troades*

the hands of the Greeks. Elaine Fantham remarks that this final pronouncement serves as Astyanax's epitaph,[94] which means that it confirms his exemplary status by memorialising his lineage and celebrating the combined outcome of his biological and moral inheritance.

Despite all of these similarities, though, it is abundantly clear throughout the *Troades* that Astyanax is *not* a perfect replica of his father. His childish weakness stands in contrast to Hector's strength, his Trojan future has been foreclosed, even his broken, dead body, which Andromache likens to Hector's mutilated by Achilles, is arrived at not via heroic single combat, but via the very different fate of leaping from Troy's battlements as a sacrifice. The more characters in the *Troades* underscore Astyanax's potential to become Hector, the greater the present gulf that appears between these two figures. Yet this dynamic, too, is part of their exemplarity inasmuch as it straddles the polarities of unique and typical, particular and general, individual and community. Astyanax qua singular, self-contained being is a small, defenceless prisoner of war, while his currency as a type, as a representation of Hector, is enormous. It is through his relationship to Hector that Astyanax begins to acquire his own, unique outlines at the same time as his identity seems to be engulfed by his father's towering reputation. The possibility of his future heroism, desired by the Trojans and feared by the Greeks, marks him out simultaneously as a copy of Hector and as a potentially powerful individual in his own right. Thus, mimetic identification between Hector and Astyanax absorbs the latter into the Trojan community, reduces him to a link in a genealogical line, as well as granting him a small measure of independent existence. In both a positive and a negative sense, Astyanax's identity depends on his descent from Hector.

It is ironic that exemplarity in Astyanax's case brings about annihilation rather than the continuity and perpetuity it is so often assumed to ensure.[95] The boy's inheritance of his father's paradigm does not, ultimately, guarantee the future of his *gens*, an

---

[94] Fantham (1982) *ad Tro.* 1110b–1117. Erasmo (2008) 49 likewise notes that the vocabulary of *Troades* 1117 – *iacet, similis, pater* – evokes the language of epitaphs.
[95] Schiesaro (2003) 201 pursues a similar argument, maintaining that 'circularity and repression pose [a threat] to the norms of continuity and linear progress' in the *Troades*.

Exemplarity

outcome that contradicts standard Roman thinking about the *exemplum*. Indeed, it is Astyanax's very urge to repeat the past that precipitates the past's – and his own – eradication. Seneca draws attention to this topic via another set of lexical correspondences, echoing Andromache's call for Astyanax to 'restore the Phrygians' name' (*nomen ... suum / Phrygibus ... reddas*, 473–4) with her subsequent 'bestowal of final rites on [her] son' (*officium ... / nato supremum reddo*, 761).[96] Likewise, Andromache's hope that Astyanax 'may lead back [Troy's] citizens dispersed by flight' (*sparsos fuga / cives reducas*, 472–3) is undercut by the enemy's more forceful need to return to Greece, and therefore, to sacrifice Polyxena and Astyanax so that the gods will open up 'passages leading back home' (*reduces ... vias*, 167). Just as Astyanax both is and is not his father, so his role as *Hector redux* paradoxically ensures that Troy does not survive.

Exemplary Performances

Astyanax's exemplarity illustrates both his fictional and his implied human identity as a character within Seneca's drama. The young boy's relationship to Hector confirms his quasi-human status by drawing attention to physique, biology, and moral disposition. At the same time, this relationship can be seen to minimise Astyanax's 'humanness' in favour of his self-reflexively textual role in the play: like all fictional characters, Astyanax lays claim to an essentially typologised, restricted selfhood and has no recourse to self-determination. In the *Troades*, his behaviour also tends to be framed in specifically metatheatrical terms. His identity is a role both in the sense of its inherited transmission from another person (Hector) and in the sense of its being enacted, literally, in a play. Like Pyrrhus, whose assumption of Achilles' traits leads to dramatised re-enactment, Astyanax brings Hector back to life by performing his father's part, reproducing his visage, his gesture, his broken body.

---

[96] Pyrrhus' dark promise at *Tro* 306 – *hac dextra Achilli victimam reddam suam* – also belongs to this nexus. A reference to Polyxena this time rather than to Astyanax, it is yet another example of *reddo* being used to evoke the impossibility of Troy's *return*.

2.1 *Troades*

As discussed above, Andromache's description of her son's appearance (465–8) can also serve as a set of stage directions, with the person who plays Astyanax being asked to look 'thus' (*sic*, 466–7) or to pose or move in such a way (*talis*, 465–6) that replicates the deceased Hector's physique. Viewed from this self-consciously theatrical angle, Astyanax becomes an actor and Hector a part to be played. Nor is this the only occasion on which Astyanax is asked to perform: when Andromache, reluctantly, calls him from his hiding place towards the end of Act 3, she urges the boy, in a last, desperate bid for his salvation, to 'play the captive and, on bent knee ... [to] copy [his] mother's tears' (*gere captivum positoque genu / ... / matris fletus imitare tuae*, 715–17).[97] Although in this instance Astyanax's immediate model is Andromache herself, not Hector, intergenerational exemplarity can still be seen to underpin the performance, because the little boy's gesture is meant to remind Ulysses of the youthful Priam supplicating Hercules: *vidit pueri regis lacrimas / et Troia prior, parvusque minas / trucis Alcidae flexit Priamus* ('once before, Troy also witnessed the tears of a boy-king, and small Priam turned aside fierce Alcides' threats' 718–20). Just as Andromache hopes – in vain – that her son will one day surpass his grandfather's longevity (702) and live to wield his grandfather's sceptre (771–2), so she wills him to evoke Priam through his present supplicatory performance. Here, the expectation of ancestral exemplarity merges with the imitation practised by actors in the theatre; Astyanax must follow Priam both as a role model and more literally as a role.

To complement this theatrical display, Ulysses is urged to take up the position of spectator. Andromache continues to stage-manage the scene by establishing an implicit parallel between Troy witnessing Priam's tears (*vidit*, 718) and Ulysses watching Astyanax plead. As the object of Ulysses' evaluative gaze, Astyanax resembles not only an actor but also a character, a *dramatis persona* whose tragic performance will succeed only

---

[97] The self-conscious theatricality of *Troades* Act 3 has been noted especially by Boyle (1997) 76 ('a tragedy within a tragedy'), and Volk (2000) 202 ('a string of mini-dramas in which each protagonist tries to be the better actor'). For detailed analysis of Andromache's and Ulysses' respective performances, see Aygon (2016) 231–8.

if Ulysses responds with the requisite amount of pity. This patently metatheatrical encounter further highlights Astyanax's status as a fabricated identity, that is, as a figure constructed by Seneca for the express purpose of eliciting certain reactions from the play's external – as well as internal – audience.

Ulysses, too, is implicated in this nexus of acting and exemplarity, because besides being a spectator, he is also impelled to occupy Hercules' role and to play the merciful conqueror to Astyanax's Priam. Such enactment would, Andromache hopes, alter Ulysses' disposition, hence she exhorts him to 'learn Hercules' gentle anger' (*discite mites Herculis iras*, 730).[98] Here, the *exemplum*'s moral-didactic function – implied by *disco* – blends into an explicitly theatrical form of imitation, so that Hercules becomes simultaneously a paradigm for Ulysses' personal conduct and a paradigm for his dramatic performance. As in Astyanax's case, role and role model overlap.

The climax of this performative exemplarity comes in Act 5, when the messenger tells the assembled crowd of Trojan women how Astyanax died. As has often been noted, Seneca frames the dual sacrifice of Astyanax and Polyxena in theatrical terms: the Greeks are called spectators (*spectator*, 1087; *spectat*, 1129); the locale of Astyanax's death is surrounded by a hill (1078–9), a towering cliff (1080), and high ruins (1084–5) that make it resemble a theatre or amphitheatre; and the landscape bordering the site of Polyxena's sacrifice has hills that rise *theatri more* ('like a theatre', 1125).[99] Situated beside the sea and enclosed by a natural slope, the latter of these two locations actually approximates to a classical Greek theatre building, with Achilles' tomb as its central feature.[100] Moreover, since Achilles' tomb is mentioned in Talthybius' report in Act 2 of the *Troades*, and since Hector's definitely appears on stage in Act 3, the play's external audience can be said already to have experienced this location as a dramatic

---

[98] Andromache's plural verb, *discite*, is directed at all of the Greeks, but as their representative in this scene, Ulysses is the most immediate target.
[99] Ahl (1986) 22–3; Boyle (1997) 119–21; Shelton (2000); Benton (2002); Erasmo (2008) 47–9.
[100] Seneca's description recreates the conventions of the Greek tragic stage, where tombs were often treated as the equivalent of altars and occupied a correspondingly central position: see Arnott (1962) 60–2; Taplin (1977) 117; and Rehm (1988) 264–74 and n.6.

2.1 *Troades*

space: what the messenger asks the Trojan women to imagine in terms of a theatre, the audience of Seneca's *Troades* has already witnessed *in the theatre*.

As regards Astyanax's death, Seneca reverses the standard visual relationship of Trojan city versus Trojan plain, so that the victorious Greeks gaze upon Troy's battlements rather than being, as in Homer, the objects of Trojan *teichoskopia*. The city and its inhabitants are now *documenta ... quam fragili loco / starent superbi* ('examples of how unstable is the place occupied by the proud', 5–6), as Hecuba remarks at the play's outset. Thus, a clear parallel is established between the Greeks and the *Troades*' external audience, with the former group pausing to witness Troy's death throes – this tragedy played out against the backdrop of the city – just as the latter group has done for the drama's entire duration. The setting alone is enough to emphasise Astyanax's fictional, performed identity: he is a character in a play, a part assumed by an actor to provoke emotional responses from internal and external audiences alike. His brave death impresses and saddens the Greeks, as it is meant to impress and sadden those watching the play: *moverat vulgum ac duces / ipsumque Ulixem. non flet e turba omnium / qui fletur* ('he moved the crowd and the leaders and Ulysses himself. He does not weep, though bewept by the whole throng', 1098–100).

The boy's pursuit of exemplarity contributes further to this climate of self-conscious enactment, partly because his death, like Polyxena's, is itself portrayed as an *exemplum* of admirable behaviour,[101] and also because the specific manner of his dying enables him to achieve final, total identification with his paradigmatic father. Andromache anticipates just such an outcome when she laments, 'the walls will witness something more pitiable than great Hector's death' (*flebilius aliquid Hectoris magni nece / muri*

---

[101] Astyanax and Polyxena are clearly held up to other characters as laudable examples of courage and defiance in the face of enemy brutality, but their deeds may also be interpreted as instances of Stoic morality, that is, as paradigms for the *Troades*' external audience. Thus Pratt (1983) 111: 'the stance of equanimity and submission to what is to be is the ultimate Stoic shield against adversity. More than this, when Astyanax interrupts Ulysses' ritual and leaps, when the dying Polyxena assaults Achilles' grave, they are in effect committing legitimate Stoic suicide in the grandest manner, pitting their spirits against brute force.'

videbunt, 784–5), implying that Astyanax's end will both approximate to and exceed his father's model, and that it will do so in the presence of onlookers, like a performance. The messenger, too, alludes to exemplarity by pointing out that Astyanax leaps from the same tower where, as a baby in Priam's arms, he used to watch Hector fighting on the plain below (1071–4). Besides emphasising the bitterness of Troy's reversed fortunes, the image suggests a correlation between Hector's past and Astyanax's current achievements, with the young boy's death matching the level of his father's heroism. A fearless end is now the only way for Astyanax to assert his glorious parentage, and although the fall damages his visage to the extent that it removes individual traces of his resemblance to Hector (*illas nobiles patris notas*; 'those noble marks of his father' 1113), it does so in the name of consolidating a broader, more significant resemblance of behaviour and disposition. Both father and son prove their heroism by dying bravely at the hands of the Greeks: this – not just bodily similarity – is what Andromache refers to when she concludes, in questionable taste, *sic quoque est similis patri* ('in this way, too, he is like his father', 1117). The overall effect, for Seneca's audience, is once again to have attention focused on Astyanax as a version of Hector, a version achieved specifically via enactment and validated by spectators. Even Andromache's response to the messenger at 1117, her final words in the play, serves to remind listeners that Astyanax's part is performed, because the adverb *sic* recalls her earlier evocation of the boy's appearance (*sic tulit ... / sic celsus ... sic ... minax*, 466–7), a passage in which, as we have already seen, physical and moral similarity coincide with practised theatrical gesture. Just as Astyanax the actor/role reproduces Hector's distinguishing bodily features in Act 3, so in Act 5 he performs a death scene *sic*, to match his father's.

In fact, Astyanax's performance throughout the *Troades* rests on complex conceptual underpinnings. To the extent that he identifies with his father and assumes Hector's corporeal or dispositional characteristics, Astyanax does the work of an actor, whose profession requires precisely such identification of the self with another. In much the same way that Astyanax blends into Hector, stage artists blend into their roles, merging their bodies and thoughts

2.1 *Troades*

with those of an imaginary or absent other, so that the relationship of performer to character is not a simple case of 'either/or' but 'both/and'. Seneca's Astyanax cannot be separated from the exemplary part he undertakes (or is urged to undertake), and in this respect his performance may be seen as confirming his quasi-human status. By engaging in an act of mimetic identification, albeit under extreme duress, Astyanax shapes himself as an individual being. In equal degree, however, the young boy's performance of multiple roles in an explicitly theatricalised setting suggests that he has little or no identity apart from being a *dramatis persona*, a Hector-template, a Priam-template, even an Astyanax-template, whose brave response to Greek cruelty furnishes a model for others.

The *Troades*' theme of intergenerational exemplarity likewise promotes a fluid exchange between the implied human and fictional aspects of characters' identities. On the one hand, Achilles and Hector constitute moral-didactic models for their sons, models intended to influence Pyrrhus' and Astyanax's conduct as quasi-people within the world of the play. Emulation of a celebrated parental paradigm is meant to improve Pyrrhus' disposition either by fostering heroic valour or by dissuading him from cruelty. For Astyanax, Hector likewise represents heroism and bravery, and even though fate affords the boy scarcely any opportunity to pursue his parent's *exemplum*, the relationship nonetheless centres upon learning and self-improvement. It is implied that Astyanax will become the right kind of person principally by adopting Hector's model. The didactic and transformative effect of this *exemplum* can be seen in the simple fact that Astyanax grows up over the course of the play, changing from timid child in Act 3 to solemn, courageous youth in Act 5, seemingly as a result of Hector's paradigmatic authority.

On the other hand, Astyanax exhibits only the most minimal presence as an implied human figure in this tragedy, and more often than not, his emulation of Hector overrides his quasi-humanity in favour of producing a copy or a type. Exemplarity's analogical bent encourages the audience to regard Astyanax as just one instance of an infinitely repeatable, and therefore detachable, identity. The child is at once Hector's moral, physical, and biological

Exemplarity

duplicate; his status as a representation is confirmed by his own ghostliness, and by the ghostly traces of other characters – Aeneas, Ascanius – discernible within his story. A similar situation applies for Seneca's Pyrrhus, who adopts his parent's moral model only to end up performing it as a dramatic role and quoting the 'parent' text from which it ultimately derives. Like Astyanax, Pyrrhus mimics an inherited paradigm to the point that he becomes a mimetic and literary artefact.

Bridge: Seneca

Seneca's Imago Vitae Suae

The exemplarity discussed so far in this chapter has been entwined with processes of genetic and dynastic replication. But not all Roman exemplarity is underpinned by family ties or guided by the notion that one's name or bloodline predisposes one to particular kinds of action. Pursuing paradigmatic status can also be a more self-directed and freely chosen enterprise, one that individuals undertake in the hope of themselves becoming future objects of emulation.[102] Barchiesi remarks that historical and fictive characters in early imperial literature 'increasingly anticipate their own future as *exempla*, and paradoxically imitate their future exemplarity – which is a rough and ready description for Lucan's Cato or even Caesar, and Seneca's tragic heroes and heroines'.[103] An equivalent phenomenon also occurs in Roman society: we have seen already how Augustus positions himself as the culminating point in a line of Rome's *summi viri*, thereby advertising himself as a living *exemplum* and also anticipating – even guaranteeing – post mortem conferral of paradigmatic status.[104] Seneca, too, appears to engage in exemplary self-fashioning in the later stages of his life, self-consciously pre-empting his posthumous reputation and viewing himself as a reproducible

---

[102] A practice that appears to have increased during the early principate, due possibly to the changing composition of the Roman elite, which now included more men from obscure backgrounds whose prominence was supposed less threatening to the emperor. Since these men did not belong to old, established families, the onus was on them alone to create and justify their renown; see Habinek (2000).
[103] Barchiesi (2009) 55.
[104] Above, 109–10.

type. While much of his overtly exemplary conduct still embeds itself within established traditions, it nonetheless stands out as being an expression of singular self-confidence performed more in anticipation of his becoming a future *exemplum* than in response to the inescapable pressures of the past.

The events leading up to Seneca's death epitomise such exemplarity.[105] According to Tacitus, Seneca was forbidden on Nero's orders from writing an actual will and bequeathed instead his *imago vitae suae*:

> Ille interritus poscit testamenti tabulas; ac denegante centurione conversus ad amicos, quando meritis eorum referre gratiam prohiberetur, quod unum iam et tamen pulcherrimum habeat, imaginem vitae suae relinquere testatur, cuius si memores essent, bonarum artium famam fructum constantis amicitiae laturos.

> He, not at all afraid, demanded the writing tablets for his will; when the centurion denied them, he turned to his friends and called them to witness that since he was prevented from expressing his thanks for their services, he was leaving to them the only and yet most beautiful thing he possessed, the image of his life, and if they bore it in mind, they would reap as the fruit of steadfast friendship the renown of virtuous pursuits. (*Ann.* 15.62.1–2)[106]

In a paradox worthy of Seneca's own writing, the *dying* philosopher is said to bestow his *life* upon his friends – not, admittedly, the physical existence of which he has very little left, but the identity and patterns of living that he has fashioned over the preceding sixty-odd years. By referring to this inheritance as an *imago*, Seneca adopts the discourse of exemplarity in which, as we have seen, metaphors of reflection often articulate the *exemplum*'s innate need to be copied. Seneca is at this moment both himself and an image of himself, a (still ... just) living model ready to be duplicated by those who come after. Moreover, the friends present at this deathbed scene are invited to preserve and perpetuate this example, as the ambiguous referent of *bonarum artium famam*

---

[105] In addition to the death scene, there is also clear evidence that Seneca used his *Epistulae* to establish and promote his exemplarity. The idea has been noted by Misch (1950) 421; Mayer (1991) 168; and Edwards (1997a) 23, but awaits full exploration.

[106] Some scholars interpret the death scene as ironic: see, for example, Henry and Walker (1963) 109; Dyson (1970) 77–8; Erasmo (2008) 32–3. In contrast, I follow the majority view that Tacitus' commemoration is sincere.

suggests: are these Seneca's virtuous pursuits that bestow fame on his companions simply by association, or are these the companions' own virtuous pursuits, developed in accordance with Seneca's model? Does the *fama* belong to the leader, or to the disciples? That Tacitus does not care to clarify this distinction only emphasises further the repetition germane to Rome's culture of *exempla*: Seneca will, in effect, live on after himself in his friends' behaviour as well as in their memories.

It is significant in this regard that Seneca's *imago* takes the place of an actual, written will, because both the *exemplum* and the *testamentum* dictate equivalent forms of inheritance: Seneca's paradigm will be passed down and maintained in the manner of a precious physical possession; it is even referred to as something tangible, graspable (*habeat*). In fact, the deathbed context allows Tacitus to explore further links between exemplarity and inheritance, because the conjuring of an *imago* in this scene inevitably evokes the Roman funeral mask,[107] with its attendant connotations of family role models and specific forms of behaviour preserved across generations. Like the images of ancestors displayed in an aristocratic atrium or paraded prior to someone's burial, Seneca's *imago vitae suae* is designed to commemorate his life explicitly as a spur to future achievement and emulation.

At the same time, this comparison to aristocratic *imagines* also emphasises the somewhat self-generated nature of Seneca's model in contrast to more standard narratives of familial and biological exemplarity: in place of a family,[108] Seneca has his friends clustered around his deathbed; instead of handing down an *exemplum* exclusively suited to his own *gens*, Seneca propagates a philosophical model that aspires to universal applicability; and, as a member of equestrian stock, Seneca most likely lacks *imagines* of his own, which means that his *exemplum* does not result from the

---

[107] Mayer (1991) 169; Erasmo (2008) 30; Ker (2009) 288. Santoro L'Hoir (2006) 215 seems to stretch the point when she interprets the *imago vitae suae* as referring to the theatre.

[108] The only family member present in Tacitus' account is Seneca's wife, Paulina, who is later removed from the scene at Seneca's bidding. Her role in the narrative is examined by Erasmo (2008) 27–34 and Ker (2012) 324–7.

Bridge: Seneca

pressure of a family name.[109] In comparison to, say, Marcus Junius Brutus or the second or third Decius Mus, Seneca is not expected by those around him to pursue a specific, pre-established *exemplum* in order to achieve his identity. He is at greater liberty to self-invent, to insert himself into a tradition of his choice or, more boldly, to devise one of his own. His ambition to attain paradigmatic status indicates a highly self-reflexive and at the same time detached, almost third-personal approach to selfhood; Seneca thinks of himself as 'Seneca' and models his current conduct on what he thinks that future model should do. Arguably, Marcus Junius Brutus likewise thought of himself as 'Brutus', the main difference being that Brutus imitated predecessors while Seneca copies and perpetuates chiefly himself. To borrow a phrase from Roland Mayer: 'it is in death that Seneca crowned his lifelong practice of referring to *exempla* by himself becoming one'.[110]

This is not to say, however, that Seneca's *exemplum* is entirely his own invention, since the narrative of his death adheres to an established and explicitly philosophical pattern, which in turn enables Seneca to present himself as a Stoic opposing tyranny and as someone condemned unjustly.[111] The events recounted by Tacitus at *Annales* 15.60–4 form a series of unmistakable allusions to Socrates' execution and to the suicide of Cato the Younger: like Socrates, Seneca drinks hemlock (*Ann.* 15.64.3; cf. *Phaedo* 117c); discourses with friends on philosophical topics, and has his thoughts recorded (*Ann.* 15.62–3; cf. *Phaedo* 59a-c); excludes his wife from the scene (*Ann.* 15.63.3; cf. *Phaedo* 60a); and pours a libation to Jupiter Liberator (*Ann.* 15.64.4), which recalls Socrates' request for a cock to be sacrificed to Asclepius (*Phaedo* 118a). Like Cato, Seneca's suicide articulates his Stoic defiance of a regime he perceives to be tyrannical, and it is not a smooth process, but one that occurs in several stages (veins: *Ann.*

---

[109] Mayer (1991) 169 notes that Seneca, as a man who had held curule office, had the right to leave a death mask to his descendants. But it is unlikely that Seneca himself had inherited any *imagines*. On the vexed question of which Roman nobles were granted the right to display *imagines* and under what circumstances, see Flower (1996) 53–9.

[110] Mayer (1991) 142.

[111] For Seneca's death scene as a mimicry of other models, see Griffin (1976) 369–72; Geiger (1979) 63; Mayer (1991) 142; Connors (1994) 228; Edwards (2007) 156–7; Erasmo (2008) 32–3; Ker (2009) 55–6.

15.63.2–3; hemlock: *Ann.* 15.64.3; steam bath: *Ann.* 15.64.4; cf. Cato's first and second attempts in Plut. *Cato* 70; both authors emphasise the subjects' weakness: Tac. *Ann.* 15.63.3; Plut. *Cato* 70.5).

Further, Seneca's imitative bid for exemplarity mimics that of Cato himself, who was widely recognised as having modelled his own death on Socrates': Cicero aligns the two by claiming that both men received divine sanction for their deaths (*Tusc.* 1.74); Plutarch has Cato accompanied by a small group of friends, among whom are several philosophers (*Cato* 67–70); and Cato is said to have read, and presumably taken inspiration from, Plato's *Phaedo* prior to committing suicide (Plutarch *Cato* 68.2, 70.1; Sen. *Ep.* 24.6–8).[112] This last piece of evidence underscores Cato's self-conscious intent to follow and thereby become an *exemplum*. By reading the *Phaedo* and subsequently adapting elements of Socrates' paradigm, Cato envisages for himself a future exemplarity that will lead to his story likewise being enshrined in written accounts and held up as a model for others. In effect, the Cato in Plutarch's biography perceives himself as a type already, while he is still alive, and attempts to dictate in advance how later generations will regard him. Tacitus' Seneca exercises similar concern for his posthumous reputation, and in striving to ensure his exemplarity, he condenses his identity into something that may be copied: a *testamentum*, an *imago*.

We may wonder whether the historical Cato and Seneca actually took such care to ensure their deaths complied with a well-known philosophical model – was exemplarity really their first thought in those last moments? While it is difficult to gauge the accuracy of Tacitus' and Plutarch's accounts, it seems likely that they do rest on a solid foundation of fact albeit one that has acquired accretions and embellishments over time.[113] Yet the very question of

---

[112] On the exemplary nature of Cato's death, see in particular Geiger (1979) 62–3, and Edwards (2007) 155. The afterlife and influence of Socrates' death scene across the Roman imperial period is discussed by Wilson (2007) 119–40.

[113] The historical background of the Cato narrative has received thorough treatment from Geiger (1979). While not focused solely on Seneca's death scene, Turpin (2008) makes a strong case for seeing in Tacitus' portrait the influence of Stoic approaches to exemplarity, approaches championed by Seneca himself. Mayer (1991) 169 remarks that Tacitus' account of Seneca's death must, ultimately, derive from the secretaries/

historical veracity, the attempt, that is, to disentangle the actual person from his or her characterisation in a text, gains little purchase in these circumstances precisely because these death scenes represent such an inseparable blend of life and literature. Seneca reads about Socrates and replicates Socrates before having that replication commemorated in Tacitus. How is the 'actual person' to be separated from a representation when he or she is so intent upon becoming a textually inscribed *exemplum*? Catherine Connors rightly defines the process as a kind of intertextuality whereby successive death scenes simultaneously evoke earlier people and earlier written accounts.[114] As in Seneca's tragedies, and in Roman culture more broadly, these exemplary suicides combine reiterated behaviour with textual reiteration.

In fact, this intertextual pattern reaches a pitch of *intra*textuality in Book 16 of Tacitus' *Annales*, with the deaths of Petronius (*Ann.* 16.19) and Thrasea Paetus (*Ann.* 16.34–5).[115] Thrasea, besides following the examples of Socrates and Cato, also re-enacts Tacitus' preceding portrayal of Seneca's death: he converses with a companion, Demetrius the Cynic, 'on the nature of the soul and its separation from mortal flesh' (*de natura animae et dissociatione spiritus corporisque, Ann.* 16.34.1); he dissuades his wife, Arria, from committing suicide with him (*Ann.* 16.34.2); he pours a libation to Jupiter Liberator (*Ann.* 16.35.1).[116] Just as Seneca bequeaths his *imago vitae suae* (*Ann.* 15.62), so the dying Thrasea implicitly offers himself as an *exemplum* when he tells the quaestor tasked with delivering the senate's decree, 'you have been born into an era when it may be helpful to fortify your morale with examples of constancy' (*in ea tempora natus es quibus firmare animum expediat constantibus exemplis, Ann.*

---

companions who were present at the scene and said to have recorded the event: *et novissimo quoque momento suppeditante eloquentia advocatis scriptoribus pleraque tradidit* (Tac. *Ann.* 15.63.3).

[114] Connors (1994) 228.

[115] On the intratextual repetition of death scenes in the later books of the *Annales*, see Ker (2009) 41–62.

[116] These are well-recognised parallels, discussed in varying degrees by Wirszubski (1968) 142; Griffin (1976) 370–1; Geiger (1979) 62–3; Mayer (1991) 142; Connors (1994) 228; Edwards (2007) 157–8; Ker (2009) 60–1. At *Ann.* 16.22.2, Thrasea's accusers, too, implicitly associate him with the younger Cato.

16.35.1–2). Clearly, the young quaestor is meant to learn something about virtue from witnessing Thrasea's death.

The suicide of Petronius (*Ann.* 16.19) also fits this established narrative arc, though it is clearly intended as a parody, with the dying man surrounded by friends; insisting on trivial conversation rather than philosophical discourse on the nature of the soul; letting his life ebb by degrees as he binds and unbinds his wrists; and leaving a list of Nero's crimes in place of a will.[117] In the simple act of copying (or satirising) a predecessor, each of these figures aspires to paradigmatic status, and in doing so, each merges his actual, human existence with a distinctly fictive identity: the dying Seneca is at once individual and inimitable, *and* a version of Socrates, *and* a version of Cato, *and* a version of himself, *and* an example of exemplary death preserved by Tacitus. Person, character, and type converge for the purpose of self-exemplification.

It is worth stressing once again the slight yet crucial difference between following a predominantly familial model because it is expected of one, or even regarded as the only means of proving one's inheritance, and opting to fashion oneself as a paradigm independent of any genealogical demands. Both scenarios negotiate a balance of individual versus society, particular versus general, but the latter grants the individual slightly sharper outlines. While familial exemplarity tends to focus on the past, self-directed exemplarity looks more fully to the future. The former embeds itself within extant traditions, while the latter often stands as a potential source of new traditions (influenced as Seneca is by Socrates and Cato, he also manages to inspire Thrasea and Petronius). Self-reflexive exemplification of the sort practised by Seneca further suggests an acute sense of one's uniqueness and importance: instead of dutifully preserving family customs and subordinating one's individuality to the broader demands of a *gens*, those who predict and strive after an *exemplum* of their own devising must assume in advance their singular ability to acquire a paradigmatic reputation and have it commemorated. This kind of exemplarity has a greater capacity to isolate the

---

[117] On Petronius' death as a parody of Seneca's, see Connors (1994) 228–9; Edwards (2007) 158–9; and Ker (2009) 67–8.

person in question from his or her immediate milieu, as opposed to familial patterns of *exempla*, which tend to integrate the individual within a wider social nexus.

A mild contrast between these two kinds of exemplarity may be found in Tacitus' vignettes of Seneca's and Thrasea's deaths. In each case, the wives of these men also aspire to attain paradigmatic status by dying alongside their husbands. For Arria, Thrasea's wife, the model is familial: she attempts 'to follow the *exemplum* of her own mother, Arria' (*temptantem ... exemplum Arriae matris sequi, Ann.* 16.34.2) and thus, to merge genealogical with exemplary reproduction. Like Brutus, Arria seems compelled to fulfil the expectations implicit in her name. Seneca's wife, Paulina, appears in contrast to be set on achieving her own exemplarity and on ensuring her posthumous fame, as Seneca himself acknowledges in his final address to her: 'I have shown you life's enticements, but you prefer death's glory: I will not begrudge you your *exemplum*. May the steadfastness of such a brave end be within our power equally, and may greater renown attend your departure' (*vitae ... delenimenta monstraveram tibi, tu mortis decus mavis: non invidebo exemplo. sit huius tam fortis exitus constantia penes utrosque par, claritudinis plus in tuo fine, Ann.* 15.63.2–3). While it could of course be argued that Paulina copies Seneca himself, her bid for exemplarity nonetheless appears fundamentally self-motivated and driven by a sense of her own specialness. Paulina hopes to claim individual *claritudo* (as implied by Tacitus' Seneca, at least), while Arria situates herself within a family context. One woman highlights her own singularity, the other her belonging to a group.

Such pursuit of exemplary death appears to have been particularly widespread during the early empire, when memorable departures from life were celebrated and circulated in published collections of *exitus illustrium virorum*.[118] Although none of

---

[118] Primary evidence for these publications comes from Pliny *Ep.* 8.12.4–5, where one Titinius Capito *scribit exitus inlustrium virorum*, and *Ep.* 5.5.3, about Caius Fannius: *scribebat ... exitus occisorum aut relegatorum a Nerone*. Detailed discussion of the genre can be found in Ronconi (1940).

these collections survives, they presumably resembled the compilations of protreptic and apotropaic *exempla* preserved in Valerius Maximus, whose own volume also has a section 'on extraordinary deaths' (*de mortibus non vulgaribus*, 9.12) though it has, unfortunately (ironically!), suffered severe truncation. There is good reason to believe that Tacitus drew on such compilations in order to compose the grim series of Neronian purges that occupies *Annales* 15 and 16.[119] There is equally good reason to believe that the historical Seneca, Thrasea, Petronius and others were well acquainted with the genre of *exitus illustrium virorum*, and may even have taken inspiration from it in a general way prior to preparing their own suicides.[120]

These anthologies of anecdotes served a purpose akin to martyrologies in that they commemorated individual deaths not just as praiseworthy events in themselves, but also as summative proof of a person's essential character. Gathered into handbooks, they provided guidance for those who, for whatever reason, found themselves in equivalent circumstances and needed to make a good end. As in other instances of Roman exemplarity, this tradition assumes a permeable boundary between the categories of person and typology, ethical improvement and artistic mimesis, living individual and textual representation: one reads these *exitus* not only for moral guidance, but also in order to reproduce such model behaviour in one's own life and thereby anticipate one's own commemoration. When the Seneca of *Annales* 15.60–4 constructs his own *exemplum*, he behaves as though he were already part of an anthology of *exitus illustrium virorum*. And in choosing to pursue such exemplarity in the first place, he betrays a self-centred impulse to be considered *illustris*: while friends, family, and society will undoubtedly derive some benefit from Seneca's *imago vitae suae*, the chief beneficiary in this instance is 'Seneca' himself.

---

[119] Demonstrated by Marx (1937) and Bellardi (1974). See also Edwards (2007) 132.
[120] A scenario made more likely by the fact that the genre enjoyed substantial popularity during Nero's reign, on which, see MacMullen (1966) 70–93.

2.2 *Hercules*

Hercules' Family

It is a short step from Seneca's semi-independent exemplarity to the fierce individualism of the protagonist in *Hercules*. Whereas Seneca's *exemplum* straddles two extremes, detached from family traditions yet still complying with some freely chosen models from the past, Hercules' is entirely self-generated and self-reliant. In contrast, too, to the suffocating father–son relationships portrayed in the *Troades*, Hercules' interaction with both his stepfather, Amphitryon, and his real father, Jupiter, is characterised by dissociation and dissonance. His *exemplum* represents the peak of self-reflexivity.

Rifts between Hercules and the rest of his family are most apparent in Act 5, when the hero regains consciousness following his attack of madness. The bodies of his slaughtered wife and children lie strewn around him (*Her.* 1143–4) and as he recovers from delirium to realise that he, not an external enemy, is responsible for this carnage, he resolves on suicide as the only solution to the problem of himself. A significant portion of Act 5 is occupied by Hercules searching for a means of death while Amphitryon counters and blocks these attempts to the best of his ability and with increasing levels of desperation. When Hercules demands the return of his confiscated weapons, Amphitryon responds with a formulaic but nonetheless heartfelt plea:

> per sancta generis sacra, per ius nominis
> utrumque nostri, sive me altorem vocas
> seu tu parentem …
> …
> temet reserva

> by the sanctity of family ties, by the rights
> of either of my names, whether you call me 'stepfather'
> or 'parent' …
> …
> keep yourself alive
>
> (*Her.* 1246–8; 1252)

That Amphitryon, in a moment of high emotion, asks Hercules to choose between two forms of nomenclature, *parens* or *altor*, may

Exemplarity

seem like ill-timed pedantry on Seneca's part, but the distinction actually represents a deep, personal rift between these two characters.[121] *altor* is of course the correct term in the literal sense that Hercules is Jupiter's son, and Amphitryon the step- or foster-father.[122] Yet the choice also reflects broader themes of human closeness and the value – or hindrance – of family bonds: Amphitryon invites Hercules either to acknowledge the genealogical distance separating them, or to gloss over it in favour of an unbroken social unit. Hercules' immediate response is to ignore both the plea and the invitation (*Her.* 1258–62), demonstrating his disregard for Amphitryon and for the demands of family more generally. This attitude, moreover, has direct bearing on Hercules' identity and on his role as an *exemplum* throughout the play. His surrogate relationship to Amphitryon, which Seneca takes pains to emphasise, symbolises the isolated, solipsistic quality of his exemplary status.

To grasp what is distinctive about Seneca's treatment of Hercules we must first take a brief look at Euripides' version, not with a view to formulating unfair or anachronistic comparisons between the imperial Roman tragedian and his classical Athenian counterpart, but for the simple purpose of shedding clearer light on Seneca's dramatic choices.[123] In Euripides' *Heracles*, companionship and human closeness are major themes. Amphitryon and

---

[121] Fitch (1987) *ad Her.* 1246–8 is right to note the emotional rather than purely practical connotations of Amphitryon's statement: '*altor* would mean that [Hercules] regards [Amphitryon] simply as a foster-father, whereas *parens* would imply a closer relationship'.

[122] I raise here the caveat that *altorem* at *Her.* 1247 is a widely accepted renaissance conjecture replacing the manuscript reading *auctorem*, which makes no sense in the given context. Obviously, resting an argument on a conjecture – even one as established as this – is a tricky business, but my main point still stands, because it is clear from the context that Amphitryon gives Hercules the choice between two names and hence, two kinds of family relationship. For discussion of the emendation, see Fitch (1987) *ad Her.* 1246–8 and Billerbeck (1999) *ad Her.* 1247.

[123] Thus Braden (1990) 245: 'the Athenians, and especially Euripides, still belong in any serious assessment of Seneca as a tragedian, and not merely as intimidating guardians of some corruptible greatness. If we ask the right questions, the differences between their theatre and Seneca's can measure not loss of talent, but underlying changes of vision and intent. Those changes help define Seneca as an artist in his own right'. On the similarities of Seneca's *Hercules* to Euripides' *Heracles*, see the summaries by Fitch (1987) 44–7 and Billerbeck (1999) 11–24, and the insightful comparative analysis of Zintzen (1972) [1971].

2.2 Hercules

Heracles address each other and apply to themselves affectionate terms such as πατήρ ('father'), τέκνον ('child'), and παῖς ('child'). Even though Amphitryon is not Heracles' biological father, Euripides observes no linguistic distinctions between this relationship and Heracles' to his own biological children; the same terminology is used throughout. On those occasions in the play when Amphitryon's surrogate status is evoked, emphasis falls on the connections and commonality that unite Heracles' foster-father with his real one: at 340 Amphitryon calls Zeus 'a partner in my son's begetting' (παιδὸς κοινεῶν' ἐκλήζομεν), and at 798–800, the chorus sings of 'the two related beds of the marriage, one with a mortal and one with Zeus' (ὦ λέκτρων δύο συγγενεῖς / εὐναί, θνατογενοῦς τε καὶ / Διός), with the adjective συγγενής evoking a tie so close it verges on being counted as family. Towards the tragedy's end, Heracles also reassures Amphitryon of his parental role: 'don't take any offence, old man, for I consider you my father instead of Zeus' (σὺ μέντοι μηδὲν ἀχθεσθῇς, γέρον· / πατέρα γὰρ ἀντὶ Ζηνὸς ἡγοῦμαι σ' ἐγώ 1264–5). Not once does Seneca's Hercules admit such emotional and psychological intimacy.[124]

Euripides' Heracles also cultivates a family relationship with Theseus, who is admittedly a distant relative but does not share any immediate blood or marriage ties with the hero. Their friendship becomes such a vital source of strength for Heracles in the aftermath of his attack that he goes as far as deeming Theseus a replacement for his children: 'having lost my sons, I consider you my son' (παίδων στερηθεὶς παῖδ' ὅπως ἔχω σ' ἐμόν, 1401). The closeness of this surrogate family bond is also affirmed by one of the play's most memorable similes: when Heracles returns from the Underworld, his frightened children cluster around him like little tow boats pulled along by a larger ship (631–2); later, when the same children lie dead by Heracles' unwitting hand, the hero declares that he will follow in Theseus' wake like a boat being towed (1424). Besides illustrating the absolute reversal of Heracles' fortunes, the latter of these two images equates the heroes' friendship with an actual, biological bond. Although his

---

[124] Fitch (1979) is an insightful study of Hercules' emotional limitations in the final Act of Seneca's play.

155

suffering is exceptional, Heracles is nonetheless not alone. Despite having killed his own wife and children, he achieves heroic stature in this play chiefly through his willingness to cultivate and to participate in the bonds of human society.[125]

Intergenerational and interpersonal relationships in Seneca's *Hercules* are not nearly so sympathetic. Although Seneca, like Euripides, uses equivalent terms such as *genitor*, *parens*, *pater*, and *natus* quite indiscriminately throughout the tragedy, he tends to concentrate on points of disjunction rather than union within Hercules' family group. When in Act 2, the tyrant Lycus appears on stage and undertakes to challenge claims regarding Hercules' divine ancestry (*Her.* 438–64 cf. Eur. *Her.* 148–9), Amphitryon does not gloss over the matter, or leave Zeus to answer for it, as he does in Euripides (*Her.* 170–3), but launches into a full and spirited defence of his step-son's descent from Jupiter, asserting that many gods owe their genesis to Jove's affairs with mortal women (*Her.* 449) and referring to Jove himself as 'Alcides' real father' (*Alcidae patrem* ... / ... *verum*, 440–1). The speech is meant to accentuate Hercules' semi-divine stature as a singular, exemplary hero, but its secondary effect is to acknowledge fissures within the family unit.[126] Whereas Euripides' Amphitryon refers to Zeus as a partner (340), Seneca's emphasises instead the gulf between his humbly ineffectual self and the potent king of the gods. Jupiter and Amphitryon claim no common ground in Seneca's play.

Acts 4 and 5 of the *Hercules* see the terms *genitor* and *pater* applied with increasing frequency both to Jupiter and to Amphitryon, but again without conveying any sense of shared enterprise. Rather than representing the united elements of a single family, Jupiter and Amphitryon appear in Seneca's version as disparate figures endowed with contrasting levels of authority and validity. For instance, following the death of Lycus,

[125] An argument pursued by Braden (1990) 246–9.
[126] Contra Bernstein (2017) 30, I do not see Amphitryon's speech at *Her.* 439–47 as exemplifying a 'relaxed attitude towards ancestry'. Granted, Amphitryon displays in this scene a willingness to accept and love Hercules despite the latter's illegitimacy, and to that extent, he also attempts to foster family bonds. But his far from 'relaxed' desire to prove Hercules' divine parentage also emphasises an unbridgeable division between himself and Jupiter.

2.2 Hercules

Amphitryon advises Hercules to request from Jupiter a rest from his labours: 'ask that your father put an end to your toils' (*finiat genitor tuos / opta labores, Her.* 924–5). The two-stage process – Amphitryon asking Hercules to ask Jupiter – underscores Amphitryon's own powerlessness, his at best secondary influence over Hercules, and the enormous distance between the capacities of these two father figures, a distance only increased by the ineffectiveness of Amphitryon's request: Hercules does not in fact proceed to pray for the cessation of his work (*Her.* 937–9). Further divisions within Hercules' family are emphasised when the hero, in the process of offering sacrifice in gratitude for his recent victory over Lycus, calls upon Jupiter's other male offspring, but excludes any son born from Juno: 'may he be present … whichever brother of mine inhabits heaven, but not a brother born from my step-mother' (*adsit … / … / fraterque quisquis incolit caelum meus / non ex noverca frater*, 903; 907–8). Unlike Euripides' *Heracles*, who is willing to class even Theseus as an honorary family member, Seneca's maintains an attitude of exceptionalism and a readiness to foster estrangement in place of concord; possible sources of connection become instead irreparable divisions.

Similar family tensions simmer beneath Amphitryon's question to Theseus at 761: does Hercules bring Cerberus back from the Underworld 'as a gift from his willing uncle, or as spoils?' (*patrui volentis munus an spolium refert?* 761). Inclusion of *patruus* draws attention once again to Hercules' divine ancestry but also to the fact that his Underworld mission brings him into conflict with a member of his own kin. Theseus' response, which includes an animated account of the battle between Hercules and Cerberus (782–806) implies that while Hades gave nominal consent to the act, the three-headed hound really is more of a *spolium* than a *munus*.[127] Allegorically, Hercules' Underworld battle enables him

---

[127] I concur with Fitch (1987) *ad Her.* 761, against Lawall (1983) 12, that Seneca depicts Hercules' underworld labour as a violent, hard-won victory. Juno's comments in the prologue confirm the idea that Cerberus is a *spolium*: *effregit ecce limen inferni Iovis / et opima victi regis ad superos refert. / vidi … / … Dite domito spolia iactantem patri / fraterna* (*Her.* 47–8; 50–2). Hercules' own remarks, upon his return, also suggest his total conquest of Hades (and by implication, spoils): *si placerent tertiae sortis loca, / regnare potui* (*Her.* 609–10).

Exemplarity

to achieve a (temporary) victory over death;[128] literally, it leads him to act in an aggressive, domineering manner towards a close relative.

Hercules' emotional distance from his family is thrown into even sharper relief by Amphitryon's persistently loving, paternal behaviour. The stepfather defends his stepson against Lycus' slander (439–89); is overjoyed at the latter's safe return from Hades (621); and more than once expresses his sadness at Hercules' frequent absence (249; 1256–7). Amphitryon stands out among Seneca's *dramatis personae* for being able to speak tenderly, not furiously, of another person; as John Fitch remarks, Seneca's Amphitryon 'values the natural affection between father and son'.[129] But Hercules, for his part, repeatedly pushes this affection aside, disregarding or overriding Amphitryon's gentle suggestions (e.g. at 918–22, when Hercules refuses to follow Amphitryon's advice about cleaning his bloodied hands before performing a sacrifice), even refusing the offer of his embrace: *differ amplexus, parens* ('postpone your embraces, father', 638).

Nor does Hercules achieve any closer relationship with his true progenitor, Jupiter, though his semi-divine qualities may induce the audience to expect otherwise. When, in Act 5, the recovering Hercules calls upon the king of the gods to wreak vengeance for his crime, the lack of divine response only increases our sense of the hero's isolation: 'now thunder angrily, father, from every part of the sky; forgetful of me, at least avenge your grandsons with your all-too-slow hand' (*nunc parte ab omni, genitor, iratus tona; / oblite nostri, vindica sera manu / saltem nepotes, Her.* 1202–4). Such requests for Jupiter's thunderous reaction are frequent and always unfulfilled in Senecan tragedy (*Phaed.* 671–4; *Med.* 531–7; *Thy.* 1077–85), but the trope acquires added poignancy here, because Ju<u>piter</u> *is* Hercules' *pater*, and because fathers typically wield a lot of influence over their offspring in Seneca's plays, even when they are not physically present. Jupiter's silence, at this moment, only serves to widen the existing chasm between Hercules and his immediate family members.

---

[128] On the allegorical role of the Underworld in this play, see Galinsky (1972) 171–2.
[129] Fitch (1979) 242.

2.2 *Hercules*

Besides being isolated from his divine parent, Seneca's Hercules also cuts himself off from the family he himself has produced. John Fitch notes that in comparison to Euripides' hero, Seneca's protagonist spares no time upon his return from Hades to reconnect emotionally with his wife and children; as soon as he hears about Lycus, he rushes off.[130] Complementing this emotional isolation is the obvious fact that Hercules also kills Megara and their mutual offspring in the fit of insanity brought about by Juno, but here, too, Seneca makes an added effort to highlight Hercules' detachment. The moment comes when Megara, in a last, desperate attempt to save her youngest son, exhorts the raving father to recognise the boy's physical resemblance: 'this son reflects your face and bearing' (*natus hic vultus tuos / habitusque reddit, Her.* 1017–18). Once again, Seneca evokes potential communality only to reject it in favour of division: Hercules disregards all evidence of biological ties; he sees not his son, but a *monstrum* (1020), which he duly eradicates.

Megara's brief, fraught plea to her rampaging husband also hints at the discourse of exemplarity, especially in the terms explored by Seneca's *Troades*, where the physical similarity of sons to fathers anticipates similarity of temperament. Hercules' bloodline figures fleetingly as a possible source of exemplary repetition. But *exempla* in this play tend to discourage rather than foster mimetic identification between family members or, more broadly, members of the same society; the balance between particular and general, individual and group tips towards the former of each pair. Hercules' detachment from his family symbolises the correspondingly detached quality of his *exemplum*, which operates largely in a vacuum, self-regarding and self-sustained.

The closest Hercules himself ever comes to following a parental model is in his fit of madness, when he threatens to unseat Jove:

> vincla Saturno exuam,
> contraque patris impii regnum impotens
> avum resolvam. bella Titanes parent
> me duce furentes

> I'll set Saturn free from his chains
> and against my immoral father's unbridled rule

---

[130] Fitch (1979) 242.

> unleash my grandfather. Let the raging Titans
> prepare war; I'll lead them
>
> (*Her.* 965-8)

In one regard, Hercules' mad wish seems to epitomise the characteristics of exemplary *aemulatio*. Just as Jupiter once ousted Saturn in order to establish himself as ruler of the gods, so Hercules now hopes to oust Jupiter; like father, like son. Hercules' proposed enlistment of the Titans, however, indicates his divergence from and outright contesting of paternal exemplarity, since victory in the gigantomachy constitutes one of Jupiter's greatest and most definitive achievements. The son hopes to undo what the father has done. The competitive impulse inherent in all exemplary activity (to a greater or lesser degree) becomes, in this instance, overt conflict, and Hercules' rapport with this divine parental paradigm seems rocky at best.

Sole Exemplar

In place of expected ancestral precedent, Seneca's Hercules looks almost exclusively to himself for guidance, for evaluation of his conduct, and for formulating his identity. In one respect, this self-reliance is part and parcel of Hercules' established role as an *exemplar virtutis*: in mythology, in literature, in philosophy, Hercules embodies a model for others but does not himself appear to follow other people's paradigms.[131] In Seneca's *Hercules*, however, this exemplary exceptionalism approaches an extreme of self-reflexivity and self-implosion, because when Hercules finds himself needing moral guidance and needing to re-establish his identity in the wake of madness, he has no model to turn to apart from his own. As Juno remarks in the prologue, this Hercules is peerless: *quaeris Alcidae parem? / nemo est nisi ipse* ('You seek Alcides' equal? There's no-one, apart from himself' 84–5). Gordon Braden is surely right to detect in Juno's claim an allusion to Roman practices of self-*aemulatio*, like that pursued by Plutarch's Julius Caesar: τὸ μὲν πάθος οὐδὲν ἦν ἕτερον ἢ ζῆλος αὐτοῦ καθάπερ ἄλλου καὶ φιλονεικία τις ὑπὲρ τῶν μελλόντων πρὸς τὰ πεπραγμένα ('the feeling was nothing other than zealous emulation

---

[131] On Hercules' role as an exemplification of abstract values in ancient literature and philosophy, Galinsky (1972) 101–52 remains a useful summary. See also Billerbeck (1999) 25–9.

2.2 *Hercules*

of himself as though he were another man, and rivalry between what he planned to do and what he had achieved' *Caesar* 58.5).[132] The contours and consequences of such self-exemplification are explored in full in a subsequent section of this chapter; for now, it suffices to affirm that whenever Seneca's Hercules cites the model of his own achievements, he does so in the implicit context of exemplarity. The protagonist of the *Hercules* is obsessed not just with himself,[133] but more precisely with his own *exemplum*.

One of the most telling instances of Hercules' solipsism comes in Act 5, when Amphitryon has exhausted all other arguments against the hero's intended suicide, and resorts instead to emotional blackmail:

> **Amph:** sic statue, quidquid statuis, ut causam tuam
> famamque in arto stare et ancipiti scias:
> aut vivis aut occidis. hanc animam levem
> fessamque senio nec minus fessam malis
> in ore primo teneo. tam tarde patri
> vitam dat aliquis? non feram ulterius moram,
> senile ferro pectus impresso induam:
> hic, hic iacebit Herculis sani scelus.
> **Herc:** iam parce, genitor, parce, iam revoca manum.
> succumbe, virtus, perfer imperium patris.
> eat ad labores hic quoque Herculeos labor:
> vivamus.
>
> **Amph:** Whatever you decide, decide on the understanding
> that your case and reputation stand in delicate, dubious balance:
> either you live or you kill me. I hold this frail spirit, tired out by age
> and no less by troubles, on the edge of my lips. Does anyone
> grant life to his father so slowly? I won't bear delay any more,
> I shall press the sword-point against my aged breast and plunge it in:
> here, here will lie the crime of Hercules sane.
> **Herc:** Stop now, father, stop, withdraw your hand.
> Submit, courage, endure your father's command.
> Let this task, too, be added to Hercules' labours:
> that we live.
>
> (*Her.* 1306–17)

---

[132] Braden (1985) 13–14.
[133] This self-obsession is, in any case, remarkable, even against stiff competition from some of Seneca's other protagonists. Fitch and McElduff (2002) 25 note that Hercules cites his own name twelve times over the course of the tragedy, more than any other Senecan character does. Similarly, Fitch (1979) 243 n.10 observes that Seneca's Hercules uses the pronoun *ego* a staggering twenty-one times in Act 5 alone.

Exemplarity

What is it in Amphitryon's speech that motivates Hercules' change of heart? The passage has received a lot of scholarly commentary, with Bernd Seidensticker and Gilbert Lawall asserting that Hercules' concedes his step-father's request out of a long-buried sense of *pietas*: the hero has spent most of the play disregarding his family's needs, but here he finally recalls and capitulates to the demands of filial duty.[134] Another, equally optimistic, interpretation maintains that Hercules comes to understand *virtus* as a moral rather than purely physical quality, and hence reframes his feats of brute strength in terms of peaceful, ethical principles.[135] In place of his victories over nature's monsters, Hercules now achieves a far superior moral victory over himself: he learns self-control; he learns to rein in his vicious impulses, and to brush them aside in favour of obeying *ratio* and *natura*. What Juno envisaged at the outset as a violent, physical form of self-defeat – *se vincat* ('let him conquer himself', 116) – becomes instead a moment of spiritual self-conquest and moral regeneration.[136] On this reading, Hercules ends his tragedy either a fully Stoic hero,[137] or at the very least an admirable man equipped with deeper knowledge of moral precepts and of his own, all-too-human fallibility.

Each of these theories, however, posits too radical a change in Hercules' disposition, especially as regards his attitude to those around him. John Fitch remarks that understanding of Act 5 'has often been distorted by presuppositions about what *ought* to take place' as scholars reach after the same dynamic of fellowship and redemption found in Euripides' version.[138] In response to such positive views, Fitch and Braden argue that Hercules remains self-centred and emotionally detached throughout the exchange and yields to Amphitryon not out of any newly found sense of *pietas* or *virtus*, but out of an over-riding, all-consuming regard for his own

---

[134] Seidensticker (1969) 118; Lawall (1983) 20–1. Galinsky (1972) 173 also leans towards this interpretation.
[135] A popular view: Zintzen (1972) 205–6; Shelton (1978) 67–73; Motto and Clark (1981) especially 112–13; Pratt (1983) 118; Okell (2005) 188–90. Contrasting negative assessment of Hercules' *virtus*, even in Act 5, is presented by Henry and Walker (1965).
[136] Lawall (1983) 21–2.
[137] While currently unfashionable, arguments in favour of Hercules as a Stoic hero form a persistent strain in Senecan scholarship: see Egermann (1972) [1940], 47–8; Marti (1945) 224–5; Motto and Clark (1981); Lawall (1983); and Billerbeck (1999) 30–8.
[138] Fitch (1987) 35.

2.2 *Hercules*

reputation.[139] When Amphitryon threatens suicide and declares the deed will be commemorated as *Herculis sani scelus* (1313), he finally lights upon the hero's true priorities. The point at issue is what it means to be 'Hercules' and how others will define or remember the hero in the future. If Amphitryon's life hangs in the balance at this moment, it does so only for the sake of making Hercules' *fama* hang in the balance as well. Hercules' response confirms where his interests lie: he will add the achievement of living to the list of his previous feats; to continue being Hercules is a Herculean task in itself. He even characterises his action as obedience to *imperium*, just as he has previously obeyed the *imperium* of Eurystheus (*Her.* 42: *laetus imperia excipit*; 398: *disce regum imperia ab Alcide pati*; 433: *imperia dura*). Hercules does here what he has done all along: behaves and thinks of himself solely as the hero of the labours.

The phrasing of Amphitryon's plea acquires particular significance in this regard because its third-personal construction encourages Hercules to view himself as a symbol, a reproducible *exemplum*, an instance of 'Hercules' and of all that name typically entails. Concomitantly, the expression *Herculis sani scelus* (1313), alludes darkly to the play's title, *Hercules Furens*, thereby inviting Hercules to adopt a detached, metatheatrical view of himself as a character within his own story. Whatever action the hero opts to pursue at this juncture, Amphitryon implies, may become the subject not only of future reputation, and so, possible emulation, but also of future literary works. Amphitryon catches Hercules' attention and manages to persuade him by citing the one thing that really matters to the hero: his future commemoration as an admirable paradigm.

Such self-reflexive exemplarity is a particularly crucial theme in Act 5 of the *Hercules* because it is at this point that the protagonist must reconcile his former with his current self.[140] Reeling from the

---

[139] Fitch (1979) and (1987) *ad Her.* 1300–1313, and more fully, 35–8; Braden (1990) 249–57. A more recent proponent of the view is Mader (2014) 128–31.

[140] Crucially, Hercules himself does not experience his madness and sanity as contiguous states, so the fifth Act is largely occupied with issues of self-reconstruction. From the audience's perspective, however, there are manifest similarities between Hercules' behaviour while mad and while sane: see below, 174–6. On Hercules' mediation of past and present, Mader (2014) 129 makes some insightful remarks.

knowledge of his crime and fumbling to regain some form of mental equilibrium, Hercules relies on *exempla*, and specifically on their ability to mediate between past and present, in order to reassemble and to promote a clear sense of his identity. Hence, when he contemplates suicide as a first response to his crimes, he rouses himself to the deed by calling it *ingens opus, labore bis seno amplius* ('a huge enterprise, greater than the twelvefold labours' *Her.* 1282). He also pledges to rid the earth of his presence as though he were one of the monsters he has previously conquered: *purgare terras propero. iamdudum mihi / monstrum impium saevumque et immite ac ferum / oberrat* ('I hasten to cleanse the earth. For a long time now this wicked, cruel, pitiless, wild monster has roamed free before me' 1279–80). Similar obsession with his past achievements underpins his question to Amphitryon at 1301 – *pande, quid fieri iubes?* ('Speak, what do you command to occur?') – because obeying and fulfilling *iussa* is a key characteristic of the former Hercules (*Her.* 41–3; 211; 235; 596; 604; 831; and especially 1268: *laudanda feci iussus*, 'I did praiseworthy things under orders'). Amphitryon, for his part, attempts to dissuade the hero by citing his well-known capacity for endurance, once more framed in terms of a pre-established reputation: *nunc Hercule opus est: perfer hanc molem mali* ('now Hercules is needed: endure this mass of evil' 1239).[141] Who Hercules was dictates who Hercules should be now: the self-referentiality of this process is yet another factor highlighting Hercules' isolation in this play. He does not follow parental models, and he proves stubbornly unreceptive to his stepfather's pleas. The only family connection Hercules cultivates in this drama is that of himself to himself. The social and biological divide between Amphitryon and Hercules deepens into an emotional and psychological one as well: the protagonist does not

---

[141] Seidensticker (1969) 112 rightly compares this line to Theseus' exhortation in Euripides' *Heracles* 1250: ὁ πολλὰ δὴ τλὰς Ἡρακλῆς λέγει τάδε; ('does Heracles, having suffered so much, say these things?'). There is a difference between the two treatments, however, inasmuch as Euripides' Theseus cites Heracles' name and heroic stature as a way of underscoring the universality of human suffering, while Amphitryon uses Hercules' name to emphasise the hero's uniqueness, his solitary ability to bear the burden of this misfortune.

2.2 *Hercules*

display any intrinsic care for family bonds when deciding how best to handle his wretched situation.

To some extent, Hercules' self-obsession resembles the *decorum* and *constantia* pursued by figures such as Atreus and Medea: it links past to present; it relies on repetitious behaviour; it fosters acute consciousness of the self qua reputation.[142] It is also inherently concerned with exemplarity, not least because of Hercules' pre-established role as a paradigmatic figure. Having no one to follow or copy, Seneca's Hercules hones his identity solely via reference to his own model. His sense of self relies not on his identification with others, but on solipsistic resurrection of his own past deeds. His isolated exemplarity is both a symptom and cause of his emotional and physical detachment from those around him, detachment that often spills over into outright aggression.

Hercules in Character

Hercules' preoccupation with what he symbolises, and with what it means to be 'Hercules' encourages the play's audience, too, to regard him as a symbol, a textual representation, and ultimately, a dramatic character. Just as the protagonist worries about his *fama* in Act 5, so the rest of the tragedy focuses attention on how that *fama* is created and sustained, and concomitantly, how its very existence influences our perception of Hercules' identity. Seneca achieves this end via a striking (and possibly, unique) form of dramaturgy that couples short bursts of Hercules' stage action with lengthy spoken accounts of the hero's accomplishments. Critics have not been slow to note that the *Hercules* exhibits a ponderously static quality, especially for a play that encompasses multiple murders and a scene of madness: Act 1 comprises Juno's aggrieved monologue (1–124); Amphitryon opens Act 2 with a protracted summary of his son's labours, and of the present, grim situation prevailing in Thebes (205–78); Theseus' *ekphrasis* of the

---

[142] Fitch and McElduff (2002) 29–30 link Hercules, Medea, and Atreus as three Senecan characters inclined to assess their actions according to their own past precedents.

underworld occupies the bulk of Act 3 (650–829).[143] Hercules himself does not appear on stage until 592, only to vanish again between 641 and 895; despite being the play's titular character, he is rarely present before the audience, and even more rarely engages in dialogue with the tragedy's other figures.[144]

In lieu of Hercules himself, Seneca has other characters talk about the hero, and particularly about his defining activity, the twelve labours: Juno mentions the Nemean lion and the hydra (46), Cerberus (46–63), and Hercules accepting the weight of the globe from Atlas (70–4); Amphitryon recites a full catalogue of the twelve tasks at 222–48, several items of which the chorus reprises at 529–49; Megara, Amphitryon, and Lycus pursue a three-way debate over whether Hercules' deeds merit the label of *virtus* (422–89); Theseus' description of the underworld features cameo appearances by some of Hercules' erstwhile monstrous opponents (778–81) and concludes with the hero himself defeating Cerberus (782–829). Seneca's audience spends most of the play encountering Hercules via other characters' narratives.[145]

The traditional view attributes these narrative passages to the demands of *Lese-* or *Rezitationsdrama* on the basis that an audience of listeners would require, and even enjoy, hearing descriptions of events they cannot see.[146] Composing for the recital hall rather than for the stage – if this really was Seneca's objective – is assumed to result in looser dramatic form and general disregard for the conventional restrictions pertaining to onstage action. A less charitable approach simply dismisses Seneca as an unskilled,

---

[143] Seneca's preference for narrative in the *Hercules* has been addressed piecemeal by Zwierlein (1966) 112–13 and 119–20, while fuller, more up-to-date treatment of the issue can be found in Von Glinski (2017). Of Theseus' *ekphrasis*, Fitch (1987) *ad Her.* 592–829 remarks that such scenes in Seneca 'displace, or at least overshadow, scenes of more traditional dramaturgy'. Tarrant (1976) *ad Ag.* 392a–588 voices a similar opinion.

[144] His frequent absence from the onstage world is well noted by Von Glinski (2017). On Hercules' inclination for monologic speech, see Fitch (1979) 243–4.

[145] A crucial yet seldom acknowledged point: see Seidensticker (1969) 113, and Lawall (1983) 10–11.

[146] In the words of Zwierlein (1966) 60: 'Die pedantische Beschreibung ... mußte einem Zuschauer, der dies ja selbst sähe, albern erscheinen; dem Hörer kann sie helfen, sich das Bild plastisch vorzustellen' (The pedantic description ... must appear silly to a viewer, who sees these things for him/herself; but it can help the listener imagine the physical representation'). Fantham (1975) 3 n.3 pursues a similar argument.

2.2 *Hercules*

third-rate playwright.[147] But, whether performed or recited, the dramatic structure of the *Hercules* fulfils a distinct purpose in compelling the audience to contemplate Hercules chiefly in terms of his reputation, just as the protagonist himself does. How heroic is Hercules? Does he live up to the *exemplum* that precedes him? Can the figure that appears on stage be reconciled with the one we have – literally – *heard* so much about? The play's structure invites the audience to pose such questions in the same way that Hercules' misfortune pushes him to measure the distance between his past and current sense of self.

Seneca further implies that Hercules owes his exemplarity, and hence a significant aspect of his identity, to acts of narration. When Amphitryon punctuates a list of his son's labours with the rhetorical *quid memorem?* ('why should I speak of?' 226), he draws attention to the fact that he is currently celebrating Hercules' paradigm in speech, and by extension, that spoken and/or written records are the principal means of preserving – even of generating – such *exempla*. As a *rei gestae ... comm<u>emo</u>ratio*, a 'record of achievements', the definition proffered by Quint. *Inst.* 5.11.6, the *exemplum*'s existence depends upon its being talked about (*memorare*). Thus, Hercules' labours are twice referred to as *memoranda facta* ('memorable deeds / deeds worth speaking about', 442; 1265–6), and Theseus commences his account of Hercules' *katabasis* by protesting, <u>memorare</u> *cogis acta securae / horrenda menti* ('you compel me <u>to narrate</u> deeds that make my mind shudder even now, in safety' 650–1). The narrative passages in this play repeatedly draw links between Hercules' paradigmatic feats and others' accounts of them. Even Juno, in the prologue, grudgingly admits that the hero *toto deus / <u>narratur</u> orbe* ('<u>is talked about</u> as a god throughout the entire world' 39–40), a claim we later see substantiated when Amphitryon invokes his son as though he were a deity (277; 519–20).[148]

As this last point demonstrates, Seneca also endeavours to link the play's various narrative accounts of Hercules to the

---

[147] Witness, for example, the perceptive but unnecessarily harsh judgements made about the *Hercules* by T. S. Eliot (1999) [1927] 69–70.
[148] Fitch (1987) *ad Her.* 520–2 notes in addition that the natural phenomena described by Amphitryon 'suggest the imminent epiphany of a *numen*'.

Exemplarity

protagonist's subsequent activity on stage.[149] The effect once again is that Seneca induces his audience to compare the stage Hercules – bodily present, speaking and acting – with the reputation that surrounds and precedes him. Guided and informed by other characters' perspectives, the audience is able to see in this actual Hercules traces of his pre-established paradigm. Like the practice of exemplarity in Roman society and politics, Seneca's dramaturgical trick configures Hercules as simultaneously himself and a copy of himself, a unique individual and a reproducible type, Hercules the quasi-person and 'Hercules' the *exemplum*. Viewed from one angle, the protagonist's materialisation on stage asserts his personal, contingent singularity in contrast to the infinitely repeatable paradigm of 'Hercules' sustained in others' narratives. From another angle, the stage Hercules comes to seem an extension or even a replica of the one other characters talk about. Hercules the *dramatis persona* re-performs entire sequences of action in a manner reminiscent of a Brutus or a Decius Mus replaying the deeds of his ancestors. The crucial difference, of course, is that Seneca's Hercules only ever replays himself.

This theme of self-repetition is present from the very beginning of the play, in Juno's prologue. Here, the vengeful goddess relates in aggrieved detail how she watched Hercules emerge from the underworld with Cerberus cowering in tow (59–63). The event occurs again, this time on stage, when Hercules makes his first appearance at 592, dragging Cerberus behind him. Connections between the two passages are clear and strong: Juno affirms in the prologue that she has witnessed Hercules' conquest of Hades (*vidi ipsa*; 'I myself saw it', 50) and the capture of its canine guardian (*terna monstri colla devincti intuens*; 'looking upon the bound monster's triple neck', 62), while Hercules himself, at the opening of Act 3, asserts that only he and Juno may gaze upon the *nefas* that is Cerberus' presence in the upper world: *hoc nefas cernant duo / qui advexit et quae iussit* ('let two look upon this sacrilege: he who fetched the dog and she who ordered it', 603–4). Each speaker also alludes to the potentially polluting effect this sight has on the sun.

---

[149] Lawall (1983) 10–11 notes the technique, though he argues that Seneca employs it as a source of contrast, not comparison.

2.2 Hercules

Juno declares, 'I saw the day sinking and the Sun frightened by the sight of Cerberus' (*viso labantem Cerbero vidi diem / pavidumque Solem*, 60–1), while Hercules begs, 'forgive me, Phoebus, if your visage has seen anything unlawful' (*da, Phoebe, veniam, si quid inlicitum tui / videre vultus*, 595–6). What Juno reports as happening in the time of the prologue happens again in the real time of the play.[150]

The result, for Hercules, is that he appears to be acting on cue, not just matching his conduct to the contours already outlined by Juno, but even repeating something he has already done, returning from the underworld while she watches and then doing it again while the audience looks on. Strictly speaking, of course, Hercules emerges from Hades only once over the course of his story, but the drama's temporal repetition gives the impression of the activity being infinitely reproducible, like all *exempla*. Furthermore, Juno's role as prologue speaker places her in a quasi-directorial position: she is the metatheatrical dramatist whose purpose it is to ensure that Hercules follows the script.[151] Thus, the structure of the *Hercules* draws attention to its protagonist as a fabricated dramatic *persona*, a character acting in character. In following his own paradigm, Hercules causes himself to become a version, a type, a detachable, imitable role. But in the *Hercules* this role is neither passed on to nor assumed by others; Hercules alone *resumes* it, repeatedly. He imitates himself, which only further underscores the selfishness of his exemplarity.

Besides seeking to reproduce the behaviour essential to his paradigm, Seneca's Hercules also displays concern for the items specific to it, namely his weaponry. When the hero sinks into a stupor at the close of Act 4, Amphitryon commands servants to confiscate his bow and arrows (1053). One of Hercules' first

---

[150] Shelton (1975) and (1978) 17–25 examines the temporal dislocation of the *Hercules* in considerable detail, though her conclusion, which attributes this dramatic structure to Seneca's interest in personal psychology, is unsatisfactory. Seneca's curious manipulation and/or repetition of stage time has also been noted by Owen (1970).

[151] Von Glinski (2017) 215. On prologue speakers as substitutes for the playwright/ *didaskalos*, see Easterling (1993) 80.

thoughts upon waking is to wonder what has become of his usual equipment and costume:

> cur latus laevum vacat
> spolio leonis? quonam abit tegimen meum
> idemque somno mollis Herculeo torus?
> ubi tela? ubi arcus? arma quis vivo mihi
> detrahere potuit?
>
> Why is my left side bare?
> Where is my lion skin? Where has it gone, that protection of mine,
> and soft bed for Hercules' sleep?
> Where are my weapons, my bow? Who could strip me of my arms
> while I'm alive?
>
> (*Her.* 1150–4)

Like his repeated citation of the labours, Hercules' search for his weaponry symbolises the painful process of self-reconstruction in the wake of madness. In Rosie Wyles' words, 'Seneca makes use of the idea that Heracles' iconic pieces of costume embody his identity.'[152] The passage has the metatheatrical effect of highlighting Hercules' status as a dramatic role generated through props and particular items of apparel.[153] Concomitantly, Hercules' costume also symbolises the exemplary status conferred upon him by his labours: the pelt of the Nemean lion is both a commemorative trophy (*spolio leonis*, 1151) and synecdoche for Hercules qua hero.[154] Implicit in Hercules' wondering who could possibly have stolen these items is the vague worry that another, more exemplary hero has managed to overpower him (cf. 1168: *victor Alcidae, lates?* 'Are you in hiding, conqueror of Alcides?') Hercules regards his weapons, like his deeds, as belonging to him alone; in the same way that nobody can live up to his *exemplum*, so nobody, Hercules feels, should expect to wield his bow

---

[152] Wyles (2013) 194. See also Bernstein (2017) 46–50.
[153] Thus Wyles (2013) 182: 'His costume is used to reflect on ancient theatre's dependence on costume for the construction of its stage characters.'
[154] Dionysus' assumption of the lion skin in Aristophanes' *Frogs* is an obvious example of the costume's ability to represent the hero. Another example comes from Theseus' *ekphrasis* in the *Hercules*, where the hero's fight with Cerberus is represented as an encounter between a dog and a lionskin: *solvit a laeva feros / tunc ipse rictus et Cleonaeum caput / opponit* (797–9). Fuller treatment of the costume's symbolism can be found in Wyles (2013).

2.2 *Hercules*

and arrows. Of course, the only conqueror of Hercules in this play is Hercules himself, a self-reflexive feat that confirms the circularity of his *exemplum*. Despite his being a role and role model, Hercules emerges as the only figure able to undertake this part.

Self-aemulatio

As noted in a preceding section, Seneca's Hercules spends most of his eponymous tragedy in competition with himself. His feats of strength cannot be equalled let alone surpassed, and his exceptional heroism makes him the only man capable of overthrowing himself. While not categorically wrong, this activity threatens to unseat the *exemplum*'s primary purpose of fostering interpersonal and intergenerational emulation in the name of social and moral continuity. Despite the centuries separating Lucius from Marcus Junius Brutus, the former's model is maintained and perpetuated by the latter. But the exemplarity of Seneca's Hercules achieves the opposite effect inasmuch as it confirms his isolation from his surrounding community rather than enabling him to claim a place within it.

The phenomenon of self-*aemulatio* is a minor yet persistent theme in Roman letters, typically appearing in panegyric passages and, following the establishment of the principate, typically applied to emperors.[155] I have cited already, above, Plutarch's comments about Julius Caesar's ambition and energy reaching such heights that he had nobody to contend with apart from himself (Plut. *Caes.* 58.5). Pliny voices a comparable idea when praising Trajan's performance in battle:

Non tibi moris tua inire tentoria, nisi commilitonum ante lustrasses, nec requiem corpori nisi post omnes dare. Hac mihi admiratione dignus imperator ⟨vix⟩ videretur, si inter Fabricios et Scipiones et Camillos talis esset; tunc enim illum imitationis ardor semperque melior aliquis accenderet. Postquam vero studium armorum a manibus ad oculos, ad voluptatem a labore translatum est, postquam exercitationibus nostris non veteranorum aliquis cui decus muralis aut civica, sed Graeculus magister adsistit, quam magnum est unum ex omnibus patrio more

---

[155] For a full list of references to self-*aemulatio* in Latin literary sources, see Oakley (1997) *ad Liv.* 6.6.9.

Exemplarity

<u>patria virtute laetari, et sine aemulo [ac] sine exemplo secum certare, secum contendere</u> ac, sicut imperet solus, solum ita esse qui debeat imperare! it was your habit to inspect your comrades' tents before you retired to your own; the last man must go off duty before you would take a rest yourself. Such were the great generals of the past, bred in the homes of Fabricius, Scipio, and Camillus; if they have a lesser claim upon my admiration it is because in their day a man could be inspired by keen rivalry with his betters. But now that interest in arms is displayed in spectacle instead of personal skill, and has become an amusement instead of a discipline, when exercises are no longer directed by a veteran crowned by the mural or civic crown, but by some petty Greek trainer, <u>it is good to find one single man to delight in the traditions and the valour of our fathers, who can strive with none but himself for rival, press on with only his own example before him</u>, and since he is to wield authority alone, will prove that he alone is worthy. (*Pan.* 13.3–5 trans. Radice)

The passage describes a complex balance between the community of common soldiers and lesser commanders, and Trajan as their ultimate, outstanding leader. Pliny depicts the emperor as leading by example and, at the same time, as reviving exemplary practices from the republican past. Trajan features as the military heir of model commanders from the ranks of Fabricii, Scipiones, and Camilli. Up to this point, the emperor's exemplarity can be said to strengthen social bonds, both within the immediate context of his own army and within the broader context of social and historical continuity.

But Pliny also acknowledges a wide gap separating Trajan from his republican predecessors: they belonged to a time period (and implicitly, a social structure) in which it was possible for them to vie with and imitate each other (*tunc enim illum imitationis ardor semperque melior aliquis accenderet*, 13.4). Because Rome's republican oligarchy allotted governmental power to more than one individual, it cultivated an environment of elite *aemulatio* in which a host of aristocrats would jostle to claim the best places in the hierarchy. For all its manifest failings and restrictions, this political system entailed a degree of plurality, which in turn encouraged the competitive, interpersonal pursuit of *exempla*. In contrast, Trajan's position at the very peak of an autocratic hierarchy leaves him – at least in theory – without any superior

2.2 Hercules

paradigms to emulate.[156] Since nobody, by definition, can be better than Trajan, Trajan has nobody to imitate aside from himself. The panegyric topos of incomparability merges with the cold, hard fact of Trajan's absolute power: he competes with himself because competing with anyone else would mean a diminution not just of his talents, but also of his political rank. The exemplarity of an autocrat spirals inwards and has the distinct potential to broaden rather than narrow the distances between ruler and ruled.

Self-*aemulatio* likewise appears as a topos in Seneca's exhortation of Nero in the *de Clementia*. Hoping to ensure his pupil's continued good behaviour, Seneca congratulates the young emperor on his exemplary style of government: *nemo iam divum Augustum nec Ti. Caesaris prima tempora loquitur nec, quod te imitari velit, exemplar extra te quaerit; principatus tuus ad gustum exigitur* ('nobody now speaks of the divine Augustus, nor the bygone times of Tiberius, nor seeks an example other than yourself for you to imitate; your principate is made to conform with the taste you have already given' *Clem.* 1.1.6). Like Pliny, Seneca articulates a delicate balance between the competing demands of dynastic tradition and autocratic self-sufficiency: Nero must remain aware of Augustus' good *exemplum* even though he is no longer required to follow it. As a persuasive tactic, Seneca's and Pliny's praise of self-*aemulatio* fulfils the dual purpose of encouraging their addressees to uphold good government by caring for their people's needs, and conversely, of admitting that their power makes them unanswerable to anyone apart from themselves. Their *exemplum* may be self-contained but, these texts imply, it should not also be self-serving. What better way to persuade Nero than to tell him that his good conduct is peerless?

While self-*aemulatio* is especially suited to autocratic contexts, it does also appear in republican ones. Livy, for instance, depicts Camillus as being 'in competition with himself' (*certantem secum ipsum*, 6.6.9), and Cicero confesses that he need not exhort Dolabella to follow the examples of famous men because

---

[156] The transition from pluralist republican *exempla* to the centralised, autocratic *exemplum* of the emperor has been ably studied by Kraus (2005).

Exemplarity

Dolabella is already famous enough to be his own model and contend with himself (*te imitere oportet, tecum ipse certes, ad Fam.* 9.14.6). Cicero inverts the topos, too, when denouncing Verres for exceptional cruelty: *nam si cum aliorum improbitate certet, longe omnes multumque superabit: secum ipse certat, id agit ut semper superius suum facinus novo scelere vincat* ('in competition with other scoundrels he would easily leave them all far behind. But he is his own competitor; with each new crime his aim is to break his previous record.' *Verr.* 2.5.116 trans. Greenwood). Although none of these individuals is – strictly speaking – unanswerable to others in the same way as Nero or Trajan, the topos is nonetheless intended to evoke their potential separation from the surrounding community. Instead of modelling himself on other *clari viri*, presumably from the Roman past (*Fam.* 9.14.6), Dolabella is invited to cultivate a purely self-reflexive *exemplum*. Such exceptionalism can easily lead to tyrannous self-absorption.

In *Hercules*, Seneca illustrates the perils of the protagonist's self-*aemulatio* in two main ways. The first concerns the ambiguity of Hercules' heroism. As many scholars have remarked, Hercules' madness and sanity appear to exist on the same continuum; much of the behaviour he exhibits while hallucinating corresponds to the attitudes and conduct he displays before and after the attack.[157] Significantly, he frames his assault upon heaven as a logical extension of his earlier labours: *perdomita tellus, tumida cesserunt freta, / inferna nostros regna sensere impetus: / immune caelum est, dignus Alcidae labor* ('earth is conquered, the swollen seas have yielded, the kingdoms of the dead have felt our attack: heaven has escaped so far – a labour worthy of Alcides' *Her.* 955–7).[158] The same sequence of thought characterises his

---

[157] A line of argument pursued by: Henry and Walker (1965); Bishop (1966); Owen (1968) 303–4; Shelton (1978) 58–73; Fitch (1987) 24–33 and 35–8; Braden (1990) 249–52; Motto and Clark (1994) 269–72; Harrison (2014b) 623.

[158] Seneca's language creates additional links between Hercules' labours and his meditated conquest of heaven. His return from the Underworld is ambiguously described as a *viam ad superos* (318), which implies both that he will reach the upper world and that he will reach heaven. Megara then uses *supera* to mean 'the heavens' at 423, and Hercules uses *ad superos* with the same meaning at 970, in the midst of his madness. Metaphorically speaking, Hercules follows the same path from Hades, to earth, to his

2.2 *Hercules*

sacrificial prayer to Jupiter (926–39), in which Hercules celebrates his civilising mission. Here, his initial, ambitious hopes for universal peace (927–31) rapidly devolve into an expansive vision of future tasks, where Hercules calls upon himself as much as upon Jove to ensure that 'no storm troubles the sea' (*nulla tempestas fretum / ... turbet*, 931–2); that 'poisons may be eradicated' (*venena cessent*, 935); that 'tyrants may not hold sway' (*non ... / regnant tyranni*, 936–7); and cheekily, that Jove himself may not hurl lightning bolts when angered (*nullus irato Iove / exiliat ignis*, 932–3).[159] As if to confirm that he is the ultimate recipient of his own prayers, Hercules concludes this catalogue with the ironically appropriate desire to oppose any of the world's remaining monsters: *si quod etiamnunc est scelus / latura tellus, properet, et si quod parat / monstrum, meum sit* ('if the earth is going to bring forth any wickedness even now, let it hurry, and if it is preparing some monster, let it be mine' 938–9). Though Hercules' megalomania and encroaching insanity blind him to the line's nuance, Seneca's audience comprehends that the protagonist himself has become this last *monstrum*,[160] his desire for conquest having spun out of control and reached a self-destructive extreme.

One effect of Hercules' mad scene, therefore, is to illustrate the destructive potential of a self-sufficient *exemplum*. Because Hercules imitates and vies with himself, there are no external moral checks placed upon his exemplarity; Hercules justifies his conduct solely with reference to Hercules. The self-*aemulatio* that encapsulates and celebrates his supreme heroism becomes, at the same time, a dangerous source of self-serving aggression.

It is of course possible to argue that Juno assumes full responsibility for Hercules' madness: as the one who brings destruction on the hero, she, not Hercules himself, is ultimately to blame for the perversion of his *virtus*. In contrast to the pessimistic scholarly view of Hercules' heroism inducing its own destruction, some take

---

final, imagined assault on the gods. Fuller discussion of this motif can be found in Henry and Walker (1965) 16–17.
[159] Shelton (1978) 64 remarks of this passage: 'Hercules ... boasts that he shares Jupiter's role of maintaining universal peace'. See also Paratore (1966) 23–4 and n.29.
[160] An irony well noted by Shelton (1978) 65; Lawall (1983) 18; Fitch (1987) *ad Her.* 937–9; Motto and Clark (1994) 269–70.

Exemplarity

the optimistic tack of exculpating the hero for crimes committed at Juno's vengeful behest.[161] Yet, Juno's involvement does not really lessen the ominous impact of Hercules' self-reflexive *exemplum*, because her revenge takes the form of causing Hercules to fight himself: *bella iam secum gerat* ('let him wage war with himself' 85); *se vincat et cupiat mori* ('let him defeat himself and long for death' 116). Like Seneca's Atreus, whose preferred method of vengeance is 'Thyestes himself' (*ipso Thyeste, Thy.* 259), Juno engineers her enemy's downfall by exploiting his chief weakness, in this case, the overweening power and loneliness generated by his heroism. If anything, Juno simply provides a catalyst for the already dark, destructive potential of Hercules' *exemplum*.

Seneca's second critique of self-*aemulatio* comes in the form of a striking parallel between Hercules and the tyrant Lycus. Although this usurper of the Theban throne plays a relatively minor role in the tragedy, Seneca makes a clear effort to depict him as the protagonist's *doppelgänger*.[162] A brief review will serve to demonstrate the points of correspondence: Lycus enters the stage in the aftermath of violence he has committed against Megara's family; his hands are described as 'spattered with blood' (*sanguine aspersam manum*, 372), though the comment is more metaphorical than literal at this point in the play; his proposals for peace and reconciliation are undercut by his propensity for physical aggression; he attributes *clara virtus* to himself (340) and identifies himself as *victor* (398–9; 409); he prepares to immolate Megara and her children as they take refuge in a shrine (514–15), an act that is planned to occur while Lycus himself offers votive sacrifice to Neptune (514–15); finally, he exempts Amphitryon from death, counting it a greater punishment to sentence the old man to life (509–13).

Lycus' resemblance to Hercules is not far to seek: Hercules, too, arrives on stage following deeds of violence, in the first instance

---

[161] Major proponents of the view include Motto and Clark (1981) and Lawall (1983). Bernstein (2017) 20–1 expresses a more balanced view that goes some way towards reconciling the two camps.

[162] Noted by Owen (1968) 304 and explored more fully by Rose (1979–80) and OKell (2005). Littlewood (2004) 33–6 pursues a similar idea by connecting Megara and Lycus, which likewise suggests the fallibility and agressiveness of Stoic values: 'we are encouraged to see her obduracy as the image of his'.

2.2 Hercules

after abducting Cerberus from the underworld (592–612), and in the second, after murdering Lycus (895–9); his hands 'drip with the blood' of this recent slaughter (*manantes ... / manus cruenta caede*, 918–19), but he ignores Amphitryon's plea for him to cleanse them prior to conducting sacrifice (920–4); like Lycus, he describes himself as a *victor* (898), and his aspirations for universal peace (927–30) are rapidly overthrown by his own brutality; *virtus* is his attribute *par excellence*; madness overtakes him as he performs a votive sacrifice to Jupiter (926–52), and while mad, he regards his killing of Megara and the children as an offering to Juno (1036–7); like Lycus, he refers to his children as a *grex* (1037 cf. 507); finally, Hercules, too, refrains from killing Amphitryon, if only because his fit of madness subsides just as the old man steps forward to present himself as the final victim (1039–52).[163]

It should be clear by now that aside from simply resembling Lycus, Hercules actually takes his place. In slaughtering his wife and offspring, Hercules completes in Act 4 the task Lycus commenced in Act 2. The association grows closer still when Hercules hallucinates that he is killing Lycus' children (in Euripides, by contrast, he thinks they belong to Eurystheus): *sed ecce proles regis inimici latet, / Lyci nefandum semen. inviso patri / haec dextra iam vos reddet* ('but look, here hide the children of a hostile ruler, / Lycus' wicked seed. This right hand will return you, now, to your hated father' 987–9). With this declaration, the roles of Lycus and Hercules eclipse into one, and Seneca implies that the latter is the real *invisus pater*. The implication is reiterated, with even more ironic force, just a few lines further down, when the mad Hercules remarks 'I see hidden here the son of a wicked father' (*hic video abditum / natum scelesti patris*, 1001–2). Where Hercules sees Lycus' child, the audience of course sees Hercules' child, and the hero becomes the *scelestus pater* he imagines himself as fighting. Of course, in the world outside Hercules' disordered brain, Lycus does not in fact have any children; he remarks in Act 2 that he plans to get them through forced union with Megara (494). But

---

[163] Many, though not all, of the parallels I list here have been ably traced by Rose (1979–80) 137–8.

such information points once again to the potential interchangeability of Lycus and Hercules, since with this claim Lycus aims to occupy Hercules' role just as Hercules later occupies Lycus'.

The links connecting these two characters are crucial for understanding, on a number of levels, how Seneca has chosen to represent Hercules' exemplarity. Like the arbitrary power of an absolute ruler, Hercules' *exemplum* asserts the capacity to self-regulate, and that capacity, in turn, reinforces the hero's isolation. While he may feel responsible for his family, on occasions, he is nonetheless set apart from them; his example is an exception rather than a rule, a point of disjunction rather than union and tradition. Granted it is not identical to tyranny, but it certainly has the potential to foster tyrannical behaviour.

It is telling that Lycus, too, shares this quality of self-contained isolation. Immediately upon entering the stage, he boasts about his lack of family name and inherited wealth:

> non vetera patriae iura possideo domus
> ignavus heres; nobiles non sunt mihi
> avi nec altis inclitum titulis genus,
> sed clara virtus. qui genus iactat suum,
> aliena laudat

> I do not lay claim to the old laws of an ancestral home
> as a lazy heir; I do not have noble grandfathers
> nor a lineage distinguished by lofty titles,
> but illustrious courage. He who boasts about his lineage,
> praises others

(*Her.* 337–9)

The assertion has a distinctly Roman flavour to it, as though Lycus were a *novus homo* proudly proclaiming his ascent to the very top of the *cursus honorum*. But in a play so fixated upon family divisions and strained or estranged family relationships, Lycus' claim takes on other colouring as well. Like Hercules, Lycus rests a large part of his self-definition on being a solitary figure. Although his reference to a *genus* implies that he does have some family members somewhere, he appears in the context of this drama to be entirely a lone wolf: he never mentions any parents, and we gather from later comments that he does not have any children; he appears to be personally, socially, and

2.2 Hercules

politically self-sufficient. While Lycus makes no explicit reference to intergenerational exemplarity in this passage, his proud independence from familial and dynastic tradition certainly taps into the tragedy's theme of self-*aemulatio*. Like Hercules, Lycus relies on himself instead of following an ancestral paradigm, and this sense of independence seems to find a parallel in the ruthlessly autocratic nature of his rule. The autonomous quality of his self-definition, figured as an absence of family members, slides into his desire for despotic hegemony. This is the mirror in which Seneca reflects the danger of Hercules' detached, self-reflexive *exemplum*.

Conclusion

The act of adopting and imitating role models entails a delicate balance between self-abnegation on the one hand, and self-assertion on the other. As Seneca's *Troades* shows all too brutally, exemplarity requires a degree of displacement in which children re-embody their parents and recapitulate past actions rather than develop independent identities. The self qua *exemplum* tends to be derivative, which explains in turn its close conceptual links to biology, family lineage, and literary tradition. Just like an unavoidable set of hostile genetic traits, or like an unalterable narrative detail, *exempla* in Senecan tragedy oppress characters under the weight of inherited precedent.

Yet to the extent that one *chooses* to follow an *exemplum*, the process can also be an affirmation of selfhood. Pyrrhus celebrates his descent from Achilles as the core of his identity; Marcus Junius Brutus imitates Lucius because he, too, wants to acquire the title of liberator; Seneca copies Socrates in order to gain an equally enduring posthumous reputation. Each of these figures employs the *exemplum* for the deliberate purpose of self-fashioning; by eliding or aligning their identity with someone else's, they also assert essential aspects of themselves. Who you are, in this regard, depends upon whom you duplicate.

With Seneca's Hercules, however, this delicate balance of self and other collapses as the *exemplum* fails to find a reference point beyond its own exceptionalism. Whereas the traditional purpose of the *exemplum* in Roman society was to mediate between the individual and the community, the singular event and the general rule, the older and younger generations, Hercules' paradigm both stems from and ends with himself, and the only mediation it performs is between the Hercules we see on stage and the reputation he has so far accumulated. Hercules' *exemplum* is simultaneously vital to his sense of self, and responsible for his insurmountable isolation; the more he aspires to fulfil it, the more he cuts himself off from family and friends.

CHAPTER 3

APPEARANCE

From the patterns of social and behavioural identification embedded in Roman exemplarity, I turn now to issues of physical identification, that is, to the ways in which individual bodies reveal or conceal, communicate or misrepresent elements of their owners' identities. The central dynamic here is one of interior versus exterior, first-person versus third-person, as the body's visible qualities are assumed to channel information outwards from the private realms of psychology, emotion, and intent. Corporeal surfaces gain significance as meeting points of internal and external selfhood, and of subjective self-knowledge pitted against the appraisal of onlookers. In Senecan tragedy, this dynamic derives from a potent combination of Stoic materialism – which elides emotional with physical states – physiognomy, and awareness of enactment, all three of which perceive the body as an index of intangible, psychological traits. Just as the physiognomist and, in related ways, the Stoic infer character from a person's gait, or gestures, or face, so the actor's body is tasked with conveying to audiences information about the character it represents. The face blends into a mask and the mask a face, since on stage and off it claims the same capacity to signify. In all three cases, the body is assumed to offer itself for analysis, analysis that simultaneously heightens 'humanness' by inferring the presence of a private interior consciousness, and lessens it in favour of the body's primarily semiotic surface, its similarity to a text.

Bodily identity is of course an enormous topic spanning disciplines from Theology to Neuroscience.[1] Mind–body interaction is at once the most fundamental and the most contested aspect of human selfhood. Does identity reside in an individual's mind / soul / cognitive faculties, or in his or her embodied existence (or

---

[1] For overviews of the various disciplines and issues involved, see Coupland and Gwyn (2003) 1–16; Turner (2012) 1–17; and Westphal (2016). On the mind–body debate as it relates to theatre, see Conroy (2010) 41–57.

both)?[2] Seneca's approach largely elides the two, for while he follows Stoic orthodoxy in regarding the soul as the ultimate repository and pre-requisite of human existence, his emphasis on embodiment and on the corporeal reality of even abstract qualities leads him to situate many components of identity in the *corpus* as well. This chapter begins by considering how Seneca's Stoic precepts underpin the tragedies' numerous instances of physical description, before proceeding to examine the relationship of corporeality to internal emotional or psychological states in the *Phaedra*. Questions of bodily identity acquire particular urgency in this play, where beautiful *corpora* break apart under the strain of moral ugliness, and mental suffering is seen to imprint itself on flesh. In a process both paradoxical and comprehensible, Phaedra and Hippolytus are granted inner realms chiefly because of their envelopment in a body. But, at the same time, the *corpus*' essentially external orientation, its constant exposure to view, leaves audiences wondering about the truth and presence of what lies beneath.

As mentioned, physical description and physiognomic analysis can also have the opposite effect of augmenting a body's textual qualities, translating skin and bones into symbols and literary tropes. Seneca, too, often portrays the *corpus* as an assortment of marks, signs, and indications, a legible surface inviting decipherment. In the tragedies, this technique highlights characters' fictional nature, for instance, when Hippolytus' disjointed frame comes to resemble a series of poetic fragments that Theseus qua reader must recompose. Such 'textual' corporeality gains further prominence in Seneca's *Oedipus*, the second play discussed in this chapter. Here, characters and audience alike are called upon to decode the manifest signs of the protagonist's body. As an omen, a sacrificial victim, a piece of well-known poetry, Seneca's Oedipus claims his identity from the symbols his *corpus* displays to others, and the play's continual process of interrogation heightens audience awareness of Oedipus qua dramatic construct, a body composed by Seneca, whose identity does not extend beyond the surface of text and enactment.

---

[2] A question tackled superbly by Frow (2014) 264–96, with particular emphasis on its exploration in literary texts/film.

3.1 *Phaedra*

Senecan Bodies

Act 2[3] of Seneca's *Phaedra* contains the lengthiest physical description in all of Seneca's tragedies. It begins with the chorus leader inquiring about the progress of the queen's malady. In reply, the Nurse launches into an elaborate account of Phaedra's bodily and mental state:

> torretur aestu tacito et inclusus quoque,
> quamvis tegatur, proditur vultu furor;
> erumpit oculis ignis et lassae genae
> lucem recusant; nil idem dubiae placet
> artusque varie iactat incertus dolor:
> nunc ut soluto labitur moriens gradu
> et vix labante sustinet collo caput,
> nunc se quieti reddit et, somni immemor,
> noctem querelis ducit; attolli iubet
> iterumque poni corpus et solvi comas
> rursusque fingi: semper impatiens sui
> mutatur habitus

> She is seared by secret heat and, locked inside,
> though covered up, passion reveals itself on her face;
> fire springs from her eyes, and her tired gaze
> shuns the light; she wavers, nothing pleases her,
> and restless pain makes her body toss and turn at random:
> now she sinks to the ground on weakened legs, as though dying,
> and scarcely can her head find support from her drooping neck,
> now she takes her rest and, forgetting sleep,
> drags out the night in weeping; she orders us to lift her body
> and lay it down again, and to undo her hair
> and do it up again: she keeps changing her mien,
> perpetually discontent
>
> (*Phaed.* 362–73)

The Nurse continues in this vein for a further ten lines, reporting to the chorus and to the play's audience her observations about

---

[3] Boyle (1987) 134, following Heldmann (1974) 71, argues the case for dividing the *Phaedra* into six Acts instead of the usual five, with lines 1–84 and 85–273 comprising Acts 1 and 2 respectively. But I follow Coffey and Mayer (1990) in treating all of lines 1–273 as Act 1, on the basis of there being no choral division. I also maintain – this time against Coffey and Mayer (1990) *ad Phaed.* 1–84 – that Act 1 of the *Phaedra* is not unique in comprising two separate scenes, since the same occurs in Act 2 of the *Troades*.

Phaedra's present eating habits, her bodily strength and complexion, and the appearance of her tears. Dramatic action is suspended while Phaedra's symptoms are catalogued, and it recommences only when Phaedra herself emerges from the palace at 384. This is unusual theatrical practice, to say the least. Seneca could just as easily have foregone the Nurse's narrative and had Phaedra enact her suffering directly before the audience, or cause it to emerge gradually through dialogue, as happens in Euripides' *Hippolytus* (129–250).[4] That Seneca rejected both of these options raises questions about the role of description, especially physical description, in his plays.

Phaedra 360–83 is not an isolated example. Lengthy narrative accounts have long been recognised – and often deplored – as hallmarks of Senecan drama. To many critics' fascination and dismay, Seneca interrupts the progress of events on stage to have his characters chronicle past experiences, report on their natural surroundings, and, as in the example cited above, describe each other's bodily features or gestures.[5] Uniquely, some of these ekphrastic passages also form 'running commentaries' in which the character being described is simultaneously present on stage: at *Medea* 380–96, the Nurse catalogues the symptoms of Medea's emotional condition in the heroine's presence, as does the chorus with Cassandra's frantic movement at *Agamemnon* 710–19; *Hercules* 1042–50 sees Amphitryon describe Hercules as the hero sinks into unconsciousness on stage, and it is quite possible that Amphitryon's earlier reports in this scene are likewise accompanied by Hercules' performance.[6] Narrative

---

[4] In fact, Barrett (1964) 36, followed by Coffey and Mayer (1990) *ad Phaed.* 358–9, attributes Seneca's arrangement of material to inept adaptation of the Euripidean model, namely his having Phaedra confess the source of her passion in Act 1 only to revisit the issue, this time with physical symptoms, in Act 2. I am inclined to give Seneca more credit, though: he deviates from Euripides not out of dramaturgical clumsiness but in order to suit his own aesthetic purposes.

[5] The role of description in Senecan tragedy has been studied in detail by Tietze Larson (1989) and (1994). Other treatments of the topic include Evans (1950); Herington (1966) 433–43 and 447–52; Zwierlein (1966) 56–63; Zimmerman (1990) 161–7; Zanobi (2014) 89–127 and 147–99; and Aygon (2016) 179–91 and 207–19.

[6] According to Zwierlein (1966) 42 and n. 8; Fitch (1987) *ad Her.* 895–1053; and Zanobi (2014) 104–5, Hercules exits the stage at 1001, reappearing briefly in pursuit of Megara at 1008–18, exiting again with Megara at 1018, and reappearing at 1035. Sutton (1986) 47 and Kohn (2013) 103–5 take the slightly more conservative approach of having Hercules offstage continuously from 1001–35.

3.1 *Phaedra*

descriptions, even in the midst of stage action, are such a distinctive trait of Seneca's dramatic style that they feature also in the work of his early imitator, the unknown author of the pseudo-Senecan *Oetaeus*. This play contains a scene like that of *Phaedra* 360–82, in which the Nurse relays the offstage event of Deianira's frenzied physical and emotional reactions to Iole's arrival (*H.O.* 238–55).

Greek tragedy, by comparison, lacks such extended ekphastric passages; with the notable exception of the messenger's *rhesis*, it employs description sparingly, either to convey information crucial to the plot (witness Jocasta's brief portrayal of Laius at *O.T.* 742–3), or to signal the entrance of a specific character.[7] Even the conventional messenger's speech, which Seneca's accounts of offstage action may reasonably be expected to resemble, exhibits fundamental differences in length, temporality, and plot relevance.[8] Seneca's descriptions are a unique phenomenon in extant ancient drama and, viewed in relation to works of classical Athenian tragedy, they can seem both superfluous to and disruptive of a play's enactment. This singularity has prompted numerous attempts to explain their presence and function within Senecan drama, with older generations of scholars labelling them a regrettable outgrowth of florid rhetoric, or a symptom of Seneca's misplaced enthusiasm for epic narrative, and for Ovid's *Metamorphoses* in particular.[9] Another, more influential approach is Otto Zwierlein's *Rezitationsdrama* theory, which cites Seneca's descriptions as evidence of his composing tragedies for the recital hall rather than the stage, on the assumption that these passages provide vital, visual guides to the action unfolding in the purely nominal

---

[7] Comparison of Seneca's descriptions to those of the Attic tragedians can be found in Tietze Larson (1989) and (1994) 19–44, and Zwierlein (1966) 57.

[8] As charted by Zanobi (2014) 111.

[9] Lucas (1922) 57 dismisses Seneca's descriptions as 'purple patches'; Eliot (1999a) [1927] 71 calls them 'beautiful but irrelevant'; for Mendell (1968) [1941] 108 they are 'of an overstated character, showing at times an exaggeration of the exclamatory monologue, at times too much the influence of epic'. Good summary of these (typically outdated) scholarly attitudes can be found in Faber (2007) 427–8. The descriptions' 'epic' quality has also been proposed, more recently, by Aygon (2016) 193–220 and by Tietze Larson (1989) and (1994) who, however, uses the term a little differently, in the Brechtian sense of 'epic theatre'. For more detail on Seneca's appropriation of Ovid, see Jakobi (1988).

theatre of Seneca's – and the audience's – imagination.[10] In Zwierlein's words, 'wir vernehmen den Dichter, der seinem Hörer beschreibt, welches szenische Spiel er sich vorzustellen hat' ('we hear the poet describe to his listener which scenic action he has to imagine').[11] For proponents of this theory, narrative descriptions in Senecan tragedy represent clumsy, non-theatrical tactics for circumventing the problems inherent in dramatic recitation.[12] Yet a third group of scholars advances the contention that Seneca's *ekphrases*, especially his 'running commentaries', could have been designed for pantomime performance, because this wildly popular early imperial genre entailed a split between a dancer's silent, physical enactment, and a singer's or chorus' verbal narrative.[13] Lengthy descriptions would, on this basis, not disrupt the performance so much as provide actors with opportunities for virtuoso physical display.

While many of these propositions boast a degree of plausibility and validity, there is to my mind only one explanation that accounts fully for the effect of Seneca's bodily *ekphrases*, and that is Stoic physics. Scholars have often noted that Senecan drama elides the moral with the material universe such that evil manifests itself as cosmic disruption and psychological disturbance becomes meteorological as well.[14] The same holds true for bodies in these plays: they reflect characters' turbulent passions and deep-seated anxieties; they communicate psychology via the flesh. Whenever *dramatis personae* in these tragedies surrender themselves to the irresistible tug of immorality, in the words of John Herington, 'the result is at once visible and concrete (such is the instant causal connection between moral and material realities): the regular lineaments of the human face collapse into the contorted mask of mania'.[15]

---

[10] Zwierlein (1966) 56–63.
[11] Zwierlein (1966) 63.
[12] For example Fantham (1982) 40–2 and Goldberg (2000) 223–5.
[13] An idea first proposed by Zimmerman (1990) 161–7 and elaborated substantially by Zanobi (2014) esp. 89–127 and 147–99. Slaney (2013) similarly envisages pantomimic performance for the choral lyrics of Senecan tragedy.
[14] Evans (1950); Herington (1966); Mastronarde (1970); Pratt (1983) 50, 81, and 162; Rosenmeyer (1989) esp. 93–159; Tietze Larson (1994) 135–68.
[15] Herington (1966) 434–5.

3.1 *Phaedra*

The chief reason for this convergence is Seneca's materialist worldview, his Stoic belief in the corporeality of even such abstract ethical categories as vice and virtue. For the Stoics, every movement and state of the soul was corporeal; mind and body were not regarded as ontologically distinct substances and their essential difference was claimed to lie in dichotomies of active versus passive, or divine versus terrestrial, not material versus immaterial.[16] Against the dualism of Platonist metaphysics, the Stoics propounded more of a monist theory in which both God and matter constituted *corpora*.[17] In this worldview, psychology *is* bodily: Cleanthes and Zeno are reported to have believed that ἦθος could be known from εἶδος (*SVF* 1.618; Diog. Laert. 7.173); Chrysippus maintains that the passions are perceptible (*SVF* 3.85). According to Seneca himself (*Ep.* 106.5–6), one should not doubt 'whether emotions are corporeal' (*an adfectus corpora sint*) since they accomplish physical changes such as furrowed brows and blushes; what happens in the interior realm of the psyche rapidly impresses itself upon the surface of the flesh.

Seneca is particularly taken with this idea of embodied emotions and visible psychology, returning to it repeatedly across the arc of his entire oeuvre. Recalling in *Epistle* 66 his recent meeting with an old classmate, Claranus, Seneca remarks that the man's sturdiness of spirit all but eclipses his frail and feeble physique: 'I think Claranus has been produced as an example, so that we can understand that the soul is not disfigured by the body's ugliness, but rather, that the body is adorned by the soul's beauty' (*Claranus mihi videtur in exemplar editus, ut scire possemus non deformitate corporis foedari animum, sed pulchritudine animi corpus ornari, Ep.* 66.4.). As a corporeal entity, goodness can lend a certain amount of physical grace to even the most unattractive of flesh and blood *corpora*. Correspondence of ethical with bodily states likewise underpins Seneca's thinking in *Epistle* 115.3, where he imagines the visibly radiant beauty of a good man's soul, and in

---

[16] For an overview of Stoic materialism and how it shapes Stoic concept of mind–body interaction, see Smith (2014) 343–61, and the more cursory treatment of Pratt (1983) 46–51. Also useful in this context is the oft-cited statement of Long (1968) 341: 'Stoic ethics is ultimately parasitical upon physics.'

[17] Vogt (2009) is an informative comparison of the two schools' views on this issue.

Epistle 52.12, where he catalogues the gestures indicative of specific moral temperaments. *Epistle* 114.3 equates intellectual dissipation with soft, flabby bodies;[18] *Epistle* 11.10 describes the wise man as someone whose face expresses what is in his soul; *Epistle* 106.6–7 charts some of the *notae corporis* produced by, and therefore signalling, vicious and virtuous behaviour, while in Book 6 of the *de Beneficiis*, Seneca anticipates Liberalis' question on the grounds that his countenance communicates his thoughts (*intellego iam, quid velis quaerere; non opus est te dicere; vultus tuus loquitur*, 'I know what you want to ask; there's no need to say anything; your face speaks for you', *Ben* 6.12.1). The idea of the face as a text for the heart, as a barometer of one's personal, emotional atmosphere is a standard trope in ancient literature, but here it acquires the additional significance of complementing Stoic precepts.[19] It is the material nature of the universe that ultimately enables Liberalis' intent to be inferred from his expression.

The two culminating examples of this Senecan obsession come from the *de Ira*, 1.1.3–5 and 2.35.3–36.2. Both passages describe the symptoms exhibited by irate and unhinged people, with a view to identifying shifts in internal, psychological conditions. Seneca diagnoses those affected by *furor* as displaying 'a bold and threatening countenance, grim brow, savage features, rapid step, restless hands, altered complexion, fast and laboured breathing' (*audax et minax vultus, tristis frons, torva facies, citatus gradus, inquietae manus, color versus, crebra et vehementius acta suspiria*, *Ira* 1.1.3). As for those experiencing *ira*, 'their eyes flare and sparkle, redness suffuses their face ... lips shake, teeth are ground together ... breathing is forced and harsh ... they groan and bellow' (*flagrant ac micant oculi, multus in ore toto rubor ... labra quatiuntur, dentes comprimuntur ... spiritus coactus ac stridens ... gemitus mugitusque*, *Ira* 1.1.4). Once again, the corporeal quality of emotional states causes the body to disclose the movements of the soul almost involuntarily. Anger cannot remain hidden; it forces its way onto the visible planes of the face

---

[18] Graver (1998) 612.
[19] Remarked by Tarrant (1976) *ad.* Sen. *Ag.* 128, with a full list of comparanda.

3.1 *Phaedra*

(*Ira*. 1.1.5). An angry person's physical conduct is a direct reflection of his or her inner state: the angry soul is just as deformed as the angry body (*Ira* 2.36.2). So fascinated is Seneca by this interplay of internal and external realms that he even disregards, momentarily, the central tenets of Stoic materialism, declaring, 'if the mind could be made visible and shine forth in some material form its black, blotchy, seething, twisted, swollen appearance would stun viewers' (*animus si ostendi et si in ulla materia perlucere posset, intuentis confunderet ater maculosusque et aestuans et distortus et tumidus*, *Ira* 2.36.2 trans. Kaster). Such temporary aberration from Stoic precepts is not just an example of Seneca employing common sense terminology, as Robert Kaster would have it,[20] but also a hyper-development of his interest in the body qua cipher for psychological activity. What one experiences in the private domain of one's own mind or soul, the body renders public. As much as a materialist worldview makes this exchange possible, for Seneca it also highlights the fact of constant dialogue between inner and outer expressions of self.

Significantly, for the purposes of my present investigation, *de Ira* 1.1.3–5 exhibits demonstrable similarities to a lengthy physical description in the tragedies, namely, *Medea* 382–96.[21] Here, the Nurse produces a running commentary on the heroine's agitated mindset: Medea 'runs back and forth' (*recursat huc et huc*, 385), 'draws deep breaths' (*spiritum ex alto citat*, 387), 'issues threats' (*minatur*, 390), 'groans' (*gemit*, 390), displays a 'fiery expression' (*flammata facies*, 387) and a changeable mien that 'takes on the appearance of every emotion' (*omnis specimen affectus capit*, 389). In like fashion, those suffering from *ira* and *furor* display a 'rapid step' (*citatus gradus*, *Ira* 1.1.3), their breathing is 'fast and laboured' or 'forced and harsh' (*crebra et vehementius acta suspiria*, *Ira* 1.1.3; *spiritus coactus et stridens*, *Ira* 1.1.4), they 'act out anger's enormous threats' (*magnas ... irae*

---

[20] Kaster and Nussbaum (2010) 119. Using common cultural assumptions as a basis for further ethical reasoning appears to have been regular Stoic practice: see Long (1996) [1971] 139 and Inwood (1995) 20. Roller (2001) 76–7 and 87 argues that Seneca mixes common sense with Stoic registers when he writes, for the purpose of 'getting off the ground', even if this sometimes leads to inconsistencies.

[21] Parallels amply documented by Marti (1945) 229–34; Costa (1973) *ad Med.* 382ff; Pratt (1983) 90; Tietze Larson (1994) 140–1; and Hine (2000) *ad Med.* 380–96.

minas agens, *Ira* 1.1.4), they issue 'groans' (*gemitus*, *Ira* 1.1.4), and exhibit a 'bold and threatening countenance' (*audax et minax vultus*, *Ira* 1.1.3). Beyond basic lexical correspondences, both passages present the body as a reliable index of internal emotional activity. Movements and changes to facial expression are documented in quasi-medical fashion[22] and presumed to function as a set of codes or signifiers: Medea's face bears the 'signs' (*signa*, 386) of her emotional condition, and the Nurse claims to 'recognise the marks' (*novimus ... notas*, 394) of her charge's now habitual anger; similarly, Seneca prefaces his list of symptoms at *de Ira* 1.1.3–5 by calling them 'definite clues' (*certa indicia*, 1.1.3) and 'signs' (*signa*, 1.1.4). The *corpus* resembles a text capable of conveying to onlookers crucial information about the individual who inhabits it. Seneca elides emotional with physical *motus* to show how feelings of *ira* body forth in specific gestures and actions.

The body's power to signify also necessitates a viewer, someone to interpret and decipher the symptoms on display. *corpora* in Senecan tragedy are always being seen and reported through somebody else's eyes, and Seneca is at pains to demonstrate how individuals, on stage or in life, employ corporeal clues to fashion judgements about each other. It is this emphasis on interpretation, on 'reading the body', that requires a narrator's presence, even at the expense of smoother dramatic sequence. The Nurse's commentary at *Medea* 382–96 fulfils just such a need, and this seems to me a fundamental if overlooked reason for the passage's narrative quality. At very least, the close resemblance of *Medea* 382–96 to *de Ira* 1.1.3–4 weakens the *Rezitationsdrama* argument, because the *de Ira*'s description is not there to help an audience visualise an unperformed theatrical scene, but to provide a visual diagnosis of internal, emotional pathology. The *de Ira* furnishes a catalogue of symptoms chiefly in order to explore the relationship between bodies and emotions, the latter of which cannot be disclosed without the former. Why, then, could Seneca not be pursuing the same aim in the *Medea*, and indeed, in all of his tragedies' bodily descriptions? Though we need not discount

---

[22] Robin (1993) 108 and Hine (2000) *ad Med.* 380–96.

3.1 *Phaedra*

entirely recitation's possible influence, Stoicism still seems the most immediate, most plausible source of Seneca's narrative passages.

Keeping this Stoic background in mind, I return now to the passage cited at the beginning of this section, *Phaedra* 362–83. Here, too, the body plays a major role in disclosing the individual's psychological and emotional state. The Nurse's account of the queen's malaise elides emotional with physical suffering, to suggest that whatever Phaedra experiences in the private realm of her mind finds corresponding expression on the public surfaces of her body.[23] Phaedra is 'seared by secret heat' (*torretur aestu tacito*, 362) and that *aestus* represents at the same time lust for Hippolytus and debilitating corporeal fever; her *dolor* (366) similarly designates both mental anguish and physical pain.[24] Equally ambiguous is Phaedra's *habitus*, which she is said to change repeatedly (*semper* ... / *mutatur habitus*, 372–3). Commentators and translators are divided over whether to render this word as 'clothing' – since Phaedra *does* change her outfit when she subsequently appears on stage at 387–403 – or as something more abstract: 'mood', or 'condition'.[25] Most likely, however, Seneca is not forcing readers to choose but instead taking advantage of the word's polyvalence, in order to show how Phaedra's mental instability translates into sartorial fussiness; the *habitus* on Phaedra's body represents and communicates the *habitus* of her

---

[23] Cf. the illuminating remarks of Ruch (1964) 362 – though I would stop short of labelling Seneca's description 'realism': 'le langage de la psychologie amoureuse se meut aux limites du physique et du mental, de la sensation et du sentiment, ou plutôt le sentiment s'exprime en premier lieu par la sensation; le corps y joue un grand role: c'est la marque du réalisme de Sénèque, observateur averti des 'symptômes' du phénomène affectif' ('the language of the psychology of love pushes itself to physical and mental limits, limits of sensation and feeling, or rather, feeling is expressed primarily through sensation; the body plays a large role here: it is the mark of Seneca's realism, his keen observation of the 'symptoms' of an emotional condition').

[24] Ruch (1964) 356 describes Phaedra's *dolor* as 'à mi-chemin entre le physique et le moral' ('halfway between physical and moral').

[25] Boyle (1987) 66 translates 'moods'; Fitch (2002) 479 'condition'; Wilson (2010) 'clothes'. Lawall, Lawall, and Kunkel (1982) do not mention clothing but give their student readers the full choice of 'condition, habit, deportment, nature, character', while Coffey and Mayer (1990), though they do not provide a translation, obviously lean towards 'dress' as per their comment *ad Phaed.* 371–3. A similar use of *habitus* to mean 'mood' or 'condition' is found at Juvenal *Sat.* 9.18–20: *deprendas animi tormenta latentis in aegro / corpore, deprendas et gaudia; sumit utrumque / inde* habitum *facies*.

mind. What we and the Nurse see on the outside tells us what Phaedra is like on the inside.

The Nurse's account further augments this interplay of interior with exterior selfhood by characterising Phaedra's psychology as a hidden, internalised space. The queen experiences a 'secret heat' (*aestu tacito*, 362); her *furor* is 'locked inside' (*inclusus*, 362) and 'covered up' (*tegatur*, 363) only to be betrayed by her expression (*proditur vultu*, 363); even her eyes are said to 'emit fire' (*erumpit oculis ignis*, 364) as though conduits for the spiritual *aestus* she endures. By implication, Phaedra's emotional states would be inaccessible to others were it not for the unbreakable bond that the mind shares with the body. Phaedra's *corpus* is simultaneously a covering for her self – something that creates a private, inner realm – and a reliable revelation of that self to others. So intimate is the link between psychological and physical states in Senecan tragedy that Phaedra cannot, though she tries, succeed in dissembling: her body inevitably displays how she feels.

Thus, Seneca charts Phaedra's physical reactions chiefly in order to show how her body communicates aspects of her identity. Deploying Stoic precepts, Seneca invites the play's audience to accompany the Nurse in deciphering Phaedra's symptoms. Additionally, his detailed portrayal of her expression and physique endows Phaedra with quasi-human selfhood, principally by generating illusions of psychological depth and privacy.[26] The Nurse's narrative encourages the play's audience to think beyond Phaedra's immediate surface, or more precisely, to imagine that *there is something* beyond her surface: a consciousness, a mind. Like a person, Phaedra is assumed to possess greater profundity and complexity than immediately meets the eye. This essentially penetrative act of interpretation that divines Phaedra's secrets

---

[26] Psychological interiority has long been a contentious topic in Seneca scholarship. Eliot (1999a) [1927] 70 famously claimed that Seneca's characters 'have ... no "private" life', a position also upheld by Hook (2000). Of Seneca's physical descriptions, Tietze Larson (1994) 61 avers, 'They are not revelations of "inaccessible privacy" but authorial descriptions, appropriate to an omniscient narrator, placed into the mouths of the dramatic characters themselves.' But these are minority views. The majority of scholars working on Seneca understand the playwright to have had an abiding interest in internal psychological and emotional states; see, for instance, Herrmann (1924) 488–92; Regenbogen (1927/28) 187–218; Ruch (1964); Segal (1986) esp. 1–38; and Boyle (1997) esp. 15–84.

3.1 *Phaedra*

from her face necessarily implies that Phaedra *has* both secrets and an interior realm in which to hide them.[27]

It may, of course, be objected that as a dramatic character Phaedra lays no real claim to inner selfhood: the face and body she presents are themselves products of a play script, while in performance, her inner realm is a mere fantasy adumbrated by an actor's skilful gestures. Some critics go as far as arguing that Greco-Roman traditions of masked drama preclude *any* possibility of interior revelation; the mask, they maintain, is all surface and no depth – a public, changeless face.[28] Yet there is far less difference between interpreting fictional and actual bodies than critics tend to believe. Whether we watch an actor playing a role or a person just being him/herself, whether we witness these scenes in a theatre or read them on the page, in every instance we absorb the same set of corporeal clues which we then use to build judgements about internal moral character, even if the person in question is fabricated and his or her inner realm a mere mirage.[29] Just because Phaedra lacks real human psychology does not prevent an audience from making assumptions about it, and such willingness to assume, to become invested in a character's quasi-humanity, is essential to the play's overall effectiveness. Although Phaedra's *persona* may be no more than skin deep, Seneca encourages spectators and readers to approach it via the same methods they would apply to actual people: gesture; physique; clothing; mannerisms.

---

[27] My analysis here approximates the 'mental character models' described by Eder, Jannidis, and Schneider (2010) 13: 'in contrast to objects, characters have mental states, such as perceptions, thoughts, feelings, and aims. Accordingly, characters have both an outer appearance and an inner state of psyche that is not visible from the outside'.

[28] A position argued forcefully by Jones (1962), and pursued by Gould (1978) 49, 'in masking we lose the flickering procession of ambiguous clues to inaccessible privacy'. Seidensticker (2008), 340 is one of its more recent manifestations: 'the mask cannot (as the human face) be used to reveal the character of the "inside"'.

[29] In this regard, claims like those made by Garton (1972) 15 are only partially right: 'the attributes of a *persona* [i.e. dramatic character] differ from those of a person in that the sum of them is totally accessible'. True, in that an audience's quantifiable knowledge of a dramatic character is circumscribed by a play's contents. But a lot of audience knowledge about characters is not so readily quantifiable: it comprises inferences, extrapolations, and emotional reactions, all of which enable audiences to imbue characters with levels of human meaning and human motivation impossible to measure in strictly academic terms.

The same arguments may be used to overturn the mask/face distinction, which seems needlessly artificial. First, ancient masks were not immobile but supple, expressive objects capable of imparting a range of emotions according to the angle at which they were positioned.[30] In emotional terms at least, the Greco-Roman theatrical mask was far from being unchangeable. Second, the mask's various components were intended to relay information about a given character in a manner equivalent to a face. Granted that even the most naturalistic mask could never match the sheer complexity and range of the human *vultus*, nevertheless it performs the same basic significatory function, for instance by using tilted eyebrows to convey anger, or an upturned mouth for happiness. In fact, it could be said that all actors wear masks, no matter their era or their style of performance. For the face that has been trained to imply certain emotions or dispositions via subtle tweaks in expression does the same duty as a mask, even though it is made from real flesh and blood. The human body may be *naturalistic* in performance, but it is never purely *natural*. Hence it is difficult to maintain that the mask denies interior selfhood, since it operates on precisely the same plane as the human face, even more so in the context of the theatre.

In sum, Phaedra's fictional existence does not preclude her implied interiority. Granted her inner realm displays none of the uniqueness and idiosyncrasy that modern audiences have come to associate with individual selfhood, but neither does that of the angry man described in the *de Ira*, and he clearly possesses quasi-human status within Seneca's text. Moreover, Seneca's materialism naturally inclines him to produce typologised sketches because it assumes the body's universal legibility, which in turn relies on an accepted catalogue of fleshly traits. To the extent that these physical characteristics specify psychological ones, psychology too is standardised, but that is no barrier to its (implicit or

---

[30] The mask's visual versatility is championed by Meineck (2011) and (2018) 79–119, and Johnson (1992); Marshall (1999) 189 assumes it as a given. Though all of these studies focus on fifth-century Attic theatre conventions, it seems unlikely – Cicero's caveats at *de Orat.* 3.221 notwithstanding – that the Roman mask was more restricted than the Greek in its range of expression (see, e.g. Ballio remarking on Pseudolus' *acuti oculi* at *Pseud.* 1219, in what is clearly a reference to a mask).

3.1 *Phaedra*

actual) existence. Phaedra's body matters for what it tells audiences about her mind/soul, even if that information is somewhat generic.

Physiognomy and Stoic Physics

Seneca is hardly alone among the writers and thinkers of antiquity in making the body a cipher for mental and emotional states. Inferences from appearance are, in fact, so widespread across the various authors, eras, and philosophical schools of the ancient world as to suggest a shared social discourse of codifying and interpreting individual physical qualities.[31] One result of this interest is an intermittent yet persistent stream of works about physiognomy: the earliest surviving text is the Pseudo-Aristotelian *Physiognomica*, which dates from the third century BC; the most famous treatise was Polemon of Laodicea's work, produced in the early second century AD and surviving in a Greek abridgement by Adamantius (fourth century AD) and an Arabic epitome (the original completed *c.* eighth–tenth AD) as well as constituting the main source for the anonymous Latin *Physiognomia* (fourth century AD). From Socrates to Apuleius, physiognomic ideas were prevalent and its practice popular.[32]

---

[31] The premise of Corbeill (2004), on Roman gesture. Weiler (1996) similarly speaks in terms of 'naïve physiognomy' that may owe more to folk traditions than to official treatises. Evans (1969) wants to see the popularity of drawing inferences from appearance as evidence for the pervasive influence of physiognomic doctrine, but the trend is likely more diffuse than this. See also the survey of material in Misener (1924) 103–23, and for more recent discussion, the collected essays in Cairns (2005).

[32] Evans (1969) provides a comprehensive overview in addition to which the following selective list of scholarship merely confirms the wide dissemination of physiognomic precepts in Greco-Roman antiquity. On Socrates' reputed encounter with the physiognomist Zopyrus, see Boys-Stones (2007) 23–6. In a different context entirely, Xenophon has Socrates voice quasi-physiognomic ideas to the painter Parrhasius: καὶ τὸ μεγαλοπρεπές τε καὶ ἐλευθέριον καὶ τὸ ταπεινόν τε καὶ ἀνελεύθερον καὶ τὸ σωφρονικόν τε καὶ φρόνιμον καὶ τὸ ὑβριστικόν τε καὶ ἀπειρόκαλον καὶ διὰ τοῦ προσώπου καὶ διὰ τῶν σχημάτων καὶ ἑστώτων καὶ κινουμένων ἀνθρώπων διαφαίνει ('nobility and dignity and baseness and servility and wisdom and understanding and insolence and tastelessness are made known in people's face and through the body's poses when still or in motion', *Mem.* 3.10.5). Wiles (1991) 85–90, followed by Petrides (2014) 138–50, argues for physiognomy's significant role in shaping the semiotics of the New Comic mask. Pertsinidis (2018) considers Theophrastus' use of physiognomy in his character sketches. Gleason (1995) investigates physiognomy and paradigms of masculinity in the oratorical practices of the Second Sophistic. Barton (1994) considers the function of

Appearance

There can be little doubt that Seneca was acquainted with its general principles, even though the majority of formal physiognomic works postdate him. More specifically, Seneca's Stoic approach to bodily signals appears to have a lot in common with ancient doctrines of physiognomy, and since physiognomy has been proposed as a possible influence on Seneca's plays,[33] this relationship needs to be explored in greater depth. Doing so will not only help to clarify the purpose of Seneca's physical descriptions but also elucidate more fully the relationship Seneca envisages between bodies and personal identity.

The most significant aspect of ancient physiognomy – as concerns my present study of Seneca – is its emphasis on intrinsic and supposedly unalterable character. Extant ancient treatises on the topic are uniform in the attention they devote to innate physical characteristics, which they tend to classify on the model of animals. The pseudo-Aristotelian *Physiognomica* lists three possible methods of bodily interpretation: an ethnological approach, based on people's racial and geographic origins; a zoological one, from analogies with animals' appearance and behaviour; and a pathognomic approach that deals with transient expressions of emotion (805a20–805b1). The central method is preferred as being both subtler than ethnology and more reliable than pathognomy. Hence, the text abounds with observations such as, 'to hold one's shoulders straight and stiff and roll them as one walks and to have weasel-arms is haughty, on the analogy of the horse; but to roll the shoulders if one stoops a little forward means a proud soul, as in the lion' (οἱ δὲ τοῖς ὤμοις ἐπισαλεύοντες ὀρθοῖς ἐκτεταμένας γαλιάγκωνες <γαῦροι·> ἀναφέρεται ἐπὶ τοὺς ἵππους. οἱ τοῖς ὤμοις ἐπεσαλεύοντες ἐγκεκυφότες μεγαλόφρονες· ἀναφέρεται ἐπὶ τοὺς λέοντας, 813a10).[34] Since physiognomy takes an essentialist

---

physiognomy alongside medicine and astronomy in imperial Rome. Rohrbacher (2010) argues for Suetonius' eclectic use of physiognomy in his biographical portraits of the emperors, while Opeku (1979) and Mason (1984) examine the presence of physiognomic concepts in Apuleius. Weiler (1996) reads Juvenal 10.356 – *orandum est ut sit mens sana in corpore sano* – against the background of physiognomic thought both ancient and modern.

[33] Evans (1950).
[34] The text and translation are those provided by Swain (2007). For analysis of the pseudo-Aristotelian *Physiognomica*, its context and its influence, see Evans (1969) 6–17, and Boys-Stones (2007) 44–75.

3.1 *Phaedra*

approach to questions of identity, and aspires to delineate inborn characteristics, it tends accordingly to focus on unalterable elements of individual bodies. For example: the pseudo-Aristotelian *Physiognomica* declares, 'an ill-proportioned physique indicates a rogue' (οἱ ἀσύμμετροι πανοῦργοι 813b35-814a1 trans. Swain), while Polemon's *Physiognomy* contains such curious, almost comic, details as, 'very small nails indicate villainy' (μικροὶ πάνυ ὄνυχες πανουργίας σημεῖον, Adamantius *Phys.* B4 trans. Repath).

In contrast, an orthodox Stoic approach to bodily signals employs the pathognomic method rejected by the Pseudo-Aristotelian text (805b1-10). Given their abiding interest in emotional states as evidence of vice and virtue, Stoics focus chiefly on the acquired or transient elements of facial and bodily expression, as opposed to immutable characteristics. When Seneca charts the symptoms of anger and madness at *de Ira* 1.1.3-5, or Medea's derangement at *Med.* 382-96, he traces the progress of temporary, albeit intense, emotions that – arguably – need not indicate anything fundamental about the personalities of those who experience them. As the author of the Pseudo-Aristotelian *Physiognomica* remarks, 'a man may at times wear an expression that is not normally his: for instance, a morose person will now and again ... assume a cheerful countenance, while a naturally cheerful man, if he be distressed, will change his expression accordingly' (κατὰ χρόνους τινὰς τὰ ἤθη οὐ τὰ αὐτὰ ἀλλὰ ἑτέρων ἔχουσιν· δυσανίοις τε γὰρ οὖσιν ἐνίοτε συνέβη ... τὸ ἦθος λαβεῖν τὸ τοῦ εὐθύμου, καὶ τοὐναντίον εὔθυμον λυπηθῆναι. ὥστε τὸ ἦθος τὸ ἐπὶ τοῦ προσώπου μεταβαλεῖν 805b5-9). From a strictly physiognomic viewpoint, what Medea and the angry man feel at any given moment may not tell us much about *who they are*. From a Stoic viewpoint, discerning the corporeal presence of the passions is a crucial step towards curing them: Stoics differ from physiognomists in believing that the body and the person can change.

Should it be said, then, that Stoics judge emotion rather than identity per se, or can physiognomy and pathognomy claim some common ground? In fact, despite divergent precepts, the two schools of thought actually arrive at some similar conclusions.

The divide separating pathognomy from physiognomy narrows upon closer inspection, especially when we consider that repeated indulgence of particular emotional reactions can lead to the formation of habits, and habitual behaviour – as discussed in Chapter 1 – as a core constituent of identity.[35] Many Stoics attributed the development of dispositional traits such as boldness or timorousness to the habit-forming effects of emotion; Seneca at *de Ira* 1.4.1–2 likewise distinguishes between being merely angry and being irascible.[36] Medea's Nurse reaches an equivalent conclusion when she admits to seeing the marks of her mistress' 'old anger' (*irae novimus veteris notas*, *Med.* 394): the heroine does not experience a transient emotional state, but instead displays the corrosive effects of a perpetually recurring passion, one that has moulded her face and her identity over many years. The dark shadow that clouds Medea's features is proof of an ingrained trait that other characters in the tragedy would do well to heed. So, in Seneca's work at least, pathognomic observations do not preclude judgements about the person as a whole, about his or her major attributes and sense of self. Contrary to the physiognomists' claims, what the characters of Senecan tragedy *feel* does actually tell us a lot about who they *are*, and about who they have *become*.

I hasten to add that these similarities should not be taken as evidence for any deliberate physiognomic basis or borrowing in Stoic thought, especially since true physiognomic doctrine contradicts some core Stoic tenets. After all, the self-improvement of the *proficiens* would be a futile exercise if both physical and moral character were unalterable, and Stoic writers do not characterise the *sapiens* as being any more beautiful in his appearance despite his moral perfection.[37] Instead, it could be said that Seneca's

---

[35] In similar fashion, Baumbach (2008) 36 counsels against drawing too strict a line between innate physical traits and temporary changes wrought by emotion, because 'repetitive actions of a particular pathognomic expression are prone to inscribe themselves into one's physiognomy'.

[36] See Graver (2007) 133–71 on the relationship of emotion to disposition in Stoic thought.

[37] These and similar objections to physiognomic influence on Stoic thought are raised by Boys-Stones (2007) 79. Plutarch *Mor.* 1058a and Seneca *Ep.* 66.4 both seem to suggest – I say 'seem' because the Plutarch passage is lacunose – that wisdom beautifies a person without actually altering his bodily features. The point Seneca stresses in *Ep.* 66 is that Claranus' virtue overshadows and almost causes one to forget his manifest physical defects.

3.1 *Phaedra*

descriptions are 'small-p' physiognomic inasmuch as they share some of the school's methods without adhering to or promoting its precepts.

Stoic preoccupation with the body as a marker of identity is likewise present in Zeno and Cleanthes' reported belief that ἦθος ('character') could be known from εἶδος ('appearance', *SVF* 1.618; Diog. Laert. 7.173). As told by Diogenes Laertius, this tenet comes from an anecdote in which some young men try to trick Cleanthes by bringing before him a *cinaedus* whose body has been toughened up through agricultural labour. Despite Cleanthes' touted expertise in judging moral character from appearance, the philosopher is stumped and sends the man away. But just as the man turns to leave, he sneezes, whereupon Cleanthes cries out, 'He's a *cinaedus*!' (Diog. Laert. 7.173; Dio 33.53–4). The story shares several elements with physiognomic discourse and has sometimes been taken as proof of Stoicism's engagement with physiognomy.[38] The tale stresses the body's involuntary revelation of character despite an individual's strenuous efforts at concealment (more on this topos below), and it pivots around the notion of immutable character traits – the *cinaedus* cannot help being what he is even if his body presents misleading signals.[39] It can and has been argued that the anecdote downplays the relevance of innate physical characteristics because it is not the set of his jaw or the width of his brow that gives the *cinaedus* away, but a simple sneeze.[40] Yet the notion that sneezes can designate effeminacy is present in the fourth-century AD anonymous Latin *Physiognomia* (Anon. Lat. 11) and was most likely a standard trope of physiognomic advice as far back as Polemon's second-century work.[41] The sneeze, too, can be considered innate, and even if we count it as learned behaviour instead, (in the sense that its quality – pitch, noise level and spluttering – may be acquired and changed), it does not differ significantly from, say,

---

[38] Evans (1969) 10–11 and Petrides (2014) 147 treat the anecdote as purely physiognomic. Boys-Stones (2007) 78–80 refutes the assumption.
[39] Augmenting the anecdote's 'physiognomic' character is its similarity to the tale of Zopyrus and Socrates reported by Cicero *Tusc.* 4.80 and *Fat.* 10, and by Diogenes Laertius 2.45.
[40] Boys-Stones (2007) 79.
[41] On the origins and relevance of the sneeze in physiognomic literature, see Boys-Stones (2007) 78 n.133.

the acquired qualities of a person's walking style, which is also an issue of great concern to physiognomists (e.g. Ps-Arist. *Physiognomica* 813a1–20; Adam. *Phys.* B39–40; Anon. Lat. 75–6). A Stoic view – if one can be attempted from such slender evidence – might by contrast be more inclined to count the effeminate man's sneeze as a kind of physical habit developing alongside and in direct relation to the moral habit of effeminacy.

Clearly, the anecdote is insufficiently forthcoming to be pushed too far in either direction and, as I have noted in the preceding section of this chapter, Cleanthes' belief, however reductively reported by Diogenes Laertius, can also be used as evidence of Stoic materialism. The point worth emphasising here is that Stoic notions of corporeal identity lend themselves easily to physiognomic colouring, which only increases their bearing on the detection and definition of individual psychological qualities. Although in the realm of the body Stoic materialism focuses chiefly on the passage of emotions, it is not as though such emotions leave the core of the individual untouched; ἦθος ('character') is not immune to πάθος ('passion/emotion'). In Seneca's case, bodily features, expressions, and reactions are not mere epiphenomena but primary indications of a person's mindset. If Seneca's work sometimes resonates with quasi-physiognomic sentiments that is because he regards people's *corpora* as integral to their personal identity.

For his part, Seneca also associates ἦθος ('character') with εἶδος ('appearance'), when he counsels Lucilius on assessing men's dispositions prior to selecting the correct moral guide:

Omnia rerum omnium, si observentur, indicia sunt, et argumentum morum ex minimis quoque licet capere: inpudicum et incessus ostendit et manus mota et unum interdum responsum et relatus ad caput digitus et flexus oculorum; inprobum risus, insanum vultus habitusque demonstrat. Illa enim in apertum per notas exeunt

If you take note, all actions are significant, and proof of character can be ascertained even from the smallest things: the lascivious man is indicated by his gait, by the movement of his hand and occasionally, by a single reply, by his raising a finger to his head and by the slant of his gaze. The rascal is revealed by his laugh; the madman by his face and bearing. These traits are made known through identifying marks. (*Ep.* 52.12)

3.1 Phaedra

Like the anecdote about Cleanthes and the *cinaedus*, this passage describes the physical revelation of deviant qualities that individuals would, presumably, prefer to keep hidden. Gesture, posture, expression and movement are classified as an *argumentum morum*, that is, as proof of customary (repeated and thus somewhat ingrained) behaviour, not just transient emotional reactions. The passage also shares with physiognomic literature an interest in the body's semiology. Physical and/or gestural quirks offer themselves up to scrutiny (*si observentur*) and furnish evidence (*ostendit; demonstrat*) in the form of meaningful signs (*indicia; notae*). Physiognomic treatises likewise tend to speak of bodily traits and gestures as inherently communicative; they are σημεῖα ('signs'), σύμβολα ('symbols'), *signa, indicia / indices*, and *notae*.[42] For Seneca as for the physiognomists, the body is a visual object and a readable one; it invites decoding.

The body's involuntary disclosure of private information is another core trope that Seneca's work shares with physiognomic texts. A frequent theme in these treatises is the unmasking of deceptive identities achieved through precise attention to corporeal signals.[43] For instance, Adamantius' epitome of Polemon declares that even if androgynous men pretend otherwise, 'thinking to hide their lewdness ... the deviation of their eyes, the noncoordination of their feet ... and the screaming of their voice denounce them' (οἴονται τὴν μαχλοσύνην ἐπικρύπτειν, κατηγοροῦσι δὲ αὐτῶν ... ὀφθαλμῶν παρατροπὴ καὶ ποδῶν παραφορὰ ... καὶ φωνῆς κραυγή, Adam. B21 trans. Repath). The anonymous author of the Latin *Physiognomia* similarly avers, 'the attentive practitioner will detect even the man who is taking precautions' (*et praecaventem attentus artifex detegat*, Anon. Lat. 11 trans. Repath), because the sound of his voice reveals the sybarite, the sneeze the effeminate man, and the abuser 'betrays (*prodidit*) his desire by tears when others start up the abuse' (Anon. Lat. 11 trans. Repath). Seneca uses the same verb to describe Phaedra (*proditur, Phaed.* 363) as she strives unsuccessfully to conceal the desire she feels for her stepson; in fact, it is not hard to see how this extended portrait (*Phaed.* 362–83, above)

---

[42] Noted more or less implicitly by Gleason (1995) 55–81.
[43] See Gleason (1995) 76–81, who refers to 'the X-rays ... of physiognomical insight'. Also, Petrides (2014) 147.

coincides with elements of physiognomic discourse. The same idea of mute, corporeal revelation recurs elsewhere in the tragedies as well. Atreus worries that his children, Agamemnon and Menelaus, may inadvertently reveal his scheme to Thyestes simply through their expression: 'a fearful face often reveals a lot, and great plans <u>betray</u> a person even against his will' (*multa ... trepidus solet / detegere vultus, magna nolentem quoque / consilia <u>produnt</u>, Thy.* 330–2). In similar fashion, Clytemnestra's Nurse tells her 'though you yourself are silent, all your pain is in your face' (*licet ipsa sileas, totus in vultu est dolor, Ag.* 128), while Jason uses almost identical phrasing of Medea: 'she bears her anger before her: all her pain is in her face' (*fert odia prae se: totus in vultu est dolor, Med.* 446). The unknown author of the *Hercules Oetaeus* appears to have understood such remarks as characteristically Seneca, since he imitates them in the chorus' address to Deianira: 'although you yourself deny it, your face announces whatever you cover up' (*licet ipsa neges, vultus loquitur quodcumque tegis, H.O.* 705).

Of Stoicism's relationship to physiognomy it could therefore be said that the two schools are neither entirely incompatible nor identical in their approach to the body. Both assume the body's fundamental honesty and reliability – that it will disclose the truth even when its owner is trying to lie. Both also envisage the body as a collection of signals that articulate an unbreakable bond of mind and flesh, identity and appearance. Although at a deeper level Stoics and physiognomists quickly part company, the similarities that Seneca's work displays to physiognomic discourse are indispensable for understanding his notion of bodily identity. Most importantly for my present study, the quasi-physiognomic quality of Seneca's corporeal descriptions indicates their pertaining to the individual as a whole and not just to the fleeting passage of emotions across the skin's surface. In Senecan tragedy, *how* one seems and *who* one is are inextricably bound.

The Inner Worlds of Seneca's Phaedra

As we have seen already in the description of Phaedra's malaise, Seneca's fascination with bodily signals and with the soul's influence over fleshly form draws his attention inwards to the private

3.1 *Phaedra*

spaces of selfhood, where individual mores are constituted and from which they emanate. Physiognomic notions of bodily revelation complement this motif by urging observers to see through or strip away the body's layered wiles in order to reach an inner, essential truth. For observers in Seneca's tragedies, the body provides precious access to another person's secluded interior while at the same time acting as a covering, a potentially obstructive and misleading screen intended, usually unsuccessfully, to conceal a person's true qualities. Movement from inside to out, outside to in, typifies Seneca's thoughts about physical appearance.[44]

This pull towards the (possibly) unfathomable, secretive interior of the self is a powerful theme in the *Phaedra*, where it articulates both the forbidden nature of the protagonist's passion and also her implied human characteristics, generating an illusion of depth that makes Phaedra seem more than the sum of words and actions dictated by the playwright. The spatial metaphor features chiefly in depictions of Phaedra's love, which 'burns inside like the heat billows out of Aetna's cavern' (*ardet intus qualis Aetnaeo vapor / exundat antro*, 102–3). Its flame 'devours her innermost marrow deep within and courses through her veins, submerged in her vitals and hiding in her bloodstream' (*intimas ... vorat / penitus medullas atque per venas meat / visceribus ignis mersus et venis latens*, 641–3).[45] The chorus refer to *amor* as a 'furtive fire' (*igne furtivo*, 280),[46] and Phaedra protests to the Nurse that she does not fear the consequences of her passion because, 'I bear within me Love's great kingdom' (*Amoris in me maximum regnum fero*, 218). Corporeal and spiritual sensation merge to the extent that it is not always clear where Phaedra's

---

[44] Relatedly, metaphors of inner space typify Seneca's thoughts about the soul: see Bartsch (2009) 201–4 and Traina (1974) 20–3, who remarks, 'il linguaggio dell'interiorità ... è forse il maggior contributo di Seneca alla terminologia filosofica dell'occidente' ('the language of interiority ... is perhaps the greatest of Seneca's contributions to the vocabulary of Western philosophy').

[45] There are several issues of transmission affecting *Phaed.* 641–3: Zwierlein (1986a) brackets 642 for deletion since it does not appear in the *E* branch of MSS; he also sides with the Gronovian emendation of 641 – *intimis saevit ferus* – and has *venas* rather than *venis* in 643. In contrast, I follow the text of Boyle (1987), which in this instance, I feel, deviates less radically from manuscript tradition. In any case, both versions succeed in conveying Seneca's emphasis on interiority.

[46] *Phaed.* 280 has also been bracketed for deletion by Zwierlein (1986a), but I am inclined to agree with Boyle (1987) that it should be kept on the basis of the lexical and thematic links it displays to other sections of the tragedy.

metaphors end and where they begin. The 'insides' she refers to are at once literal and figurative, a collection of *viscera, medullae, venae* and an intangible psychic space beset by imaginary flames. Whatever takes place in this interior realm imprints itself rapidly on the surface of Phaedra's flesh. *Amor* leads her to waste away: 'anxiety ravages her limbs, her steps falter, and her radiant body's delicate beauty has collapsed' (*populatur artus cura, iam gressus tremunt, / tenerque nitidi corporis cecidit decor*, 377–8). Infatuation for Hippolytus' renowned *decor* (657; 1096; 1173) causes Phaedra to lose her own. In fact, such is the reach of love's virulence that Hippolytus as well loses his beauty to it, in exact echo of Phaedra's misfortune: *cecidit decor* (1270).[47]

Critics have been quick to point out that Seneca's portrayal of Phaedra's love draws inspiration from two famous predecessors: Euripides' Phaedra and Vergil's Dido. The latter, like Seneca's heroine, experiences love as a deep-buried destructive disease that devours her from the inside, physically and psychologically. Elaine Fantham charts the main parallels: in Vergil's portrait of the Carthaginian queen, lines such as *vulnus alit venis et caeco carpitur igni* ('she nourishes the wound with her veins and is consumed by hidden fire', *Aen.* 4.2) and *est mollis flamma medullas / interea et tacitum vivit sub pectore vulnus* ('meanwhile a flame eats at her soft marrow and a hidden wound thrives in her breast', *Aen.* 4.66–7) find clear echoes in the love that afflicts Seneca's Phaedra: *alitur et crescit malum* ('the evil is nourished and grows', 101); *vorat tectas penitus medullas* ('it devours the marrow hidden deep within', 282); *torretur aestu tacito* ('she's seared by silent heat', 362).[48] Both sets of descriptions have their origins in the elegiac trope of love as illness,[49] and like Vergil's, Seneca's images of secretive internalised desire are meant to

---

[47] Although he does not record this particular parallel, Boyle (1985) 1302 notes other verbal correspondences between the scenes describing Phaedra's illness and subsequent reactions to / accounts of Hippolytus' death.
[48] Fantham (1975) 4–6. Prior to Fantham, connections between *Aen.* 4.2 and *Phaed.* 101 had also been noted by Ruch (1964) 361.
[49] Coffey and Mayer (1990) *ad Phaed.* 363 cite as parallel the portrait of the lovesick stepmother in Apul. *Met.* 10.2, but in addition, the Nurse's account of Phaedra's suffering also demonstrates more diffuse elegiac undertones. On the play's interaction with Ovidian elegy, see Davis (2012) 449–51 and Trinacty (2014) 67–93; and for its interaction with elegiac poetry more generally, see Littlewood (2004) 264 and 274–85.

3.1 *Phaedra*

arouse the audience's sympathy by emphasising the character's quasi-human quality. Repeated allusions to a private psychological landscape, however overwrought in Seneca's version, create the impression of consciousness, as though Phaedra herself laid claim to inwardly constituted subjectivity, independent of the dramatist's pen.

However, just because Seneca's images owe a debt to Vergil does not preclude them from serving their own, independent function within the text, chiefly as a means of interrogating how identities are fashioned and interpreted. In Seneca's *Phaedra*, motifs of psychological interiority do not just build the impression of a character but also, on a more abstract plane, articulate a complex relationship between exterior and interior manifestations of selfhood: whether the body covers or discloses one's inner thoughts and whether one's appearance really matches the reality of one's personal qualities.

In this regard, Seneca can be seen to build upon Euripides, whose tragedy on the same topic likewise considers the hermeneutic and revelatory power of the body, albeit in a less comprehensive fashion. In the scene following the first choral ode, Euripides' Nurse remarks to the chorus leader that Phaedra will not disclose the cause of her troubles (πάντα ... σιγᾷ τάδε; 'she keeps quiet about everything', 273) and that she 'conceals her suffering [from Theseus] and denies she is ill' (κρύπτειν γὰρ ἥδε πῆμα κοὔ φησιν νοσεῖν, 279). When, in response, the chorus leader wonders why Theseus cannot 'deduce it by looking at her face' (ὁ δ'ἐς πρόσωπον οὐ τεκμαίρεται βλέπων; 280), Euripides activates the contending claims of verbal and visual evidence that structure this play's events.[50] He also activates the idea of the body as a semiotic object that can be deciphered (cf. τεκμαίρεται) and so provide

---

On the elegiac resonance of Vergil's Dido, see in particular Cairns (1989) 129–50 (esp. 142, on the symptoms of lovesickness).

[50] Thus, Nikolsky (2015) 32: 'In *Hippolytus*, vision turns out to be ... [a] key motif, which develops in parallel and constant juxtaposition with the motif of words.' Characters in Euripides' version are inclined to treat speech with suspicion and to believe all too readily the evidence set before their eyes. The play's linked themes of concealment, misinterpretation, and the instability of verbal and physical signs are also explored by Segal (1988) and (1992).

evidence of internal character.[51] Like Seneca's Phaedra, Euripides' heroine is implied to have difficulty disguising what she really feels: the body will betray what the tongue holds back. The idea surfaces again at *Hippolytus* 416–18, where Phaedra wonders how adulterous women manage to 'look at their husbands face-to-face ... unafraid that the chambers of the house may at some point cry out' (βλέπουσιν ἐς πρόσωπα τῶν ξυνευνετῶν / ... / τέραμνά τ' οἴκων μή ποτε φθογγὴν ἀφῇ). Besides evoking such women's brazen lack of shame, Phaedra's imagery here suggests that the face may inadvertently communicate one's secrets, just as the house, another voiceless entity, may reveal what has gone on inside it. These are auxiliary motifs in Euripides, but, thanks largely to the influence of Stoicism, they become the driving force of Seneca's *Phaedra*, underpinning the characters' knowledge of and judgements about one another, as well as the audience's insight into the figures presented on stage.

To complement this notion of private subjectivity, moreover, Seneca employs throughout his tragedy images of interior space, secrecy, and concealment.[52] The heroine hopes fervently that she may be able to 'hide [her] crime with the torch of marriage' (*forsan iugali crimen abscondam face*, 597) and begs Hippolytus to receive her confession 'confidentially' (*secretus*, 600). Earlier, the Nurse argues that it will not be easy for Phaedra 'to cover up such great wrongdoing' (*tegere ... tantum nefas*, 153), and that even if 'the gods' favour were to conceal' the crime (*numinum abscondat favor*, 159), Phaedra's father would not 'allow it to hide in secret' (*latere ... occultum sinet*, 151) nor would Phaedra herself 'manage to evade [her] all-seeing ancestors' (*effici, / inter videntes omnia ut lateas avos*, 157–8). Parallel lexical choices convey close thematic links: Phaedra aspires to conceal her transgressions (*latere*, 151; *lateas*, 158) at the same time as

---

[51] For Segal (1992) 435, this is one of the *Hippolytus*' main structural themes: 'discovering our inner being beneath the outer covering of what we seem to be'. Jones (1962) 239–70 detects in Euripidean drama a broader trend of exploring discrepancies between internal moral character and external markers of honour/social status.

[52] Segal (1986) 29–37 offers an insightful though far from exhaustive study of these motifs in the *Phaedra*.

3.1 *Phaedra*

passion conceals itself in her veins (*latens*, 643); the body qua *covering* for her psyche is further evoked through her attempts to *cover up* her wayward lust. Repeated references to interiority and secrecy accentuate the drama's oppressive atmosphere. The guilt and shame that Phaedra feels inside her person find counterparts in the buried sexual misdemeanours of her mother, Pasiphaë, and the resulting labyrinthine home of the Minotaur that lies beneath the Cretan palace like a murky Freudian subconscious.[53] While Euripides' Phaedra imagines fearfully that the house itself could speak her secrets, the characters of Seneca's version return again and again to visions of the Cretan labyrinth sheltering its hideous occupant. Phaedra remarks of Daedalus that he, 'confined our monster in a sightless dwelling' (*nostra caeca monstra conclusit domo*, 122), and Hippolytus alludes to the maze in his tirade against the corrupting effects of wealth. Whoever pursues a simple life of rustic purity, he claims:

> non in recessu furta et obscuro improbus
> quaerit cubili seque multiplici timens
> domo recondit: aethera ac lucem petit
> et teste caelo vivit
>
> does not seek out adultery, shamelessly, in hidden nooks
> and darkened couches, nor hides away, scared,
> in a labyrinthine house: he seeks the air and the light
> and lives under heaven's gaze
>
> (*Phaed.* 522–5)

in recessu, obscuro, se ... recondit: this is the same web of visual symbolism that entwines Phaedra herself, a continuity that shows Seneca identifying the psyche with the murky corners of private rooms.[54] Whatever suspicious activity takes place under this knot of roofs is on par with the shameful thoughts concealed in Phaedra's mind. Granted, elaborate houses are commonplace in

---

[53] Segal (1986) pioneered a Freudian/Lacanian reading of the *Phaedra* and the success of his study initiated a trend of psychoanalytic Senecan criticism, for example, Schiesaro (2003) and (2009); Staley (2010); Rimell (2012). Detailed justification for applying such frameworks to Senecan tragedy is given by McAuley (2016) 272–80.

[54] A good parallel is *Epistle* 43.4–5. Using buildings to symbolise personal *mores*/interior selfhood is a notable Senecan tactic, for example *Epp.* 12, 55, and 86, with Henderson (2004).

Appearance

Seneca's denunciations of wealth and overweening power (cf. *Thy.* 455–7; *de Clem.* 6.1: *multiplicibus ... muris turribusque*), but in the context of the *Phaedra*, and in such close conjunction with *furta*, the *multiplex domus* irresistibly conjures images of the convoluted Cretan palace.[55] Rather than become trapped in this sinful tangle, Hippolytus opts for the open air, by which he also implies a life free from deception. His rage against Pasiphaë's sexual misconduct grows more explicit when he addresses Phaedra later in the same scene:

> tamen tacitum diu
> crimen biformi partus exhibuit nota,
> scelusque matris arguit vultu truci
> ambiguus infans

> but the birth exposed
> the long hidden crime, through its double form,
> and the hybrid child proved by its savage face
> the guilt of its mother.

(*Phaed.* 690–3)

With its emphasis on the body's *nota* or 'imprint', and on the face as capable of revealing closely guarded secrets, Hippolytus' description of the Minotaur recalls even if it does not quite replicate the quasi-physiognomic assessments of bodies performed elsewhere in Seneca's *Phaedra*. Moral transgressions are reified in corporeal monstrosity, and what is patently visible on the outside points towards what is hidden within. Mention of a *tacitum crimen* also looks back to Phaedra's preceding experience of *tacitus aestus* (362) and to her plea that Hippolytus heed the entreaties of her 'silent mind' (*tacitae mentis*, 636),[56] a set of lexical links that further associate what is silent and concealed with what is internal and subjectively experienced.

Psychological interiority, therefore, is often paired with the threat of deception in the *Phaedra*, and this pairing makes sense

---

[55] Confirming this connection, Coffey and Mayer (1990) *ad Phaed.* 523–4 note that Seneca probably borrowed the phrase *multiplex domus* from Ovid's description of the Labyrinth at *Met.* 8.158.

[56] Against Axelson's emendation, *pavidae mentis*, accepted by Zwierlein (1986a), I prefer the manuscript reading, *tacitae mentis*, printed by Boyle (1987), Coffey and Mayer (1990), and Viansino (1993). For discussion of the issue, see Morelli (1995).

3.1 *Phaedra*

because both motifs imply hidden depth. Just as a person's psyche is assumed to lie beyond or behind the screen of his/her face and body, accessible only in mediated form, so deceptive behaviour presupposes veiled intentions that observers must delve to uncover. Phaedra's hope of hiding her love affair (*tegere*, 153) points also to the sensations of *amor* eroding her <u>tectas</u> *medullas* (282) and culminates in her ambiguous gesture of veiling her face in Theseus' presence (*op<u>tegis</u>*, 887); the act of decoding her movements and bodily condition coincides with the push to reveal her potential falsity. Deception and secrecy are used not just by Seneca but by many writers of fiction to convey the elusive, unreachable nature of individual consciousness and thereby to endow characters with quasi-human features. Another example from this tragedy centres around the participle *abditus*: Theseus uses it to decry – mistakenly, it turns out – Hippolytus' misleading behaviour and the shameless lust supposedly hidden beneath the young man's serious visage (*abditos sensus geris*: 'you keep your true feelings hidden', 918); he also uses it in his promise to hunt down Hippolytus 'even though [he] is hidden deep in the far-most corner of the earth' (*licet in recessu penitus extremo abditus*, 933); the word is also applied, by the Nurse, to Theseus himself, 'submerged in the underworld' (*Lethaeo abditum*, 147) for the underhand purpose of helping Pirithous abduct Persephone; and by the chorus to describe, in obviously Ovidian fashion, the seductive perils of the noontime woodland (*te nemore abdito, / cum Titan medium constituit diem, / cingent turba licens Naides improbae*; 'in a secluded forest glade, when Titan halts the day at its height, a lustful crowd of wanton Naiads will encircle you' 778–80).[57] Again, literal acts of hiding and supposedly deceptive appearances are paired with the seemingly unfathomable depths of personal psychology, an association reinforced by *de Ira* 1.1.5 where Seneca likewise uses *abditus* to denote internally experienced passions not readily noticeable to others (*in abdito alere*). In this quasi-physiognomic schema, personal character is inwardly situated. As Cicero remarks in the *de Legibus* 1.26, *tum [natura] speciem ita formavit oris, ut in ea <u>penitus reconditos</u> mores*

---

[57] On the Ovidian quality of this *topos*, see Segal (1986) 68.

Appearance

effingeret ('nature shaped the appearance of the face so as to reproduce in it the disposition <u>hidden deep inside</u>'). Seneca's *Phaedra* pursues much the same idea, via multiple images of bodies enveloping minds and of people attempting to hide themselves or their intentions (cf. *se . . . / . . . recondit*, *Phaed.* 523–4).

As a brief epilogue to this section, it is worth noting that the dramaturgy of Seneca's *Phaedra* complements this theme of inwardness by drawing the audience's attention towards private, offstage space. When Phaedra is presented before the audience following the Nurse's physiognomic report at 360–83, 'the stage action of showing the queen languishing in her palace interior enacts the process of revealing the mystery of passion hidden in her soul'.[58] Likewise, Theseus' aggressive desire to gain entry into Phaedra's chamber (863) mirrors his more protracted attempt to discover what lies behind his wife's intention to commit suicide (864–85). The queen's location within the enclosed space of the palace matches her reticence: *haud pandit ulli; maesta secretum occulit* ('she unfolds nothing; sorrowfully she covers up her secret', 860). It is equally fitting that Phaedra's two great scenes of confession take place outdoors, first in the woodland with Hippolytus (589–718) and later, outside the palace, in front of Theseus and the gathered citizenry of Athens (1155–98). In echo of the play's quasi-physiognomic themes, the spatial placement of stage action guides audiences to interrogate the relationship between inside and outside, between the private, internal regions of the psyche and the public, readily accessible planes of the body. The extent to which they correlate or diverge forms the subject of the next two sections.

Deceptive Appearances

Ultimately, Phaedra's attempts at concealment prove ineffectual, as does her body's task of veiling her psychological states. This happens not just as a consequence of the tragedy's spiralling revelatory impulse towards catastrophe, but also through its monist, material treatment of the mind–body relationship. If in the

---

[58] Segal (1986) 48.

3.1 *Phaedra*

Senecan universe passion is always involuntarily made manifest somewhere on an individual's body, then successful acts of physical deception become more or less impossible. That the body does not, *cannot*, lie is a central theme both in Stoic and in physiognomic narratives: misleading appearances are partial at best and typically due not to the *corpus* itself, but to the misinformed eye of its beholder. For Seneca, symptoms are reliable; it is their interpreters who make mistakes.

Much of the action in Seneca's *Phaedra* pivots around such questions of whether and to what extent the body can actually deceive its witnesses. Hippolytus' ascetic beauty is claimed to belie the ugliness of his conduct (915–22); Phaedra is accused of accentuating her distressed appearance for the fraudulent purpose of condemning her stepson (826–8); Theseus misconstrues the meaning of his wife's gestures (886–7) and of the sword she presents to him as an evidential token (898–900). From these sinister ambiguities disaster unfurls like waves across the shore, with Phaedra in particular being held culpable for displaying a dishonest façade. Scholars of Senecan tragedy tend to label the heroine as duplicitous: they point to her changeability, her inconsistency and uncertainty that lead her to play numerous roles throughout the drama, as proof of her falsity.[59] Phaedra's appearance is assumed not to accord with her intentions at critical points in the play, a dissonance that is further assumed to highlight her status as a dramatic character, an enacted part, a theatrical performance. There is some substance to these views, especially because, as Christopher Trinacty notes, Seneca uses the same verb, *fingo*, to describe Phaedra's changeable hairstyles (*solvi comas / rursusque fingi*; 'undoing her hair and doing it up again', 371–2) and her false accusation of rape (*mentita finxi*; 'I fashioned lies', 1194).[60] Since *fingo* can also denote 'playing a part',[61] the constellation of theatrical performance, contrived

---

[59] An argument pursued in various forms by: Trinacty (2014) 45–6 and 67–93, and (2017) 180; Kirichenko (2013) 51–9; and Fitch and McElduff (2002) 32–6. On the incongruities and possible duplicity in Phaedra's conduct, see also Hill (2004) 159–75, and Coffey and Mayer (1990).
[60] Trinacty (2014) 45–6.
[61] *OLD s.v. fingo* entry 9c.

physical appearance and deliberate falsehood begins to look convincing. Fabricated behaviour is posited as the natural correlate of a fake guise, on the model of actors donning costumes to express what they do not personally, individually, feel. How, if at all, can this be squared with the principles of Stoic materialism?

Surprisingly, it can be, in much the same way that Atreus' superficially deceptive conduct does not preclude behavioural consistency. The clue lies in the erroneous equation of acting with pretence, for the body on stage does not merely *pretend* to be someone else, but also, through its posture and movement, communicates to the audience a given character's inner state. Granted the actor's body lies in respect of not (or not wholly) representing the actor's own, internal psyche, but in respect of displaying a character's disposition, it very much tells the truth. In Colette Conroy's formulation, 'it is important to recognise that actors are not *copying* behaviour, but are performing it in a way that involves a formal and aesthetic relationship to the play, the conventions of theatre and the world outside the theatre'.[62] Audiences use essentially the same set of codes to interpret bodies both on stage and off. Like the body in Stoic physics or in physiognomy, the *corpus* on stage is a meaningful, legible object providing onlookers with information crucial to their deciphering a character's traits, inclinations, and emotional states.

Hence, belief in the coincidence of moral character and physique informs the practice of performing fictional roles in the theatre almost as much as it informs the pursuit of physiognomy. An actor's gesture, an actor's body, symbolise the psychology, emotions, and intentions of the *dramatis persona* he or she has assumed. This happens even in the case of duplicitous characters, for without such information an audience would not be able to judge whether the character in question was in fact duplicitous. The body on stage can therefore be remarkably sincere, and we should be wary of presupposing that all instances of Seneca's characters performing their identities necessarily entail a divorce

---

[62] Conroy (2010) 40. The distinction between acting and pretence is stressed by Zamir (2014) 33–8.

3.1 *Phaedra*

between internal motivation and external display. Contrary to common scholarly belief, performance can actually unite the two. This sincerity of bodily signals is key to understanding Seneca's Phaedra, since the queen passively exploits ambiguities at least as much, if not more, than she practises active deception.[63] All responsibility lies with the interpreter of these physical cues, who, like a well-schooled Stoic or capable physiognomist, must exercise corporeal knowledge in order to reach the truth. When the queen sits stunned in the aftermath of her ill-conceived attempt at seduction, the Nurse plots a cover-up by declaring Phaedra's shattered appearance evidence of pre-meditated assault at Hippolytus' hands. 'Leave her pulled hair and torn tresses as they are', she admonishes the servants, 'the marks of so great a crime' (*crinis tractus et laceratae comae / ut sunt remaneant, facinoris tanti notae*, 731–2). Certainly, the Nurse's aim is dishonest, and her instructions seem to acquire a metatheatrical tint as she stage-manages Phaedra's appearance in the manner of a director. Yet this dishonesty and pretence need not falsify the state of Phaedra's body, which really does bear the *facinoris tanti notae*, even if the *facinus* in question is attempted adultery, not attempted rape. Hippolytus *has* wrenched Phaedra's hair (707–8: *crine contorto ... / laeva*; 'with her hair twisted back in my left hand') and threatened her with violence (706–9). Thus, the *notae* exhibited on her body are fundamentally reliable, and it is only a slight slant in context that makes them convey a misleading impression.

It is at the end of the play's second chorus that Seneca comes closest to crediting Phaedra with actual physical deceit. The speakers protest that Phaedra 'is preparing heinous charges against an innocent youth' (*nefanda iuveni crimina insonti apparat*, 825), in the service of which she deliberately composes her looks, for maximum effect: 'see her villainy! With her torn hair she seeks to be believed; she spoils her head's full beauty, drenches her cheeks: she sets her trap with every feminine wile' (*en scelera! quaerit crine lacerato fidem, / decus omne turbat capitis, umectat genas: / instruitur omni fraude feminea dolus*, 826–8). With its excitable

---

[63] For this perspective on Seneca's Phaedra, see in particular Davis (1983) and Roisman (2000).

en! the chorus indicates the performative quality of Phaedra's appearance: her corporeal distress is a spectacle both for the audience and for other characters within the tragedy. As a piece of theatre, moreover, this staging of the body is assumed to lack truthfulness; Phaedra's desire for belief (*fides*) only accentuates the absence of trustworthiness (*fides*) from her looks. Her interior and exterior are assumed not to correspond.

Yet Phaedra's bodily state may be more genuine than the chorus would have us believe because her disordered visage recalls not just Hippolytus' violence (707–8 and 732, above) but also the queen's own distraught reaction to the disastrous encounter with her stepson, which leaves her 'clawing at [herself]' (*te ipsa lacerans*, 734 cf. *lacerato*, 826). Her tears are likewise a standard symptom of her suffering, and in the play's second Act the Nurse cites them as reliable evidence of Phaedra's lovesickness: 'tears fall down her face and drench her cheeks in perpetual dew' (*lacrimae cadunt per ora et assiduo genae / rore irrigantur*, 381–2). Lexical and visual associations between the chorus' and these earlier descriptions of Phaedra's physical condition suggest that the chorus has misjudged the queen's physiognomy. Her symptoms may well be reliable indications of something other than what the chorus chooses to see; her distress may be genuine, not counterfeit, even though it is being directed towards an underhand purpose.

From the better-informed perspective of the audience, moreover, Phaedra's performance of crying and tearing at her hair can actually convey a high level of sincerity. Since the audience knows about the queen's distressing encounter with Hippolytus, it is able to ascertain the potential *fides* linking her external bodily signals to their internal correlatives: the pain displayed on the surface of Phaedra's skin communicates the psychological pain she experiences underneath. Like an actor using his or her body to convey a character's ethos, Phaedra performs her suffering in a manner arguably no less reliable for being deliberate. Admittedly, Seneca provides too little detail in this passage to allow full resolution of the issue, but the clear distance separating the chorus' interpretation from the audience's more sophisticated understanding shows that for Seneca misconceptions rather than outright falsehoods are indeed the central concern of this tragedy.

3.1 *Phaedra*

Despite allegations of pretence, then, Phaedra's appearance tends throughout the play to demonstrate the logic of her feelings. A good example is the elaborate scene near the beginning of Act 2 where she exchanges her royal robes for the compact kit of an Amazonian huntress (387–403). Christopher Trinacty interprets the new costume as evidence of Phaedra's desire to re-invent and therefore contrive her appearance along with her *persona*; he cites in support the chorus' preceding comment that love compels even the gods to undergo metamorphosis and visit earth 'in disguise' (*vultibus falsis*, 295).[64] Following hard upon the chorus' tales of Apollo as a herdsman (296–8), Zeus as a bull (303–8) and Hercules in women's garb (317–24), Phaedra's change of outfit may well seem to realise the deceptive effects of passion. It may also seem to highlight Phaedra's inconstant performance of multiple roles, as it does in the case of Thyestes exchanging exilic rags for royal drapery at *Thyestes* 524–6. To some extent this is correct: Phaedra's change of clothing indicates a changeable disposition and draws attention to her status as a fabricated, enacted character. But it is also true that her sartorial transformation is not unfaithful to her internal state, both in the sense that it illustrates her struggle to escape love's physical oppression – as Charles Segal has shown[65] – and also in its leading her to resemble Hippolytus' mother, a similarity that only confirms the incestuous, transgressive nature of her desire.[66] The queen's exterior thus reflects her interior even when she seems at her most fickle.

Events in the latter half of the *Phaedra* are likewise driven by misinterpretation far more than by active deceit. The problem of bodily communication grows more acute by the middle of Act 3, when Theseus struggles to prise an explanation from his wife, and subsequently misreads his son's character from his looks. Having gained access to Phaedra's chamber at 863, Theseus tries to access her worries as well, only to be greeted with obdurate silence. He falls back on endeavouring to decipher her gestures instead, but in

---

[64] This view is actually a combination of Trinacty (2014) 73–4, with n.44 in particular, and Trinacty (2017) 180.
[65] Segal (1986) 30–2.
[66] An association noted by Davis (1983) 115, Kirichenko (2013) 52, and, far earlier, by the anonymous interpolator of *Phaed.* 398: *talis severi mater Hippolyti fuit*.

Appearance

this regard, too, he remains at a loss: *quidnam ora maesta avertis et lacrimas genis / subito coortas veste praetenta optegis?* ('why do you turn away your sorrowful face and why hold up your robe to veil tears suddenly sprung from your eyes?' 886–7). Like the preceding examples discussed in this section, this act of veiling could be construed as a deceitful move, especially in its visual echo of the Nurse's earlier proposal to 'cloak crime with crime' (*scelere velandum est scelus*, 721), that is, to salvage Phaedra's reputation by accusing Hippolytus. Certainly, the gesture fits within the play's economy of hidden intentions and physiognomic revelation; Phaedra's move to cover her face is at once a bid for concealment and a publicly available sign of what her psyche contains.[67] The latter point deserves stressing: Phaedra's body language still communicates her state of mind even as, or *because*, it tries to shroud it. Essentially, Phaedra's body reifies her psyche even against its owner's will (cf. 363: *quamvis tegatur, proditur vultu furor*); the act of covering her face may, paradoxically, uncover a dishonest intent. In Seneca's Stoic universe, cerebral deception need not translate into bodily falsehood.

But neither Theseus nor the play's audience has sufficient information at their disposal to decipher this action, and so Seneca throws us back into questions of how and with what degrees of success bodily signals are interpreted. Theseus seems to regard the veiling as a gesture of grief, which is not an unreasonable guess given the conventions of the Greco-Roman tragic stage.[68] Still, Phaedra's gesture is more multivalent than Theseus allows. Michael Coffey and Roland Mayer suggest that the veiling signifies Phaedra's intent to lie under oath.[69] Anthony Boyle points out that Phaedra's gesture resembles her earlier behaviour when the Nurse revives her following her confrontation with Hippolytus: *quid ... omnium aspectus fugis?* ('why do you avoid everyone's glance?' 734).[70] Both instances may be intended

---

[67] Thus Cairns (2011) 19–20: 'as well as drawing attention to and expressing emotion ... veiling creates a personal space, a barrier behind which the emotional self can be protected ... the veil is a symbol ... for what the character is feeling inside: what we see makes manifest what we cannot see'.
[68] On veiling and grief, see Cairns (2011).
[69] Coffey and Mayer (1990) *ad Phaed.* 887.
[70] Boyle (1987) *ad Phaed.* 886.

3.1 *Phaedra*

to illustrate Phaedra's acute sense of shame, an explanation that seems especially plausible when we consider that Euripides' lost *Hippolytus Kalyptomenos* had the protagonist veil himself in response to the shame he felt at Phaedra's overtures,[71] and also that Euripides' extant tragedy on the same myth has Phaedra, at the height of her lovesickness, command that her veil be removed (*Hipp.* 201) and later replaced (*Hipp.* 243–4) when she regains her sense of sexual propriety. The extent of Phaedra's covering indicates the measure of her modesty, and this equation may apply equally well to Seneca's as to Euripides' heroine.[72] For Seneca's, moreover, a sense of shame may be caused by acknowledgement of her illicit lust, recent experience of assault, the intention to lie, or any combination thereof. But Theseus does not pause to pursue any such reasoning, nor to recognise let alone choose between these multiple significations. He proves himself a poor student of physiognomic analysis.

Theseus' emphatic yet ineffectual desire to decipher his wife's movement further underscores the observer's role in (mis)construing identity. He is just as hasty and imprecise in his treatment of Hippolytus. When he demands that Phaedra reveal what has happened to her, she recounts her misfortune in elliptically ambiguous language: *temptata precibus restiti; ferro ac minis / non cessit animus; vim tamen corpus tulit* ('I stood firm though assailed by entreaties: my mind did not yield to threats of violence, but my body endured assault' 891–2). Theseus takes this to mean that Phaedra has been raped, though of course, her words can equally well refer to the *ferrum*, *minae* and *vis* Hippolytus *did* visit upon her, and also to the more figurative *vis* she has suffered at the

---

[71] Boyle (1987) *ad Phaed.* 886 is surely right to suggest, 'There may be some counterpoint here with Eur.'s first *Hippolytus* (*Kalyptomenos*).' Given Seneca's (and indeed all Roman dramatists') preference for Euripidean material, some interaction with the *Hippolytus Kalyptomenos* seems likely, though it should not be overstated. Beginning with Leo (1878) 173–83, there developed in late nineteenth and early twentieth-century German scholarship a trend of linking Seneca's *Phaedra* to Euripides' lost *Hippolytus*, whereas later scholars, for example Grimal (1963) and Barrett (1964) 16–17 and 29–45 correctly advise extreme caution in deriving any of Euripides' plot details from Seneca.

[72] Covering the head to express shame/modesty is of course a common gesture in ancient tragedy. See, for example, Euripides' *Herakles* 1160–2 and 1199–201, with Cairns (2011) 20–2.

hands of Cupid.[73] Like her physical appearance, Phaedra's pronouncement does not exactly lie even though it is liable to misinterpretation. Her next move is just as cryptic: she accuses Hippolytus not by speaking his name, but by handing the young man's sword to her husband. Theseus must now decode yet another set of visual clues, and his interrogation of the sword substitutes for his interrogation of the actual person:

> quod facinus, heu me, cerno? quod monstrum intuor?
> regale patriis asperum signis ebur
> capulo refulgent, gentis Actaeae decus.
> sed ipse quonam evasit?
>
> Alas, what crime is this I see? What monstrosity before my eyes?
> Royal ivory embossed with ancestral symbols
> gleams on the hilt, the glory of the Actaean clan.
> But he – where did he go?
>
> (*Phaed.* 898–901)

Theseus' reading of the sword is quasi-physiognomic in the sense that he pays careful attention to the object's *signa* (*patriis ... signis*, 899), which he uses to form a judgement about his son's character. Here Seneca establishes an analogy between bodies and material objects in respect of their mutual ability to represent an individual. The sword stands in for Hippolytus himself, not just because it belongs to him, but also because it evokes masculine sexuality and even more literally, the penis.[74] The weapon's symbolism equates it with Hippolytus' flesh and physique. Further, in calling the sword *gentis Actaeae decus* (900), Theseus alludes to Hippolytus' own much-praised physical *decus* ('beauty': 659; 741; 1110) and the phrasing he employs could just as easily apply to Hippolytus qua person as to the sword's decoration.[75] The sword's interchangeability with Hippolytus' actual *corpus* highlights once again the body's role as a symbolic, spectatorial object in physiognomic discourse. In a simplistic sense, Theseus

---

[73] These lines' multiple ambiguities have been examined by Seidensticker (1969) 149; Davis (1983) 122–3; Boyle (1987) 31–2 and (1997) 80; Mayer (2002), 57; and Hill (2004) 170.

[74] A standard metaphor: see Adams (1982) 19–22. On this specific scene, Segal (1986) 134 remarks, 'in her false accusation of Hippolytus, the sword is indeed an instrument of desire. It replaces the phallus metonymically as well as metaphorically'.

[75] Refer to Chapter 1, 80, for other examples of *decus* being used to denote individuals.

3.1 *Phaedra*

reads the item correctly – the sword really does represent Hippolytus. But his judgement from appearances is ill-informed, with the result that the body's truthfulness is undercut by poor discernment. Things really are what they seem, just not what they seem to Theseus.

It is worth stressing once more that I do not deny the deceitful quality of Phaedra's actions in the latter half of the play. She gives Theseus misleading information, she does not correct his erroneous inferences, and she complies with the Nurse's underhand plot to accuse Hippolytus. Throughout these events, though, Phaedra's body remains a reliable index of her emotions and experiences. For the most part, it seems to indicate how and what she actually feels, and even its changeability is reliable for alerting onlookers to her potential duplicity. In line with Seneca's Stoic views, in line also with physiognomic assumptions, Phaedra's *corpus* does not lie even when she herself does.

Hippolytus' Face

As ought to be clear from the preceding discussion, corporeal descriptions in the *Phaedra* highlight, often simultaneously, the fictional and quasi-human aspects of characters' identities. On the one hand, Seneca's portrayal of bodily surfaces intensifies audience awareness of what lies behind these surfaces, namely the inferred, invisible presence of motives, emotions, intentions, and psychology. The play's incorporation of Stoic physics and 'small-p' physiognomy further accentuates the characters' quasi-human aspect because it applies in a fictional setting paradigms developed for the actual, offstage world: Phaedra and Hippolytus invite and receive the same kind of analysis as any real, living and breathing physiognomic subject. On the other hand, though, Seneca's descriptions draw attention to the body's enactment on stage and hence, to a character's identity as a constructed dramatic role. The body acquires a strong tint of metatheatricality: it may be moulded and fashioned to elicit the desired response from its audience, its clothing may serve the same purpose as a costume, and the face a mask. It can even be likened to a literal text, inscribed as it is with *notae* and *indicia*.

Appearance

This combination of ethical and textual identity comes notably to the fore in the play's treatment of Hippolytus' face. Enraged at the crimes he believes have been committed against his wife, Theseus decries a perceived mismatch between Hippolytus' appearance and his conduct:

> ubi vultus ille et ficta maiestas viri
> atque habitus horrens, prisca et antiqua appetens,
> morumque senium triste et affectus graves?
> o vita fallax, abditos sensus geris
> animisque pulchram turpibus faciem induis:
> pudor impudentem celat, audacem quies
> pietas nefandum; vera fallaces probant
> simulantque molles dura
>
> Where is that countenance, and the man's feigned dignity
> and the unkempt clothing, imitating ancient custom,
> his austere and gloomy habits, and harsh character?
> O treacherous life, you hide your true feelings:
> you put a fair face on foul thoughts:
> shame conceals the shameless man; placidity, the reckless;
> respect, the wicked; liars sanction the truth
> and the feeble pretend to be tough
>
> (*Phaed.* 915–22)

With the participle *ficta*, Theseus affirms not only the supposed falsity of Hippolytus' morals, but also their constructed quality, as part of a *fictional* text. Hippolytus' character and Hippolytus *as a character* have been composed (*fingere*, OLD entry 6a) in a work of poetry. The theme of literary and more specifically, dramatic composition extends to the verb *induo*, which often refers to the assumption of a part, a costume, or a mask. For instance, Seneca's Medea, in her opening speech, urges herself in overtly metatheatrical terms, *inhospitalem Caucasum mente indue* ('clothe your mind with [the behaviour of] the inhospitable Caucasus', *Med.* 43), while the phrase *induere personam* is a common theatrical metaphor for Latin writers.[76] Arguably, such a context could elicit the association of *facies* (919) with its root meaning, *facere*, thereby implying that the face may be designed and shaped like

---

[76] On the metatheatrical resonance of *Med.* 43, see Boyle (2014) *ad loc.* Seneca uses *induere personam* at *Ben.* 2.17.2. Other pertinent examples from Latin texts include Cic. *Cael.* 35.1 and *Tusc.* 5.73.3, and Quint. *Inst.* 3.8.50 and 12.8.15.

3.1 *Phaedra*

any other object of manufacture.[77] Hippolytus' face may be constructed, either by Hippolytus himself as an implied human individual, or by his author, Seneca.

Moreover, the passage's repeated emphasis on the face as an index of personal character draws attention to the purpose and quality of the theatrical mask. Does Hippolytus veil his true feelings the way a mask is assumed to shroud the face? Is there a discrepancy between his exterior and his interior, or does the face that he wears provide reliable information about his disposition? The audience knows, of course, that Theseus is mistaken, and that Hippolytus' austere appearance really does convey his *mores*: witness the Nurse's earlier attempt to have Hippolytus swap his grimace for a smile on the basis that 'a grim brow befits an old man' (*frons decet tristis senem*, 453), not a young one. But the audience's background knowledge only accentuates the conflation of metatheatre with physiognomy, textual with quasi-human modes of identification in *Phaedra* 915–22. Hippolytus' mask *is* his face, and vice versa: it is the front-on, visible, legible surface that communicates to viewers what kind of character Hippolytus is. As discussed earlier in this chapter in connection with Phaedra, the actor's face is performative and physiognomically legible regardless of whether a mask is worn.[78] The same goes for the character's face: it provides clues about the intangible, invisible aspects of a *dramatis persona*'s disposition. An audience's interpretation of the mask runs parallel to the physiognomist's (and in Seneca's case, the Stoic's) interpretation of actual, human faces. In fact, rising popularity of physiognomic discourse appears to have influenced mask-making in Hellenistic times, albeit only in the genre of New Comedy.[79] Such

---

[77] Bettini (1996) 184–9 remarks on the connections ancient etymologists would draw between *facies* and *facere*. See also Baumbach (2008) 68.
[78] Thus, Baumbach (2008) 130 links the face and the mask: 'both point to something *beyond* the visible and act as ciphers awaiting a diligent reader to unfold their meaning'.
[79] The topic has been explored at length by Wiles (1991) 85–90 and Petrides (2014) 138–50. Magli, quoted by Frow (2014) 260, remarks an 'odd coincidence' between the 'stiff facial masks of ancient actors, which set expressions according to a few symbolic representations, and ancient physiognomics with its interest in the stable and lasting traits of a face, as separate from the passions that might move it'. Physiognomy, for its part, also draws connections with masks, for example Anon. Lat. 72: *Aristoteles addit etiam hos esse versutos, qui habent inflexa supercilia, sicut sunt in personis senum comicorum*. The objections of Poe (1996) notwithstanding, it seems that a solid case can be built for physiognomy interacting with Hellenistic mask design.

Appearance

overlap between the physiognomist's and the dramatist's art collapses notions of mask–face dualism, that persistent yet often erroneous 'dichotomy of inner truth and conventional exterior'.[80] Just as Phaedra's body reveals her thoughts and feelings, so does Hippolytus' visage indicate his character, both at the level of conscious dramatic enactment and at the level of implied human existence. In the words of Roland Barthes, 'the temptation of the absolute mask (the mask of antiquity, for instance) ... implies less the theme of the secret (as is the case with the Italian half mask) than that of an archetype of the human face'.[81]

The interchangeability of mask and face is likewise key to Phaedra's interaction with Hippolytus at the close of Act 2. When Phaedra confesses her love for her stepson, she does so in elliptical language that rationalises her passion at the same time as underscoring its incestuous bent. 'Hippolytus', she says, 'it is like this: I love Theseus' face, the looks he once bore as a young man, long ago' (*Hippolyte, sic est: Thesei vultus amo / illos priores quos tulit quondam puer*, 646–7). She proceeds to recall the hero's appearance and to trace its outline in Hippolytus' form:

> tuaeque Phoebes vultus aut Phoebi mei,
> tuusve potius – talis, en talis fuit
> cum placuit hosti, sic tulit celsum caput.
> in te magis refulget incomptus decor.
> est genitor in te totus et torvae tamen
> pars aliqua matris miscet ex aequo decus:
> in ore Graio Scythicus apparet rigor.

> His face was like your Phoebe's, or my Phoebus',
> or rather, like yours – this, this is how he was
> when he beguiled his enemy, he held his head high, like this.
> Unkempt beauty shines more brightly in you.
> All of your father is in your face, but also some part
> of your wild mother, mixed in, with equal grace:
> Scythian ruggedness in a Grecian countenance.
>
> (*Phaed.* 654–60)

In her use of the terms *sic* (656) and *talis* (655), Phaedra not only conflates her memory of the father's face with the present form of

---

[80] Frow (2014) 248.
[81] Barthes (1972) 56.

3.1 *Phaedra*

the son's, but also behaves like a director instructing an actor in how to pose. Like Andromache's portrayal of Hector/Astyanax at *Troades* 465-8, discussed in Chapter 2, Phaedra's description blends metatheatrical self-consciousness with explicit confirmation of biological descent.[82] It is by standing and, given the dramatic context, *performing* in such a way that Hippolytus reinforces his resemblance and family relationship to Theseus. Once again, the concept of the theatrical mask and its evocation of specific character traits forms an undercurrent in the passage: the *vultus* Hippolytus displays to his internal and external audience is a totalising vision of his self. It is tempting to speculate that, were the play staged in ancient Rome, Theseus and Hippolytus would wear similar masks, or even be played by the same actor, staging choices that would bring another layer of poignancy to this scene. But even without such ingenious dramaturgy, Phaedra's speech still gives prominence to the face as a dramatised, visual symbol of identity: this is Hippolytus as a *persona* in a play.

At the same time, though, Hippolytus' *vultus* can also be said to convey who he is as an implied human individual, the habits and choices (*volo*) that comprise his personal attributes.[83] The wildness and austerity that appear in his countenance correspond to the texture of his preferred lifestyle, while his physical similarity to Theseus points to the more troubling aspects of his nature, which he shares with his father: a propensity for violence, wilfulness, hostility towards women (e.g. *Phaed.* 226-9; 927). Most importantly, his *vultus* affirms his quasi-human status by corroborating his bloodline: Hippolytus is Theseus' offspring in looks as well as character.

Performance, even just the *idea* of performance, is one more element contributing to Hippolytus' quasi-humanity in this scene, because the face Phaedra touches on stage is attached to a real body, a real person, regardless of the mask's stylised presence. I remarked in the Introduction to this book that live performance endows dramatic character with an additional layer of human

---

[82] Boyle (1987) *ad Phaed.* 655 notes the correspondences between these two passages.
[83] Bettini (1996) 181-4 argues that *vultus*, for Roman writers, evoked interiority and personal disposition, chiefly via association with *voluntas*. On the association of *vultus* and *volo* in Seneca's *Phaedra*, see Bexley (2011) 385-6.

resemblance.[84] The simple fact of their embodiment grants *dramatis personae* an extra degree of reality, completeness, and selfhood. In Hippolytus' case, actual physicality is overlaid by and merges with Phaedra's projections, making the young man's *vultus* both a tangibly present object and an incorporeal image, a simultaneous marker of his implied personhood and his fictional status. When Phaedra gives stage directions to Hippolytus (*talis*, 655; *sic*, 656) and proceeds to describe the beauty of his countenance, there is an actual body on stage beside her, ready to receive and perform these directives. Metatheatrical language, in this instance, only emphasises the physical reality of what is being presented: Hippolytus' embodied identity, his 'personal' existence. And even if the scene is not staged but merely read, the text's dramatic form is such that it cannot avoid evoking embodiment and the sort of physical identity that brings literary characters closer to the human sphere. Arguably, these associations would be all the more immediate to Seneca's contemporary audience whose familiarity with ancient stage conventions would enable them to envisage such embodiment even in the context of a dramatic recital.

From sapiens *to Shapelessness*

Immediately following Phaedra and Hippolytus' encounter in the woods, the play's second chorus devotes itself to celebrating the young man's unrivalled *forma*. The speakers insist that Hippolytus's 'beauty shines more brightly just as the moon glitters more clearly when its orb is full' (*pulchrior tanto ... forma lucet, / clarior quanto micat orbe pleno / ... / ... / ... Phoebe*, 743–4; 747). They then proceed to issue gnomic warnings about beauty's transience – *res est forma fugax* ('beauty is a fleeting thing', 773) – and about the trouble it can cause: *anceps forma bonum mortalibus* ('beauty is a dubious boon for mortals', 761). After reviewing some cautionary tales of divine attraction (777–94) and stark images of natural decay (764–72), the chorus compares Hippolytus' beauty to that of the gods, whom he easily outstrips

---

[84] Introduction, 18–19.

3.1 *Phaedra*

(795–811) and concludes by wishing that his beauty go 'unpunished' (*impunita*, 821) and survive to 'display the imprint of ugly old age' (*deformis senii monstret imaginem*, 823). Repetition of the term *forma* enables Seneca to achieve several aims: first, it contrasts Hippolytus' beauty with his final, gruesome fate of shapelessness, his ultimate lack of any discernible *forma*, and second, it focuses attention on the issue of Hippolytus' less than attractive behaviour and whether that behaviour should, in Seneca's Stoic scheme, imply an uglier exterior. The two topics are, at base, interrelated.

Of course, from a Stoic perspective, physical beauty need not imply virtuous behaviour, nor is there any expectation that achieving *virtus* ameliorates the appearance of an unattractive body. But there is in Seneca's work the persistent idea that immoral qualities that corrupt the soul will have a correspondingly deleterious effect on an individual's *corpus*. Writing about the physical symptoms of anger, Seneca avers, 'you would not know whether it is a more detestable vice, or an ugly one' (*nescias utrum magis detestabile vitium sit an deforme*, *Ira* 1.3.4). He continues to refer to its *deformitas* sporadically throughout the *de Ira* (2.11.2; 2.35.3; 2.36.1–2), adding, 'no emotion disturbs the face more than this one: it spoils the most beautiful countenances, it turns the most calm visages into savage ones; all physical grace deserts the angry' (*non est ullius adfectus facies turbatior: pulcherrima ora foedavit, torvos vultus ex tranquillissimis reddit; linquit decor omnis iratos*, *Ira* 2.35.3). Such *deformitas* also befalls Hippolytus, albeit in a much more literal way: Theseus describes his son's broken body as 'lacking shape' (*forma carens*, *Phaed.* 1265) and the messenger reporting the details of Hippolytus's death wonders incredulously, 'is this beauty's glory?' (*hocine est formae decus?* 1110). Significantly, Hippolytus' face is ravaged when he falls from his chariot (1095–6) and Phaedra, in her struggle to comprehend the extent of his physical destruction, asks, 'which bi-formed bull, fierce and horned, tore you apart?' (*quis ... / ... /taurus biformis ore cornigero ferox / divulsit?* 1170; 1172–3). Like a reification of beauty's dubiety (*anceps forma*, *Phaed.* 761, above) the double-bodied Minotaur that Phaedra imagines attacking Hippolytus symbolises the threat of formlessness, of the disproportion and distortion that sabotage beauty's implied balance. In the end, Hippolytus' *forma* is worse than merely *anceps*; it is countless bloody pieces.

Does Seneca then imply that Hippolytus is morally responsible for his own disintegration? This is a tempting line of argument, especially since Hippolytus admits to the possibility of *furor* underpinning his hatred of women (567) and since his character appears quick to anger.[85] Relatedly, scholars of Senecan tragedy have often noted that Hippolytus' accounts of his Golden Age idyll in the forest reveal unsettling undercurrents of destruction and discontent: the young man seems more at war with nature than at one with it.[86] Although he compares his sylvan lifestyle to an innocent *prima aetas* in which the earth spontaneously nourished men and which men subsequently destroyed through greed, rage, and warfare (525–68), Hippolytus hunts with the very weapons whose invention he condemns. He criticises the corrupting influence of city life that, among its many sins, teaches men to lie (*verba fingit*, 497) and contrasts this immorality with the harmless forest-dweller who 'knows only how to set clever traps for beasts' (*callidas tantum feris / struxisse fraudes novit*, 502–3), but the two activities are presented as equivalent in a way that begins to undermine Hippolytus' point: the forest still teaches him a form of trickery, the only difference being that he does not perpetrate it against fellow men.[87] Although he decries both intra-familial murder (553–8) and sacrifice (498–500), his immediate response to Phaedra's revelation is to combine the two (706–9). Hippolytus' stance is contradictory at best, and by the end of the play, the natural world he so reveres turns on him, transforming him from hunter to hunted, victor to victim.[88] He cannot, it seems, preserve his ideals.

---

[85] When Theseus accuses Hippolytus of rape, he similarly attributes the young man's misdeeds to an inherited impulse of Amazonian *furor* (*Phaed.* 909).

[86] Davis (1983) 126 and n.21; Segal (1986) 60–105; Boyle (1987) 18–24 and (1997) 64; Roisman (2000) 77–82. Notwithstanding the objections of Mayer (2002) 54–7, the overall approach is a convincing one.

[87] Cf., however, the comments of Mayer (2002) 55: 'tricks were morally satisfactory if directed towards securing your dinner, they are obviously wrong when used against your fellow man'.

[88] Boyle (1985) 1302–3 is an insightful study of these motifs.

3.1 *Phaedra*

But assuming his utter moral *deformitas* would be unfair both to Hippolytus and to Seneca. Like many of the tragedies' waverers, Hippolytus is a complex figure:[89] he desires a life in the forest but cannot fully achieve it; his austere self-control unravels; his desperate attempts at self-coherence and self-containment meet with literally shattering defeat.[90] He bears mild resemblance to Thyestes in his profession of, yet ultimate failure to maintain, Stoic or Stoic-sounding principles. His dismemberment is, in many ways, the physical realisation of this failure, just as Thyestes' faltering body illustrates his inconstancy. What we see in Hippolytus' *deforme corpus*, therefore, is not just moral weakness but also his failure to attain a consistent, fully integrated identity. The fate of Hippolytus' celebrated *forma* mirrors, and to some extent evolves from, the tensions and contradictions in his personality itself. Once again, the body tells an essential truth about its owner's traits: lack of moral and lack of corporeal unity go hand-in-hand, as Hippolytus' lost *forma* also symbolises his ineffectual pursuit of *sapientia*.

Hippolytus' fate similarly illustrates his ultimate lack of individual autonomy. He cannot control how others – specifically, how Phaedra perceives his beauty, nor when and how that beauty will fade. The idea that Hippolytus' body will undermine as well as encapsulate his identity recurs throughout the play. When the chorus wishes him *deforme senium* ('shapeless/ugly old age', 823) as the best possible outcome for his *forma*, it acknowledges time's inevitable, inexorable extinction of his corporeal selfhood. What happens by the tragedy's conclusion is an even more radical instance of lost bodily integrity: Hippolytus' *forma* is pulverised by natural forces beyond his control. From the monstrous, sea-birthed bull to Phaedra's sexual obsession, wild and often hostile *natura* threatens to destroy Hippolytus' physical boundaries. In Seneca's tragic *corpus*, where self-definition and self-determination are such persistent concerns, the end of the *Phaedra* raises pressing questions about the extent to which

---

[89] Coffey and Mayer (1990) 28 are surely misled in their assertion that 'the presentation of Hippolytus is uncomplicated'. He may, as they note, be prone to 'angry rhetoric', but his characterisation reveals its complexity via multiple layers of internal contradiction.

[90] On Hippolytus' potential for self-coherence, see Kirichenko (2017) 279.

individuals can actually govern their own identities. To the degree that Hippolytus is an embodied self, he actually has very limited command of how that self is constructed, not to mention how long that construction lasts.

Admittedly, Hippolytus' body is only one element of his identity overall, and there is a strong sense in which his memory, reputation, and representation survive the bull's attack. But, as Glen Most points out, Stoic materialism makes dismemberment a particularly problematic event, because if everything that exists is a *corpus* 'at what point [does] the mutilation of a body lead to the loss of personal identity of that body's owner?'[91] If Hippolytus' *forma* is one of his most identifying features, what happens to 'Hippolytus' when that shape is gone? Conversely, who or what is Hippolytus if this shapeless mass, *forma carens* (1265), most accurately represents him? When Phaedra bends over the young man's mangled remains and asks, 'Hippolytus, is this your face I gaze upon? Is this what I have done to it?' (*Hippolyte, tales intuor vultus tuos / talesque feci?* 1168–9), and when she later wonders, 'where has your beauty fled?' (*quo tuus fugit decor*, 1173), her perplexity articulates a deeper philosophical quandary. At an emotional level, Phaedra struggles to come to terms with her loss; at a grimly literal level, she is unsure whether the pieces of flesh set before her really do come from Hippolytus' face;[92] at a far more abstract level, her questions prompt the audience to consider precisely what bodily form constitutes the person and character of Hippolytus. Seneca does not provide definite answers to these

---

[91] Most (1992) 406.
[92] The sequence of events here has caused some confusion. At *Phaed.* 1105–14, the messenger reports that servants are scouring the woods to bring back what remains of Hippolytus' body; at *Phaed.* 1159–98, Phaedra emerges to lament and kill herself over these remains; and at *Phaed.* 1247–74, Theseus commands the servants to bring in Hippolytus' broken pieces before proceeding himself to lament and assemble them. Are these actions coherent? Zwierlein (1966) 15–24 regards the scenes as inconsistent and not composed for stage performance. Sutton (1986) 52–3 envisions the remains brought on at *Phaed.* 1156, the beginning of Act 5. Kohn (2013) 76–8 has them brought on at *Phaed.* 1247 and thus has Phaedra lament over an *imaginary* corpse. From personal experience of staging this play, I see no problem with some remains being brought on during the end of the messenger's speech, and some more being brought in response to Theseus' command at *Phaed.* 1247. True, they sit around on stage for a long time, but there is nothing dramaturgically problematic about that, and this arrangement means that Phaedra really *is* addressing some part of Hippolytus (face or not) when she speaks lines 1168–9.

3.1 *Phaedra*

questions – that is not his purpose in the play – but by bringing them into such visually impressive focus, he demonstrates how the body, with its seemingly limitless capacity for abjection, can elude control and destabilise the concept and the fact of individuality. Hippolytus' body is simultaneously an important index of his identity and a potential betrayal of it.

Identifying Hippolytus

Besides highlighting the fragility of Hippolytus' embodied identity as a quasi-human, the young man's *forma* also highlights his textual status as a constructed, fictional figure. His appearance is the result of poetic composition, it is a rhetorical creation (*forma, figura*), while its devastation reflects and is reflected in the disjointed style of the *Phaedra*'s final scene.[93] This last episode, in which Theseus endeavours to recompose Hippolytus' broken body, has not always been granted a favourable reception. Barrett dismissed it as a 'grisly jigsaw', and many others have criticised it for including unnecessarily grotesque detail, and for being either implausible, impossible, or simply laughable to stage.[94] But the Act's thematic relevance to the preceding events of this tragedy make it a fitting – if also arresting and unsettling – finale to Phaedra and Hippolytus' story.[95] For a play that has stressed the significance of bodily and facial expression, it seems perfectly appropriate to conclude with a scene in which Theseus painfully and methodically reassembles his son's fragmented frame, an action that is at once an attempt to comprehend what has happened, and to ascertain, if possible, precisely *who* Hippolytus was. As Theseus puts his son's limbs back together, he struggles to come to terms with his son's identity, to sort it out, to make sense of it. The act of arranging body parts in an attempt to

---

[93] See Segal (1986) 215–20.
[94] Barrett (1964) 44. The scene's detractors include Beare (1945) 14; Zwierlein (1966) 24; Coffey and Mayer (1990) 17–8 and *ad Phaed.* 1256–61; Mayer (2002) 31–2. For defence of its potential enactment on stage, see Fortey and Glucker (1975) 713–15; Sutton (1986) 52–3; and Kohn (2013) 76–8.
[95] The thematic importance of the *Phaedra*'s final Act has been explored by Segal (1982) 215–20, and Most (1992) 394–5, and touched upon more lightly by Davis (1983) 117; Boyle (1985) 1304 and 1332–4; and Bexley (2011) 389.

fashion a coherent whole evokes simultaneously a process of literary composition and of quasi-physiognomic corporeal interpretation. It is here in this last scene that Hippolytus's fictional and quasi-human identity finally, fully coincide.

Faced with his son's fractured remains, Theseus turns at once to matters of identity, leaning over the limbs to wonder, *Hippolytus hic est?* ('Is this Hippolytus?' 1249). As Glen Most points out, the question is multivalent, since it articulates Theseus' distress – like a futile cry of 'why?' – but also unfolds the complex issue of how selfhood relates to bodily integrity.[96] Like Phaedra, who expresses similar perplexity over how and whether these limbs can signify Hippolytus, Theseus struggles to reconnect such scattered pieces with the (former) person of his son. To what extent can these parts still symbolise Hippolytus even though Hippolytus the individual has evidently been destroyed? One of the question's many effects is to stress Hippolytus' current role as interpretive material, and concomitantly, Theseus' – and any observer's – role as 'readers' of these corporeal fragments. Hippolytus' body resembles a text, a set of signs that must be scrutinised and assembled if they are to yield any meaning. Theseus' activity, by extension, is analogous to rhetorical or literary interpretation, or even composition, as he examines in turn each body part, to ascertain its place within the larger structure of Hippolytus' frame.

Appropriately enough, Theseus' speech is replete with literary vocabulary, an issue explored briefly by Charles Segal and Glen Most,[97] but worth reprising and elaborating here. The grieving father places Hippolytus' pieces 'in order' (*in ordinem*, 1257) and 'counts the limbs' (*membra ... adnumerat*, 1264); the *locus* of the body's final arrangement (1257–8; 1268) blends into the literary *locus* of the play's final speech, both articulating an uncomfortable sense of burial and closure.[98] Seneca also has Theseus 'fashion the body' (*corpus fingit*, 1265), as though fabricating the text of Hippolytus' limbs just as a poet writes verse. The link is further facilitated by a long tradition of Greek and Roman writers using corporeal metaphors to furnish terminology for rhetorical and

---

[96] Most (1992) 409.
[97] Segal (1986) 215–20 and Most (1992) 407–8.
[98] Erasmo (2008) 53–61 discusses the scene's association with Roman burial rituals.

3.1 *Phaedra*

literary composition and criticism: *membra, caput, corpus, oculi* all claim places within rhetorical discourse alongside the vocabulary of assembling, joining, cutting, and dissecting.[99] Horace famously says of breaking up the sequence of an Ennian line (*Ann.* 7 frag. 13 Manuwald-Goldberg), 'you would find the limbs of a poet even when he had been dismembered' (*invenias etiam disiecti membra poetae, Serm.* 1.4.62). It is tempting to hear an echo of this comment in Theseus' self-exhortation, *disiecta, genitor, membra laceri corporis / in ordinem dispone et errantes loco / restitue partes* ('Father, place in order the torn body's dismembered limbs and restore to their place these scattered parts', 1256–8). Hippolytus is now little more than a set of clauses and metrical feet.

A closer and equally rhetorical parallel to Theseus' activity comes from Seneca's own prose, specifically *Epistle* 89.1, in which Seneca extols the benefits of making philosophy more manageable and accessible: *rem utilem desideras ... dividi philosophiam et ingens corpus eius in membra disponi; facilius enim per partes in cognitionem totius ducimur* ('you desire a useful thing ... namely, dividing up philosophy and arranging its huge body into limbs; for through the parts we are brought more easily into comprehension of the whole'). Although Theseus at this point in the tragedy is recomposing rather than dividing Hippolytus' body, his activity seems likewise geared towards comprehension of the matter at hand. Seneca hopes to lead his readers *in cognitionem totius*, and Theseus, as he gazes at the parts arrayed before him, proceeds to discern not only their specific physical features – *laevi lateris agnosco notas* ('I recognise the marks of your left side' 1260) – but also the broader sequence of events and culpability that has led to this conclusion: *crimen agnosco meum* ('I recognise my crime' 1249). Like the readers of *Epistle* 89, Theseus strives for global comprehension of the material laid before him, though arguably with less success.

Motifs of recognition in this passage also contribute to this sense of Hippolytus' textual constructedness. I remarked in

---

[99] Most (1992) 407–8 stresses the key role of bodily rhetoric / rhetorical bodies in Neronian literature. Useful collation of such rhetorical/bodily terms can be found in Svenbro (1984). See also Kennerly (2018).

Chapter 1 that recognition scenes can invite a semiotic approach whereby the person being recognised is assimilated to an interpretive object, a conglomerate of signs and symbols.[100] The well-known scenario from New Comedy, in which birth tokens are presented to a Nurse or to a long-lost relative, equates the person with the tangible memento, such that the latter signifies the former and enables the individual to be 'deciphered' in terms of social status and background. Another common scenario, exemplified this time by Sophocles' (and Seneca's) Oedipus, conflates the person completely with the recognition token, since the object to be deciphered is the body itself. Seneca's *Hippolytus* represents an extreme version of such bodily recognition: the marks/signs that designate his left flank (*laevi lateris ... notas*, 1260) imply a specific set of physical features that help Theseus to recognise this body part, and, at the same time, evoke letters inscribed on paper, written communication (*notae*).[101] Instead of an aged servant presenting the estranged father with objects that prove his children's paternity, the servants in Seneca's *Phaedra* scour the fields and carry back to Theseus pieces that represent, that *stand in for*, the son he once had. Recognition, for Theseus, is an act of semiotic reconstruction in which he pulls together his son's actual and inscribed *corpus*.

Significantly, the term *nota* likewise correlates the body to a text in physiognomic discourse. When Seneca lists degenerate character types and behavioural traits in *Epistle* 52.12, he declares that they *in apertum per notas exeunt* ('are made known through identifying marks'). In *de Ira* 1.1.5 he similarly uses *notae* to denote the warning signs of aggression in animals, which he likens in turn to bodily expressions of anger in humans. The anonymous Latin *Physiognomia*, too, has recourse to this term, for example 11: *denotabit*; 16: *notat*; 105: *denotatur*, albeit with less frequency than its equivalents, *signa* and *indicia*. Common to all of these passages, nonetheless, is the idea that physical features and gestures have the same ability to signify and to generate meaning as

---

[100] Chapter 1, 27–8.
[101] *OLD s.v. nota* entries 1 and 6. Seneca uses *notae* to mean 'writing' at *Epistle* 40.1: *quanto iucundiores sunt litterae, quae vera amici absentis vestigia, veras notas adferunt?*

3.1 *Phaedra*

letters on a page or words in a sentence.[102] In the *Phaedra*, Theseus performs a quasi-physiognomic act by perceiving and interpreting the *notae* on Hippolytus's body (1260), while the servants sent to fetch those scattered limbs engage in a subordinate process of textual assemblage by tracking down 'the bloody imprint [that] signifies the long path' of Hippolytus' final journey (*longum cruenta tramitem signat nota*, 1107). The metapoetic language of the tragedy's last Act combines literary inflections with the *Phaedra*'s persistent interest in physiognomic observation; in fact, it shows how the former often underpins the latter.

At the same time, any physiognomic and recognition motifs present in this scene also bolster Hippolytus' quasi-human status as an individual within the world of the play. By examining the *notae* (1260) and by recognising/acknowledging (*agnosco*, 1249; 1260) parts if not all of his son, Theseus tries to confirm his personal as well as metapoetic knowledge of Hippolytus. The verb at the root of both words, *noscere*, indicates not just Theseus' cognisance of a fact or study of a text, but also his final, painful attempt to understand his son's character. Just as a physiognomist reads bodily surfaces in order to divine the type of person situated behind them, so Theseus discerns through his careful recomposition of Hippolytus' *corpus* the young man's true nature, which he had earlier misread. Unlike the recognition scenes in *Medea* and *Thyestes*, this episode really does hinge on a *dramatis persona*'s acquisition of new knowledge and on the realisation of a drastic reversal in fortune. The *facies* that Theseus previously condemned as a false covering for deviant conduct he now sees as a true index of Hippolytus' physical and moral *forma* (1269), although its radical destruction also implies that Theseus may never quite succeed in his task of comprehensive knowledge. Thanks to his fragmented form, Hippolytus remains just as elusive and ambiguous a figure in death as he was in life; his reconstitution can only ever be partial.

Hippolytus' implied humanity is similarly conjured via Seneca's simple yet emotive technique of using second-person forms in this

---

[102] Baumbach (2008) 98 is particularly perceptive in this regard: 'Physiognomy is above all an art of *reading*, of deciphering and interpreting a text.'

speech. 'I destroyed you', Theseus admits to his son's remains (*ego te peremi*, 1250), and later, in grim puzzlement, 'I don't know what part of you this is, but it is part of you' (*quae pars tui sit dubito; sed pars est tui*, 1267). The tone is affectionate as well as sorrowful. Its sense of intimacy only makes Hippolytus' absence all the more shockingly palpable: by having Theseus talk 'to' his lost son, Seneca points to the unbridgeable chasm separating the 'person' Hippolytus was just lately from the 'parts' that exist now. Hippolytus is no longer 'you', he can no longer respond to such a form of address, and Theseus' use of it accentuates this loss of selfhood, of *being*. Though Hippolytus' component parts lie available for reassembly, they lack the agency that once animated them, helped them cohere, and gave them meaning. Like the compositional, textual elements of literary character, they cannot hope to convey the impression of a person without the addition of some extra, almost ineffable human colouring. All the pieces are there, but Hippolytus isn't. And his absence, indicated so clearly by these second-person forms, only confirms his implied human status in all of his preceding appearances in the tragedy: this was a figure endowed with sufficient agency, psychology, and individuality to merit being called 'you'.

Such contemplation of Hippolytus' absence brings us back again to the multiple meanings of the question, *Hippolytus hic est?* (1249, above). Besides evoking the limbs' ability to signify and querying the extent to which they succeed in encapsulating the person to whom they once belonged, this plain yet remarkably resonant question also interrogates what, in the first place, made Hippolytus who he was. Obviously, this collection of bloody limbs both is and is not Hippolytus: it stands in for the person who was always, in any case, accessed via the external surfaces of his body, and it signals the lack of defining features – both corporeal and psychological – necessary to Hippolytus' selfhood. Interpreted at an extra-dramatic, meta-literary level, the question also prompts us to consider how actor, character and person coincide. Is Hippolytus the actor who plays the role (and who is now, concomitantly, absent from the scene)? Or is he the role itself, fabricated by Seneca, assembled from language, rhetorical tropes, and a range of pre-existing literary components? Finally, is Hippolytus the person we see within the world of the play, the individual now broken by fate and lamented by Theseus? The answer, of course, is that Hippolytus is all three, and that all three layers – the metatheatrical, the metapoetic, and the intra-dramatic – telescope together to present Hippolytus' identity as simultaneously fictional and quasi-human. Hippolytus is an illusion created by poetry and its enactment on stage; he is also an implied human personality capable of being subjected to suffering and to physical devastation. As depicted by Seneca, the young man's corporeal ruin articulates the gap separating singular body parts from the whole, integrated, embodied person,[103] *and also* the gap separating singular rhetorical or literary components from the final, finished poetic product. Close examination of Hippolytus' pieces, such as that performed by Theseus, functions almost as a metaphor for the ways in which character is built, and the ways in which it may be dissected.

Bridge: Character Portraits

Physiognomy and Literary Portraiture

It is a profitable exercise to consider how the *Phaedra*'s various physical descriptions relate to the literary technique of character portraits, not only as a means of elucidating their effects, but also for the sake of further contextualising their representation of fictional people. Typically, character portraits are designed to mediate between a character's interior and exterior, using the latter to define the former and assuming that inner nature can be perceived from outward form.[104] While they do not always refer explicitly to the private worlds of characters' psychology, as Seneca does, they nonetheless adhere to broadly physiognomic principles of bodily and mental states coinciding.

The most plentiful and representative examples of character portraits come from the eighteenth and nineteenth-century novel,

---

[103] Thus, Slaney (2016) 31: 'The human body is here reduced to components and deprived of the formal unity which now appears at the very least transient and unreliable, if not downright illusory.'
[104] Heier (1976) 321.

Appearance

in which abundant descriptions of physical appearance are used to enhance narrative realism. These depictions evolved from the belief that additional corporeal detail would produce more lifelike characters, partly through making them seem unique and psychologically complex. In fact, the era's and the genre's interest in literary portraiture derives much of its momentum from one specific source, the physiognomic handbook of Johann Caspar Lavater, which galvanised the reinstatement of physiognomy as a scientific discipline as well as influencing swathes of European novelists, inspiring them to contemplate mind–body interaction in their narratives.[105] The character portraits resulting from this trend generate the illusion of personality by enticing readers into inferring psychological traits from physical ones, and tempting them into thinking that a character's façade necessarily implies – and may even give access to – the labyrinthine structure of personality qualities lying behind it.[106] We may think, for instance, of Charles Bovary, whose ill-fitting, ill-matched clothes and ill-considered haircut conjure the awkwardness, hopelessness, and rustic ignorance that will define him throughout the novel.[107] Similarly, Nelly Dean's observations in *Wuthering Heights* uphold the notion of dialogic exchange between mind and body, such that reading a person's surface equates to comprehending his or her moral character and vice versa.[108] Nelly says of Heathcliff, 'personal appearance sympathised with mental deterioration; he acquired a slouching gait, and ignoble look' (Chapter 8), and of Hareton, 'his brightening mind brightened his features, and added spirit and nobility to their aspect' (Chapter 33). A major purpose of these passages is to motivate readers to engage in the same pursuit as Nelly. When she treats others' bodies as symbols of internal, psychological activity, readers are likewise meant to extrapolate

---

[105] The most comprehensive study of Lavater's influence on literature is Tytler (1982). See also Heier (1976) 324–5.

[106] The comments of Segal (1986) 23 on the *vraisemblance* of literary character are instructive in this regard: 'we inevitably endow a character with a three-dimensional life of thoughts and feelings like our own, through our sympathetic identification with another human being'.

[107] Further discussion of Charles Bovary can be found in Tytler (1982) 221.

[108] Tytler (1982) draws frequent examples from *Wuthering Heights* and stresses Lavater's influence on Brontë.

depth from façade, and to imagine a fully rounded personality hidden behind the narrator's descriptive plane.

Hence, the paradox of character portraits in eighteenth and nineteenth-century novels is that, by focusing so closely on visual data, they manage to imply that there is more to a given literary figure than immediately meets the eye. Diversity of somatic and sartorial detail creates a sense of characters' individuality, as though they were not forever bound within a specific, iterable text, while the interplay of external and internal features often conveys an impression of subjectivity, of individual consciousness, and of the distance separating a first-person from a third-person viewpoint. Character portraits are capable of drawing attention – again, paradoxically – to a private, internalised world of conscious thought: Heathcliff's movement and posture grants us, as readers, privileged access to how he, personally, feels. To the extent that character portraits achieve any or all of these effects, they can be said to perform the mimetic function of enabling literary figures to approximate to actual humans.

This mimetic quality becomes even more sharply defined in light of physiognomy's own dialogic relationship with literature. In his handbook, Lavater exhorts the would-be physiognomist to learn from 'die Menge physiognomischer Züge, Charaktere, Beschreibungen, die man in den grössten Dichtern so häufig findet' ('the mass of physiognomic sketches, characters, and descriptions which one so often finds in the greatest poets').[109] Such remarks reveal Lavater's inclination to treat fictional characters as pseudo-people, as templates to be applied in real-world situations. At the same time, they signal the literary quality of physiognomic analysis, virtually to the point of aligning physiognomists with readers or poets. Just as ancient Greek and Roman physiognomists describe the body as a set of legible signs, so Lavater directs readers to employ fictional paradigms for the decoding of actual people. Character and person overlap. In each case, identity is thought to depend on much the same clusters of corporeal information.

---

[109] Lavater, in Tytler (1982) 5.

Appearance

Besides emphasising characters' quasi-humanity, though, literary portraits also draw attention to their textual construction, chiefly via self-conscious dependence on internal readers and narrators. Again, *Wuthering Heights* provides pertinent examples in the form of Catherine's diary and of Nelly Dean's reminiscences. A particularly telling instance of literary self-consciousness occurs when Nelly leads Heathcliff to the mirror and teaches him the meaning of his countenance (Chapter 7):

> 'Oh, Heathcliff, you are showing a poor spirit! Come to the glass, and I'll let you see what you should wish. Do you mark those two lines between your eyes; and those thick brows, that, instead of rising arched, sink in the middle; and that couple of black fiends, so deeply buried, who never open their windows boldly, but lurk glinting under them, like devil's spies? Wish and learn to smooth away the surly wrinkles, to raise your lids frankly, and change the fiends to confident, innocent angels, suspecting and doubting nothing, and always seeing friends where they are not sure of foes. Don't get the expression of a vicious cur that appears to know the kicks it gets are its desert, and yet hates all the world, as well as the kicker, for what it suffers.'
>
> 'In other words, I must wish for Edgar Linton's great blue eyes and even forehead', he replied. 'I do—and that won't help me to them.'

An acute observer of physiognomy, Nelly instructs Heathcliff in how to 'read' his own face. The mirror's reflection facilitates the novel's self-reflection on the techniques used to convey character, the lines drawn on the countenance and the personality inferred thereby. At the same time as Nelly schools Heathcliff, she also instructs the novel's external readers in how best to process and interpret physiognomic signs. We have seen already a similar presence of physiognomic narrators in Senecan tragedy: the Nurse describing Phaedra (*Phaed.* 362–83); the Nurse describing Medea (*Med.* 382–96); the chorus describing Cassandra (*Ag.* 710–19). Despite vast differences in genre and era, these Senecan examples share with *Wuthering Heights* an emphasis on decoding psychological states via external, corporeal observation; narrators as interpreters are paramount. Hence, as I remark above, Seneca relies on narrative passages even though they stall dramatic action.[110]

---

[110] Nor is Seneca the only dramatist to employ such techniques, although he does so at greater length than most: see, for example, Baumbach (2008) 98–178 on Shakespeare's physiognomics.

Of course, Seneca's approach also differs in some fundamental respects from that of the eighteenth and nineteenth-century novel. The pathognomic portraits in the tragedies do not envisage a bilateral exchange between mind and body; influence proceeds from the soul to the *corpus*, not the other way around, and this is in line with Stoic as opposed to physiognomic thought. Whereas ancient physiognomists happily entertain notions of two-way mind-body interaction (e.g. Ps.-Arist. *Physiognomy* 805a1–10), as do many of the novelists inspired by Lavater, Seneca sees only unidirectional causation: in *Epistle* 66.4 he states outright that the soul 'is not disfigured by the ugliness of the body' (*non deformitate corporis foedari animum*). No matter how much the body may dictate another person's judgements, it is always, ultimately the soul that is being judged.

Another crucial difference, which emerges from the *Wuthering Heights* passage in which Nelly directs Heathcliff to the mirror, is the concept of fixed personalities existing under unalterable exteriors. By complaining that he cannot swap his black eyes for blue ones, or make his forehead more even, Heathcliff covertly acknowledges the impossibility of changing his disposition as well. In contrast, Seneca's stance, thanks largely to its Stoic background, permits such change: even if most of his characters exhibit ingrained dispositions that have come to define them through a combination of literal and literary iteration (viz. Medea's anger), there is still the possibility, typically proffered by a Nurse or confidant, of altering one's emotional responses and following a different path. In the puzzling second Act of Seneca's *Agamemnon*, the Nurse declares that Clytemnestra's countenance communicates her distress in place of speech: *licet ipsa sileas, totus in vultu est dolor* ('Though you yourself are silent, all your pain is in your face', *Ag.* 128). By the end of this conversation, when the Nurse appears to have prevailed on Clytemnestra's sense of shame and convinced her to return to her husband, the queen's countenance changes accordingly: Aegisthus wonders why 'pallor spreads over [her] trembling cheeks, and [her] gaze is downcast, dazed, [her] face weary' (*sed quid trementis circuit pallor genas / iacensque vultu languido optutus stupet? Ag.* 237–8). Although Seneca never clarifies the depth or integrity of this change,[111] the very fact of its existence indicates the possibility of altering one's countenance and concomitantly, one's mindset. That most of Seneca's dramatic characters deliberately ignore such possibilities is a key part of their tragic fates.

One final point of divergence concerns personal distinctiveness and idiosyncrasy, qualities prized by eighteenth and nineteenth-century novelists but credited with far less importance in Senecan tragedy. Against the widespread and comparatively modern assumption that increased interiority and privacy equals increased individuality and uniqueness,[112] Seneca presents his audience with character portraits that are at once internally focused and reasonably generic. Though descriptions of Phaedra are rife with references to her internal psychological state, they do not reveal a complex singularity so much as a standard, recognisable pattern of emotional symptoms. Phaedra's feelings resemble a disease that can be classified and catalogued, much as ancient physiognomic thought catalogues types rather than individuals: the devious man; the gluttonous man; the stingy man; the flatterer. Stoicism likewise specialises in emotional and psychological typology because it shares – at least superficially – physiognomy's aim of *diagnosis*: anger, lust, and other diseases of the spirit must, from Seneca's perspective, be detected and cured. This means, as I observed briefly in the very first section of this chapter, that Seneca's portraits convey a sense of interiority and internally situated identity without concomitant expressions of singular selfhood; the two are not mutually interdependent – something modern audiences and scholars really need to keep in mind when assessing Seneca's dramatic work.

---

[111] Is Clytemnestra's change of heart sincere or motivated by a desire to deceive Aegisthus? Critics are divided. Supporting the former option are Herrmann (1924) 411–13, Herington (1966) 454, and Tarrant (1978) *ad Ag.* 239ff, who suggests in addition the two scenes' lack of dramatic connection. Schiesaro (2014) 180 seems to support the sincerity hypothesis, though, to be fair, this is far from the focus of his paper. Advocating for the latter option are Croisille (1964) 487 and Calder (1976) 32. The debate appears to have been largely abandoned by recent scholarship.

[112] A phenomenon tackled by Sennett (1974) with particularly insightful results. For the literary consequences of this turn towards individuality, Trilling (1973) remains a classic study.

Bridge: Character Portraits

Even when they are not directly prompted by physiognomy, all character portraits obey implicitly physiognomic principles of encouraging observers to deduce behaviour from, or match it with, appearance; this is just as true of Homer as it is of Dickens. In fact, Homer's portrait of Thersites is a perfect example of physiognomic reasoning uncoupled from any immediate doctrinal influence. The most detestable of Homer's Achaeans is presented as an ungainly, ill-shaped body:

> αἴσχιστος δὲ ἀνὴρ ὑπὸ Ἴλιον ἦλθε:
> φολκὸς ἔην, χωλὸς δ' ἕτερον πόδα: τὼ δέ οἱ ὤμω
> κυρτὼ ἐπὶ στῆθος συνοχωκότε: αὐτὰρ ὕπερθε
> φοξὸς ἔην κεφαλήν, ψεδνὴ δ' ἐπενήνοθε λάχνη.

> This was the ugliest man who came beneath Ilion. He was bandy-legged and went lame of one foot, with shoulders stooped and drawn together over his chest, and above this his skull went up to a point with the wool grown sparsely upon it.
> *(Il.* 2.216–19 trans. Lattimore)

Here, physical description follows rather than precedes an account of the character's behaviour, as though to ensure the audience's dislike of this particular figure; Thersites' ugly physique is meant to confirm the ugliness of his conduct. Although it is highly unlikely that this passage owes any debt to ancient physiognomy, its correlation of body and behaviour nonetheless displays affinities with physiognomic principles.[113] Thersites' propensity for 'disorderly words' (ἔπεα ... ἄκοσμά, 2.213) and for speaking 'in a disorderly fashion' (οὐ κατὰ κόσμον, 2.214) is reified in his jumble of mismatched body parts, which are themselves far from being κατὰ κόσμον ('orderly'). Likewise, his inclination for strife (ἐριζέμεναι, 2.214) complements the obvious lack of harmony in his own physique – bandy legs, stooping shoulders, pointy skull, and sparse hair.[114] The impression is of

---

[113] Evans (1969) 58–9, and Weiler (1996) 163, regard Homer's Thersites as an early example of physiognomic thought. Boys-Stones (2007) 20 n.4 counters these suggestions: 'one might take Thersites' ugliness as further proof of the gods' disfavour towards him, rather than an indication of his character'. I prefer the approach of Thalmann (1988) who sees in the portrait a correlation of moral worth and physical appearance, but does not posit any specific *doctrinal* influence from physiognomy.

[114] I follow standard practice in translating φολκός (*Il.* 2.217) as 'bandy-legged', though Kirk (1985) *ad loc.* suggests 'dragging one foot'.

241

a man who not only falls far below the standard of heroic beauty in Homer[115] but worse, whose body has not even been fully formed. With his disproportionate limbs and immoderately ugly appearance (not merely αἴσχρος but αἴσχιστος, 2.216) Thersites mirrors in his body the 'endless volubility' (ἀμετροεπής, 2.212) attributed to his character; he exceeds acceptable limits both in his physical features and in his conduct.[116] True, Homer makes no mention of Thersites' interior; this is not a view into his psyche. But the portrait does imply a link between his disposition and his physique, a link that Homer stresses at the level of lexis and imagery.

There is, then, a strong sense in which Seneca's corporeal descriptions may be considered a variety of character portrait, both for their connection of internal with external states and for their loose association with physiognomic ideas. Like countless other fictional bodies from Homer's Thersites to Brontë's Heathcliff, the *corpus* in Senecan tragedy is a means for audiences inside and outside the play to identify and comprehend individual characters, whether at the level of psychology and emotions, or more simply in terms of matching a name (and face/body) to a deed. Identifying characters in the former sense is a major, unifying theme in Seneca's *Phaedra*, where beautiful bodies give way to monstrous passions and psychological turmoil finds rapid parallels in physical ruin. In the following sections of this chapter, by contrast, I examine how the depiction of bodies in Seneca's *Oedipus* repeatedly – often ironically – identifies the protagonist more as an object than a subject. Moving away from the secluded world of internalised dispositions and consciousness, I examine how Oedipus' bodily characteristics designate an almost wholly external identity: his belonging to certain social and familial categories, his pre-established dramatic part, his formation from words. While Oedipus' surface *does* indicate his particularity – as 'Oedipus' rather than anyone else – Seneca is not much concerned with the depth of what lies behind this façade.

---

[115] Kirk (1985) *ad Il.* 219.
[116] He also threatens to exceed narrative constraints, on which, see Woloch (2003) 4–5.

3.2 Oedipus

Oedipus' Body

Investigation of bodies and bodily qualities is a major motif in the *Oedipus*. Tasked with discovering Laius' killer, Tiresias proceeds to scrutinise the physical signs revealed in an extispicy. He commands a bull and a heifer to be slaughtered and proceeds to interpret (as best he can) the information relayed to him by his daughter, Manto. This scene, with all of its Roman peculiarities, not to mention the challenges it poses for performance, has been much remarked on by scholars as a distinctively Senecan contribution to Oedipus' well-known tragedy.[117] Several critics have shown in addition how the imagery of the extispicy provides proleptic evocation of Oedipus' own fate and the fate of his sons. Thus, for example: the sacrificed heifer is pregnant in an unnatural way, signifying Jocasta (371–5); smoke from the altar settles in a ring around the king's head, designating his kingship and self-blinding (325–6); the sacrificial flame splits in two and fights itself, designating Eteocles and Polynices (321–3); further signs of the impending Theban civil war are found in the liver, which has seven veins – the seven gates of Thebes (364) – and two nodes, indicating shared power (359–60).[118] Most important to my present discussion are the features that relate specifically to the bodies of Oedipus and Jocasta: the heifer 'launches herself upon the sword' (*ferro semet opposito induit*, 341) just as Jocasta will later commit suicide, and blood leaks from the bull's wounds and gushes from his eyes: *huius exiguo graves / maculantur ictus imbre; sed versus retro / per ora multus sanguis atque oculos redit* ('this one's heavy blows are stained with a small trickle; but much of the blood, turned back again, flows out through the

---

[117] Boyle (2011) *ad Oed.* 291–402 asserts that the scene is entirely Seneca's invention. Bexley (2016) 367 n.35 notes a possible connection to the episode of divination at Sophocles' *Antigone* 998–1114, an idea elaborated by DeBrohun (2017). Seneca's deviation from Sophocles, especially in the addition of the extispicy scene, has been emphasised by Paratore (1956) 111; Mendell (1968) [1941] 3–21; Töchterle (1994) 9–18; Ahl (2008) 120–3; Trinacty (2014) 230. On the challenges – and possibilities! – of staging it, see: Zwierlein (1966) 24–5 and 31–2; Sutton (1986) 23; Rosenmeyer (1993); Fitch (2000) 9–11; Ahl (2008) 119–20; Dodson-Robinson (2011); Boyle (2011) *ad loc.*

[118] Pratt (1939) 93–8; Paratore (1956) 119; Bettini (1983) and (1984); Boyle (2011) *ad Oed.* 303–80.

Appearance

mouth and eyes', *Oed.* 348–50).[119] The latter image hints at Oedipus' self-inflicted blindness not just through the simple combination of eyes and blood, but also through the term *imber*, which Seneca uses again at 978 to describe the 'filthy rain' (*foedus imber*) that drenches Oedipus' wounded face, and the collocation of words for 'returning' – *versus, retro, redit* – which evoke throughout the tragedy Oedipus' return to Thebes, his (re)union with his mother, and his overturning of nature's laws.[120] The bull's body symbolises Oedipus' own. More significantly, it suggests that Oedipus' identity can and will be known via specific physical characteristics that mark him out as the very individual he seeks. Although Tiresias declares the extispicy's venture inconclusive because 'it cannot call up a name' (*nec ... potest / ciere nomen*, *Oed.* 391–2), the culprit's name turns out to be less consequential than the body from which it, in any case, derives. As in the *Phaedra*, bodies are the primary means by which characters in this tragedy become accessible and identifiable to others around them.

Further examples of physical evocation in the extispicy scene include the bull turning his face from the light (339), just as Oedipus will later consign himself to permanent darkness (971–3) and of it 'rushing uncertainly, to and fro' (*huc et huc dubius ruit*, 343) after having received two blows from the axe. The importance of this latter phrase lies in the word *dubius*, which has previously been used by Jocasta in the context of encouraging her husband's firmness of purpose:

> regium hoc ipsum reor:
> adversa capere, quoque sit dubius magis
> status et cadentis imperi moles labet,
> hoc stare certo pressius fortem gradu:
> haud est virile terga Fortunae dare.

> This I regard as regal:
> seizing hold of adversity, and the more uncertain

---

[119] Allegorical correspondences noted by Davis (1991) 157–9, Fitch (2004) 48 n.21 and Boyle (2011) *ad Oed.* 341 and 348.
[120] See, for example, *Oed.* 238, *turpis maternos iterum revolutus in ortus*; *Oed.* 371, *natura versa est*; *Oed.* 869–70, *rape / retro reversas generis ac stirpis vices*; *Oed.* 943, *natura in uno vertit Oedipoda*. Further discussion: Davis (1991) 157–8.

3.2 *Oedipus*

> the situation, the more the mass of power teeters on the brink,
> the more firmly you should stand, strong, sure of step:
> it is not manly to turn your back on Fortune.
>
> (*Oed.* 82–6)

While Jocasta employs *certo gradu* and *dubius* in a figurative sense, it is impossible not to hear in her words an echo of the very literal condition of Oedipus' body: his stance is anything but *certus* given the swollen feet that presumably impede his movement.[121] Oedipus's *status* really is *dubius* both in the literal sense that his physical stance is hampered by the ancient wound in his ankles and in the sense that his circumstances are far from unambiguous: he is simultaneously son and husband, father and brother, stranger and long-lost relative. That *certus* and *dubius* can also signify paternity (cf. *Thy.* 240; 1102) further corroborates their applicability to Oedipus qua individual, for his origins are the clue to his identity. Thus, the inherent uncertainty of Oedipus' body affirms and underpins the broader uncertainty of who Oedipus is as a person and where he fits within a social, familial context.

So besides being a striking piece of Senecan innovation and/or a particularly gory instance of Neronian baroque, the extispicy scene in the *Oedipus* concentrates audience attention on the body as a cluster of indispensable physical signs. Twice in this episode Tiresias remarks upon the importance of corporeal *notae*, first when he declares, *solet ira certis numinum ostendi notis* ('the gods' anger is usually revealed through definite signs', 331), and again when he asks Manto to describe what she sees in the entrails: *ede certas viscerum nobis notas* ('report to us the innards' definite signs', 352). Crucially, Oedipus applies the same phrase to himself when he commands the Corinthian messenger, *nunc adice certas corporis nostri notas* ('now state in addition the definite marks on my body', 811). The repetition suggests Oedipus' status as quasi-extispicial material: his body may be analysed by others in

---

[121] An interpretive point captured by Ahl's 2008 translation: 'Being a king, I think means this: coming to grips / with what confronts you. The harder it is / to stand, the more power's burden slips and slides, / the more determinedly you must take / your stand. Be brave! Step confidently now!' The passage's wordplay has also been noted more recently by Stevens (2018) 583.

a manner parallel to the bull's.[122] It affirms the legibility of his physical presence and implies that his body, at least, is a reliable source of information even when everything else pertaining to Oedipus is so uncertain. In fact, Seneca's repeated emphasis on *notae* conjures the distant shadow of physiognomy and likens Oedipus' body to an object of physiognomic analysis inasmuch as it can be read for proof of his personal identity.

This connection between bodily and personal identity grows closer still when we consider how the term *notae* relates to Oedipus' name. As I observed above in the 'Identifying Hippolytus' section, the word's derivation from *noscere* leads Seneca, consciously or unconsciously, to associate it with moments of recognition. The idea is especially prominent in Act 4 of this tragedy, where Oedipus asks the Corinthian messenger whether he could 'recognise [the old shepherd] by his face and looks' (*potesne facie noscere ac vultu virum?* 819), to which the Corinthian replies, 'Perhaps I would recognise him. Often a minor sign summons back a memory faded and buried by time' (*fortasse noscam. saepe iam spatio obrutam / levis exoletam memoriam revocat nota,* 820–1). In wordplay that evades translation, the Corinthian shows how marks on the body facilitate initial knowledge of another person. Although the Corinthian refers here to the aged shepherd, Phorbas, who once delivered the injured baby Oedipus into his care, his remarks can also be taken as conjuring an image of Oedipus himself, the man recognised via his *notae*, and the man whose face, for the audience at least, will be one of his defining physical features. As happens so often in this tragedy, evocations of Oedipus' physical characteristics underlie descriptions of other bodies. Moreover, *noscere* is doubly significant because it recalls one of the possible etymologies of Oedipus' name, from οἶδα, 'to know'.[123] Seneca is familiar with the pun and advertises it clearly when he has Oedipus assert his power to solve riddles: *ambigua soli noscere Oedipodae datur* ('to Oedipus alone has been granted the skill in understanding ambiguities', 216).[124] The

---

[122] Bexley (2016) 367–8.
[123] For the etymological roots of Oedipus' name and specifically, Sophocles' punning on them, see Goldhill (1986) 216–19 and Segal (1993) 56.
[124] Wordplay noted by Frank (1995) 129, Fitch and McElduff (2002) 26 and Boyle (2011) *ad Oed.* 215–16.

3.2 *Oedipus*

'knowable' marks on Oedipus' body thus reflect the 'knowing' that is built into his name. While *notae* is a common term in Seneca's corporeal descriptions, it gains additional meaning in the context of the *Oedipus*.

Throughout this tragedy, Seneca stresses Oedipus' transition from riddle-solver to riddle, knowing to being known. A man once capable of defeating the Sphinx, Oedipus has now become 'a monster more convoluted' than her (*magis... monstrum Sphinge perplexum*, 641). He is a prodigy, an omen (*monstrum*) that must be subjected to others' scrutiny. Despite his persistent desire to interpret events as he sees fit, Seneca's Oedipus always ends up being interpretative material for others – characters in the play, the audience – to exercise their minds upon.[125] Once again, *noscere* and its cognates are important means for Seneca to signal this transition, as Oedipus' attempt to comprehend his situation collapses into others dictating and analysing it for him. Thus, the Delphi oracle, reported by Creon at 233–8, refers to Oedipus elliptically as *Phoebo iam notus et infans* ('known to Phoebus even as a child', 235). The passive form expresses not only Oedipus' lack of interpretive authority, but also his role as an object of inquiry. It is yet another instance of Oedipus' identity being closely linked to his body: both Oedipus qua individual and Oedipus qua *corpus* are scrutinised from an external perspective, the man's *notae* making him readily *notus*.[126]

I remarked above that Seneca's *Oedipus*, unlike his *Phaedra*, rarely treats bodies as sources of psychological information. There is one, minor exception to this: the doubtfulness that plagues Oedipus' mind and defines his physique throughout the play. The topic has received a fair amount of critical attention ever since Donald Mastronarde first alerted scholars to the importance of *dubius* as a keyword in the tragedy.[127] For my purposes, a brief survey accompanied by some expansion of current views will suffice to show how Oedipus's mind complements his bodily qualities.

---

[125] Bexley (2016).
[126] Once again, Ahl's 2008 translation alerts readers to the significance of Seneca's vocabulary: 'marked out as an infant by Phoebus'.
[127] Mastronarde (1970) 292–4. See also Curley (1986) 91–100 and Boyle (2011) *ad Oed.* 1. Allendorf (2013) 121–3 charts the play's more general motif of incertitude. Hesitancy and fear are two of the main traits characterising Seneca's Oedipus, on which, see Henry and Walker (1983); Edmunds (2006) 61; Seo (2013) 97–101.

Appearance

The protagonist's uncertainty tends to be reflected in the world around him. Oedipus commences the play by remarking on the wavering sunlight (*Titan dubius*, 1) that constitutes daybreak in plague-ridden Thebes. As Mastronarde observes, *Titan dubius* is a projection of Oedipus' own hesitancy and opaque sense of guilt.[128] It is also an instance of Stoic *sympatheia*, that is, of the physical universe responding to the dubiety, the sinful double-ness of Oedipus' incestuous identity. Similarly, Manto reports in Act 2 that the sacrificial flame flickers and changes so much that 'you would doubt which colour is and is not present' (*quis desit illi quive sit dubites color*, 318), its multiplicity along with the viewer's perplexity evoking Oedipus' inherent ambiguity. The protagonist's own emotional uncertainty comes to the fore in the tragedy's final Act, when Jocasta asks him, 'What should I call you? "Son"? You hesitate? You are my son.' (*quid te vocem? / gnatumne? dubitas? gnatus es*, 1009–10). As in Jocasta's earlier comments about bravery and surefootedness (*Oed.* 82–6, cited above), this question combines an emotional/psychological context with a distinctly physical one. Oedipus hesitates because, it seems, he cannot bear the idea of any further contact with Jocasta, even though her request attempts to evade their husband–wife relationship.[129] On a more literal level, he can also be said to hesitate because that is the nature of his movement – a blind, crippled man feeling his way around the stage. Although Seneca does not use the language of interiority/exteriority here, as he does in the *Phaedra*, he nonetheless implies that Oedipus' psychological state matches his corporeal one.

Seneca's Oedipus certainly does not wish to be *dubius*, and he tries throughout the play to quash all uncertainty in himself and in his attendant circumstances. When Creon warns Oedipus of the Delphic oracle's *respona dubia* ('ambiguous answers' 212), Oedipus replies that he will resolve this uncertainty just as he once solved the Sphinx's riddle (215–16). In his second encounter with Creon, in Act 3, Oedipus accuses his brother-in-law of conspiring to usurp the throne and asserts, against Creon's

---

[128] Mastronarde (1970) 293.
[129] Frank (1995) 124 notes this subtlety in Jocasta's address to her son.

3.2 Oedipus

repeated protestations of innocence, *omne quod dubium est cadat* ('everything suspect must fall', 702). The phrase is not just indicative of Oedipus' authoritarian attitude; it also feeds into the play's economy of bodily images, because falling in death is what happens to the plague victims (*cadunt*: 63, 70), and because Oedipus, staggering blindly in the final scene, warns himself 'not to fall on [the body of his] mother' (*ne in matrem incidas*, 1051).[130] The claim *omne quod dubium est cadat* (702) may even be taken as referring to Oedipus himself, the ambiguous individual who tumbles from power and stumbles offstage at the play's end, who can only with difficulty be prevented from collapsing to the ground.

Hints about the state of the protagonist's body recur throughout Seneca's *Oedipus*, and those hints reveal in turn crucial aspects of his identity. Who Oedipus is and how he may be recognised depends largely upon the signals his *corpus* displays to others, and on whether they can interpret those signals correctly. The audience is best suited to picking up these clues because of its prior knowledge of Oedipus' story, which it employs to decipher both the protagonist's physique and his social/familial status as an implied person within the world of the play.

Oedipus' Face

Like Hippolytus' face, treatment of Oedipus' visage in this tragedy combines fictional with quasi-human aspects of character. On the one hand, the protagonist's countenance communicates what he is feeling, which is key to his representation as a human analogue and to his concomitant engagement of the audience's sympathy. On the other hand, Oedipus' face, alongside references to other faces in the tragedy, serves as a constant reminder of his dramatic role and mask and thereby, of his textually constrained existence.

---

[130] The significance of this final phrase has been remarked on by Henry and Walker (1983) 130, Boyle (2011) *ad Oed.* 1051 and most recently, Trinacty (2017) 176–7: it echoes and provides ring composition with *Oed.* 14: *in regnum incidi*. For the symbolic and lexical significance of *cadunt* at *Oed.* 63, see Littlewood (2004) 83 and Töchterle (1994) *ad loc.*

Appearance

In Act 3, Creon returns from the necromancy to undergo interrogation from an increasingly irate and impatient Oedipus. 'Although your face itself displays signs of sorrow,' says the protagonist, 'reveal whose life must be given to placate the gods' (*etsi ipse vultus flebiles praefert notas, / exprome cuius capite placemus deos*, 509–10). The keyword *notae* not only indicates that the face is a legible surface disclosing emotional and psychological information to those nearby, but also hints at the significance of Oedipus' own face, a *vultus* that will not just bear *notae* but be *known* for them. Understandably, Seneca focuses attention on faces throughout the tragedy, each one being in some way a reflection of or reference to the protagonist's own. When Oedipus questions the Corinthian in Act 4, he asks whether he can recognise the doddering shepherd, Phorbas, by his countenance: *referesne nomen ac vultum senis?* ('do you recall the old man's name and face?' 840). The Corinthian equivocates in reply, rather unhelpfully: *adridet animo forma; nec notus satis, / nec rursus iste vultus ignotus mihi* ('his appearance is familiar; that face of his is not really known but then again not unknown to me' 841–2). The conjunction of *notus* and *vultus* evokes once more the visage by which Oedipus comes to be known, as well as the 'knowing' incorporated into his name. It is Oedipus' own recognition that lies behind this almost comical exchange concerning old men's faces.[131] Both passages, moreover, direct the audience to concentrate on Oedipus' face as a major locus of his identity and of what he may be feeling at any given moment.

It is not until the messenger's speech that Seneca focuses directly on Oedipus' visage. The distraught ruler rushes into the palace:

> vultus furore torvus atque oculi truces,
> gemitus et altum murmur, et gelidus volat
> sudor per artus, spumat et volvit minas
> ac mersus alte magnus exundat dolor

---

[131] This seems to be the case in other parts of the play as well, for example when Manto describes the sacrificial flame as having *non una facies* (*Oed.* 314), the line could be taken as referring obliquely to Oedipus himself, who will exhibit two versions of his face over the course of his tragedy. In a more abstract sense, it could also evoke Oedipus' fluctuating identity. Likewise, the choral account of the plague victims' eyes – *multo . . . genas sanguine tendit / oculique rigent* (*Oed.* 186–7) – looks forward (pun intended!) to the fate of Oedipus' own countenance.

3.2 *Oedipus*

> his face is grim with rage, his eyes fierce
> there are groans and a deep roar, and chill sweat
> flows over his limbs, he foams and reels off threats
> great pain gushes forth from deep inside
>
> (*Oed.* 921–4)

There are clear similarities between this passage and the lengthier, diagnostic accounts of the passions in *Phaedra* (362–83), *Medea* (380–96) and *de Ira* (1.1.3–5). Oedipus' physical symptoms betoken his present psychological condition and the entire process is envisaged as a dialogue between depth and surface, interior and exterior. His *dolor*, like Phaedra's, straddles bodily and emotional realms and bursts into view from some hidden chamber of his being (*mersus alte*). This is a representation of Oedipus as an implied human figure whose facial expressions and bodily reactions betray the presence of a private, internal psyche, however sparsely conveyed. As an index of his emotional state, moreover, Oedipus' face is meant to provoke a reaction, a sense of human engagement from the audience, whether that reaction comes in the form of horror, pity, fear, disapproval, or anything else. Just as the messenger employs this description to impress upon his internal audience the severity of Oedipus' fate, so Seneca employs it to motivate viewers and readers to judge Oedipus specifically in terms of human suffering. Despite our manifest awareness that Oedipus is a text, we respond to him – superficially, temporarily – as if he were a living, breathing entity. Even if we take the Stoic line that Seneca's ideal audience should condemn Oedipus' passions and strive to avoid them, this still means treating him as an implied human personality complete with human capacities and foibles.

Like Hippolytus', Oedipus' *vultus* also contributes to his quasi-humanity by reifying his wishes (*vult*). The damage he inflicts upon his eyes symbolises and communicates his desire to punish himself appropriately for the crime he has committed. Motifs of blindness and insight, so prominent in Sophocles' version, are granted at best secondary importance in Seneca's. Instead, Oedipus blinds himself as a way of achieving 'a night worthy of [his] wedding' (*thalamis digna nox ... meis*, 977) and of dying without joining the world of the dead: 'find a way not to mix with the dead yet to wander banished from the world of the living: die, but on this side of your father' (*quaeratur via / qua nec sepultis mixtus et vivis tamen / exemptus erres: morere, sed citra patrem*, 949–51).[132] As I have signalled in the Introduction, the significance of Oedipus' punishment lies in its ambiguity, which matches his own ambiguous status: he is both son and husband, living and dead. The act of removing his sight has not literally killed him, of course, but the darkness he will endure from now on does conjure up death, more so if we think of it in the epic sense of 'darkness covering his eyes'. Thus, Oedipus creates for himself a face that exhibits core facets of his identity and the choices – conscious or otherwise – that have produced that identity. By the tragedy's end, his countenance expresses the process of reasoning and recrimination proceeding from his self-discovery, that is, it tells the audience and other characters something about how Oedipus *thinks*.

Interpreting Oedipus' *vultus* is more important to the external audience than to the other characters in the play, however, and this is where the balance starts to shift towards self-conscious theatricality. While the *dramatis personae* within the tragedy recognise Oedipus by his feet, his most distinctive corporeal feature for the play's audience is his face, the face that that will end up wounded, eyeless, and presumably represented by an appropriately bloodied mask.[133] This, rather than his swollen ankles, is what makes Oedipus fully recognisable to those reading or (better) watching the tragedy. From being 'grim with rage' (*furore torvus*, 921), Oedipus' countenance will forthwith display the permanent results of that rage in the form of gouged, gory eye-sockets. I have mentioned already in the Introduction that when the protagonist returns to the stage in Act 6 and declares, 'this face befits Oedipus'

---

[132] For more discussion of 'appropriateness' in this scene, see Introduction, 20–1.
[133] It is generally assumed that Sophocles' Oedipus would have changed his mask before returning to the stage for the final Act – see, for example Webster (1956) 50 and more recently, Marshall (2012) 191 – although Seeberg (2002–3) 60–3 argues on the basis of extant archaeological evidence that blind masks probably were not used on stage and that if they ever *did* make an appearance, it was probably from the Hellenistic period onwards. Full change of mask is not, however, absolutely necessary for conveying Oedipus' countenance; paint mimicking bloodspots would work just as well. In Seneca's case, we possess too little evidence about staging to conjecture either way, but at least his version of the tragedy fits within the (post-)Hellenistic timeframe for blind masks.

3.2 *Oedipus*

(*vultus Oedipodam hic decet*, 1003), his comment presumably gestures towards the mask, just as the citation of his own name gestures towards the role he is playing.[134] Notably, the phrase also brings Oedipus' face and feet into close conjunction: *vultus Oedipodam*. The juxtaposition is yet another of Seneca's methods for distinguishing between internal and external levels of recognition in this play: the audience, equipped with prior knowledge of Oedipus' story, is invited to agree that this *is* indeed the face it expects Oedipus to wear, while the tragedy's *dramatis personae*, enfolded in the dramatic illusion of living this story for the first and only time, cannot really say that they anticipated Oedipus' blindness, not, that is, without breaking the fourth wall and acknowledging their own fictive status. If they recognise anything, it is his feet.

It is possible to see this interchange of Oedipus' face and mask at other points in the play as well. When the messenger describes the king's countenance as 'violent, daring, angry, fierce' (*violentus audax vultus, iratus ferox*, 960) the sense conveyed is not only of an emotional state, but also of the distinguishing characteristics displayed by a mask. *iratus* and *ferox* are standard tragic attributes (e.g. *iratus Atreus*, *Thy.* 180; *Medea ferox*, Hor. *Ars* 123) and their combination with *vultus* could be seen as working proleptically to signify the qualities of the mask in which Oedipus will shortly re-emerge onto the stage. The conversation between Oedipus, Phorbas, and the Corinthian (819–21; 840–2) likewise acquires a mildly metatheatrical dimension when we consider that the two old men would, in performance, have worn quite similar masks: what methods can Phorbas and the Corinthian really use to recognise each other, and are there any features that encourage a distinction between them? How does reading this artificial, theatrical face help someone acquire knowledge of the person beneath its surface? When the Corinthian remarks, 'often a minor sign summons back a memory faded and buried by time' (*saepe iam spatio obrutam / levis exoletam memoriam revocat nota*, 820–1), his reference to *notae* combines the signifying potential of the mask with the face's physiognomic capacity to

---

[134] Boyle (2011) *ad Oed.* 1003.

disclose specific personal qualities. Marks on the face can designate a particular *persona* in just the same way as lines on a mask; in performance, the two surfaces achieve the same ends. Thus, as in Hippolytus' case, mask and face often seem to coincide in this tragedy, since both fulfil the same function of making the bearer 'legible' to others.

Oedipus Text

As I have noted several times already in this chapter, the body's and the face's legibility assimilates them to texts,[135] which in turn emphasises characters' status as constructed, fictive entities. Such readability is a prominent theme in Seneca's *Oedipus*, as the protagonist is constantly scrutinised by others and turns, eventually, to scrutinising himself. Vocabulary of reading and interpreting saturates this play, likening Oedipus to poetic material, to extispicial matter, and to omens, all of which claim the power to signify.

One of Seneca's main inventions in his version of *Oedipus* is to depict the protagonist as a sacrificial victim. Not only does his body bear *notae*, which are previously associated with the extispicy (331; 352), but it also invites analysis in ways equivalent to this sacrificial ritual. For example: Tiresias begins the rite by declaring, *fata eruantur* ('let fate be dug out' 297) and Manto utters the exhortation *scrutemur* ('let us search' 372) as she probes the pulsing entrails. The same terms recur in the messenger's speech to describe the punishment Oedipus visits upon himself: he searches out his eyes (*scrutatur*, 965) and digs at his sockets (*eruentis*, 961). The parallels encapsulate Oedipus' transition from active inquirer to if not quite passive at least self-reflexive interpretive matter. He performs the same activity on his mutilated face as Manto and Tiresias do on the cattle's dissected bodies. Like the sacrificed animals, Oedipus is imagined as an assemblage of legible, interpretable signs.

---

[135] A point stressed by Conroy (2010) 14 in relation to all kinds of dramatic performance: 'bodies and their actions may appear within theatre as objects of analysis. That is to say, bodies may be thought of as texts'.

3.2 *Oedipus*

Furthermore, Seneca merges the terms' literal and figurative meanings, so that the physical act of searching or digging (*scrutor*; *eruo*) through body parts accompanies the abstract quest of searching for truth, rooting out information. Both verbs can be used for acts of reading and/or literary analysis, as for instance in Quintilian's description of rhetorical emphasis: *cum ex aliquo dicto latens aliquid eruitur* ('when something hidden is extracted from some phrase' *Inst.* 9.2.64). Oedipus, like an ambiguous text, must be scoured for latent meaning. Religious signification slides into the poetic – hardly surprising when one considers that many Romans, and Stoics in particular, treated interpreting natural signs and interpreting literary texts as analogous activities.[136] Cicero places the two side-by-side in his *de Divinatione*: *interpres, ut grammatici poetarum, proxime ad eorum, quos interpretantur, divinationem videntur accedere* ('men capable of interpreting seem to approach very near to the prophecy of the gods they interpret, just as scholars do when they interpret the poets', *Div.* 1.34). Although Seneca makes no such explicit comparison in his *Oedipus*, the tragedy's imagery certainly suggests a correlation between the poetic and the prophetic, extispicy and text. For Oedipus, this results in his body being as much a literary artefact as a sacrificial one, since both procedures assume the ultimate readability of his physique.

A similar effect emerges from Oedipus' brief recollection of his encounter with the Sphinx, whom he describes as *viscera expectans mea* ('waiting for my innards', 100). In any other context, the image may convey little more than the Sphinx's characteristic aggression, but in the world of Seneca's *Oedipus*, where details of religious ritual occupy almost a third of the drama, the Sphinx's activity cannot help but mirror that of Tiresias and Manto. As a poet/prophet figure who utters a *carmen* (98; 102) and 'weaves words in blind rhythms' (*caecis verba nectentem modis*, 92), the Sphinx bears some resemblance to Tiresias, the blind *vates* (522; 571; 670) who likewise recites *carmina* (561). Altogether, this nexus of lexical parallels suggests that the Sphinx is just as

---

[136] Struck (2004) is particularly insightful regarding the relationship between divination and allegorical interpretation of poetry, which was practised by a number of prominent Stoics (among others) and doubtless contributed to the Roman notion of *vates* as both poet and prophet.

intent on 'reading' Oedipus' *corpus* as Tiresias is on deciphering the obscure signs present in the extispicy. Of course, both interpreters fail in some essential way, but Oedipus' status as potential reading matter remains constant throughout the play. Laius, too, characterises Oedipus as interpretable religious/poetic material when he denounces his son as *implicitum malum / magisque monstrum Sphinge perplexum sua* ('an intertwined evil, a monster more perplexing than his own Sphinx', 640–1). Images of enmeshing are apt for the man who has doubled back on himself to marry his mother and produce his own siblings/children with her. They are also, simultaneously, images that Seneca applies to poetry and poetic activity in this play: Oedipus calls the Sphinx's song *nodosa* ... *verba et implexos dolos* ('knotted words and entwined trickery', 101) and Creon says of the Pythia's arcane pronouncement, *responsa dubia sorte perplexa iacent* ('the replies are uncertain, the oracle tangled' 212). Hence, Laius' language associates Oedipus with the twisted, complex content of the Pythia's and the Sphinx's poetry: he himself is the one riddle he cannot solve. Seneca uses this technique to draw attention to Oedipus as an element of other people's poetry and thus, as a fictive creation. The drama's protagonist is a textual entity available for others to interpret in the same way as a literary work. Not only is his body portrayed as a legible, semiotic object, but Oedipus qua character is also shown to be – to some extent – a figure of others' verbal ingenuity.

The protagonist's semiotic qualities even extend into his being a *monstrum* (641), that is, a terrifying prodigy that offers itself for analysis. Whether derived from *monstrare*, as the ancients thought, or *monere*, as most modern linguists claim, the *monstrum* is something that explicitly invites interpretation.[137] In the words of Jeffrey Cohen, 'the monster exists only to be read ... a glyph that seeks a heirophant'.[138] This is certainly the case for Seneca's

---

[137] For the ancient etymologies of *monstrum*, see Maltby (1991) 391–2. Lowe (2015) 8–14 surveys the development of the *monstrum*'s cultural meaning in ancient Rome. On the term's significance in Seneca tragedy, see Staley (2010) 96–112, and Bexley (2011) 367 and 387–90.

[138] Cohen (1996) 4. In a similar vein, Garber (1988) 30, remarks how Thomas More's description of Richard III treats the king's 'deformed body as readable text'; like the

3.2 *Oedipus*

Oedipus, whose characterisation as a *monstrum* casts him once more in the role of riddling religious material, a puzzle that requires careful investigation in order for its full meaning to be revealed. Like the components of an extispicy, the *monstrum* functions as a metaphor; it communicates indirectly, via symbols. It is not merely the case that Oedipus' actions have *caused* Thebes' plague, but that they also *represent* it, conceptually: the protagonist's coupling with his mother is reflected in the indiscriminate damage of the disease that 'mingles young with old, parents with children' (*iuvenesque senibus iungit et gnatis patres*, 54).[139] The gloomy sky that hangs over plague-ridden Thebes evokes the permanent gloom that will eventually descend upon Oedipus' eyes. The plague and Oedipus are symbolically linked, just as the extispicy and Oedipus are. In fact, Seneca's heavy reliance on metaphor and symbolism in this tragedy could be seen as deriving from the very rituals he chooses to include, because extispicy itself (and, for that matter, the analysis of oracles) is an exercise in decoding figurative meaning. It is apt, though most likely coincidental, that Martial refers to reading the stories of Oedipus and Thyestes as 'reading monsters' (*monstra legis*, 10.4.2), by which he not only flags the typically hideous nature of tragic events, but also hints at the *monstrum*'s inherent legibility; it is something one *reads*. In Seneca's *Oedipus*, such legibility operates simultaneously at an extra-dramatic level (how the audience interprets Oedipus' symbolism), at an intra-dramatic one (how characters, including Oedipus himself, interpret it) and at a socio-historical one (how the rituals themselves rely upon symbolism). Although the term *monstrum* occurs but rarely in Seneca's *Oedipus*, it certainly qualifies as the leitmotif of the play.

So far in this section I have discussed the related ideas of Oedipus' body being a text and of Oedipus himself occupying the role of a poetic/prophetic symbol; I conclude by examining the ways in which this tragedy highlights Oedipus' textual identity as a literary and more specifically, dramatic character. As several critics have noted, Seneca's *Oedipus* features a number of

---

monstrum of Seneca's Oedipus, Richard III's physical disparities are assumed to indicate moral depravity, and vice versa.

[139] A connection spotted by Littlewood (2004) 23–4.

Appearance

surrogate poet figures – the Sphinx; the Pythia; Tiresias; Laius – many of whom concentrate on portraying Oedipus in their verse.[140] Although the content of the Sphinx's riddle is not reported in Seneca's version, the audience would have known its relevance for Oedipus himself, the man whose destiny begins as a baby crawling on all fours and who will leave Thebes hobbling, guided by a stick. Next, the Pythia's verse *is* reported, verbatim, by Creon (233–8), and provides a dense summary of the protagonist's main traits. After deeming Oedipus an 'exiled guest, guilty of the king's murder' (*profugus ... hospes / regis caede nocens*, 234–5), the oracle proceeds to a second-person address: *nec tibi longa manent sceleratae gaudia caedis: / tecum bella geres, natis quoque bella relinques, / turpis maternos iterum revolutus in ortus* ('the joy of this criminal slaughter will not last long for you: you will wage war with yourself and leave war to your sons, having returned once more, wretch, to your maternal origins' 236–8). Like the extispicy, the plague, and so many other elements of this tragedy, the Pythia's pronouncement depicts Oedipus metaphorically: the protagonist wages war with himself both in the sense that he has violated family boundaries and in his subsequent act of self-harm; he has returned not just to the city of his birth but to the very woman who gave birth to him.[141] Via a standard tactic of foreshadowing, Seneca invites the audience to read the oracle in ways that Oedipus himself cannot.

Such cleverness is not the only purpose of this passage, however, since by inserting a description of Oedipus into the mouth of a surrogate poet, and by having that surrogate employ the same kinds of imagery used elsewhere in the tragedy, Seneca highlights Oedipus' own status as a fictive creation. The Oedipus constructed by the Pythia's verse is equivalent to the Oedipus depicted in Seneca's tragedy overall; both are the products of language, symbolism, poetic inspiration. Seneca achieves this effect chiefly by having Creon quote the oracle directly instead of summarising its content. When Creon breaks into dactylic hexameter and uses

---

[140] Schiesaro (2003) 9–12; Trinacty (2014) 214–31; Bexley (2016). Contra: Staley (2014) 117–18.
[141] The significance of the Pythia's allusions is explored by Pratt (1939) 92 and Boyle (2011) *ad Oed.* 233–8.

3.2 Oedipus

the second-person forms typical of oracular utterances,[142] he confronts the play's audience with a separable poetic text containing a miniature portrait of Oedipus. And if Oedipus cannot be considered a fully formed *character* in the Pythia's verse, he is at least a textual *figure*. The segment of verse is therefore mirrored by and echoes in the larger work that is Seneca's tragedy: the Pythia stands in for Seneca himself, her poetry creating an Oedipus just as Seneca's does.

A similar effect is achieved in Creon's account of the necromancy, where Tiresias raises Laius from the dead. Here Tiresias resembles a poet figure, as Alessandro Schiesaro has shown, and the incantation he utters gives rise to a specifically *literary* cast of spirits: Zethus and Amphion (611–12); Niobe (613–15); Agave and Pentheus (615–18). Schiesaro remarks that Tiresias' action 'powerfully re-enacts what poetry and poets do'; it revivifies – and in Laius' case, endows with speech – *personae* that otherwise have no agency of their own.[143] Furthermore, the poetry Tiresias generates belongs to the genre of tragedy above all: Zethus and Amphion featured in Euripides' lost *Antiopa*, and in Pacuvius'; Niobe in plays by Aeschylus and Sophocles; Pentheus and Agave most famously in Euripides' *Bacchae*. By conjuring this group of chiefly tragic characters, Seneca creates yet another situation in which the play's embedded poetry reflects upon his own activity as a tragedian. His Oedipus is likewise a revivified figure from earlier literature, summoned back to life in order to replay his tragic tale.

In fact, Seneca builds several literary/dramatic layers into this scene by having Creon report the entire necromantic event, including Laius' speech, in full and vivid narrative. As he does with the Pythia, Creon quotes Laius directly rather than in summary or indirect statement. The effect is not just to intensify the scene's dramatic immediacy, but also to have Creon assume a multivalent role as creative[144] poet, skilled actor, and archetypal tragic messenger.[145] The sheer length of Creon's report – 128 lines! – its detail and its

---

[142] As used, for example, in the oracles quoted in Herodotus 1.65 and 1.85.
[143] Schiesaro (2003) 9.
[144] The idea comes from Ahl (2008) 20, who associates Creon with the Latin verb *creo*, 'I create.'
[145] As remarked by Boyle (2011) *ad Oed.* 530–658.

segments of speech-in-speech (*Oed.* 571–3; 626–58) afford opportunities for virtuosic, self-consciously theatrical performance, while also allowing Creon to seem more actively engaged in moulding and framing the event he has just witnessed. Whereas a perfunctory report would permit the speaker to remain relatively unobtrusive, this long, direct piece of communication flaunts its own artistry, and hence, the artistry of the one delivering it. Even if taken as a species of messenger speech, the passage verges on being a meta-example of this convention: the speaker begins by protesting his reluctance (*Oed.* 509–29), thereby drawing attention to his role as messenger; it conveys events that happen offstage in a drama where even the most implausible things tend to happen *on stage*; it situates Laius' prophecy in an undeniably tragic environment. Creon effectively 'performs' the messenger and in doing so, he increases our awareness of the entire scene as a performance.

Such self-reflexivity has obvious consequences for how an audience receives Oedipus' identity. When Laius describes the play's protagonist, and when Creon quotes that description, Oedipus seems once again to be the product of poetic composition, an explicitly literary character generated through the verse of these substitute poets. As it listens to Creon, the audience is encouraged to measure the Oedipus on stage against the one portrayed in the report, to see points of coincidence between the person and the text. Creon's dramatic enactment of the speech is also significant, because it heightens audience perception of the storyline as a theatrical event and of Oedipus as a *dramatis persona*. Hence, Oedipus' textual identity is underscored both in the internal world of the play – as other characters seek to decipher his body – and at the level of external reception. Oedipus' *corpus* cannot be separated from the symbols, the marks, the *words* that describe it. It is constructed and interpreted by others, even to the point of demanding such construction in order to acquire proper existence. Seneca's play turns Oedipus rex into Oedipus text.

Conclusion

Given Seneca's interest in mind-body interaction, and given his Stoic approach to *corpora*, it is not surprising to find him exploring

3.2 *Oedipus*

such topics through the medium of theatre, for all theatrical performance, at its core, deals with the representation of the mind via the body, and with the body's need to be decoded by an audience. Stage enactment encapsulates in miniature the problem of understanding another person's interior via his or her exterior. To quote Colette Conroy: 'The question of *where* thinking takes place is important because thinking seems to be an invisible activity, but humans must think audibly or visibly if they are to communicate with each other at all, let alone create theatre.'[146] An actor's body – its gestures and movements – is the visual, audible evidence of what a given character thinks and feels. This aspect of performance exhibits deep conceptual links with Stoic notions of material or embodied psychology: emotions are *corpora*; they are responsible for physical changes by which they make their presence known (and for the Stoics, thus make their diagnosis possible). The physiognomic views explored in this chapter also follow a similar line of reasoning and demonstrate equal – if slightly different – affinity with theatrical performance because they, too, make the body the primary site of characterological information. Traits, preferences, dispositions must all be embodied in some way – whether through clothing or gait or physical features – if they are to be communicated in the theatre. Physiognomy and dramatic performance may even rely on much the same corporeal typologies: noble and pompous characters walk upright while crafty ones are bent over, or hook-nosed, and so forth. For Seneca, the corporeal semiotics of the theatre provided the perfect opportunity for examining the personal, somatic consequences of Stoic materialism.

These concerns manifest themselves differently in the *Phaedra* and the *Oedipus*. The former of these two tragedies returns obsessively to the revelation of internal states on the external, visible surfaces of the body. As spectatorial objects, the bodies and faces of Seneca's *Phaedra* both *perform* emotion and *communicate* it reliably to onlookers. As is the case with so many other aspects of Senecan drama, *corpora* in the *Phaedra* are simultaneously theatrical and genuine, fabricated and quasi-human. In the *Oedipus*,

---

[146] Conroy (2010) 23.

however, the balance shifts more towards textual identity: the protagonist's body is imagined repeatedly as an assortment of legible symbols while his claim to supreme interpretive ability is turned back, cruelly, upon his own physique. Seneca's Oedipus is a man more known than knowing. While his body, like Phaedra's and Hippolytus', does on occasions communicate the intangible, internal facets of his being, it is more often treated as a semiotic surface and poetic creation, a fictional, signifying object that not only invites interpretation but requires it in order to be fully reified. Oedipus' body seems to be constructed almost entirely by others: by seers, and poet-figures, by Seneca, and by the play's audience. It is as much their creation and their possession as it is his.

CHAPTER 4

AUTONOMY

Forming an identity implies the ability to do so. In more profound terms: self-definition, of the kind discussed throughout this monograph, is predicated upon individuals' relative autonomy and agency, their capacity to effect changes in their own lives and in the world around them, to act in accordance with their own wishes, to avoid undue social, bodily, or moral constraints imposed from outside. The obverse also holds, because compromised autonomy is typically accompanied by a disruption or diminution of personal identity, with the oppressed individual becoming, at worst, an object, a vessel, an instrument.

Autonomy constitutes a, if not *the*, major distinction between the categories of 'character' and 'person', because fictional beings claim no real capacity for self-determination, no matter how full or dominant their personalities may seem. Characters are trapped within texts, at the mercy of authors and readers alike, and have no contingent futures on which to exercise their powers of choice – they have no powers of choice. Instrumentality, object-status, is their inescapable fate, a point brought home all the more forcefully in Senecan tragedy where *dramatis personae* openly acknowledge their positions within pre-existing and concurrent literary traditions, their identities predicated not just on authorial invention, but also on the demands of genre and of prior poetic models. Against such a background, their notorious tendency for self-assertion may seem a pitiful mirage. However often Medea affirms herself as Medea, or Hercules as Hercules, they remain unable to alter themselves or their circumstances. The desire of so many Senecan protagonists to push forward and dare the undareable, do the impossible, acts as a foil to the agency they do not ultimately possess. They may rant as much as they wish: it won't change anything.

Autonomy

That is, of course, a reductive view of the tragedies, and deliberately so, because it signals the impression conveyed by Seneca's characters of violently insistent selfhood, pitted against all opposition, bursting through constraints and achieved whatever the cost to the world's moral and social fabric. A combined love of force and control, along with ambitions of absolute sovereignty are some of Seneca's characters' most defining traits. Even their habit of self-citation, so patently metapoetic, can be interpreted as bullish solipsism and imperious self-confidence, a sense of importance so great that it evaluates itself in the third person, as though from the perspective of an awestruck spectator.[1] One question, therefore, is how to balance these two views of selfhood in the tragedies: do characters cede autonomy to their literary pedigrees, or do they pursue it in spite of – or by means of – the traditions lying in their wake? A second, and related issue is how to measure these tragic characters' pursuit of autonomy and agency against the ideas set out in Seneca's philosophical writings, because that will help elucidate the degree of importance and seriousness accorded to them in the tragedies. This does not mean entering upon questions about free will,[2] since those are, at base, irrelevant to fictional beings. Instead, this chapter focuses on the topics of personal and political sovereignty and freedom, and self-sufficiency as indices of an individual's capacity for uninhibited action. Following an initial discussion of autarky in the prose and dramatic works, I examine how Senecan concepts of autonomy play out in adjacent themes of revenge and suicide. Bids for power and control, in Seneca, almost invariably lead to destruction, whether of others or of the self. The concept of sovereignty displayed in both the tragedies and the philosophy is essentially a zero-sum game in which freedom is achieved by rendering others

---

[1] The position adopted by Braden (1985) 13–14 and 33–4 in his treatment of Senecan illeism. A useful parallel, in this regard, is Suetonius' Nero, whose citation of his own name (*Ner.* 23) implies more an inflated sense of self than fulfilment of a pre-established role.

[2] In any case, Inwood (2005) 132–56 argues for the relevance of 'will' but not 'free will' in Senecan Stoicism. Nor should concepts of freedom, such as those expounded by Seneca, be conflated with free will: see Bobzien (1998) 242–3 and Inwood (2005) 303. For deeper discussion of the issue: Frede (2011) 31–48 and 66–88.

4.1 Freedom

subordinate and powerless. Self-definition and self-assertion come at a heavy price.

While autarkic selfhood is by no means a new topic in studies of Senecan drama, most of this scholarship comes from the field of English Literature rather than Classics,[3] and there remains substantial scope for fresh investigation, especially on the theme of revenge, which has received surprisingly little treatment given its outsized role in Seneca's tragedies, and more broadly still, in Seneca's thought. The present chapter not only expands on existing ideas of Senecan *autarkeia*, but also brings a new dimension in the form of characters' autonomy, that is, how Seneca's interest in actual, human self-determination intersects with his characters' awareness of their purely fictional ontology. Their pushing against the boundaries of their texts coincides with their impulse to pursue ever greater criminal acts as expressions of their unassailable agency. And their pursuit of sovereign control – over their own bodies and reputations, over events and other people – mirrors in unsettling ways the *sapiens*' lonely reign in his self-conferred kingdom of virtue. This Senecan ideal of autonomy is distinctly problematic, not because of the difficulty involved in attaining it, but because it lays waste to its surroundings. Self-determination happens amid the ruins.

4.1 Freedom

Sages and Other Tyrants

To begin this investigation, we need to ask whether Seneca's characters really can claim autonomous, autarkic selfhood, or whether it is a delusion born of their spiralling criminality. From a strictly Stoic point of view, it has to be the latter, because true freedom for Stoics lies in exercising *ratio* to make correct judgements, following the dictates of *natura*,

---

[3] The main studies are Braden (1984) and (1985), which have in turn influenced Gray (2016) and (2018). As Gray (2016) 213 points out, all of these approaches owe something to T. S. Eliot's essays on Seneca and Shakespeare. From the side of Classics, only Littlewood (2004) 15–69 deals in any substantial way with the issue of autarkic selfhood in the tragedies but see also Johnson (1988) 93–7 on Seneca's Medea. At the opposite end of the spectrum, Calabrese (2017) cautions against reading Seneca's characters in purely solipsistic terms, but her arguments are largely unconvincing.

265

and expunging the passions, all of which Seneca's *dramatis personae* fail to do on a spectacular scale. Fired by anger, jealousy, fear, and greed, they assent to undertake monstrous acts and attribute immense value to the kinds of external concerns – power, wealth, reputation – that Stoics classify as 'indifferent'.[4] Seneca's characters are in this regard slaves both to fortune and to their own unchecked desires, which can make their pursuit of autonomous selfhood seem like a wry joke on the part of their author, a negative *exemplum* of how misguided priorities cloud the mind.

This is correct up to a point, but Seneca's celebration of autonomy also displays deeply negative elements, which, like his treatment of *constantia*, leave it open to misappropriation and misuse. Gordon Braden and Cedric Littlewood both detect in Seneca's *sapiens* a marked tendency for solipsistic superiority, Braden comparing the wise man to the madman, and Littlewood comparing him to the tyrant.[5] Each presents a valid argument, and the purpose of this section is to tease out their ideas in more detail, as a prelude to understanding the tragedies' quasi-Stoic representation of autonomy.

Certainly, Seneca's vision of autarky is extreme. He glorifies the *sapiens* as a figure of supreme independence and self-containment, someone who stands apart from regular human society – in a moral and, more often than not, in a physical sense – and someone whose indifference to the loss of possessions, family, or even body parts makes him untouchable. The *sapiens* aspires through virtue to equal the gods, and his moral outlook is such that he can never really be harmed, victimised, oppressed, or enslaved. This prospect of spiritual indomitability must have held deep appeal for disenfranchised members of society (Epictetus, we may recall, was a slave),[6] and especially for the Roman elite, who felt

---

[4] Lesses (1993) 62 gives a succinct summary of the concept. The exact relationship between Stoic ἀδιάφορα and virtue is a thorny issue, useful overviews of which can be found in Brennan (2005) 119–31 and Klein (2015) 227–81.
[5] Braden (1985) 5–27; Littlewood (2004) 18–36. Gray (2018) 1–46 holds a similar position, mostly expanding on Braden.
[6] Cf. Eliot (1999b) [1927] 131, 'a philosophy most suited to slaves'. We should not, however, idealise Stoicism's promise of empowerment because the majority of disenfranchised individuals in Roman society would neither have had nor have been permitted access to philosophical learning. For instance, despite the rosy image of Nussbaum (1994) 320–58 on Stoic approaches to women's education – a view revised but still optimistic in Nussbaum

4.1 Freedom

disenfranchised by the principate.[7] Yet the very fact of this appeal also points to a combative element in Stoic ethics, its encouragement of individuals to flout oppressive conventions and claim a kingdom for themselves, however immaterial that kingdom may be. Braden describes this aggressive trait as the residue of Stoicism's Cynic focus, 'a commitment to the self's superiority to all public ambitions and intimidations'.[8] Littlewood similarly identifies in the Roman Stoics an appetite for moral conflict and isolationism that puts them on a par with autocratic rulers.[9] The resemblance does not go unremarked in the ancient world either, albeit meant in more positive terms. Diogenes Laertius reports the Stoic belief that, 'not only are the wise free, they are also kings; kingship being unaccountable rule, which none but the wise can maintain' (οὐ μόνον δ' ἐλευθέρους εἶναι τοὺς σοφούς, ἀλλὰ καὶ βασιλέας, τῆς βασιλείας οὔσης ἀρχῆς ἀνυπευθύνου, ἥτις περὶ μόνους ἂν τοὺς σοφοὺς συσταίη, 7.122 trans. Hicks). Cicero expresses a parallel idea in the *de Officiis*, in the context of describing how some wise men retreat from public affairs: 'they had the same aim as kings, to lack nothing, <u>to obey nobody</u>, to enjoy liberty, that is, essentially, <u>to live as one pleases</u>' (*his [philosophis] idem propositum fuit quod regibus, ut ne qua re egerent, <u>ne cui parerent</u>, libertate uterentur, cuius proprium est <u>sic vivere ut velis</u>*, 1.69–70).[10] Although this comment about kings may be no more than a gloss on the *quality* of philosophical freedom and the expectations it entails,[11] nonetheless Cicero constructs a troubling parallel between the sage's self-sufficiency and that of an autocrat.[12] Theoretically, there is no danger in the Stoic

---

(2002) – it is unlikely that many women managed to access Stoic philosophy (cf. *Helv.* 17.4 where Seneca's own mother is prevented from such study).

[7] Undoubtedly the main reason for Stoicism's popularity with Roman *equites* and senators. On this topic, Roller (2001) 64–123 is a superb study of how Senecan Stoicism reconfigures and internalises elite values in the wake of their displacement by the principate.

[8] Braden (1985) 17.

[9] Littlewood (2004) 18–25.

[10] Comparanda in addition to the Diogenes Laertius passage are given by Dyck (1996) *ad Off.* 70.

[11] As construed by Dyck (1996) *ad Off.* 69b–70.

[12] Thus Pohlenz (1934) 47: 'das Freiheitsstreben des apolitischen Philosophen ebenso unsozial ist wie die Herrschsucht des Tyrannen' ('the apolitical philosopher's striving for freedom is just as antisocial as the domination of the tyrant'). The gist is accurate, even if we follow Büchner (1967) 61 in qualifying Pohlenz's claim, on the basis that *rex*

living as he or she wishes, because what he or she wishes will always be virtuous, but the comparison with monarchs emphasises free agency and absolute self-determination over any moral concerns. By citing both *sapientes* and kings as the epitome of supreme freedom, Cicero highlights (presumably unintentionally) the possible negative consequences of Stoics transcending standard morality and not feeling the loss of social bonds. Such autonomy has the potential to become, or to seem like, hostile, arbitrary wilfulness.

Seneca, too, enjoys comparing the *sapiens* to an absolute ruler. 'If you wish to subject everything to your authority, submit yourself to reason; you will rule many if reason rules you' (*si vis omnia tibi subicere, te subice rationi; multos reges, si ratio te rexerit, Ep.* 37.4). Submission is the path to domination: even though this implies a degree of humility, Seneca's notion of self-control rapidly extends to control over others (*multos reges*, not *multa*).[13] The *sapiens*' inward, self-reflexive concern for his own morality is unsettlingly comparable to a monarch's institutionally sanctioned egotism. If, at base, an absolute ruler has subjects chiefly as material on which to exercise his power, the same applies to Seneca's view of life's moral and physical adversities.

Permutations of this *sapiens*–monarch binary are found throughout Seneca's prose. *Epistle* 114.23 declares the soul a king (*rex noster est animus*), while *de Beneficiis* 7.6.2 avers that the wise man possesses everything 'in the manner of a king' (*regio more*) meaning that he has power over everything.[14] In *Epistle* 108.13, Seneca reports that one of his teachers, Attalus,

has more positive connotations than *tyrannus*. As must be clear already, I do not agree with Dyck (1996) *ad Off.* 69–70 dismissing the issue. Granted, the main thrust of Cicero's line is a comparison between *otiosi* and *reges*, but these *otiosi* are introduced (*Off.* 69) as comprising philosophers and 'certain stern and strict men' (*quidam homines severi et graves*), which leads us back to the idea of moral self-sufficiency resembling autocratic government, though framed, as Dyck maintains, by discussion of the active versus the contemplative life.

[13] A move Edwards (2009) 155 attributes to the exclusiveness of the master–slave dichotomy in Seneca's thought: there is no third possibility; 'each of us is either one or the other'. While I concur, I also believe that this dichotomy is part of Seneca's deeper, sometimes troubling preoccupation with absolute power.

[14] This is in the context of Seneca discussing different forms of ownership. Revealingly, he elaborates his proposition about the *sapiens* via the analogy of Caesar having power over everything but *owning* specific things: *et universa in imperio eius sunt, in patrimonio propria* (*Ben.* 7.6), with Griffin (2013) 327. As so often in Seneca's work, the sage and the emperor are parallel.

4.1 Freedom

'called himself a king' (*ipse regem se esse dicebat*) and that Seneca thought him 'more than a king, because he was entitled to pass judgement on kings' (*sed plus quam regnare mihi videbatur, cui liceret censuram agere regnantium*, trans. Gummere). Once again, terrestrial concerns usurp Stoic claims of metaphorical rulership. Attalus' paradox that the wise man is a true king (because, presumably, he exercises strict dominion over himself and minimises his earthly needs cf. *Ep.* 108.14–15), becomes in Seneca's mind the power of regulating public morals in the manner of a *censor* (*censuram, Ep.* 108.13). The authority acquired through Stoic renunciation aspires to civic supremacy; jurisdiction over the self is thought to justify jurisdiction over others.

It is telling that another permutation of this motif occurs in the *Thyestes*, where the second chorus lauds the simple life as 'a kingdom [that] each man grants to himself' (*hoc regnum sibi quisque dat, Thy.* 390). Like the paradox expressed by Attalus, the line may be taken as a comment on the benefits of Thyestes' exilic poverty, to the effect that his quiet sylvan existence has conferred upon him a kingship more meaningful than his prior rule in Argos.[15] Yet, no sooner do we recognise this quasi-Stoic attitude than Thyestes himself reveals an ingrained desire for the Argive throne, praising its wealth in terms that all but confess his greed.[16] Does this contradict the chorus' vision? Is the choral ode a foil for Thyestes' later conduct? I would argue that the two inclinations – to rustic simplicity and to tyranny – are not as mutually exclusive as they seem. They are, rather, points on a spectrum of autarkic aspirations, since in each case Thyestes chases the freedom to live as he pleases. Senecan autonomy lends itself well to absolutist claims.

The same logic emerges from the anecdotal encounters between tyrants and their victims that pepper Seneca's prose.[17] In the

---

[15] Certainly, the ode's portrayal of kingship reflects on both Atreus and Thyestes: see Tarrant (1985) 137 – the summary of the second choral ode – and Boyle (2017) *ad Thy.* 336–403. For more detail on its relevance to Thyestes: Calder (1983) 190; Davis (1989) 426–9; and Boyle (1997) 48.

[16] *Thyestes* 404: *optata patriae tecta et Argolicas opes*. As Tarrant (1985) *ad loc.* remarks, *Argolicas opes* can be construed as 'wealthy Argos' and, with *optatas* supplied from *optata*, 'longed-for wealth of Argos'. The latter 'more accurately represents Thyestes' feelings'.

[17] Hill (2004) 152 calls these confrontations 'ethically paradigmatic'.

context of praising self-sufficiency in *de Tranquillitate*, Seneca reports that a tyrant threatened the philosopher Theodorus with death and Theodorus replied, 'you have ... the right to please yourself, you have within your power only half a pint of my blood' (*habes ... cur tibi placeas, hemina sanguinis in tua potestate est, Tranq.* 14.3 trans. Gummere). Essentially, Theodorus limits the tyrant's power by declaring himself unaffected by physical pain; the prospect of death is recast as a petty half-pint of blood. The philosopher's autarky enables him to triumph over the tyrant, to hold sway over the tyrant (even if only in an abstract sense), and this, at base, is what Seneca's anecdote celebrates: the sage slipping through the ruler's grasp, proving that terrestrial absolutism is not so absolute after all. Seneca explores a similar idea in the very next story, of Julius Canus, whom Caligula had sentenced to death. Not only does Canus react calmly to the announcement of his impending execution, but, when the guards arrive at his house, they find him playing *latrunculi*, a battle-game somewhat like chess (*Tranq.* 14.4–8). The metaphor is clear, but Seneca spells it out anyway: 'do you think Canus was playing a game? He was making mockery!' (*lusisse tu Canum ... putas? Inlusit! Tranq.* 14.8). The encounter between philosopher and emperor is figured as a competition in hegemony, a zero-sum game in which one achieves control by wresting it from one's opponent. Canus' composure belittles the emperor's power, and even goes as far as allowing him to 'win' at the game of absolutism. Both the sage and the tyrant aspire to moral autonomy, but the sage does it better.

The most detailed example, and the final one I wish to consider in this section, is that of the quasi-Cynic, quasi-Stoic philosopher Stilbo, whose story Seneca tells in *Epistle* 9.[18] Stilbo's home city of Megara has been destroyed by Demetrius Poliorcetes, but the sage accepts his loss with equanimity:

Hic enim capta patria, amissis liberis, amissa uxore, cum ex incendio publico solus et tamen beatus exiret, interroganti Demetrio, cui cognomen ab exitio

---

[18] A favourite tale of Seneca's: he tells it again at *Const. Sap.* 2.6. On the episode's importance in Seneca's thought: Littlewood (2004) 19; Gloyn (2014) 233–5, reprised in Gloyn (2017) 168–9. Brief summary of Stilbo's background and influence is provided by Richardson-Hay (2006) *ad Ep.* 9.1

4.1 Freedom

urbium Poliorcetes fuit, numquid perdidisset, 'omnia' inquit 'bona mea mecum sunt'. Ecce vir fortis ac strenuus! ipsam hostis sui victoriam vicit. 'Nihil' inquit 'perdidi': dubitare illum coegit an vicisset. 'Omnia mea mecum sunt'; iustitia, virtus, prudentia, hoc ipsum, nihil bonum putare quod eripi possit.

This man, his homeland captured, his children and wife lost, when he emerged from the general conflagration alone yet happy, and Demetrius, whose last name, Poliorcetes, referred to his destruction of cities, asked whether he had lost anything, this man said: 'all my goods are with me'. What a brave and tough fellow! He vanquished his enemy's victory. 'I have lost nothing', he said: he forced Demetrius to wonder whether he had actually conquered. 'All my goods are with me'; justice, virtue, wisdom, in other words, he considered nothing that could be taken from him to be a good. (*Ep.* 9.18–19)

Placed in the position of a victim, standing amid the rubble of conquest, loved ones gone, and brought face-to-face with his sardonic enemy, Stilbo vaunts his freedom. The narrative indulges in a cheeky bit of misdirection, designed to upset our assumptions about conqueror and conquered. Has Stilbo lost anything? *Omnia . . . bona mea . . . mecum sunt.* Demetrius, we may assume, could reasonably have expected to hear the first three of those words, but the last two come as a surprise. Stilbo's solution to victimhood is to move the goalposts; in refusing to attribute true value to any of life's externals, he empties Demetrius' conquest of meaning. He also destabilises the conqueror's claim to autonomous action, since Demetrius' role as conqueror depends on Stilbo's acceptance of victimhood, whereas Stilbo depends on nothing. The philosopher's self-contentment at once reflects and exceeds his oppressor's power, enabling him to triumph over Demetrius (*ipsam hostis sui victoriam vicit*) and to undermine his opponent's sense of superiority (*dubitare illum coegit an vicisset*). Seneca imagines Stilbo as the equivalent of a bellicose tyrant, who, brave and tough (*fortis ac strenuus*), asserts his unassailable agency and self-determination in the context of violent desolation.[19] Both figures in the anecdote are defined by their separation from social bonds, the one because he destroys them, the other because he functions despite their loss. Both claim the

---

[19] Littlewood (2004) 19. Richardson-Hay (2006) *ad Ep.* 9.18 notes the motif of 'wise man as moral victor' but misses the deeper significance of Stilbo's and Demetrius' equivalence.

271

power not to be affected by the wreckage around them, both retain their self-possession (and in Stilbo's case, this may be more than self-possession of the psychological/emotional kind, given the very real prospect of enslavement after one's city has been captured).[20] In the confrontation between sage and tyrant, the sage emerges victorious, not just because he evades the ruler's grasp, but because he beats him at his own game. This need to 'win', which comes across so strongly in Seneca's accounts of Stilbo and Canus, seems to contradict the sage's professed disregard for 'indifferents'; why would Canus or Stilbo, and above all, why would Seneca *care* who emerges victorious?

It is this competitive dominance that gives the lie to Seneca's vision of virtuous self-government. While one could argue that Stilbo represents the laudable moral equivalent of Demetrius' sovereign independence, that very equivalence leaves Stilbo tainted by association. His interior hegemony of soul and spirit is less a foil to Demetrius' external rulership than a version of it. Granted Stilbo is unlikely to raze a city – he is not about to become a second Poliorcetes – but Seneca's military language indicates an aggressiveness embedded in Stilbo's autarkic ideals, which are, of course, Seneca's autarkic ideals. Essentially, Senecan autarky celebrates power and control so much,[21] and celebrates it so persistently on the model of worldly autocracy, that it risks valuing absolutist tendencies over morally informed independence. Both Stilbo and Demetrius aspire in their various ways to dictate the very shape and meaning of the world around them; the similarity may present an enticing prospect for disempowered individuals, but it is also a moral problem for Seneca's definition of freedom.

Nor is this problem solved by accepting Seneca's sporadic distinction between kings as beneficent rulers and tyrants as

---

[20] Although more of a background theme in the Stilbo anecdote, slavery is a standard trope in Seneca's treatment of self-possession: see, for example, Edwards (2009) and Degl'Innocenti Pierini (2014) 175. On the related and equally Senecan concept of the self *as* a (legal/physical) possession, see Thévanaz (1944) 191–2.

[21] Thus, Braden (1985) 20 (who ascribes such emphasis to all Stoics, not just Seneca): 'Throughout Stoicism the operative values are ... power and control: we restrict our desires less because they are bad in themselves than in order to create a zone in which we know no contradiction.'

4.1 Freedom

cruel autocrats.[22] According to this line of reasoning, if the soul is a king, and by extension the wise man is too, then however monarchical its rule, it is nonetheless founded upon virtue. Perceptive readers will have noted that the excerpt I cited above, from *Epistle* 114, was an opportunistically truncated version of the full passage, which reads: *animus noster modo rex est, modo tyrannus. Rex, cum honesta intuetur, salutem commissi sibi corporis curat, et nihil imperat turpe, nihil sordidum. Ubi vero impotens, cupidus, delicatus est, transit in nomen detestabile ac dirum et fit tyrannus* ('our soul is at one time a king, at another a tyrant. A king, when it has regard for honourable things, cares for the health of the body in its charge, and gives no disgraceful, no base commands. But when it is uncontrolled, greedy, self-indulgent, then it changes into that detestable and dire term and becomes a tyrant' *Ep.* 114.24). This seems at first blush to resolve the ambiguities of Senecan autonomy, by granting true authority and freedom only to those pursuing Stoic self-control. Philosophical self-government is virtuous; the passions, in contrast, usurp power like tyrants. But even here there is a snag that threatens to unravel Seneca's logic: the verb *imperat*, which situates the virtuous soul in the realm of supreme military and political command. Senecan autarky is a form of *imperium*, all the more absolutist for being self-granted: *imperare sibi maximum imperium est* ('command of the self is the greatest empire', *Ep.* 113.31).[23] Although it can and has been argued that Seneca reinvents *imperium* as an internalised, intangible alternative to the principate's expanding power,[24] still the term belongs to the discourse of autocracy and as such, it establishes a competitive relationship between *sapiens* and monarch, not separation. In the words of Gordon Braden: '*imperium* remains the common value, the desideratum for both sage and

---

[22] Obviously based on the Greek *basileus–tyrannos* dichotomy but complicated by the negative connotations of *rex* in Roman political thought. Seneca's usage is not always clear cut: see Griffin (1976) 206–10 and Rudich (1997) 47–51 and 69–70.

[23] Gray (2018) 8 detects a similar dynamic, to which he ascribes a Senecan origin, in Shakespeare's portrayal of Roman statesmen: 'they see only two ways to attain the *imperium* they seek: either objective rule over others or a retreat from public affairs altogether, in order to focus instead on subjective self-control over their own experience'.

[24] See in particular Star (2012) 23–36.

emperor.'[25] Time and again, Seneca's concept of moral autonomy cannot break free from terrestrial, political paradigms. As a result, his definition of true, Stoic autarky begins to look a lot like its opposite, the false, immoral freedom claimed by tyrants.

Overlap between these two categories is therefore the main issue, and one that has important consequences for our understanding of Senecan tragedy. The wise man's freedom *from* oppression, deprivation, the torments of appetite, is imagined on the model of freedom *to* oppress, deprive, torment. Because Seneca depicts the *sapiens*' autonomy in terms of imperialist conquest and forceful domination it can easily be mistaken for the earthly independence exercised by those in power. The reverse applies as well: political autarky comes to resemble Stoic self-sufficiency. For Seneca's *dramatis personae*, this means that even the most ruthless, unscrupulous pursuit of independence can take on Stoic colouring and lend itself to analysis in (at least partially) Stoic terms. If the would-be *sapiens* aspires to absolute control over his circumstances and indeed, over his opponents, then the same can be said of the tyrant. If the *sapiens* revels in his supreme isolation, celebrates unfettered individual agency, and regards his moral life as a self-conferred kingdom, then how different are the attitudes and aspirations of Seneca's Atreus, or Medea, or Hercules? Like the *sapiens*, the characters of Senecan tragedy refuse to be dominated by others, they grasp at omnipotence, they exercise fierce (if misguided) self-control to achieve their desired ends. In this regard, it is not only valid to discuss their criminality in terms of autonomous selfhood; it is necessary.

All by Yourself

Before turning attention to the tragedies, however, I wish to consider one other, crucial aspect of Senecan autarky: solitariness.[26] For Seneca, solitude provides the right environment for self-determination and self-assertion, and these activities, in

---

[25] Braden (1985) 21.
[26] A condition, in fact, of all autarky, not just Seneca's version. Thus Arendt (1998) [1958] 234: 'sovereignty, the ideal of uncompromising self-sufficiency and mastership, is contradictory to the very idea of plurality'.

4.1 Freedom

turn, breed yet more solitude. Social entanglements are often presented as damaging to virtue; Seneca urges withdrawal. He treats family relationships and friendships with a similar degree of detachment: specific individuals are replaceable, and the true sage will avoid any interdependence likely to expose him to their loss. The *sapiens*' insulation from all contingency means that he stands alone, exercising supreme subjectivity and sovereignty, godlike not just in his virtue, but in his invulnerability and capacity for self-directed action. Once again, these characteristics form an important background for Seneca's *dramatis personae*.

Retreat from public life is such a varied and pervasive theme in Seneca's writings[27] that the following discussion does not aspire to comprehensive coverage. Rather, I examine the specific issue of how solitude affects and protects the autonomy of the Senecan self. At the core is Seneca's concept of self-sufficiency, which is fundamentally introspective, and thus presents a substantial deviation from earlier, Ciceronian traditions of personal autonomy coupled with political involvement.[28] For Seneca, public life represents perilous enslavement to other individuals, to the pursuit of wealth, power and influence, to the many endless and (from a Stoic perspective) pointless demands of the workaday world. There may seem nothing remarkable in this – similar opinions can, for instance, be found in Lucretius and in Roman satire – but Seneca's portrayal is distinctive for its emphasis on subjectivity and personal sovereignty. A brief glance at the *de Brevitate Vitae*, for instance, shows men devoted to business and politics becoming objects of passional forces (both grammatically and figuratively): *alium ... tenet avaritia, ... alium mercandi praeceps cupiditas ... ducit; quosdam torquet cupido militiae* ('greed ensnares one, reckless desire for trade propels another; passion

---

[27] Seneca's varied stance on retirement is encapsulated by the contrasting views given in *de Brevitate Vitae* and *de Tranquillitate Animi*. Although *Tranq.* 17.3 is often cited as evidence that Seneca did not advocate full withdrawal from public life – for example by Inwood (2005) 351, I agree with Griffin (1976) 323–4 that this passage serves a different purpose, namely advice about observing the mean in social conduct. Seneca explores retirement again in the *de Otio*, and in *Epistles* 14, 19, 36, and 68 (although references recur across the entire collection of *Letters* – understandable given that Seneca composed them after having withdrawn from Nero's court). Griffin (1976) 315–66 is an able summary of this aspect of Seneca's views.

[28] Hill (2004) 57 and 148–57.

for war torments others' *Brev. Vit.* 2.1). Public life requires one's subordination to other, more powerful people (*Brev. Vit.* 2.2) while throngs of clients curtail one's freedom on a spiritual as well as physical level (*Brev. Vit.* 2.4). Men embroiled in such situations are 'never able to return to their true selves' (*numquam illis recurrere ad se licet, Brev. Vit.* 2.3). In the helter-skelter of public life, Seneca concludes, 'no-one belongs to himself' (*suus nemo est, Brev. Vit.* 2.4). By contrast, Seneca elsewhere describes Stoic autarky as an act of self-ownership: *te dignum putas aliquando fias tuus* ('you think yourself worthy of at last becoming your own master' *Ep.* 20.1); *ubicumque sum, ibi meus sum* ('wherever I am, I am my own master' *Ep.* 62.1). *Epistle* 75 concludes with a particularly forceful version: *absoluta libertas [est] ... in se ipsum habere maximam potestatem. inaestimabile bonum est suum fieri* ('absolute freedom [is] ... holding supreme power over oneself. Being master of oneself is a priceless good.' *Ep.* 75.18).

The upshot is that the Senecan self rarely, if ever prospers in the public sphere.[29] Withdrawal from social and political duties is carried out less with the aim of forming one's own alternative social group (like an Epicurean circle of friends) than for the sake of cultivating the self's inner sanctum, a lonely and self-absorbing task. Implicit throughout Seneca's descriptions is the idea that public life interferes with one's capacity for self-government, hence his use of reflexive language to explain the philosopher's autarky. While Seneca's propensity for reflexive phrasing has often been remarked as a novel development in self-awareness and self-care,[30] I believe its chief purpose is more grammatical and

---

[29] Thus, Hill (2004) 152: 'The public realm is, for Seneca, simply redundant to the moral excellence of the individual.'

[30] A strand of scholarship originating from Foucault (1986) 46, who was the first to draw real attention to Senecan reflexivity. Though his views on Seneca have rightly been qualified – by, for example, Hadot (1995) 206–13; Veyne (2003) ix–x; Gill (2006) 330–44; and from a rather different angle, Porter (2017) – there is still much of value in them, as demonstrated, for example by Bartsch (2006) 246–7 and 251–2. Contra this trend of magnifying the issue of selfhood in Seneca, Inwood (2005) 322–52 argues that there is little by way of philosophical innovation in Seneca's talk of the self, but that it leaves an impression upon readers because it is a striking literary artefact. Between these two poles, I am inclined to agree with Setaioli (2007) 335, that Seneca's style, and especially his reflexive language, 'imparts distinctive nuances to his thought, which are precious in order to understand Seneca's ... attitude as regards a number of problems'.

4.1 Freedom

political than ethical or aesthetic. First, it celebrates the philosopher's unfettered subjectivity by making him the subject and object of his own action; he is under his own dominion, not another's, and with the responsibility of such self-monitoring comes the freedom of being in charge.[31] Second, many of Seneca's reflexive phrases originate from the juridical language of ownership: *vindica te tibi* ('claim yourself for yourself', *Ep.* 1.1); *suum esse* ('to be master of oneself', see *Ep.* 20.1; 62.1; 75.18, above); *se habere* ('to possess oneself' *Ep.* 42.10; *Brev. Vit.* 5.7).[32] By implication, the philosopher's judgement is superior to the institutional control exercised by courts, and it duly supplants them. These phrases affirm the philosopher's supreme will and power by insisting on his inviolable claim to be his own person. When the Senecan philosopher withdraws into his introspective domain, he forsakes worldly institutions only to set up superior versions within his own soul. Like the competition between philosopher and absolute ruler, explored in the preceding section, Senecan ideals of seclusion invest the sage with unbridled personal sovereignty.

Thus, philosophical autonomy exceeds terrestrial power in the act of its retreat as well as in moments of confrontation. It is, for instance, this idea that motivates Seneca's portrait of Augustus in section 4 of the *de Brevitate Vitae*, where the *princeps* is described as longing to retire from government and enjoy contemplative *otium*: *hoc labores suos ... oblectabat solacio, aliquando se victurum sibi* ('he would make his work pleasant via this consolation, that one day he was going to live for himself' *Brev. Vit.* 4.3). Reflexive language brings us back to the self-contained realm of the Senecan *sapiens*, whose access to

---

[31] Similarly, Foucault (1986) 41, remarks of the broader phenomenon of self-care, which he regards as having emerged during the Hellenistic period, that it represents 'an intensification of the relation to oneself by which one constituted oneself as the subject of one's acts'.

[32] Traina (1974) 12–13 notes the juridical resonance of *se vindicare* and *suum esse*; Cancik (1998) 341 makes the same observation for *suum esse*. See also Armisen-Marchetti (1989) 108 and Edwards (2009) 139 and 154–5. *se habere* is less immediately obvious as legal language but see Berger (1953) 484. Pairing *habere* with a reflexive pronoun and an adverb to express disposition or emotional state is common in Latin – for example Ter. *Eun.* 634 *male me habens* and Suet. *Aug.* 87.2 *vapide se habere* – but by removing the adverb, Seneca transforms the concept into literal self-ownership.

autonomy and solitude outstrips even that of the world's most formidable ruler. Augustus' lonely post at the peak of Rome's hierarchy is nothing compared to the philosopher's self-appointed aloofness.

One last example should suffice to clinch my point. *Epistle* 14 contains one of Seneca's many exhortations to shun public life, in this case chiefly with the aim of evading *vim potentioris* ('the violence of the stronger' *Ep.* 14.4). The worst of all our terrors, Seneca maintains, originates *ex aliena potentia* ('from other people's power' *Ep.* 14.4), which he proceeds to depict in terms of mob violence, torture, and public execution (*Ep.* 14.4–6). Besides illustrating the intemperate nature of worldly might, these examples are significant for turning human individuals into depersonalised objects, literally *dividing* them into limbs and fluids. The philosopher, however, escapes such violation through a combination of physical retreat and spiritual inviolability: 'let us withdraw into ourselves in every way' (*undique nos reducamus, Ep.* 14.10 trans. Gummere). Once again, reflexive language positions the philosopher as arbiter of his own personal circumstances, while the evocation of the immaterial inner realm, in contrast to the tangible facts of bodily penetration, affirms the philosopher's ultimate unassailability; no-one can reach this private, internal region, not even the fiercest tyrant. Withdrawal from public life is accompanied by withdrawal behind the barriers of one's spirit. This is the best, indeed the only, method of asserting one's subjectivity, whereas full engagement with the social world will only lead to one's enslavement and oppression, whether physical or spiritual or, most likely, both.

Similar assertions of subjective control inform Seneca's views on friendship, albeit in more moderate fashion. While it would be wrong to think that Seneca denies the value of having friends – on several occasions, he actually affirms their importance for a full and joyous human life (e.g. *Ep.* 9; 19.10; 48.2; *Ep.* 109) – nonetheless his Stoic beliefs involve a certain amount of indifference. One must not grieve for a friend's death or absence, and such bereavement will not in any way affect the sage's happiness, nor will it curtail his ability to function as a self-sufficient

4.1 Freedom

individual and paragon of virtue.[33] One friendship can be substituted for another (*Ep* 9.5–6) and even though friends are not exactly interchangeable – since memory ensures their distinctness[34] – the value of their company and converse will be the same as that with any other sage.[35] As is apparent in Seneca's Stilbo anecdote, the specifics of personal attachment must be approached with equanimity, no matter how inherently worthwhile such attachments are as a facet of lived experience.[36] Significantly, Seneca argues against the Epicurean view that friendships are formed for the purpose of help and comfort:

> Sapiens etiam si contentus est se, tamen habere amicum vult, si nihil aliud, ut exerceat amicitiam, ne tam magna virtus iaceat, non ad hoc quod dicebat Epicurus ... 'ut habeat qui sibi aegro adsideat, succurrat in vincula coniecto vel inopi', sed ut habeat aliquem cui ipse aegro adsideat, quem ipse circumventum hostili custodia liberet.

> The wise man, even though he is self-sufficient, nonetheless wants to have a friend, if for no other reason than to practise friendship, so that his great virtue does not lie idle, not for the reason Epicurus states ... 'so that he should have someone to sit by him when he is sick, to come to his aid when he has been cast into chains or has become poor', but so that he should have someone by whose sickbed he may sit, and whom he himself may free from the surrounds of hostile imprisonment. (*Ep.* 9.8–9)

There is a strong altruistic element to this: friends should not be self-serving nor should *amicitia* be purely transactional because at some point the transaction will fail its recipient. But in elaborating this principle, Seneca also emphasises the *sapiens'* agency and control: *he* is the one looking after the friend, the one freeing the friend, just as, on a more abstract plane, he frees himself. Again, the wise man occupies a superior position, a position of active

---

[33] Though I use 'indifference' to describe the sage's emotional approach to friendship, I do not thereby mean that friendship itself was reckoned among the Stoic ἀδιάφορα, on which categorisation, see Lesses (1993) 66–8 and Reydams-Schils (2005) 69.
[34] Reydams-Schils (2005) 29–34; 76.
[35] A central argument of Lesses (1993). See also Inwood (1997) 62.
[36] Although Stoic treatment of personal relationships appears heartless by modern standards – we may think, for instance, of Epictetus (*Ench.* 3) comparing the loss of wife or child to the breaking of a jug – Reydams-Schils (2005) 75–6 makes a strong case for the Stoics' positive attitude towards human bonding, pointing out that just because 'the *loss* of a friend is structurally analogous to the loss of indifferents' this does not mean that *possession* of the friend is likewise structurally analogous.

subjectivity as opposed to the status of passive object. Although the sentiment is well meant, it is not hard to see how such assumption of control reinforces notions of the philosopher's supreme sovereignty.[37] Not only does he evade the tyrant's grip and the potential degradation that accompanies much social activity, but he also slips through the knot of interpersonal interdependence, for relying on another individual exposes one to contingency, which a true Stoic will, of course, transcend.

The self comes before the friend in Seneca's thought, and although this is not a selfish principle per se, it should give us pause, nonetheless. At the close of *Epistle* 6, Seneca quotes with approval Hecato's summary of moral progress, 'I have begun to be a friend to myself' (*amicus esse mihi coepi, Ep.* 6.7). This is progress indeed, Seneca remarks, because such a man 'will never be lonely' (*numquam erit solus, Ep.* 6.7) and will be 'a friend to everyone' (*hunc amicum omnibus esse, Ep.* 6.7). The idea is that only proper self-government allows one to be a proper friend and good global citizen; one must secure one's own moral basis first, before benefitting others. But the reflexive language of self-friendship, coupled with the assurance of self-sufficient solitude, suggests that the chief beneficiary is the philosopher himself, who maintains subjective control and secluded autonomy even in contexts of social exchange. Whether making friends or losing them, the *sapiens* appears a lonely figure, self-directed and self-determined.

Along with friendship and seclusion, there is another crucial component of Senecan autarky that requires consideration, a component with substantial ramifications for the tragedies as well: divinity. In Stoic thought, the wise man is equal to a god: an entity of perfect reason, in tune with *natura*, above Fortune, needing nothing beyond itself. Although intended to elevate and celebrate human aptitude for *virtus*, this concept shares with Seneca's other thoughts on autarky the capacity to be twisted in less scrupulous directions, as its affirmation of supreme agency

---

[37] This need for unwavering control and self-possession makes love, too, unadvisable for *proficientes. Ep.* 116.5 reports Panaetius' view of love as *rem ... impotentam, alteri emancupatam*, yet another example of legal language being used to envisage the philosopher's sovereignty.

4.1 Freedom

and solitude can be co-opted all too easily into the service of megalomania. If the philosopher aspires to godhead, so do the selfish and the power-hungry, the imperialists and the madmen. Granted their motives and means of achievement are the antithesis of Stoic *virtus*, but their desire for control and invulnerability – the rewards of divinity – resemble the Stoic's in arresting, sometimes disturbing ways.

As befits his interest in absolute self-government, Seneca emphasises the concurrence between *sapiens* and *deus*. 'This is what philosophy promised me: to make me god's equal' (*hoc enim est quod mihi philosophia promittit ut parem deo faciant, Ep.* 48.11). In *Epistle* 31.9, Seneca assures Lucilius that he, too, 'will rise equal to god' (*par deo surges*) if he takes nature as his guide. Whoever attains flawless reason *deos aequat* ('is on par with the gods' *Ep.* 92.29). In fact, the *sapiens* can even be said to outstrip divinity inasmuch as he achieves rationality via his own efforts, rather than merely embodying it, as the Stoic god does. Divinity, by its very nature, cannot partake of evil, but the wise man emerges superior even to this level of perfection because he can recognise moral evil and overcome it.[38] 'There is a way in which the wise man surpasses god: god fears nothing because of nature's favour; the wise man because of his own' (*est aliquid, quo sapiens antecedat deum: ille naturae beneficio non timet, suo sapiens, Ep.* 53.11). Another permutation of the idea occurs in the *de Providentia*, where Seneca advises his imaginary interlocutor to bear misfortune bravely: 'in this respect you surpass god; he is beyond suffering from evils, you are above it' (*hoc est quo deum antecedatis: ille extra patientiam malorum est, vos supra patientiam, Prov.* 6.6). In each case, it is the sage's capacity to act on his own behalf that places him above the static, unchanging essence of the deity. Active achievement of perfection is presented as more impressive than perfection itself. On the basis of such claims, it is not surprising that later interpreters of Seneca, from Augustine to modern scholars, sometimes accuse him of hubris,[39] and although mistaken, this reaction is evidence of the megalomaniacal

---

[38] Setaioli (2007) 365–6.
[39] Setaioli (2007) 367.

281

potential embedded in Seneca's theology. The issue is of course more complex than mere disdain for divine power; it is about the philosopher's self-conferred independence, its challenge to godhead being a virtually incidental consequence, albeit one that is liable to misuse.

Agency and autarky are the key themes in Seneca's portrait of the quasi-divine *sapiens*. Not only does the sage attain the freedom enjoyed by god, but he attains it actively and self-reflexively, *suo beneficio* (*Ep.* 53.11, above), a result of the jurisdiction he exercises over himself. Seneca quotes approvingly Sextius' view that 'Jupiter has no more power than the good man' (*Iovem plus non posse quam bonum virum*, *Ep.* 73.12), where *posse* evokes raw potential for action as well as the authority that accompanies and guarantees such potential.[40] The core meaning of Sextius' claim is that the *sapiens* and Jupiter are equally capable of bestowing benefits and forgoing external possessions, which makes them equally complete in happiness. No sooner is the comparison made, however, than Seneca avers the sage's superiority in the matter of possessions, because while 'Jupiter <u>cannot</u> use them, the wise man <u>does not want to</u>' (*quod Iuppiter uti illis <u>non potest</u>, sapiens <u>non vult</u>*, *Ep.* 73.14); the *sapiens*' act of willing ranks him above Jupiter's abstention by default. This sense of superiority even originates from the *sapiens* himself (*hoc se magis suspicit*; 'in this regard he esteems himself more', *Ep.* 73.14), which makes his eclipse of divine power entirely self-directed.

In a related vein, the sage resembles a god in his invulnerability.[41] He is impervious to injury, physical or psychological, and remains unaffected by loss. This means, Seneca affirms in *de Constantia Sapientis*, that he is 'a next-door neighbour to the gods, and resides closest to them, like god in everything except mortality' (*vicinus proximusque dis consistit, excepta mortalitate similis deo*, *Const.* 8.2). Once more, the main issue here is autonomy, of which divinity represents the apex. A divine being is, in Patrick Gray's terms, *impassable*, that is, not susceptible to

---

[40] An extended version of this wordplay occurs at *Phaed.* 215: *quod non potest vult posse qui nimium potest.*
[41] Veyne (2003) 33.

being acted upon.[42] The definition is particularly useful for thinking about *de Constantia* section 8, where gods and wise men are portrayed as exempt from object status. Their inability to receive injury – because perfect *ratio* does not allow for the existence of such a category – epitomises their broader freedom from submission, oppression, others' control. God and sage, like sage and tyrant, represent a duo of sublime subjectivity and self-determination. Better yet: the sage gains the upper hand on both of these counterparts, because unlike the tyrant he is not subject to contingency and unlike the god, he actively generates his own conditions of self-government.

The Stoic sage's proximity to the divine also reinforces his solitariness, most obviously because the Stoic god is not part of a pantheon, but also because the *sapiens'* singular virtue enables him to transcend the rabble and its earthly preoccupations. *Epistle* 9 likens the philosopher's self-sufficiency during times of hardship to Jupiter's calm acceptance of *ekpurosis*: sage and god both retreat into themselves, yield themselves to quiet contemplation (*Ep.* 9.16–17). The comparison stresses the *sapiens'* untouchability, the self-containment that insulates him from worldly shocks, and makes him an essentially lonely figure even when there are other people in his life. Just as the Stoic divinity does not depend on anyone, and has no need of anything, so the Stoic philosopher aspires to a sublime level of freedom, the price of which is isolation.

Tragic Freedom

Following this lengthy but important (de)tour through Senecan autarky, I return now to the tragedies, specifically, to discussion of how Seneca's *dramatis personae* envisage and pursue freedom. The aim of the preceding two sections, besides providing expositional material, was to argue that Seneca creates accidental equations between autarky acquired through *virtus* and *ratio*, and its opposite, the irrational, immoral autarky of the tyrant or egoist. The existence of such parallels allows for – one might even say,

---

[42] Gray (2018) 8.

encourages – analysis of autarky in the tragedies. It prompts us to take Seneca's characters more seriously, and not just dismiss their desire for autonomy as a parody or inversion of Stoicism, since Seneca's Stoicism encompasses that inversion already, in its very definition.

A key example in this regard is Seneca's Hippolytus, who resembles a *proficiens* in his dual aspiration to self-mastery and independence. When the Nurse encounters him in a forest glade, halfway through Act 2, she urges him to exchange his lonely chastity for the joys of youthful love (*Phaed.* 435–82) and he replies with an encomium on the wholesome pleasures of life in the woods (*Phaed.* 483–564). Against the Nurse's vision of human intercourse, Hippolytus sets the freedom afforded by seclusion and simple needs. Granted these themes are declamatory and poetic commonplaces, they are also, in this context, reflections on Senecan autarky. The Nurse sets the tone via her cheeky appropriation of Stoic discourse, concluding her praise of sexual pursuits by commanding Hippolytus to 'follow nature, life's guide' (*vitae sequere naturam ducem, Phaed.* 481).[43] Stoic concepts are also unmistakably present elsewhere in her speech, even though they have received no scholarly attention. Thus, for instance, she speaks of 'the proper duties god has allotted' to the different stages of human life, namely that 'joy befits youth and a grim brow old age' (*propria descripsit deus / officia ... / laetitia iuvenem, frons decet tristis senem, Phaed.* 451–3), where the collocation of *propria, officia,* and *decet* cannot help but recall Stoic notions of *decorum*/τὸ πρέπον ('appropriateness') and καθῆκον ('fitting behaviour / proper function'). She enunciates an even more explicitly Senecan form of Stoicism when she tells Hippolytus, 'I am anxious with worry about you, because, hostile, you discipline yourself with harsh punishments' (*anxiam me cura sollicitat tui, / quod te ipse poenis gravibus infestus domas, Phaed.* 438–9). Though a negative attribute from the Nurse's perspective, Hippolytus' self-control (*te ipse ... domas*) epitomises the reflexive subjectivity of the Senecan sage: his withdrawal from human

---

[43] Boyle (1987) *ad Phaed.* 481 with useful comparanda, and Coffey and Mayer (1990) *ad Phaed.* 481–2, who call the Nurse's rhetoric 'good Stoic doctrine in a bad cause'.

4.1 Freedom

commerce frees him from being the object of another's power and leaves him to shape his life as he sees fit. Further, Seneca's choice of the verb *domare* does double duty in evoking, on the one hand, Hippolytus' desire for authority and power, and on the other, his eventual, fateful similarity to a wild beast.[44] His aggressive self-control will end in violence; withdrawal, in this case, spells destruction.

Hippolytus' reply picks up on this question of autarky and pursues it with a vengeance. Life in the forest is, he maintains, 'free from hope and care' (*spei metusque liber, Phaed.* 492); the forest-dweller 'serves no kingdom' (*non ille regno servit, Phaed.* 490), nor does he chase in vain after wealth and honour (*Phaed.* 491); he knows nothing of crime (*Phaed.* 494–5) nor, more importantly, of lies (*Phaed.* 496). In all respects, he is his own master, his autonomy being simultaneously a freedom *from* oppression and a freedom *to* act as he wishes. Echoes of Seneca's philosophical *otium* abound, even if both portrayals owe their genesis to standard poetic *topoi*.[45] Hippolytus, like the Stoic sage, defines his moral outlook in opposition to the popular values of society, and removes himself from that society the better to pursue his life. Also like the Stoic sage, he imagines his isolation as a supreme form of power: the forest-dweller is 'lord over empty fields' (*rure vacuo potitur, Phaed.* 501), an image not far removed from Stilbo's triumphant stance in a devastated landscape.

As my reference to Stilbo suggests, however, Hippolytus' autarky is far from being unproblematic or morally pure. His disavowal of love transforms itself all too rapidly into an exercise in hate. While Hippolytus wishes to preserve his freedom by avoiding being 'conquered' by a woman (*victus, Phaed.* 573),[46] he also

---

[44] Davis (1983) 115 on the verb's significance.
[45] Williams (2003) *ad Brev. Vit.* 2 notes Seneca's debt to satiric traditions of denouncing vice, though the material in this section owes just as much to declamation. Coffey and Mayer (1990) *ad Phaed.* 483–564 classify Hippolytus' speech as a variation on the declamatory theme of town versus country, while noting in addition its substantial debts to Vergil and Ovid.
[46] The elegiac concept of *militia amoris* is clearly in play here, as throughout so much of the *Phaedra*, but equally relevant is Seneca's standard characterisation of the philosopher as a *victor* over adversity and (in an abstract sense) over those who would subjugate him.

285

regards his mother's death as granting him 'the license to hate all womankind' (*odisse ... feminas omnes licet, Phaed.* 578–9). Several commentators note that this sentiment reworks a fragment from one of Euripides' lost *Melanippe* tragedies (498 Kannicht; 498 Collard and Cropp): πλὴν τῆς τεκούσης θῆλυ πᾶν μισῶ γένος ('I hate the whole race of women apart from my mother').[47] There is, however, an essential difference in Seneca's version: the verb *licet*, which shifts focus from misogyny per se to the fact of Hippolytus' freedom to indulge in it. Crudely put, Antiope's death removes from Hippolytus yet one more constraining social bond, which affords him the licence to behave as he pleases. Rather than being the object of someone's love (cf. the passive form, *victus, Phaed.* 573, above), Hippolytus uses his solo status to assert active control of the situation. This self-focused isolation is, moreover, a particular characteristic of the Senecan Hippolytus, who shuns all society, right down to the family unit, in contrast to his Euripidean counterpart, who refuses merely to worship Aphrodite.

Of course, the autonomy avowed by Seneca's Hippolytus is not fully Stoic. It would be too simple a syllogism to say that isolation augments Hippolytus' independence and that it does the same for the Senecan *sapiens*, therefore Hippolytus exemplifies a *sapiens*. This is not defensible, nor is it what I am arguing. Instead, the point is that Hippolytus' angry, isolated, solipsistic view of autarky does not undermine Seneca's Stoic principles so much as *extend* them. Granted Hippolytus misconstrues freedom as licence and, despite all his protestations of independence, actually enslaves himself to anger (*Phaed.* 566–8), nonetheless he embodies an extreme version of Senecan principles in his withdrawal from social activity, in his preoccupation with personal freedom, and in his condemnation of mob morality. Even his particular emotional weakness, rage, is the one Seneca confesses most likely to befall a *sapiens*: 'the wise man will not stop being angry, once he begins' (*numquam irasci desinet sapiens, si semel coeperit, Ira* 2.9.1); 'if you expect the wise man to be as angry as the shamefulness of criminality demands, he must not just grow

---

[47] Boyle (1987) *ad Phaed.* 578; Coffey and Mayer (1990) *ad Phaed.* 578–9.

4.1 Freedom

mad, but go insane' (*si tantum irasci vis sapientem, quantum scelerum indignitas exigit, non irascendum illi sed insaniendum est, Ira* 2.9.4).[48] Although unlike Hippolytus, the *sapiens* does not fall into this trap, temptation in both instances comes in the form of moral outrage. Acute awareness of vice coupled with the desire to protect oneself prompts irate withdrawal. The comparison should give us pause.[49] Hippolytus is no sage, certainly, but neither can his autarkic aspirations be dismissed as mere delusion, or as foils to the authentic Stoic views expressed in Seneca's prose. If Hippolytus' Stoic ideals are warped – and they are, undeniably – that is partly because Seneca's ideals are too.

The flipside of Hippolytus – a potential sage overlaid by angry, selfish tendencies – is Atreus, an angry tyrant with Stoic inclinations. Since I have dealt already with some of Atreus' Stoic traits in Chapter 1, I shall restrict myself to a brief summary here. I have discussed how self-knowledge and firmness of purpose lend Atreus' actions a quasi-Stoic tint; likewise, he echoes in distorted form philosophical concepts of the *summum bonum* (*Thy.* 205–6) and is presented as 'untroubled' by the chaos around him (*securus*: *Thy.* 720; 759).[50] This Stoic framework prompts – even if it does not outright confirm – the attribution of Senecan ideals to some of Atreus' other activity as well. For instance, Atreus eschews commonly accepted moral principles as a barrier to his autonomy: in response to the *satelles*, who urges honourable conduct as the only source of genuine popular support, Atreus retorts that a ruler's true power lies in being able to disregard the populace and trample on its values (*Thy.* 207–18). While the *satelles* advocates Senecan principles in this scene (to the extent that many critics, including the *Octavia*'s unknown author, have cast Seneca in the *satelles*' role),[51]

---

[48] Braden (1985) 22 notes the wise man's susceptibility to anger but draws no connection to Hippolytus.
[49] Comparison of *Phaed.* 483–564 with *de Ira* 2.9 finds further justification in the fact that both passages refer to the myth of the Ages of Man. *de Ira* 2.9 even cites Ovid *Met.* 1.144–8, which Seneca clearly draws on for *Phaed.* 555–8: see Boyle (1987) *ad loc.* and Coffey and Mayer (1990) *ad loc.* On the *de Ira*'s use of Ovid, see also Tarrant (2006) 3–4.
[50] The Stoic resonance of *securus* is noted by both Tarrant (1985) and Boyle (2017) *ad Thy.* 720, the latter with plentiful comparanda from Seneca's prose.
[51] Reading Seneca as the *satelles* (or as a combination of *satelles* and Thyestes) and Atreus as Nero has a long history, beginning with *Octavia* 377–592. Modern scholarly appraisal of the parallels is found in Pöschl (1977) 233; Calder (1983) 191 and 194–5; Bishop

287

Atreus' disavowal of them can also be read in Senecan terms. Like Atreus, the Senecan *sapiens* pits himself against prevailing, popular morality, which he regards as a threat to his autarky. Sage and tyrant coincide in their desire not to come under another's control: *qua iuvat reges eant* ('kings should go where they please', *Thy.* 218) – the sentiment needs but little modification to fit the *sapiens* as well.

Atreus also recalls the *sapiens* in his self-deification,[52] a topic I have examined in Chapter 1, and now reprise in the light of my preceding comments about Senecan theology. Significant in Atreus' case is both his equivalence to the divine (*aequalis astris gradior*, 'I stride equal to the stars', *Thy.* 885 resembles language used in *Ep.* 92.29: *deos aequat*, 'is equal to the gods'), and the fact that his status is self-conferred. By the conclusion of his revenge, Atreus' power and independence exceed those of the mythological pantheon, checked only in his inability to drag the gods back from their flight (*Thy.* 893–5). Certainly, one can see in his divine pretensions the megalomania of a figure like Caligula,[53] or more simply, the tradition of imperial deification (which was not always strictly posthumous). But the divine aspirations of the Senecan *sapiens* also belong within this nexus, since the wise man, too, is portrayed as outranking the gods in his capacity for autonomous, autarkic action, a position achieved via his own relentless effort. Here, as on so many other occasions in Seneca's work, tyrant and *sapiens* share essential aims and qualities, albeit ones that originate in vastly different value systems. This is what prevents Atreus from being pure parody; his questionable traits belong to the *sapiens*, too, just in a different guise. Thus, the juxtaposition that many scholars detect ultimately fails to hold. John Stevens, for instance, suggests that Atreus 'does not wish to join the heavenly community by perfecting his virtue, but to supplant the gods by perfecting his vice'.[54] True, up to a point, but the common goal of

---

(1985) 345–6, who deals only with Atreus, not the *satelles*. Tarrant (1985) 48 is right to caution against such overly historical interpretation of the play's characters; Schiesaro (2003) 163 calls such identifications 'superficially appealing'.

[52] Noted briefly by Morford (2000) 167 and Boyle (2017) *ad Thy.* 885–9, the theme deserves further exploration.

[53] Tarrant (1985) 48.

[54] Stevens (2018) 578. Lefèvre (1981) 36 advances a similar claim, though he applies it to Senecan tragedy overall. Seidensticker (1985) 131 epitomises the approach I am

4.1 Freedom

perfection indicates a degree of complementarity, and the idea of supplanting or somehow exceeding the divine is already there in Seneca's portrait of the *sapiens*. The wise man's relationship to the gods is just as competitive as Atreus'.

The most powerful version of this quasi-Stoic autarky is not Atreus, though; it is Medea. Her exchange with the Nurse, in particular, is laced with sentiments that would fit just as easily in the mouth of a Senecan *sapiens*:[55]

> **Med**: fortuna fortes metuit, ignavos premit.
> **Nut**: tunc est probanda, si locum virtus habet.
> **Med**: numquam potest non esse virtuti locus.
> **Nut**: spes nulla rebus monstrat afflictis viam.
> **Med**: qui nil potest sperare, desperet nihil.
> **Nut**: abiere Colchi, coniugis nulla est fides
> nihilque superest opibus e tantis tibi.
> **Med**: Medea superest: hic mare et terras vides
> ferrumque et ignes et deos et fulmina.
>
> **Med**: Fortune fears the brave, but crushes cowards.
> **Nur**: Courage must be put to the test if there is occasion for it
> **Med**: There will never not be an occasion for courage.
> **Nur**: No hope shows the way out of your afflictions.
> **Med**: One who has no hope despairs of nothing.
> **Nur**: The Colchians have gone, your spouse is unfaithful,
> nothing remains of your once great wealth.
> **Med**: Medea remains; here you see sea and earth,
> and steel and fire and gods and lightning bolts
>
> (*Med.* 159–67)

Medea is safe because nothing else can be taken from her.[56] She is self-reliant in the face of Fortune's onslaught and responds to the deprivations of victimhood – the loss of husband, home, and resources – by affirming her self-possession and freedom to act on her own behalf. Her praise of *virtus* encompasses both the

---

critiquing here: his assessment of Atreus' quasi-Stoic traits is excellent, but he takes Stoic claims of mastery, freedom, and power too much at face value, failing to see the insidious qualities these values sometimes assume in Seneca's work.

[55] As remarked, with varying degrees of emphasis and acceptance, by Hine (2000) *ad Med.* 160, 163, 176 and 520; Fitch and McElduff (2002) 37; Bartsch (2006) 265–6; Boyle (2014) *ad Med.* 161, 176, 505, 520, and 540–1; and Mader (2014) 146.

[56] Thus, Lefèvre (1981) 33: for Seneca, 'a human being is most free when he has least to lose'. The idea is central to Calder (1976).

masculine, heroic ideal of 'courage' and the Stoic ideal of moral 'virtue', which, Medea affirms, remains not just *a* but *the only* constant in any situation.[57] Line 163 – *qui nil potest sperare desperet nihil* – finds partial echo in *Epistle* 5.7, where Seneca quotes Hecato: *desines timere si sperare desieris* ('you will cease from fear if you cease from hope').[58] More broadly, Medea resembles a *sapiens* in her disavowal of 'externals' and in her ability to function fully, autonomously, without them: *fortuna opes auferre, non animum potest* ('fortune can take away my wealth, but not my spirit', *Med.* 176). Later, when Jason confronts her, she will likewise claim, 'Fortune, in every form, has always stood below me' (*fortuna semper omnis infra me stetit, Med.* 520), and, 'my mind is able and accustomed to despise royal wealth' (*contemnere animus regias ... opes / potest soletque, Med.* 540–1). Both statements could stand alone as Senecan, Stoic assertions of *autarkeia*, making Medea, on the face of it, equal to Stilbo: *iustitia, virtus, prudentia, hoc ipsum, nihil bonum putare quod eripi possit* ('justice, virtue, wisdom, in other words, he considered nothing that could be taken from him to be a good' *Ep.* 9.19).

The preceding qualifications – 'could stand alone'; 'on the face of it' – are crucial, though, because Medea's actions within the tragedy actually demonstrate an excessive, destructive concern for externals, especially for her reputation and for her hold over Jason.[59] Contrary to her disavowals of loss, she *is* affected by the drastic change in her circumstances, which she plans to rectify to her satisfaction, even if only through the emptiness of revenge. In addition, Medea's forceful self-mastery is offset by her describing herself as the object of passional forces (e.g. *Med.* 937–44), which, by strict Stoic standards, makes a mockery of her desire for independence.

And yet, as in the case of Atreus and of Hippolytus, the equation is not so simple, because what Medea hopes to regain most of all is the capacity to control her fate, and this pursuit of self-determination coincides on many levels with the philosopher's, whose inclination for terrestrial mastery I have outlined

---

[57] I disagree with Hine (2000) *ad Med.* 160 that 'the moral sense [of *virtus*] is hardly present' in these lines. For fuller exploration of Medea's *virtus*, see Battistella (2017).
[58] Costa (1973), Hine (2000), and Boyle (2014) *ad loc.*
[59] A point emphasised by Nussbaum (1994).

4.1 Freedom

already, above. Medea celebrates solitariness because it confers invulnerability and the release from being subjected to another's power. In the midst of disaster, surrounded by threats, Medea finds strength in the thought that she has herself to fall back on. Paul Veyne's characterisation of Stoic self-reliance could just as easily be applied to *Medea* 166–7 (if it is not already a citation of it): 'when all seems lost, the only thing that really counts and acts, the *I*, remains'.[60] *Medea superest: hic mare et terras vides / ferrumque et ignes et deos et fulmina* (*Med.* 166–7). The real import of these two remarkable and enduring lines[61] lies not in their evocation of Medea's magical powers,[62] nor in their self-conscious citation of her mythological-literary pedigree,[63] but in their affirmation of steadfast, autarkic selfhood. Medea, and no one else, will dictate what 'Medea' means. Just as it is in her power as a witch to summon or even to embody the natural phenomena of sea, earth, fire, and lightning, so it is within her power as an individual to shape herself and ensure her own security. The lines' rhetorical punch comes from their celebration of agency, agency in its most naked form: the pure power of sea or flame.[64] Like Seneca's *sapiens*, Medea claims to be untouchable, indomitable, at precisely the moment when she is most in danger of being dominated.

Lurking behind all of Medea's quasi-Stoic assertions is the promise of revenge, which she deems the chief means of re-establishing her autonomy. Her defiance of fortune is not just an acknowledgement of inviolable inner strength but also a guarantee that her crimes will outdo anything fortune has wrought against her, overturn it, control it. The same goes for her self-affirmation

---

[60] Veyne (2003) 32.
[61] They have been much imitated by subsequent playwrights. Corneille *Médée* 320–1 is the most well-known adaptation: see Costa (1973) *ad Med.* 166–7 and Slaney (2019) 134. Boyle (2014) *ad Med.* 166 catalogues more fully the lines' later reception in European tragedy.
[62] The standard interpretation of their meaning: Costa (1973) *ad Med.* 166; Hine (2000) *ad Med.* 166–7; Littlewood (2004) 45; Trinacty (2014) 160. Fyfe (1983) 80 interprets the lines more broadly as 'a claim to universal power'.
[63] Littlewood (2004) 46, and Boyle (2014) *ad Med.* 166 point to this line as an example of metatheatrical self-dramatisation.
[64] Johnson (1987) 74 furnishes an apt parallel in his description of Lucan's Caesar: 'He is not so much a political phenomenon, a man who wants power, as a process in nature: he wants to *be* power, he *is* power. He is a bolt of lightning destroying whatever happens to be in its way.' Fyfe (1983), Henderson (1983), and Slaney (2019) 70–9 explore Seneca's thematising of Medea as an elemental force.

in response to loss and victimhood: besides highlighting Medea's fierce *autarkeia*, lines 166–7 foreshadow the gathering storm of her vengeance, which, she avers later in the play, will uproot and flatten everything with its violent onrush (*Med.* 411–14). Paradoxically, her Stoic professions of detachment actually contribute to her earthly triumph.

Nor is this quasi-Stoic dynamic of revenge exclusive to the warped world of the tragedies; we can also see it, faintly, in Seneca's stories of sage versus tyrant, where the former's moral victory resembles a kind of retribution for what he has been made to suffer. I note above the competitive relationship Seneca envisages for these two figures, and the sage's need to 'win' at the game of possession and control. Such competition approximates retaliation in the relationship of equivalence it creates between *sapiens* and ruler: the former responds to the latter's aggression on equal and opposite terms, triumphing over his adversary because he engages in a superior version of the harm he has experienced.[65] Demetrius robs Stilbo of his city and family, Stilbo robs Demetrius of his victory; Caligula sentences Canus to death, Canus trumps Caligula's power by counting death as nothing.[66] Just as the avenger typically assumes and exceeds his opponent's characteristics, so these 'victories' are described as mimicking the rulers' military and political sway. The impression is mild, but unmistakable: the *sapiens*, like Medea, uses his self-sufficiency as a form of revenge.

4.2 Revenge

Medea: Vengeance, Identity, Autarky

It is not surprising to see Seneca's vision of Stoic autarky gravitate towards revenge, because aside from the particulars of the *sapiens*' competitive stance, vengeance itself is an exercise in

---

[65] On revenge as an act of imitation, or an 'equal and opposite' reaction, see in particular Kerrigan (1996) 6–8 and Burnett (1998) 2–3, and more generally, Miller (2005). Dodson-Robinson (2019) 1 contends that the theory has its limitations.

[66] Though this may sound more like evasion than confrontation, nonetheless it contains a strong element of retributive aggression. As Miller (2005) 144 observes, for the Stoics, like the Christians after them, 'true satisfaction lies in denying all injury ... or in forgiving admitted injury'. A peaceful approach, to be sure, but one that still aims at recompense.

4.2 Revenge

autonomy. Francis Bacon called it 'a kind of wild justice'.[67] Revenge mimics the law while occupying a space beyond its reach; it is the flipside of judicial procedure. αὐτο/νομία: independence, and more literally, taking the law into one's own hands. Linguistic derivation points to an underlying union of ideas, namely that personal autonomy is deeply implicated in the pursuit of revenge and that vengeance amounts to the search for individual – moral, political, social – freedom. As Eric Dodson-Robinson rightly recognises, revenge is a declaration of agency in response to personal disaster.[68] Being made into a victim, being made to suffer loss, dishonour, or physical damage deprives one of sovereign jurisdiction over one's own life and body. The injury endured by the victim – whether corporeal, psychological, social, or any combination thereof – represents his or her helpless submission to external forces and a consequent distortion of authentic selfhood. Vengeance is a means of reasserting control over one's life, reclaiming one's capacity to act, and reconfiguring one's identity in response to its (often) violent disfigurement at another's hands. The avenger seeks to transform him- or herself from passive object into active, aggressive subject; such reciprocal retaliation could just as easily be called 'a kind of wild self-fulfilment'. And crucially, a bid for self-determination. There is much in the impulses of vengeance that reflects the desires of the Senecan sage, even if he employs vastly different means to realise them.

This section moves away from Stoic preliminaries, however, to consider how Medea's vengeance shapes her autonomy and identity as a quasi-human within the fictional world of her play. Successful retaliation grants Medea the freedom to define herself, and her sexual and social status, as she wishes. It enables her to reassert control over her body, her future, even over the record of her past. And, like so many other instances of Senecan autarky, it leaves her adrift in a solitude of her own making.

Every element of Medea's revenge is geared towards recalibrating her sense of self in the wake of Jason's betrayal. In both the Euripidean and the Senecan version, Medea's vengeance works

---

[67] Bacon in Kiernan (1985) 16–17.
[68] Dodson-Robinson (2019) 1–14. On the interrelationship of autonomy, agency, and revenge, see also Belsey (1985) 111–16, on Renaissance drama.

through exact reciprocity to deprive Jason in the same way his actions would have deprived her. He abandons their marriage; she prevents his remarriage. More specifically, her murder of Creon and Glauce/Creusa sabotages Jason's prospective kinship ties and his place within Corinth's socio-political order, just as his remarriage meant severing ties with Medea and jeopardising her sociopolitical status to the point of consigning her to exile. Having left her homeland, abandoned her father and murdered her brother all for Jason's sake, Medea takes as recompense Jason's future father-in-law and adopted home.[69] Since Jason had intended to keep the children from their marriage, leaving Medea bereft, she pre-empts him and bereaves him of them permanently. She ensures that Jason, too, will have to endure wandering in exile, tainted by criminal associations, shunned by other kings and communities. By the time her revenge is complete, the only connection remaining to Jason is the only one he tried to break: his union with Medea.[70]

Such acts of reciprocal, pre-emptive desolation are Medea's ways of recovering her status and identity and reaffirming her capacity for self-determination. As Gianni Guastella has demonstrated in a perceptive article on the revenge dynamics of Seneca's version, Jason's plans imperil the social roles Medea has built for herself. Not only would his remarriage invalidate her position as spouse and – to a lesser extent – as mother, it would also render meaningless all of Medea's prior, often criminal actions in the service of Jason's safety; if she loses him, her past loses its purpose.[71] Thus, when Seneca's Medea asks her husband *coniugem agnoscis tuam?* ('do you recognise your wife?' *Med.* 1021), she is – besides the other interpretations discussed in Chapter 1 – emphasising her faculty of self-definition and ensuring Jason acknowledges it as such. He has tried to change her status, to remove her role as wife; she has wrested back that power.

---

[69] Seneca's Medea is so exacting as to wish that Jason had a brother she could kill in return: *utinam esset illi frater!* (*Med.* 125).
[70] Burnett (1973) 14 summarises the reciprocity of Medea's revenge in Euripides. Mastronarde (2002) 13–18 discusses broader issues of symmetry and repetition in the tragedy's revenge-plot. On the balance of payback in Seneca's version, see Guastella (2001) 201–3.
[71] Guastella (2001) esp. 198–200.

4.2 Revenge

Similar logic drives her infanticide, since Medea asserts possession of her children by disposing of them as she wishes (there is, perhaps, a hint of this in *Med.* 935: *pereant, mei sunt*; 'let them perish, they are mine')[72] and at a deeper, unspoken level, by fixing them as hers for all eternity: they will never grow up, never leave, never change. Empty victories, of course, but that is the price of revenge, which activates the victim's agency and confirms his or her identity at the expense of the social bonds that constitute that identity in the first place.[73] Retaliation reinstates Medea qua Medea, but, paradoxically, without the relationships that made her so.

Identity formation through vengeance is a pervasive theme in the play, and, as the preceding example of *Medea* 1021 indicates, it is especially noticeable in the heroine's habit of self-reflexive speech. Repeated utterance of her own name and role represents for Medea a self-exhortation to retributive action, a totemic guarantee of what she is capable of and *who* that capability marks her out as being. Often overlooked in favour of metapoetics and dramatic self-awareness, this aspect of Medea's illeism is equally as crucial for our understanding of Seneca's composition. When, for instance, Medea goads herself to 'embark on all that Medea can do, and all she cannot do' (*incipe / quidquid potest Medea, quidquid non potest*, *Med.* 566–7), a meta-literary interpretation would highlight the character's acknowledgement of her own abilities and storyline, as well as Seneca's ambition for his Medea to surpass all her previous incarnations. On this reading, the lines' self-reflexivity would be a combined declaration of poetic aspirations, belatedness, and anxiety of influence. It is all of these things. Yet it is also the heroine's promise to attain self-definition via successful pursuit of revenge: what Medea can and will *do*, after all, is harm Jason, an act that reinstates her sense of

---

[72] I follow standard punctuation of this line, as opposed to that of Nussbaum (1997) 450. Medea's expression is so compressed as to be slightly ambiguous here: does she mean that the children must perish because in belonging to her they also belong to Jason, as Nussbaum (1994) 450 suggests? Or because of the guilt they inherit from her, as suggested by Hine (2000) *ad Med.* 934–5? *Quot grammatici tot sententiae*. I am more inclined to treat *pereant* as a direct consequence of Medea's ownership, *mei sunt*: Medea claims control over her children to the point of deciding whether they live or die.

[73] As observed by Dodson-Robinson (2019) 10.

self by allowing her to control her fate. The two readings tend to pull in opposite directions: either Medea is caught in a cycle of pre-scripted activity or, as a human analogue, she uses revenge to achieve self-government and fully realised subjectivity. Both interpretations are valid; each identifies one of the lines' fundamental features. But we should be wary of stressing metapoetics to the detriment of Medea's implied humanness, because, besides acknowledging her literary pre-destination, *Medea* 566–7 is also a fierce celebration of individual agency in which Medea qua person promises to overturn all checks and limitations, to exceed all constraints, and to achieve something beyond the expected, beyond even the pedestrian realm of the possible. Aspiring to do what she cannot (currently) do is Medea's way of attaining greater autonomy and freedom, and of realising her selfhood via the absolute independence to act as she wills. In a similar vein, the famous *Medea— fiam* ('Medea— I shall become her' 171) is not just a promise to fulfil a pre-existing dramatic role, but a guarantee of Medea's ability to fashion her own identity as she, and she alone, wishes, no matter what anyone else tries to do to her (we might want to stress the first-person: 'Medea— *I* shall become her'). Such affirmations of sovereignty reveal the self-creation inherent in the heroine's project of revenge: she and no other will decide what 'Medea' represents and who Medea is.

In addition to recalibrating her future, moreover, revenge also confers control over the production of her past. It dictates how she will be remembered – not as the victim, but as the perpetrator, the active party in the event (e.g. *Med.* 52–3; 423–5). Likewise, it facilitates the recuperation and reformulation of what she has lost, as in her counterfactual claim to have regained father, brother, homeland, and virginity (*Med.* 982–4).[74] While none of these things has (or can!) be reinstated in actuality, they encapsulate the autonomous self-fashioning and self-legitimisation afforded by Medea's vengeance. By re-establishing her dominance, revenge enables her to believe in and to impose whatever version of the past best suits her. History belongs to the winner.

---

[74] See also the discussion of this passage in Chapter 1, 58–9.

4.2 Revenge

The autarkic impulse of Medea's vengeance extends further still, from the immaterial realm of her reputation to her flesh-and-blood presence as a maternal body. Of all the uniquely Senecan elements in this play, many of which bear directly on the interlinked issue of vengeance and identity, her vow to scour her womb for any remaining embryos ranks as one of the most memorable: 'if any love pledge still lies hidden in the mother, I shall search my womb with a sword and drag it out' (*in matre siquod pignus etiamnunc latet / scrutabor ense viscera et ferro extraham*, *Med.* 1012–13).[75] In one vicious image, Medea sums up the agency conferred by revenge. If children symbolise a diminution of her autonomy – through her dependence on a spouse, lack of control over her own body, and pledged bond (*pignus*) to another person – then the prospect of abortion represents its reinstatement. As a woman, Medea achieves independence from socio-political constraints by first achieving independence from corporeal ones. Her willingness to engage in self-harm also verges on Stoic contempt for bodily pain, as though Medea has to subjugate herself to herself, and refuse the lure of externals in order to become fully autarkic.[76] Moreover, like Senecan concepts of individual sovereignty, Medea's self-government hinges on increased removal from human society: the image of abortion shows her cutting ties to Jason at a most visceral level. Once again, her project of revenge acquires a quasi-Stoic dimension, as her desire to obliterate damaged personal relationships amounts to a fiercely defended form of self-mastery.

Such defiance of limitations, Medea's assertions of agency, her self-fashioning and desire to dictate her future – all of this activity draws attention to her status as an implied human figure. Even though vengeance is built into her story, still she pursues it on the

---

[75] Though the language of *Med.* 1013 bears some similarity to Ov. *Am.* 2.14.27 – see Hine (2000) and Boyle (2014) *ad loc.* – its application to this particular context seems distinctly Senecan. Granted, one must be careful when making claims about Senecan uniqueness: it is difficult to trace the borders of originality in the tragedies when so much intervening material has been lost. But Medea's illeism, her quasi-Stoic expressions, her desire to reinstate the past— all of these echo sentiments and styles found elsewhere in Seneca's work, so I attribute them to his ingenuity, in the absence of any evidence to the contrary.

[76] Nussbaum (1994) 440, one of the only scholars to have paid serious attention to the meaning of *Med.* 1012–13, likewise asserts its bearing on Medea's self-sufficiency, though oddly does not classify it as a form of self-harm.

assumption that her circumstances are contingent, otherwise retribution would be pointless. Revenge's transformative power,[77] its promise to elevate Medea from victim to aggressor, passive to active participant, implies her possession of quasi-human agency and potential for individual change. Even her penchant for self-naming represents an assurance of future development and maturity, of control over both self and world, in addition (and contrast) to its well-recognised emphasis on the repetitive, fictional quality of Medea's being. One could, of course, ask whether Seneca's audience needs to believe in Medea's implied humanness first, before accepting these traits as evidence of it, but the question is unnecessarily chicken-and-egg (and in any case, similar acceptance of Medea's fictional status must precede awareness of her metapoetic qualities). What matters is that Medea's quasi-human characteristics should not be overlooked, not least because it is these features, rather than ironic metapoetics, that endow her rhetoric with such force, and lend her behaviour an urgent, troubling moral dimension. Medea qua textual construct may play with the contours of her narrative, but Medea qua person explores the limits of human constraint and capacity for action.

In contrast to Medea's hard-won autonomy, the Jason of Seneca's version appears perpetually subjugated and hemmed in, which accentuates his wife's power all the more; brief discussion of this binary rounds out my present analysis of Medea's revenge. Seneca's Jason is a notably weaker and more minor figure than Euripides', partly because he has fewer lines but also because Seneca depicts him as the constant victim of other people's dominance.[78] When he arrives on stage, he confesses not to have broken faith with Medea of his own free will, but under compulsion from Creon, who has forced him into a marriage alliance in exchange for protecting him and his sons from Acastus' vengeance (*Med.* 434–9). Having been duly separated from her husband and children, Medea may be handed over to Acastus for punishment, in retaliation for her prior killing of Pelias. No mere decoration, inclusion of this backstory is designed to minimise

---

[77] A phenomenon examined by Dodson-Robinson (2019) *passim*, but especially 8–10.
[78] Hine (2000) 18–20 summarises the weakness and subservience of Seneca's Jason in comparison to Euripides'.

4.2 Revenge

Jason's independence, something the chorus, too, acknowledges when it asks the gods to 'spare a man who acted under orders' (*parcite iusso*, 669). Unlike Medea, Jason seems forever unable to assume control of his situation. He complains of being bound by *fata* (*Med.* 431) whereas Medea vaunts her superiority to *fortuna* (*Med.* 520). Word-choice is significant, too, since *fatum* implies a pre-ordained sequence of events while *fortuna* designates something fickler and more changeable.[79] In contrast to Medea's confident dismissal of externals, Jason is at their mercy; he seems unable to rely solely upon himself and he constantly denies responsibility, as though he were not the source of his own actions. Far from making him an honourable or innocent figure,[80] these traits cast Jason as Medea's feeble foil, an individual whose misguided concept of security has greatly diminished his agency and independence. Whereas Jason relies on Creon (e.g. *Med.* 538–9, where he promises Creon's money rather than using his own; cf. Eur. *Med.* 610–3), Medea relies on herself. True, she strives for power over her oppressors and seeks to master fortune rather than, in Stoic guise, to conform to its demands, but her independence outstrips Jason's because she regards herself, not others, as the only real source of safety, of fairness, even of meaning. Jason may crumble, but *Medea superest*.

Revenge and Fictional Autonomy

I mentioned near the close of the preceding subsection that Medea's revenge highlights her quasi-human features chiefly by accentuating her capacity for autonomous action. The effect is hardly exclusive to Medea, or to Seneca. Rather, it is a consequence of revenge narratives more generally, which orbit around questions of self-assertion and self-determination, and which propel fictional characters into independent, largely self-motivated action. Revenge in literature distils issues of choice and intention and imbues them with particular urgency. While many

---

[79] Hine (2000) *ad Med.* 431.
[80] A favourable but ultimately untenable view of Jason proposed by Zwierlein (1978).

other fictional scenarios also achieve this variety of effects, I have chosen to focus my present discussion on revenge because it is a distinctive element of Senecan tragedy and of Western theatre more broadly.[81] Further, it has the advantage over other fictional scenarios of telescoping all these scattered facets of autonomy into one, climactic event.

The revenge plot tends to focus on control, which is perhaps the most obvious means of its emphasising characters' humanness. A major difference between fictional and actual beings is the level of mastery they exercise over their own existence, for, though both groups are inhibited by circumstance, by the demands of others, by convention, and in some belief systems, by ineluctable fate that plays itself out like a narrative, still human freedom exceeds that of characters' in its capacity for choice and change. One cannot assume control when one's context is not contingent, and to the extent that characters are imprisoned within their scenarios, they are powerless to govern their own affairs. On a metaliterary plane, the avenger's explosive anger articulates frustration at such restrictions: it crashes through the status quo, pushes beyond the expected and the possible, and rearranges its milieu radically, violently, on its own terms. From Aeschylus' Clytemnestra to Shakespeare's Hamlet and beyond, the avenger assumes a quasi-authorial, quasi-directorial role, constructing his or her own scenarios, plots (in both senses of the term!), tricks, contraptions and performances.[82] The avenger aspires to dictate how subsequent action will unfold in his or her fictional world, an act of control that imagines, simultaneously, the possibility of contingency – futures *can* be altered; circumstances and people *can* change – and its lack – all events *must* come under the command of a single, directorial will. Choice also plays a role here, because on the one hand, avengers are compelled to act by a host of forces beyond

---

[81] Perry (2015) 407 sums up the majority academic view, held especially by scholars of early modern drama: 'revenge is a theme specifically associated with Senecan tragedy'. Curiously, this characterisation persists despite ample instances of revenge in Greek tragedy, too. On revenge as a foundational motif in Western theatre, and in Western literature more generally, see Kerrigan (1996) 3–5.

[82] Thus, Dodson-Robinson (2019) 1: 'the victim becomes ... [an] auteur ... revenge in the tragic tradition is ... demiurgic'. Also, Burnett (1998) 3: 'the avenger necessarily becomes an artist who both imitates and invents'.

4.2 Revenge

their immediate control,[83] but on the other, must decide whether to accept the call to retribution and how to execute it. It is from Hamlet's indecision over whether revenge is the right course of action that his character acquires much of its complexity and depth, its illusion of intimate individualism. In a very different fashion, but still on the topic of choice, it is Atreus' deliberation over the *method* of revenge that delineates so clearly his moral and behavioural traits. The revenge plot's attention to decision-making and to eventualities accentuates the avenger's status as a human analogue while at the same time acknowledging – one might even say sympathising with – the limitations of fictional existence.

Accompanying the idea of contingent futures, moreover, is the idea of contingent selves. As I remarked in the preceding analysis of Medea's revenge, acts of retaliation typically entail self-(re)creation or development as part of the avenger's escape from victimhood. In Seneca, revenge is as much about self-discovery as it is about righting perceived wrongs. Though Senecan avengers do not undergo any radical shifts of personality, they can still be said to enlarge their capabilities and increase the sheer force of their presence over the course of the play. Medea, for instance, declares in Act 5 that her character 'has grown through evils' (*crevit ingenium malis*, *Med.* 910), where *malis* most likely signifies both the crimes she has committed against others and the prior suffering she has endured at their hands.[84] Pursuit of vengeance has increased her psychological and moral stature even if her identity has proceeded along the same continuum throughout. And in terms of social status – for this 'outward' form of selfhood is one of the avenger's prime concerns – Medea transforms herself from marginalised fugitive into a powerful manipulator of other people's fates, and, in less positive terms, moves from being wife and mother in actuality to being them in name only. In effecting a transition from victim to agent, passive to active, the fictional avenger embodies a distinctly human capacity for change, and

---

[83] A point emphasised by Dodson-Robinson (2019), who prefers to define agency as emergent and complex, the result of multiple intersecting forces both human and non, rather than, as I do, the capacity for self-directed action possessed by an independent being, fictional or otherwise.

[84] See Nussbaum (1994) 448 for the latter interpretation.

Autonomy

particularly, for self-directed, self-motivated change, which forms the basis of so much autonomous action in the non-fictional universe.[85]

Another notable consequence of the revenge plot is its filtering of events through the avenger's perspective, a focalisation that happens just as much in dramatic as in narrative literature,[86] and is especially pronounced in Senecan tragedy, where avengers dominate the dialogue and overrule all opposition with their superior wit. Of course, first-person viewpoints are far from unique in ancient literature, but revenge plots are distinctive for their sustained reliance on a single character's perception of events in a genre where focalisation is more usually dispersed across multiple speakers. The tragic avenger is our confidant and commentator: we know what Atreus and Medea are plotting, and this knowledge, besides generating ample dramatic irony, grants us privileged access to their intentional and emotional states.[87] The illusion of their humanness grows in proportion to this access, as their revenge becomes an expression of agency and individual will. Emphasis on the avenger's perceptual activity adds an intimate, private dimension to the character, as though he or she were endowed with fully functioning consciousness and such hidden realms of thought as necessarily accompany a first-personal perspective. Nor does the character have to be particularly 'round' or 'deep' for this rule to apply. Although Seneca's avengers occupy the opposite end of the spectrum from, say, Hamlet's anguished complexity, still their aggressive focalisation of the tragedies' events creates an impression of internality, of decision-making and moral sensibility, no matter how rhetorically expressed. This

---

[85] Hague (2011) 4–5 stresses the ability to change and develop as a root component of human autonomy. See also Oshana (2005).

[86] I employ the terminology tentatively; it is apt, but how and whether narratology can be applied to theatre is a contested topic: see, for example, the critical overview by Jahn (2001).

[87] I disagree with Allendorf (2013) 134 who claims, 'there is no character ... that could be relied upon for epistemic guidance in the *Thyestes*'. We are undoubtedly guided by Atreus and meant to share his perspective (however warped it is, it still represents the 'truth' in this play); see, for example, how even the messenger adopts an Atrean viewpoint and invites the chorus to do likewise: Tarrant (1985) *ad Thy.* Act IV (623–788) and Littlewood (2004) 226–40.

4.2 Revenge

internality is the wellspring of autonomy, the self behind the action, the doer behind the deed.

On the topic of doers and deeds, however, one could demur that the avenger's role as an agent of causality is no different from, say, Greimas' theory of the *actant*, a narrative element that propels action and may be instantiated by animate and inanimate objects alike, and even by abstractions.[88] While my preceding discussion takes for granted a link between agency and human or quasi-human autonomy, Greimas divorces the two categories, prioritising the former in such a way as to dismiss the latter, alongside refusing to accord any special status to fictive agency in its human as opposed to non-human forms. The avenger, on this reading, becomes a sophisticated species of plot device, an initiation (rather than the more personal 'initiator') of subsequent fictive events and of no more significance to the narrative syntax than any other catalyst for action. To take an example from Seneca's *Phaedra*, the revenge unleashed against Hippolytus is activated as much by the sword (*Phaed.* 898–900) as by Theseus himself. In Greimas' view, the two would claim equivalency as spurs to the ensuing sequence of events.

The theory falters, though, in its failure to acknowledge how central a concept of human agency is to our understanding and appreciation of fiction, so central in fact that the agency fictional works accord to objects, animals, plants, and abstract phenomena – to name just a few – tends to be framed in human terms, modelled on a broadly accepted (if culturally conditioned) understanding of human capacities.[89] Many of these fictional *actants* are endowed with intentional and emotional states or treated as though they possess them; many exhibit enduring traits, both physical and psychological. The sword in Seneca's *Phaedra* 'speaks' Hippolytus' name to Theseus (*hic dicet ensis, Phaed.* 896), despite its inanimate existence. Thus, in contrast to Greimas' equating

---

[88] Greimas (1987), esp. 71.
[89] Smith (1995) 20. The same argument may be used in response to Dodson-Robinson (2019) 2 (citing Charles Taylor), who remarks on the ascription of agency to non-human entities in actual life. His example of the corporation having the same rights and protections as natural people is a good one, but this, too, shows that the natural person is the paradigm for agency, thus confirming human salience in this regard.

fictional beings with objects and impersonal forces, the association is more likely to work in the opposite direction, as the impersonal is typically imbued with person-like qualities. Of course, the sword is not capable of self-directed action, and in this regard, its narrative agency does not lead to or derive from any impression of autonomy. But just because some agents of causality are non-autonomous does not mean that all are, and characters, as human analogues, have a special claim to being measured against human models of action. To see Theseus' vengeance purely as a narrative prop is to erase his responsibility for what happens next, and therefore to erase the audience's sympathetic involvement with his character (is he likeable, or not? Is he justified?) and besides, to erase the very thrust of *tragedy* – of an unfair fate engineered by accident – that emerges from the ensuing events.[90] To interpret the play in these terms, which is by and large a critical norm in Senecan studies, is to ascribe, tacitly, a degree of autonomy to Theseus, whereby he exercises his fictional independence to make a crucial – and damning – choice. What is true of Theseus, moreover, is true of most if not all avengers in drama, not to mention of most characters in literature more broadly. Their structural agency as elements that propel the plot is complemented to the point of being overshadowed by their thematic agency as quasi-human figures whose actions resonate across their fictional landscape. Though we must guard against overstating fictional autonomy, we must also guard against eradicating it.

Turning back to the Senecan avenger, we can see this balance in play, because besides accentuating characters' implied humanness, acts of vengeance on the Senecan stage also call attention to their status as fictional constructs. I remarked above that avengers tend to assume a directorial or authorial role within their dramas, a circumstance that summons the shadow of metatheatricality and self-conscious performance. As always, Seneca's Medea furnishes excellent examples. Her skill in magic, for one, encapsulates simultaneously her power to effect change through

---

[90] Though definitions of tragedy are notoriously difficult – see, for example Eagleton (2003) – unfairness, accident, and the individual coming into conflict with larger (social/divine) structures are indisputably core elements. On Seneca's sense of the tragic, see Staley (2010).

4.2 Revenge

vengeance and that power's circumscribed, fictional nature. Witchcraft enables her to dictate the course of events and to orchestrate Jason's downfall, activities that assimilate her to Seneca qua author. The latter half of the tragedy is a performance directed by Medea herself, in which she also plays the starring role.[91]

This authorial function is particularly evident in the magical power Seneca ascribes to Medea's voice.[92] In Act 4's spell-casting scene, the Nurse reports how Medea 'summons plagues' (*pestes vocat, Med.* 681); how a 'scaly crowd' of snakes 'is drawn forth by her magic chanting' (*tracta magicis cantibus / squamifera ... turba, Med.* 684–5); how a serpent 'is stunned at hearing her song' (*carmine audito stupet, Med.* 689). Medea, too, recognises and revels in her voice's magnetic quality: 'may Python come', she pronounces, 'at my songs' command' (*adsit ad cantus meos / ... Python, Med.* 699–700); 'I have summoned rain from dry clouds' (*evocavi nubibus siccis aquas, Med.* 754); 'the summertime earth has shivered in response to my chanting' (*aestiva tellus horruit cantu meo, Med.* 760); the forest 'has lost its shade at my voice's command' (*amisit umbras vocis imperio meae, Med.* 767); 'the Hyades are shaken by my song' (*Hyades ... nostris cantibus motae, Med.* 769). The metapoetic sense of these references is not hard to find: Medea's poetry (*carmen*; *cantus*) conjures the world into being and arranges it according to her liking. As the terminology suggests, this is solemn poetry in an elevated genre: both *carmen* and *cantare* can be used in reference to tragedy. In addition to casting her as a dramaturg, moreover, Medea's vocal abilities associate her with the actor, whose task involves 'positing the existence of fictional space and fictional objects' through the sheer power of speech acts.[93] Things happen, things exist, because Medea says so.

If Medea's vocal power symbolises her mastery – over words, over the environment, over the play's events – it also indicates her

---

[91] Trinacty (2014) 94: 'Seneca makes Medea into a quasi-author of the plot.' Also, Schiesaro (1997) 92–3 and (2003) 17–18.
[92] Many of the following examples are explored by Fyfe (1983) 83 and Slaney (2019) 86–8. Robin (1993) 109, likewise notes the prominence Seneca accords Medea's speech.
[93] Slaney (2019) 86.

ultimate lack of such control, by signalling that she, too, is the fictional product of a *carmen*, the object of somebody else's imagination, subject to somebody else's will. By fashioning her as an author/director figure, Seneca reminds his audience of Medea's fictive status as a character in his play. Her occasional similarity to an actor likewise contributes to this effect, because it celebrates her ability to manipulate spectators both internal and external to the drama (cf. her calling Jason *spectator* at *Med.* 993), while also acknowledging her subordination to a script. Thus, her magic simultaneously guarantees her autonomy and divests her of it, creating the illusion of her omnipotence only to stress that it is just that: an illusion.

While Act 4 provides the most plentiful crop of examples, Medea's quasi-authorial role is cited at other points in the play, too. When Creon denounces her as a *malorum machinatrix facinorum* ('a contriveress of evil deeds' *Med.* 266) and when the Nurse, in quaking admiration, calls her a *scelerum artifex* ('an artist of crime' *Med.* 734), each underscores her creative abilities as a practitioner of wickedness. *artifex* in particular is a word that refers not only to authors, but also to actors and stagehands (e.g. *artifices scaenae*: Sen. *Ben.* 7.20.3; Suet. *Jul.* 84.4; Gell. 3.3.14), which situates Medea's metapoetic power in a solidly theatrical context. Jason, similarly, calls her a *sceleris auctor* (979), recognising her authorship of crime via an appropriately generative metaphor, since it is through her *increase* of children that Medea achieves her *scelus*. Not only that, but her crime itself *grows* from, builds upon and extends the scale of her earlier forays into wickedness. Like Seneca's portrayal of her magic, each of these appellations articulates Medea's power as an agent of vengeance while at the same time admitting the limitations imposed by her fictional existence: she can contrive anything to suit her angry purpose ... but only at the behest of her own *auctor*, Seneca. The idea resurfaces, climactically, when Medea prepares herself for infanticide by ordering her grief to 'seek out material' for its revenge (*quaere materiam, dolor, Med.* 914). A common metapoetic marker, *materia* here signifies, all at once, the means of Medea's vengeance – the very *stuff* of her children's bodies

4.2 Revenge

and of her *mater*nal role in producing them – the content of Seneca's version, and Medea's own status as *materia* for Seneca's tragedy.[94] In other words, it expresses both her authorial aspiration to shape events and her subjugation to another's authority. Her implied humanness as an individual, purposive agent within the drama's universe is shackled to her purely fictional ontology.

Shackling and limitation are core elements of the avenger's experience and this is another reason why revenge plots convey so precisely the problem of characters' autonomy. At base, vengeance is a response to powerlessness. The avenger chafes against constraint and consequently explodes into anger against his or her perceived oppression. This quality of weakness and subjugation is fundamental, though critics often lose sight of it: we may, for instance, be inclined to regard Atreus as all-powerful from the play's outset, but he makes it clear that he feels vulnerable and victimised as a result of Thyestes' adultery. His revenge represents re-instatement, a resumption of confidence and autocratic sway (a theme explored below, in the next subsection). As an expression of fictional agency, therefore, Atreus' vengeance exalts his dominance while never once losing sight of his containment within a given literary form. His desire to surpass all kinds of limitation, crystallised in his repeated use of *modus* (*Thy.* 255; 279; 1052) combines the tyrant's with the avenger's inherent inclination to overreach, while at the same time acknowledging that his fictional power is bred of constraint.

The avenger's freedom is never complete, either, because the act of vengeance itself is always (over)determined by forces beyond the avenging agent's control. Betrayal happens, murder is committed, and the victim-cum-avenger makes a move in response. Re-venge is inherently re-active, a secondary event conditioned by other, arguably (or seemingly) freer agents and imposed upon the avenger not just by dint of circumstance but, often, by other individuals – or ghosts – seeking personal recompense via the avenger's hands.[95] Viewed from this angle,

---

[94] Trinacty (2014) 123 remarks the significance of *materia* at *Med.* 914, but not comprehensively.
[95] A topic explored by Dodson-Robinson (2019) and hinted at, incisively, by Kerrigan (1996) 4–5.

vengeance becomes a duty, and the avenger more of an instrument than an agent.[96] Although Seneca's chief avengers, Atreus and Medea, act on their own behalf and set out to gain satisfaction only for themselves, still their activity is predicated on a host of preceding events and prevailing influences that ensnare them within a particular storyline. Atreus is spurred into action by his brother's transgressions and by the spectral inspiration of Tantalus, who is in turn goaded by the Fury.[97] His presumption of individual control seems paltry against this backdrop, but that is the central dynamic of the revenge plot, in which fictional autonomy is at once granted and withheld, stimulated and suppressed by the self-same forces.

Lastly, it is helpful to think about the avenger's autonomy in a specifically theatrical context, because if the act of retaliation distils issues of individual agency, so too does stage performance, with a comparable degree of clarity and urgency.[98] Both centre upon the need for action, upon action as a determinant of identity, upon the performer's power to effect change in his or her surroundings and to manipulate an audience. As I note above, the actor resembles the avenger in experiencing a compromised autonomy. On the one hand, he or she enjoys the freedom of *doing* things on stage (δράω – drama) and of being an active subject in contrast to the audience's physical passivity as recipients of the performance.[99] In ancient Rome, where theatrical performers were typically disenfranchised and occupied the lowest rungs of society, the contrast must have been starker still, as theatre gave otherwise powerless individuals the opportunity to

---

[96] Pace Samuel Johnson's well-known assessment of Hamlet, cited by Storm (2016) 59, *all* avengers are instruments to some extent, and if Hamlet exemplifies this predicament to an extreme degree, that is because of his archetypal status as an avenger in search of (political, moral, theatrical) agency.

[97] Dodson-Robinson (2019) 38–43.

[98] Thus, Zamir (2014) 24: 'Acting ... is a form of self-animation that presents the transition from mere functionality into agency, from incomplete being into "selfing", from part object into fuller subject.'

[99] While it is unfair – and invalid – to characterise theatre audiences as 'passive', their generally sedentary state does provide a foil to the actors' task of embodying and stimulating *action* on stage. Senecan drama articulates this division in especially stark terms, with internal audiences portrayed as helpless witnesses of events they would prefer not to see, for example Jason at *Med.* 992–1021; Greek soldiers at *Tro.* 1128–9; Thyestes at *Thy.* 1004–30.

4.2 Revenge

appear as self-directed, self-determined beings.[100] Although the Roman actor's slave status classifies him, socially, as an object (e.g. Varro *Rust.* 1.17.1), he may become on stage a thinking, acting, intentional subject. On the other hand, though, this subjectivity is conferred by prevailing social and dramatic conventions, before which the actor must (literally!) bow and which imprisons him/her as the object of the audience's gaze and approval. The performer's freedom is short-lived, dependent not only on the play's duration, but also on the authority of playwright, director, and spectators. Like the tragic avenger, the actor's explosive agency reveals a relentless chafing against the very restrictions that produce it. In this respect, the tragic avenger could even be considered an Ur-figure for the actor, making it unsurprising that revenge plots underpin so much of Western drama: their obsession with agency and autonomy holds a mirror up to theatre itself.

Atreus: Vengeance, Identity, Agency

Seneca's Atreus is an avenger par excellence, in his affirmation of indomitable individual agency, and in his converse role as a product of family entanglements and an already overdetermined genre. He epitomises, simultaneously, the avenger's license to do as he pleases and his subjection to powers and processes beyond his control. He embodies what Curtis Perry defines as 'a core dialectic [of Senecan tragedy] ... in which hyper-assertive selves are set against ironizing structures of predetermination'.[101] This section and the following one examine, respectively, the autonomy Atreus pursues through vengeance and the restrictions he inherits as part of his literary and genealogical background.

Like Medea, Atreus begins his play desperate to reclaim the identity and status he feels have been stolen from him. Cuckolded

---

[100] On theatre's ability to empower the disenfranchised through performance, Conroy (2010) 30 is insightful. The issue of Roman actors' legal status is addressed most thoroughly by Leppin (1992) 71–83, but see also Dupont (1985) 95–8; Edwards (1993) 123–6 and (1997b) 66–95; and Csapo and Slater (1994) 275–9, for a collection of relevant primary sources. The idea of the powerless individual acquiring self-determination through the medium of stage performance is most obviously exemplified by the Plautine slave.
[101] Perry (2015) 411.

Autonomy

by his brother, his paternity uncertain and his kingship vulnerable, Atreus hungers to reconfirm his social, sexual, and political dominance. His sense of manhood, in particular, is a crucial though under-explored[102] aspect of this capacity for action, for it is by reaffirming his sexual vigour that Atreus prevails over Thyestes and, concomitantly, asserts himself as an actively self-determined individual. *Thyestes* is about adultery as much as it is about tyranny. Atreus' opening words of self-excoriation, *ignave, iners, enervis* ('useless, feckless, impotent' *Thy.* 176), besides criticising his present inactivity as unworthy of a tyrant, also evoke the sexual passivity to which he feels Thyestes' adultery has consigned him: he is unmanned, impotent.[103] Emasculation carries with it the entire baggage of objectification, marginalisation, and oppression that the avenger, too, experiences and fights against. For Atreus, this victimhood is the equivalent of occupying a woman's role. When, for instance, he cites the myth of Tereus, Procne and Philomela, he aligns his suffering with that of the story's female characters (*Thy.* 275–6),[104] as though Thyestes' adultery and prior usurpation of the throne qualified as acts of rape, or as though he were experiencing infidelity and its ensuing family confusion from the wife's perspective, like Procne. Either way, Atreus associates his damaged virility with the Greco-Roman woman's social and sexual subordination to men, portraying his lack of control over his marriage and kingdom as equivalent to a lack of personal autonomy. Similar hints of effeminisation emerge from his desire 'to be filled with greater monstrosity' (*impleri . . . / maiore monstro, Thy.* 253–4), a phrase that conjures images of pregnancy through its use of *impleo* (cf. Ov. *Met.* 6.111),[105] its anticipation of Thyestes' eventual fate, and its allusion to poetic inspiration, which is often depicted as a procreative act.[106] The

---

[102] Littlewood (2008) – a revised and expanded version of Littlewood (1997) – is the only full piece devoted to gender identity in the *Thyestes*. There are also scattered comments in Tarrant (1985) and Schiesaro (2003). Boyle (2017) is particularly alert to the play's themes of masculinity.

[103] Thus, Boyle (2017) *ad Thy.* 176 on *enervis*: 'the sense of "emasculated" seems prominent here'. Ovid *Am.* 3.7.15 uses *iners* to evoke impotence.

[104] See the perceptive comments by Littlewood (2008) 245 and Schiesaro (2003) 80–3.

[105] With Boyle (2017) *ad Thy.* 248–54.

[106] See Gowers (2016) 563–7 on pregnancy as a model for poetic inspiration/creation.

4.2 Revenge

implication is simultaneously positive and negative: Atreus qua avenger will swell with the productive power of his retaliation, but this is a situation made necessary by his fear of having been relegated to a sexually submissive role. Pregnancy is the perfect symbol of Atreus', and indeed of any would-be avenger's, compromised autonomy, as it destabilises everything from identity to corporeal integrity, and carries with it the stigma of female passivity, of being an object or vessel for somebody else's use. Atreus' masculinity will increase only in proportion to the agency, subjectivity and self-assertiveness proffered by revenge.

Over the course of his tragedy, Atreus carves out for himself a renewed role as a *paterfamilias*, with all its implied masculine dominance. He exchanges his initial state of enervation (*enervis*, *Thy.* 176) for harshness/hardness (*durus*, *Thy.* 763) as he hews his nephews' bodies in preparation for cooking.[107] He also stops being a vessel and assumes instead the dominant part of an impregnator: 'I shall fill up the father with the death of his sons' (*implebo patrem / funere suorum, Thy.* 890–1), he promises the audience at the opening of Act 5. It is a promise he repeats in Thyestes' presence: 'now I shall fill up the father completely with his own throng' (*totumque turba iam sua implebo patrem, Thy.* 979). This transferral of pregnancy from Atreus to Thyestes encapsulates the success of the former's revenge. To reinstate his virility, Atreus compels his brother to undergo a transformation equal and opposite to his own: Thyestes begins as *durus* (*Thy.* 299) and ends up effeminised, his bulging gut an ugly parody of a full womb (*Thy.* 999–1004; 1041–4).[108] Grotesquely, Atreus proves his manhood by burdening Thyestes with children, an act that confirms his agency at the same time as it curtails that of its

---

[107] Dodson-Robinson (2019) 43–4. Stevens (2018) 577 claims that *incubat* at *Thy.* 733 also has sexual connotations.

[108] Noted by Poe (1969) 372, and expanded by Littlewood (2008) 252–3, and Gowers (2016) 563–4, the motif of pregnancy in *Thyestes* still awaits fuller scholarly treatment. Its presence as a theme is heralded right from the play's outset, with the Fury's exhortations that crime must 'grow' as it is punished (*dum … punitur scelus / crescat, Thy.* 31–2) evoking not just the repetition of wickedness across multiple Tantalid generations, but also the perverse sense of generative increase coming from Thyestes' cannibalism. Likewise, *oriatur novum* (*Thy.* 30) and *liberi pereant male / peius tamen nascantur* (*Thy.* 41–2) conjure the gestational quality of Thyestes' full stomach, as well as referring, in the latter's case, to Thyestes' future incest with his daughter.

victim, for the female role thrust upon Thyestes renders him socially, politically, and sexually subservient to his brother, in addition to its depriving him of bodily autonomy.

Interlinked themes of sex, revenge, and personal agency also cluster around the play's imagery of fullness and gratification, especially around the term *sat/satis*, which Atreus employs throughout. In Act 2, he complains that the 'fire burning [his] breast is not big enough' (*non satis magno meum / ardet furore pectus*, *Thy.* 252–3) and declares of his proposed attack on Thyestes, 'I shall leave no outrage undone and none is enough' (*nullum relinquam facinus et nullum est satis*, *Thy.* 256). The motif returns in Act 5, when Thyestes' glut of wine and flesh (*iam satis mensis datum est / satisque Baccho*; 'enough has now been given over to feasting, enough to wine' *Thy.* 899–900) leads Atreus first to celebrate and then to doubt the fulfilment of his revenge: 'it is good, it is ample, now it is enough even for me. But why should it be enough?' (*bene est, abunde est, iam sat est etiam mihi. / sed cur satis sit?*, *Thy.* 889–90). Although he cannot compel the gods to witness his atrocity, 'it is enough that the father view it' (*quod sat est, videat pater*, *Thy.* 895). In the brothers' final clash, Atreus gloats that Thyestes will shortly have [his] fill' of his children (*satiaberis*, *Thy.* 980), while Thyestes admits his innocent enjoyment of the meal: 'I have my fill of feasting, and no less of wine' (*satias dapis me nec minus Bacchi tenet, Thy.* 973).

As an allusion to the play's theme of transgressive consumption, the *satis*-motif is well recognised.[109] It has also been studied as a technique of rhetorical/generic amplification with equal degrees of insight.[110] But its other associations have so far gone unremarked. Its evocation of psychological fulfilment, for instance, relates directly to Atreus' pursuit of vengeance, his desire to receive recompense, to achieve 'payback' (*satisfacere*), and his nagging feeling that no penalty, no matter how severe, will ever erase this sense of injury. Although the term *satisfacere* does not feature in the

[109] Poe (1969) 362–3; Tarrant (1985) *ad Thy.* 252–3; Meltzer (1988) 317; Boyle (1997) 44–6.
[110] Seidensticker (1985).

4.2 Revenge

Thyestes, the avenger's repeated use of *satis* suggests its underlying presence.[111] Similarly, the thematic centrality of food is something this play shares with broader Western cultural definitions of vengeance, many of which employ metaphors of alimentary overindulgence: the avenger experiences his lack as hunger, strives for fulfilment, and, frequently, suffers from dissatisfaction at the end.[112] What is specific to Atreus and to the play's plotline is generic to vengeance itself, something the *Thyestes*' *satis*-motif suggests by alluding not just to food, but to food *as punishment* and desire as physical appetite. Atreus sets out to sate his anger, to satisfy his soul by filling Thyestes' body, to give his brother, too, a bitter taste of victimhood. And his own fullness remains uncertain even at the play's end, a circumstance he shares with many tragic avengers. Revenge resists closure, and its perpetrators rarely feel replete.

In this last regard, the *Thyestes*' *satis*-motif is also a barometer of Atreus' autonomy, for it suggests his continued enslavement to desire even when revenge has been brought to completion. Successful retaliation may ensure Atreus' sexual domination, but does it, *can* it, ever guarantee his freedom from the impulse of vengeance itself, which tends towards addiction and imprisons its protagonists in an endless loop of wanting *more*. Like Tantalus' hunger, revenge resists gratification; its innate excessiveness always admitting the possibility of going further still and committing a yet more perfect crime.[113] Although Seneca's Atreus appears content with his final achievement (*Thy.* 1096–9), there remains a lingering sense that he could have engineered an even greater atrocity: he could have forced the gods to watch (*Thy.* 893–5), forced Thyestes to commit cannibalism knowingly (*Thy.* 1053–6; 1065–8), could, perhaps, have restored his marriage in actual rather than rhetorical fact (*Thy.* 1098–9). Every shortfall indicates

---

[111] Seneca does, however, use the term elsewhere to describe recompense, punitive or otherwise, for example *Ira* 2.32.2.
[112] Miller (2005) 140–6 surveys the metaphor's cultural breadth.
[113] Burnett (1998) 13–17 offers insightful discussion of this theme in the *Thyestes*, treating Atreus' desire for perfection as symptomatic of his 'artist's imagination', which aspires to 'make a masterpiece of his revenge'.

Autonomy

a curtailment of Atreus' agency, as though all of his sweeping anger could not overcome the barricade of its own ineradicable presence. This is a crucial caveat to my arguments about the avenger's agency: retaliation impedes autonomy just as it confers it; no matter how powerful the avenger becomes, he or she must eventually reckon with anger itself. At the same time, though, this reckoning underscores the avenger's dominance. The sheer magnitude of Atreus' aspirations, their proximity to the impossible, emphasises the extent to which his agency already reaches: he may not be able to compel the gods' return, but he *has* caused their flight. Essentially, the play's theme of satisfaction illustrates the enormity of Atreus' power by highlighting its occasional limitation. It also confirms his autonomy by establishing a contrast between active aggressor and passive victim, between the one who demands satisfaction and the one who will pay for it, for although Atreus himself is consumed by rage, he is the one in charge of Thyestes' more literal consumption: the passive *satiaberis* (*Thy.* 980) shows all too clearly where the balance of power lies.

In its evocation of food and fullness, *satis* also contributes to *Thyestes'* themes of sexual anxiety and the gendered active/passive binary. Interestingly, Petronius (75.11 and 87.1)[114] uses *satisfacere* in reference to sexual gratification, which raises the tantalising possibility of vengeance *tout court* embodying a sexual act. Of course, Atreus' revenge does have a sexual dimension, but that is due to the specifics of plot, it seems, rather than to the individual quality of revenge itself; there is too little evidence to be certain on this point. A more fruitful set of parallels, however, appears in Plautus' *Amphitruo*, where *satis* is used to characterise Alcmena's insatiable sexual appetite: she complains in her *canticum* of pleasure's insufficiency (*Am.* 633), and Jupiter, in their first scene together, asks why she cannot be satisfied with his love of her (*Am.* 509).[115] Jupiter's own indulgence is called *satietas* at *Am.* 472, and when the offended Alcmena seeks an

---

[114] See Adams (1982) 197 and 215, for further discussion.
[115] Christenson (2000) 40–2 summarises the thematic significance of *satis* in the *Amphitruo*. In an example of even greater relevance to Seneca, *satis* may also have had sexual connotations in Accius' *Atreus*, since there Atreus describes Thyestes as *qui non sat habuit coniugem inlexe in stuprum* (*Atreus* 205 Ribbeck *TRF*²).

4.2 Revenge

apology from Amphitruo, her request – <u>satis faciat mi ille</u> ('he must <u>make amends</u> to me', *Am.* 889) – acquires undeniable sexual connotations in light of her preceding characterisation. While I do not propose that Plautus influenced Seneca directly,[116] this comedy's use of *satis* is a helpful measure of what occurs in the *Thyestes*: besides configuring Atreus' retaliation as hunger, *satis* also configures it as lust, a burning desire that Atreus struggles to gratify. Further, Atreus' persistent yearning seems to place him in a sexually subordinate role, as implied by the parallel of Alcmena, and by Greco-Roman cultural norms, which tend to associate sexual insatiability with feminine lack of control. This fact of Atreus' lust, like the fact of his anger, represents a potential check to his free agency.

Unlike anger, though, the check seems temporary, because, as I explore above, Atreus manages to trap Thyestes into 'pregnancy'. The protagonist's lack of *satietas* is cancelled out by his antagonist's surfeit: *satis* finds its echo in Thyestes' being 'stuffed' (*satur est*, *Thy.* 913). Comparison with Plautus' Alcmena is instructive here, too, because the same term is used to describe her bulging pregnant belly, in the context of a joke about food (*Am.* 665–8). Just as Thyestes' overeating resembles gestation, so Alcmena's gestation resembles overeating. The parallel highlights Thyestes' increasing feminisation across the course of the drama, and the concomitant reinstatement of Atreus' dominant masculinity. Rage may not admit of full satisfaction, but lust has a generative telos.

Although a more generic form of identity than Medea's, Atreus' manhood is nonetheless pivotal to the sense of self he seeks to recalibrate in revenge. It is an integral part of his social position as a father, as the head of a household, as an autocrat, that he appear sexually powerful.[117] He says as much in his opening collage of the expectations inherent in a tyrant's role (*Thy.* 176–8): the list shows clearly what Atreus wants to be, and further, that vengeance is his chief means of achieving this identity. His political and

---

[116] The presence of Plautine themes in Seneca is, however, a large and fruitful topic that I am exploring in my current research.

[117] Dodson-Robinson (2019) 49: 'Atreus' identity is deeply vested in the legitimacy of his offspring (*Thy.* 326–329), and thus through his crime he reconstitutes himself in his role as *pater*.'

sexual statuses largely coincide in a relationship of mutual reinforcement, so that his securing of power within his immediate domestic sphere (*domus*) confirms the authority and prestige of his lineage (*domus*) as a ruling family.[118]

At the epicentre of these themes is the question of paternity, which exemplifies Atreus' combined ambition for domestic and social control, and over which Thyestes' adultery has cast a long shadow. Atreus begins the play in doubt over his sons' parentage: he worries about their 'dubious bloodline' (*dubius sanguis*, *Thy.* 240) and hopes for 'proof of uncertain paternity' (*prolis incertae fides*, *Thy.* 327) by involving Agamemnon and Menelaus in his plot. First, he aims to determine his sons' loyalty by disclosing his full intent, reasoning that if they defend their uncle, they must in fact be his offspring (*Thy.* 328–30). No sooner has he devised this primitive DNA test, however, than he discards it for fear that his children will betray him even unwittingly, through the apprehension writ across their faces (*Thy.* 330–1). Instead, he treats Thyestes' cannibalism as confirmation of bilateral legitimacy, quipping gleefully that Tantalus, Plisthenes and the un-named third boy are 'definitely' Thyestes' sons (*certos*, *Thy.* 1102) and concluding the same for his own, in a passage whose 'mixture of logic and sheer delusion'[119] still defies scholarly subdual:

> nunc meas laudo manus,
> nunc parta vera est palma; perdideram scelus,
> nisi sic doleres. liberos nasci mihi
> nunc credo, castis nunc fidem reddi toris
>
> > now I praise my handiwork,
> > now the true palm of victory is won; my crime would have been wasted
> > had you not grieved. Now I believe the children are mine,
> > now trust and chastity have been restored to my marriage
> > (*Thy.* 1096–9)

Schiesaro attempts to untangle this claim by proposing that a) Thyestes' grief proves his parentage, for he would not, presumably, lament what was not his, and b) disproves his parentage of

---

[118] On *domus* as a *leitmotif* in the play, see Tarrant (1985) 45, Faber (2007) 429–33, and more generally, Boyle (2017) *ad Thy.* 220–43.
[119] Tarrant (1985) *ad Thy.* 1098–9.

4.2 Revenge

Agamemnon and Menelaus, for he would, presumably, grieve less if he knew he still had sons remaining; ergo the children belong to Atreus.[120] It is a feasible proposition, especially given Atreus' later assertion about Thyestes' wanting to commit an equivalent crime but refraining because he thought the children were his (*hoc unum obstitit: / tuos putasti*; 'one thing stopped you: you thought they were yours' *Thy.* 1109–10).

The logic remains tortuous, though, and its rationalisation merely deflates Atreus' powerful rhetoric.[121] These claims do not arise from careful calculation but from the vicious glee of payback: Atreus feels assured of his paternity because he is victorious *tout court*, because victory guarantees his dominance and re-establishes his manhood (he *must* be the father: he is powerful and Thyestes weak), because successful vengeance grants him the power of self-determination and self-creation (he can be whatever and however he wishes), and because his political supremacy imbues his words with an almost performative quality (what he says goes). His sexual and domestic ascendancy is confirmed more through symbolism than through coherent reasoning, such as when he turns Thyestes into a quasi-female vessel. Likewise, he establishes Thyestes' paternity via equally symbolic means, as the father's ingestion of his sons represents an indissoluble merging of genetic and corporeal substance.[122] From a rational perspective, it may appear that Atreus has slim grounds for insisting on the legitimacy of his sons and the faithfulness of his marriage, but the point at issue here is that Atreus dictates reality, not the other way around. The tyrant's agency and autonomy are so vast that logic cannot restrain them (nor can time, for that matter; Atreus claims to have reversed its effects). Thus, through vengeance, Atreus assumes the authority to shape the world around him, and to shape it to his advantage.

Such autonomy breeds isolation. *Thyestes* 1096–9 shows Atreus asserting power over his family members – the power to reconstitute and redefine them according to his will – at precisely the moment he steps free from their messy interpersonal nexus.

---

[120] Schiesaro (2003) 105.
[121] Littlewood (2008) 250.
[122] Dodson-Robinson (2019) 50.

Although he declares his marriage true and chaste, he has not reconciled with his wife, who, for all her thematic significance, does not even feature as a character in the play. His children are similarly instrumental, important only to the extent that they reflect on him, as living symbols of his virility and dominance. He has, of course, cast aside any remaining ties to his brother. As is the case for Seneca's Medea, and indeed for much of Seneca's approach to matters of freedom, destructive solitude is the ultimate guarantee of Atreus' individual autonomy. In the words of Gordon Braden, for Seneca's tragic characters, 'the devastation of emotional ties is an unanswerable gain of power and control'.[123] In releasing Atreus from the danger of subjection to another person, vengeance cuts him loose from the sustaining bonds of human society. Just as the tyrant finds freedom in his radical separation from those he rules, and just as the avenger finds freedom in slicing through the social ties that ensnare him, so Atreus exalts in having reached the lonely pinnacle of self-sufficiency and individual sovereignty, states that he (and, arguably, Seneca too) imagines existing beyond the reach of societal and legal norms. Freedom, for Atreus, is just another word for tyranny, for revenge, for murder.

Political supremacy is another core aspect of Atreus' autonomy, one I have so far remarked upon only in passing. Accompanying his sexual and domestic potency, it, too, is strengthened by vengeance because even though Atreus begins the tragedy already enthroned in Argos and already capable of violent coercion, nonetheless he views his rule as unstable, under threat from Thyestes' nefarious scheming. Atreus insists throughout the play that his brother is his mirror image, devising the same crimes (*Thy.* 193–5; 201–4; 314–16; 917–18; 1105–9) and coveting the throne with the same intensity (197–9).[124] The imputations verge on paranoia, especially given that Thyestes appears in person weak and gullible, the opposite of Atreus' conniving cleverness. Still, his brother's previous usurpation makes Atreus wary of future attacks. Thyestes' prior theft of the talismanic ram, along with Atreus'

---

[123] Braden (1985) 57.
[124] See Schiesaro (2003) 139–51 on the brothers' equivalence. The chorus, likewise, treats Atreus and Thyestes as interchangeable at *Thy* 339–41 and 638–40.

4.2 Revenge

wife, Aerope (*Thy.* 222–35), is an act of public and private sabotage that disrupts the Atrean *domus* on a political as well as personal level. Atreus has experienced exile at his brother's hands (*Thy.* 237) and even though he has since regained control in Argos, the mutual nature of their conflict prevents him from feeling secure.

Consequently, while in comparison to Seneca's Medea, Atreus does not pursue vengeance from a position of total social or political marginalisation, even so he rejoices that his completed act of retaliation guarantees his absolute rule. 'Oh I am the highest of heavenly beings, king of kings' he crows upon witnessing Thyestes' meal (*o me caelitum excelsissimum / regum atque regem, Thy.* 911–12), in celebration of a power so total that it brings other rulers and gods under its sway. Later in the same Act, he announces to Thyestes, 'This is the day that confirms my kingship and establishes the solid trust of definite peace' (*hic est, sceptra qui firmet mea / solidamque pacis alliget certae fidem, Thy.* 971–2). Situated in the false context of reconciliation, the statement extends the promise of political harmony achieved through the brothers' newfound unity, with *alligo* hinting further at ties of kinship and affection.[125] Atreus' real meaning, however, is that he has restored his own supremacy by neutralising Thyestes' political threat (namely, by removing his heirs and souring his appetite for power). Lurking underneath the lines' suggestion of plurality and co-operation is the tyrant's obsessive drive for solo control. The ambiguity of Atreus' rhetoric likewise illustrates his power over language and hence, over the very shape of the world around him. Whereas Thyestes cannot seem to extricate himself from lexical and rhetorical conventions, Atreus is their undisputed master – another gauge of his autonomy.

Finally, *Thyestes* 971–2 is also notable for its conflation of political with sexual dominance, because the terms *certus* and *fides* convey distant echoes of Atreus' cuckoldry and subsequent doubts about paternity (cf. *Thy* 327 *prolis incertae fides* and *Thy.* 1099 *fidem ... toris*, above), while the *sceptrum* functions in Senecan tragedy as a symbol of patriarchal (political, sexual)

---

[125] *OLD s.v. alligo* entry 8.

power.[126] Consolidating his hold on the Argive throne is what enables Atreus to feel assured of his masculinity and position within the family: one form of autonomy ensures the other.

In sum, Atreus demonstrates his agency and autonomy by using revenge to wrest back control of his identity and to alter his situation for – as he sees it – the better. Like Medea, he pursues vengeance as a means of self-transformation and self-creation, riding its swelling tide from a position of relative passivity to one of absolute sovereign dominance: from quasi-feminine to fully masculine, from political insecurity to perfected tyranny. Implicit in the roles he assumes is the power to dictate the shape of the world around him, a power he exercises on everything from the heavens to the form of Thyestes' body. More fundamentally still, Atreus' retaliation ensures his agency because vengeance itself is 'a thrust toward action',[127] a transition from endurance to perpetration, as Seneca signals so clearly in Atreus' opening monologue. In all of these respects, revenge emphasises Atreus' quasi-human features, namely his capacity for independent action, his assertive subjectivity, his (illusion of) contingent selfhood. But this very position of control also draws attention to its own limitations, which marks Atreus', and all literary portrayals of vengeance as a straining of human capability against the restrictions of fictional form. The ensuing section takes up this question of textual identity to explore how Atreus' genealogical and literary background propel him into action.

A History of Violence

Atreus' revenge reveals its explicitly fictional dimension in a multitude of ways: it prompts the protagonist's resemblance to a playwright/director; it gestures self-reflexively to the very genre of tragedy and to vengeance as one of its principal conventions; it flags Atreus', and Seneca's, debt to prior literary models; it acknowledges, by enforcing, characters' circumscribed autonomy. The first of these items has been treated already in considerable

---

[126] Boyle (2017) *ad Thy.* 225–9 and 970–2.
[127] Burnett (1998) 10.

4.2 Revenge

detail by Alessandro Schiesaro, Cedric Littlewood, and most recently, Anthony Boyle.[128] In brief: Atreus' manipulation of his brother corresponds to a director's handling of rehearsal and performance processes. Not only does Atreus devise a role for Thyestes, in the manner of a playwright, but he also orchestrates a reconciliation, commands his brother to change garments/costume, frames the feast as an inset performance and gazes upon it as a satisfied spectator (*libet videre*; 'it is pleasant to watch' *Thy.* 903) before entering to take part in the denouement. The *nefas* Atreus plans, perfects, and commits is the very substance of the play; in fashioning his revenge, he all but writes the *Thyestes* itself, in addition to embedding his own drama within its bounds.[129]

Themes of literary and generic self-consciousness have likewise received an ample share of scholarly scrutiny, but I revisit them here because they encapsulate perfectly the conflicting dynamics of Atreus' revenge, and because they have rarely, if ever, been measured against the contours of vengeance itself, its very nature as a human act and a fictional trope. I note in my preceding analysis the tendency for Atreus' vengeance to generate dissatisfaction and yearning; another crucial formulation of these emotions, which accompanies the *satis*-motif, is the tragedy's frequent recourse to *magnus* and *maior*, alongside more diffuse expressions of magnitude. Atreus characterises his desire for revenge as a persistent longing to exceed limits and achieve something greater than what has gone before. I have already had occasion to quote *Thyestes* 253–4 – *impleri iuvat / maiore monstro*; 'I long to be filled with greater monstrosity' – in the context of discussing the play's gender roles; the lines also announce the excessiveness germane to all acts of retaliation and, at a more specific level, the relationship of Atreus' own revenge to its prior fictional and genealogical instantiations. *maior* is the key word in this regard, and it is multivalent.

---

[128] Schiesaro (2003) 45–69 is the most thorough. Littlewood (2004) 183–240 features many perceptive comments on Atreus' metatheatrical conduct, but they are piecemeal, subordinated to his broader treatment of spectatorship in the tragedies. Mowbray (2012) 401–2 likewise acknowledges Atreus' revenge as a variety of performance. Boyle (2017) revisits the topic regularly in his exegesis of the play.

[129] See Schiesaro (2003) 45–61.

First, as a metapoetic marker, it signals the 'lofty' genre of tragedy and Atreus' self-conscious operation within it.[130] In wanting to commit greater outrages, Atreus expresses a metaliterary desire both to act in accordance with his given genre and to outdo all prior dramatisations of revenge. Second, and relatedly, *maior* at *Thyestes* 254 signals the specific intertext of Accius' Atreus, who declares of his brother's heralded attack:

> iterum Thyestes Atreum adtrectatum advenit;
> iterum iam adgreditur me et quietum suscitat.
> maior mihi moles, maius miscendumst malum
>
> Once again Thyestes comes to assault me;
> now, again, he attacks me and rouses me from my rest.
> Greater trouble for me, a greater crime to concoct
> (*Atr.* 198–201 Ribbeck *TRF*²)

Excessiveness and repetition are present already in the Accian version,[131] as the threat of Thyestes' renewed hostility reiterates the brothers' earlier confrontation – when Thyestes wrested the throne from Atreus (cf. Sen. *Thy.* 222–37) – as well as reiterating this well-known story's representation in a poetic text. Reiteration is built into the myth's plotline and reinforced, metapoetically, by its multiple treatments on the tragic stage. Concomitantly, Accius' Atreus aspires to surpass his prior mythological conflict with Thyestes *and* prior fictional instantiations of his trademark aggression. And Seneca's Atreus aspires to surpass even this already overdetermined claim to greatness.

The third important feature of Seneca's *maius*-motif is its evocation of literal as well as literary genealogy. Paul Hammond remarks that *maior* at *Thyestes* 254 calls to mind the ancestral quality of Atreus and Thyestes' hatred, the *maiores* from whom the present conflict originates and to whose models Atreus looks

---

[130] The idea originates with Hinds (1993) 39–43 and Barchiesi (1993) 343–5, both of whom examine *maius* as a generic marker in *Heroides* 12. Schiesaro (2003) 34 is similarly alert to the term's metapoetic meaning in the *Thyestes*, though he frames it as an allusion to the *maius nefas* and *maius furor* of Vergil's Amata. Also informative in this regard is Williams (2012), who discusses the metapoetic sense of *maius opus* in the Medea episode of *Met.* 7, arguing that the heroine's pursuit of 'something greater' assimilates her to, and puts her in competition with, the work's author.

[131] Gowers (2016) 557.

4.2 Revenge

for inspiration (*Thy.* 242–3).[132] Tantalus in particular provides not just a template for Atreus' behaviour but also direct influence in the form of his ghostly presence, which sets the play's events in motion. This ancestral background functions alongside the lines' references to poetic tradition, in highlighting Atreus' enmeshment within larger structures of causation and agency. For all of his personal sovereignty, he cannot avoid being an instrument of forces greater than himself, whether those forces comprise the myth's pre-established patterns and its prior poetic handling, Seneca's authorial control (likewise conditional upon literary precedent), or the Pelopid family's curse and its seemingly genetic predisposition for alimentary wickedness. As the meeting point of all these vectors, Atreus' revenge begins to seem unavoidable and pre-determined, not the wild cry of independence that I (and on many occasions, Atreus himself) have characterised it as being. It becomes instead the embedded textual act of a patently fictional entity.

Such intimations of fictionality are not confined to one or two lines, either, but traverse the entire play, as Seneca's language from the very first scene indulges in a rapid spill of comparatives and images of excess. 'Let Thracian impiety happen in <u>greater</u> number', (*Thracium fiat nefas / <u>maiore</u> numero, Thy.* 56–7) roars the Fury in simultaneous allusion to the play's Ovidian intertext of Procne and Philomela (Ov. *Met.* 6.424–674), and to this myth's (re)transposition into the genre of tragedy (with *numerus* indicating not just the *number* of children Atreus will sacrifice, but also the elevated *metre* of tragic drama).[133] In echo of this hellish prologue, Atreus himself promises to perpetrate 'something that does not cleave to the limits of ordinary pain' (*nil quod doloris capiat assueti modum, Thy.* 255), describes his 'mind swelling with something <u>greater</u>, larger than normal, beyond the boundaries of human custom' (*nescioquid animus <u>maius</u> et solito amplius / supraque fines moris humani tumet, Thy.* 267–8) and confesses

---

[132] Hammond (2009) 108.
[133] The reference to metre is undeniable but slight; it cannot be pressed too far, for epic represents the most elevated genre and tragedy does not exceed it in this respect. But the generic mix of Ovid's *Metamorphoses* makes it both greater and less than a typical epic, which justifies Seneca's comparative.

that he must perform 'something greater' (*maius* ... *aliquid*, *Thy.* 274) than Procne did against Tereus. Upon hearing all of this, Atreus' minister shudders that the intended crime 'is greater than anger' (*maius hoc ira est malum*, *Thy.* 259). These examples pair the tyrant's and the avenger's shared impulse for over-reaching with expressions of metaliterary competitiveness. Atreus qua fictional construct acknowledges his confined place within a poetic tradition and admits the pressure he feels to distinguish this particular version of his story from other, similar versions, whether those versions involve him or other figures (e.g. Procne) engaged in acts parallel to his own.

As always, though, Seneca's portrayal of autonomy is more complex than mere metapoetics. While it is undeniable that Seneca employs the *maius*-motif to signal his rivalry with earlier poets and to enrich his own text by echoing them, nonetheless Atreus' desire to surpass, simultaneously, his predecessors and the confines of possibility is also emblematic of the avenger's bid for total control over his opponent and his circumstances. *maius* for Atreus represents the 'more-ness' of vengeance, and its attendant magnification of the perpetrator's agency. Essentially, the motif articulates a definition of vengeance itself, not just Atreus' particular pursuit of it, for retaliation is, by nature, an excessive act. Payback is not a matter of pure equation or recompense, but *over*payment, as the victim attempts to extract compensation for things that can never be recovered or repaired, whether they include deceased friends / family members or, at a more basic level, the very fact of one's own past suffering.[134] Atreus freely admits that his vengeance must go beyond anything Thyestes has done to him: 'you do not avenge crimes unless you outdo them' (*scelera non ulcisceris, / nisi vincis*, *Thy.* 195–6), he remarks in Act 2, half to the minister, half to himself. The idea reappears in Act 5, when Thyestes complains of discomfort in his belly:

> **Thy:** genitor en natos premo
> premorque natis; sceleris est aliquis modus
> **Atr:** sceleri modus debetur ubi facias scelus,
> non ubi reponas.

---

[134] See the insightful remarks of Burnett (1998) 3.

4.2 Revenge

Thy: Look, I, the father, crush my sons and am crushed by them; the crime has some measure
Atr: A crime needs measure when you commit it, not when you repay it.

(*Thy*. 1050–3)

This terse exchange encapsulates perfectly the dynamic of revenge. Thyestes' description of his physical state – equal parts himself and his sons – presumes the equilibrium of payback and at the same time, indicates its excessiveness, its blurring and overturning of boundaries. His comment in 1051, *sceleris est aliquis modus*, can be read either as a gauche reference to the symmetry of his bodily suffering,[135] or – as it is sometimes translated – a vain plea about crime's limits.[136] Actually, both meanings are present, and their combination points to revenge's uneasy union of balance and immoderation.

It is a union Atreus comprehends to the core, as he rebuffs Thyestes' complaint with, effectively, an explanation that despite its 're' prefix (re-venge; *re-ponas*), retaliation is no mere 'equal and opposite reaction'. Though *talio* assumes an eye-for-an-eye exchange, the reality is more like two, or even a whole face, for one. In an innovative twist on the theme of curtailment and boundary violation, Atreus proposes that the original perpetrator, not the avenger, is the one most limited in his criminal activity, presumably because the originary offence is not compelled to push beyond a prior model, whereas vengeance is, by definition, responsive and competitive in its drive to replicate while outdoing the very event to which it owes its existence. Revenge – Atreus', anyone's – outstrips established parameters in a manner that is simply not incumbent upon the initial crime.

It is no accident if this competitive repetition sounds a lot like intertextuality. To put it another way: the poetic imitation ingrained in Atreus' act is matched by, and finds direct reflection in, the avenger's need to repeat and outperform his predecessor's moves. Revenge's combination of recurrence and innovation,

---

[135] The interpretation given by Tarrant (1985) *ad Thy.* 1051. Wilson (2010) appears to follow this reading by translating 'The crime at least is balanced.'
[136] This seems to be the sense of Fitch (2004), 'There is *some* limit to crime!' Boyle (2017) captures better the line's ambiguity: 'Evil has some measure.'

confinement and transcendence, resembles the challenge faced by poets – and poems ... and characters – situated within an established tradition which they must acknowledge and defy, as these respective needs arise. The same union of opposites underpins the fictional avenger's agency: imitation of the past threatens his/her capacity for self-directed action at the same time as stimulating the desire to break free. A injures B, and B, by replying, cedes autonomy to the discourse that A has formulated and within which all subsequent action must occur. But, by expanding on A's initial deed, B asserts the ability to advance beyond mere copying and into a realm of self-conferred sovereignty. Paradoxically, it is this very dependence upon past paradigms that secures a kind of freedom for the avenger, at least in the sense that he/she can see where potential limitations lie and can work to overturn them.

In Atreus' case, the pre-established parameters that guide his vengeance include not only Thyestes' initial crime, but also the intergenerational wickedness of the Tantalid dynasty, the existence of comparable acts of vengeance in other mythological narratives, the existence of other tragedies dealing with the same topic, and the pre-determined nature of revenge as an event intrinsic to the tragic genre. Atreus knows from the outset that he is in a revenge tragedy, and consequently, that he must fulfil the demands of this particular artform (cf. *Thy.* 176–80).[137] All of this may appear to quash any possibility of his having free agency or claiming independent action, but the reality is actually more complex than this, because these forces *promote* Atreus' conduct even as they restrict it. Essentially, Atreus' recourse to prior examples, his reflexive awareness of genre and the self-consciously literary texture of his thought need not, per se, negate impressions of his quasi-human autonomy. His fictional and implied human identities are not opposites, in this instance, but

---

[137] A telling and well-known comparison is Shakespeare's Hamlet, whose hesitancy may be interpreted in metapoetic terms, as awareness of his featuring in the established genre of 'revenge tragedy' and resistance to playing its already clichéd role. Arguably, the genre was far less established when Seneca's Atreus strode the stage, but his acknowledgement of its prior existence is actually typical of how theatre deals with genre, that is, by framing it as repetition of already recognised modes: see Goldman (2000) 8; Carlson (2003) 6. On Hamlet's debt to Seneca's Atreus, see Miola (1992) 41, Burrow (2013) 175, and Perry (2015) 414–15.

4.2 Revenge

two sides of the same coin. Atreus wants to perform *greater* crimes not just out of rivalry with earlier literature, but also because the extent of his transgression verifies the extent of his power. Flouting *modus* is central to his expression of agency, but in order for this to occur, a *modus* must first be established. Audiences can appreciate Atreus' push towards domination only once they have recognised the very dynamics of that domination in Atreus' own sense of victimhood.

This intersection I propose between the mechanics of revenge and those of literary appropriation has important consequences for our understanding of fictional character in general, not just of Seneca's Atreus. Fundamentally, it demonstrates that fictional beings may seem quasi-human when they are at their most metapoetic, and vice versa. A character's status as a textual construct not only does not preclude its equally significant status as an implied human personality but may actively *give rise to it*. This is not a question of 'either/or' but 'both/and'. We may take vengeance, broadly speaking, as an event that emphasises characters' person-like aspects, chiefly because it is a *personal* act: the avenger takes his or her injury to heart – this is a deed meant and received in deeply personal terms – and targets specific individuals in return. Vengeance is meaningful violence and meaningful suffering; it is not directed against anonymous, faceless groups or institutions, nor is it performed by them. Although it may be perpetrated by groups, vengeance in literature is typically a solo act that distils in a single figure pressing human problems of justice, self-determination, and moral choice (to name but a few). Its emphasis on action and on change invites writers and audiences alike to frame the avenger in human terms despite his or her purely fictional ontology.

The consciously literary texture of much fictional vengeance – its awareness of poetic and/or dramatic tradition; its inclination for performance and role-play; its similarity to the very act of literary composition – may seem to override its 'personal' quality, but the dichotomy is false, as is the broader dichotomy from which it derives, namely that of character-as-text versus character-as-person. Granted metapoetics, metatheatrics, and intertextuality, by signalling characters' fictional fabric, prevent us from assuming too much of their motives and psychology, but these very conventions also work to frame characters' motives and psychology in the first place, to deepen their significance by placing them within a tradition. The same applies to audiences' emotional investment in and response to given fictional scenarios: while metapoetic techniques may seem, on the one hand, to curtail these by minimising readers'/viewers' sense of immersion in the events portrayed, they can, on the other hand, activate such immersion – at base, simply by imposing shape and form on what might otherwise appear meaningless, random activity. If the avenger resembles a poet/playwright in plotting retaliation, and an actor in executing it then, yes, self-awareness of fictionality may generate a certain amount of audience detachment. But it can invite involvement, too, because, as I have outlined above, the avenger's scheming focalises events from his/her perspective, encourages audiences to sympathise with his/her grievances, affirms the character's capacity for independent action, and contributes to illusions of contingency. It fosters the avenger's self-assertion as much as it potentially denies it. These two facets work in tandem; characters' textual ontology cannot really be divorced from their implied humanness, and vice versa.

A brief coda about Atreus, in light of these remarks: although vengeance against Thyestes springs from a nexus of factors, not all of which are under Atreus' direct control, it is nonetheless individually, personally meant. However much Tantalus and the Fury propel him into action, however much Procne and Philomela (and Ovid) provide him with a template, however much his actions cleave to conventions of tragic vengeance, the brutality he visits upon his brother amounts to so much more than the outcome of an impersonal or supra-personal system that uses Atreus as its instrument. Literary and genealogical inheritance may influence the form of Atreus' revenge, but they do not occlude his (relatively) autonomous performance of it. The subjectivity he (re)claims through revenge is just as much (if not more) a matter of being active and in command, of bringing matters under his control, as it is of being *subjected* to external forces, people, and sources of motivation.[138]

---

[138] On the topic of subjectivity in revenge, I both engage *and* disagree with the approach outlined by Dodson-Robinson (2019) 4–12.

4.3 Suicide

Likewise, his hatred of Thyestes is not just a mythological or literary datum, nor the inevitable result of family feuds; it is these, granted, but it is also an immediate, passionate, implied human response to the circumstances in which Atreus finds himself and to the individual he credits with creating them. To forget this latter dimension is to bleach Atreus' project – and any avenger's, for that matter – of its most fundamental colours, and to see only half of the story. Served hot or cold, vengeance is the discriminate means of satisfying individual grievance. As the saying goes, it's personal.

4.3 Suicide

Self-Enforced Endings

From vengeance I move to suicide, as a complementary and likewise deeply Senecan expression of individual agency. Though they may seem like odd bedfellows, the two acts actually have a lot in common. Like the avenger, the Senecan suicide takes action from the margins, and achieves in self-inflicted death a vital demonstration of freedom and self-government. Both acts also usurp the law, a similarity particularly apparent in the case of Roman political suicide, which often took the place of state-sponsored punishment.[139] Both represent the dissolution of oppression and victimhood, and the aggressive reinstatement of subjectivity in response to intolerable circumstances. Both strive to achieve dominion, over others or over the self. Whereas the avenger pushes outward to destroy those around him/her, the suicide turns inward to the task of making the self inviolate from all future attacks, material or immaterial. These parallels, combined with the scope of suicide's portrayal in Seneca's work, make the motif particularly apt for my present study of characters'

---

[139] Suicide's legal recognition in ancient Rome is discussed by Plass (1995) 85, and more thoroughly by Edwards (2007) 119–21. The anecdote about Caius Licinius Macer, reported in Val. Max. 9.12.7, illustrates especially clearly the idea of suicide supplanting judicial procedure. Macer was on trial for extortion; he watched over proceedings from the balcony and when it became apparent that he would be convicted, he suffocated himself. Upon learning of this fact, Cicero, who was presiding over the court, pronounced no verdict, and Macer's property was not confiscated. Cicero's silence is telling: it implies that Macer's suicide is the equivalent of a judicial sentence, and that the act confers on Macer a (temporary) status equivalent to a judge's.

Autonomy

fabricated versus quasi-human identities. It is also an appropriately closural gesture for this chapter and for the book overall, a self-chosen, self-directed ending that lends additional significance to many of my preceding arguments and promises freedom for reader and writer alike.

Let us begin this final episode by glancing back, briefly, to the *Thyestes*. When the victim understands the true contents of his meal, his first thought is to free his progeny from entombment in his belly:

> volvuntur intus viscera et clusum nefas
> sine exitu luctatur et quaerit fugam:
> da, frater, ensem (sanguinis multum mei
> habet ille): ferro liberis detur via.
> negatur ensis? pectora inliso sonent
> contusa planctu—sustine, infelix, manum,
> parcamus umbris.
>
> My guts churn inside me and an enclosed evil
> struggles with no way out; it seeks escape:
> give me your sword, brother (it has much of my blood
> already): let the blade grant passage to my children.
> You refuse? Let this bruised breast resound
> with sorrowful blows – stay your hand, wretch,
> spare the dead.
>
> (*Thy.* 1041–7)

The grotesque gesture amounts to a suicidal wish: Thyestes will spill his guts, in the process releasing what remains of his children and, just as vitally, releasing himself from the prospect of future suffering and oppression. If his current state represents a diminution of his autonomy and confusion of his individual agency, the prospect of suicide represents their dramatic reinstatement: Thyestes taking charge of his own fate, wresting control from Atreus. Though the lines themselves exhibit an undeniable debt to Ovid's Tereus, who similarly responds to revelations of paternal cannibalism by contemplating disembowelment (*Met.* 6.663–4),[140] the statement in Thyestes' mouth is wholly Senecan. It is, as Brad Inwood observes of Seneca's overall notion of suicide, 'a mark of agency even amidst misfortune'.[141] The difficulty for Thyestes is

---

[140] Tarrant (1985) *ad Thy.* 1043–4; Boyle (2017) *ad Thy.* 1041–7.
[141] Inwood (2005) 307.

4.3 Suicide

that the contents of his stomach render him incapable of self-determination, at least symbolically. For Thyestes is simultaneously himself and alien to himself; he and his children have blended together; he is not physically discrete and cannot act purely in his own interests. In a perceptive if harrowing comment on the nature of blood ties, Seneca shows how biological proximity limits Thyestes' capacity for autonomous action. If he cannot hurt himself without also 'hurting' his offspring, then Atreus has attained a complete victory over him, having foreclosed even the consolatory possibility of agency proffered by suicide.

Bolstering this interpretation of *Thyestes* 1041–7 is the famous 'ode to suicide' at *de Ira* 3.15.4, which follows directly upon the tale of Harpagus' unwitting cannibal banquet.[142] Astyages, furious at what he perceives as Harpagus' disloyalty, cooks and serves up the latter's sons. Upon the meal's completion, Astyages orders the children's heads to be brought in and presented to their father, whereupon he asks Harpagus what he thinks of his reception. Harpagus suppresses his anger and responds with flattery, a reaction that elicits first guarded approval from Seneca, then an outburst in praise of suicide's liberating power. The endless possibilities of death by one's own hand are presented as 'escapes from servitude' (*effugia servitutis*, *Ira* 3.15.4) and, by implication, as opportunities, however terminal, for autonomous action. Harpagus may be oppressed by a *dominus* (*Ira* 3.15.4) – and it is significant to Seneca's point that Harpagus lives under an autocratic regime – but suicide would enable him to regain control over himself, his life, his circumstances. Parallels to the *Thyestes* are obvious. It could even be said that Seneca treats the theme more intricately in the tragedy than in the dialogue, because he acknowledges the complex, thwarted agency of one who has just consumed the products of his own flesh.

Preoccupation with agency and autonomy underpins much of Seneca's thinking about death,[143] an association that contributes, in turn, to his vision of the *sapiens*' competitive autarky. Of

---

[142] A passage treated by Rist (1969) 248; Inwood (2005) 308–10; Edwards (2007) 102–3; Ker (2009) 267–8.
[143] As shown by Inwood (2005) 305–12, which is in many ways the most insightful treatment to date of suicide in Seneca.

course, suicide in Seneca is a well-trodden topic[144] that I do not intend to reprise here. Instead, I present a swift overview of its relationship to self-determination and self-government in Seneca's work, as a prelude to considering its bearing on characters' autonomy in the tragedies.

The paradigmatic case for Seneca, and arguably, for all aristocratic suicides in imperial Rome, is Cato the Younger, whose act is celebrated, variously, as a consummate gesture of political and spiritual freedom, of moral *virtus* and self-control, of bravery and aristocratic dignity, of Stoic contempt for 'indifferents', and of good old-fashioned republican defiance of an aspiring dictator.[145] While Seneca's recurring, multifaceted treatment of Cato touches upon all of these elements to some degree, the most relevant to my present discussion is this combined concept of political and personal *libertas*. Basically, in opting to die rather than endure the prospect of Caesar's *clementia*, Cato trumps the ruler's claim to absolute sovereignty.[146] Like the Senecan sage who outmanoeuvres the tyrant, Cato slips through Caesar's grasp, thereby demonstrating its limitations and the superiority of his self-conferred autarky in opposition to Caesar's self-conferred autocracy. In *de Providentia* 2.10–11, Seneca's Cato declares that his sword will grant him the (individual) freedom it could not grant his (collective) fatherland, and muses that it is just as disgraceful for him to seek death at another's hands as it is for him to seek life. Both assertions pivot around issues of individual sovereignty, as Cato counters the now inevitable fact of his political subjugation with the ultimate and absolute subjective agency of self-imposed death. This is a particular kind of freedom, situated at the

---

[144] Major anglophone studies include: Rist (1969) 246–50, who calls Seneca's identification of suicide as freedom 'a new emphasis in Stoicism'; Griffin (1976) 367–88; Hill (2004) 145–82; Inwood (2005) 305–12; Ker (2009) 247–79. Romm (2014) uses death, self-inflicted and otherwise, as the structuring motif of his study of Seneca. Tadic-Gilloteaux (1963) is also a useful, if dated, treatment of Senecan suicide. Griffin (1986a) and (1986b) are valuable for situating Seneca's approach in a broader Roman/Stoic context.

[145] On the 'programmatic' nature of Cato's suicide, see, among others, Griffin (1986b) 194–200; Goar (1987) 51–65; Edwards (2007) 1–5, 114–16, 121–2; Ker (2009) 55–6, 255.

[146] Similarly, Plass (1995) 108 sees in Cato's suicide 'a move to protest repression coupled with a second move anticipating the countermove of *clementia*'.

4.3 Suicide

intersection of public and private spheres, the freedom to be as and what one chooses, even if that 'being' means, finally, *not* being. Catherine Belsey remarks of suicide in Renaissance drama that it 're-establishes the sovereign subject' and fulfils the subject's desire for autonomy, 'to be not just free, but also the origin and guarantee of its own identity, the source of being, meaning, and action ... In the absolute act of suicide, the subject itself is momentarily absolute.'[147] The same judgement may profitably be applied to Cato in the *de Providentia*, who presents his self-inflicted death as the essence of what it means to be 'Cato',[148] and who frames his suicide as an explicit challenge to Caesar's absolute power. By depicting Cato's death as the alternative to political liberation (*Prov.* 2.10), Seneca hints at equivalence between terrestrial control and spiritual mastery: the sage emulates and outstrips the ruler's role, albeit only in the singular realm of the self.

Seneca further emphasises Cato's agency by calling him 'a most fierce avenger of himself' (*acerrimus sui vindex*, *Prov.* 2.11), a striking phrase that twins the projects of suicide and retaliation, imputing to each a commensurate degree of freedom. Just as the avenger reinstates his or her autonomy via retributive violence, so the suicide discovers the purest form of agency in visiting violence upon the self; self-destruction is revenge, in another sense, for the position one has been placed in and for what one has been made to suffer.

In this regard, the political aspect of Cato's suicide is relevant only to the extent that it illustrates his autonomy. What matters is not Cato versus Caesar or republic versus prospective dictatorship, but, more fundamentally, one man assuming the power to dictate another's fate. While Seneca is undeniably alert to the event's historical background,[149] and to the specific political implications of aristocratic suicide (which he himself will commit), the concept that unites this anecdote with his other portrayals of suicide is more basic: it is about the capacity to choose and control the form of one's death, thereby escaping oppression and victimhood.

---

[147] Belsey (1985) 124–5.
[148] See discussion in Chapter 1, 51–3.
[149] On Seneca's knowledge and treatment of republican history, see Castagna (1991) and Gowing (2005) 69–81.

Examples of this idea abound in Seneca's prose works, especially in the *Epistles*, where Seneca, writing in old age, is even more than usually concerned with death.[150] *Epistle* 26.10, for instance, pairs death with emancipation: *qui mori didicit servire dedidicit; supra omnem potentiam est, certe extra omnem. Quid ad illum carcer et custodia et claustra? Liberum ostium habet.* ('one who has learned how to die has unlearned servitude; he is above all external power, certainly beyond it. What do prison and guards and bars matter to him? He has a way out.') That final image of the *liberum ostium*, so difficult to capture in translation, combines concepts of physical escape – from prison, from one's own body – with social enfranchisement, the condition of no longer being subjected to another's *potestas*. Self-inflicted death is the equivalent of terrestrial autonomy. Seneca reprises the idea at *Epistle* 51.9: *Libertas proposita est; ad hoc praemium laboratur. Quae sit libertas quaeris? Nulli rei servire, nulli necessitati, nullis casibus, fortunam in aequum deducere ... ego illam feram, cum in manu mors sit?* ('Freedom is placed before me; I work towards that reward. And what is freedom, you ask? It means not being enslaved to any circumstance, to any need, to any chance; it means engaging with Fortune on equal terms ... shall I endure her, when death is within my reach?'). Here the Stoic concept of 'indifferents' is used to illustrate a freedom at once social and spiritual, mundane and transcendent, for the individual who manages to reject the false lure of earthly concerns (*res, necessitas, casus*) and to view death with detachment, as neither intrinsically good nor evil, resembles a fully enfranchised member of society, not beholden to anybody or anything else.[151] Death as physical escape is matched with the sage's less tangible freedom from life's ups and downs: both enable the individual to evade others' grasp, and to claim sovereign dominion over his/her own existence.

Fascination with personal autonomy is also the reason why so many of Seneca's anecdotes about suicide focus on slaves or

---

[150] As Edwards (2019) 3 remarks on the *Epistles*' preoccupation with death, and the tense political atmosphere in which they were composed, 'the imperial instruction to commit suicide ... cannot have been unexpected'.

[151] Hill (2004) 151–7 notes that Seneca often treats death in this way, as a means of thinking about Stoic principles of 'indifferents' and detachment.

4.3 Suicide

prisoners of war. *Epistle* 70 tells the story of a German *bestiarius* who escaped performing in the arena by choking himself with a toilet brush (*Ep.* 70.20–1), and of another gladiator who committed suicide on the way to his morning *munus* by drooping his head in feigned sleep until it was caught and broken in the wagon's spokes (*Ep.* 70.23). Seneca accords these examples significance for proving that anyone, no matter how lowly, can defy death (*Ep.* 70.19), but his choice also springs from a deeper, unexpressed premise, namely that gladiators are prime examples of social disenfranchisement and objectification. The gladiator resembles a slave (and often is one) in the lack of control he exercises over his own body and person. His subjectivity and agency are compromised to the point of being almost non-existent. His very job allows him to be wounded or killed with impunity and even if he is the one doing the killing, he does so in obedience to his trainer, *editor*, and the rules of the game. Outside the arena, he is *infamis*: open again to being beaten with impunity, debarred from public office, and unable to bring lawsuits or to represent others in court.[152] He is the object of others' gaze, the source of their enjoyment, and identified almost solely in terms of his body. Little wonder, then, that Seneca selects gladiatorial suicide as the epitome of agency and subjectivity, for here is a class of person possessing almost no opportunity for self-determined action beyond the deed of suicide. But suicide is enough to guarantee his ultimate, irreversible self-government. In the deed's self-reflexive microcosm, the gladiator discovers the freedom and subjectivity denied him by Roman society as a whole.

Much the same set of assumptions applies to *Epistle* 77's anecdote about the young Spartan prisoner of war, who dashed his brains out against a wall rather than perform the menial task of fetching a chamber pot (*Ep.* 77. 14–15). Once again, the autonomy and agency afforded by suicide are set in contrast with the slave's bodily and social subjugation, and more deeply still, with the inevitable corporeal needs and appetites that ensnare every human being. Suicide represents corporeal domination to the same extent that urinating (signalled by the chamber pot)

---

[152] On gladiators' *infamia*, see Edwards (1997b) 66–76.

represents our corporeal reliance on fluids. Self-inflicted death frees the self at every level. The obverse is *Epistle* 70's tale of Telesphorus of Rhodes, who clings to life despite having been imprisoned in a cage by the tyrant Lysimachus and treated like a wild animal (*Ep.* 70.6–7). Telesphorus' reluctance to end his own life is equated to his bestial existence as an oppressed, tormented object. His unwillingness to assert agency through suicide is not only weakness (*Ep.* 70.6), but also makes it seem as though he deserves his fate. What he suffers, after all, is merely a magnified, reified version of the curtailment experienced by anyone who places undue value on physical existence and lacks the self-control required for attaining subjectivity in death.

It may be objected, at this point, that Seneca's view of individual agency is not as clear and straightforward as I have presented it, mainly because he is also inclined to praise those who forego suicide and instead submit themselves to torture or execution.[153] He often pairs Socrates with Cato, for instance, although the former was, *stricto sensu*, executed (despite administering the poison himself), while the latter took his own life.[154] Another example, cited for other purposes earlier in this chapter, is Julius Canus, whom Seneca applauds for his calm acceptance of and submission to a death sentence from Caligula (*Tranq.* 12.4–10). *Epistle* 70.8 sees Seneca approve of people who refuse to commit suicide when faced with torture, on the grounds that enduring torment likewise demonstrates one's *virtus*. While it is true that such forms of death and suffering do not entail the absolute agency epitomised by suicide's self-reflexivity, Seneca still treats them as instances of autonomy, chiefly by accentuating the element of

---

[153] An issue flagged by Ker (2009) 250–66, but see also comments by Edwards (2007) 122 on general Roman views of suicide: 'Agency, in the sense of who did the deed, is of little significance.' Flemming (2005) 316 likewise notes in relation to Roman suicide, 'the question of agency, narrowly construed, had no bearing on the ethical, juridical or political quality of [a] death'.

[154] A point Seneca himself acknowledges at *Ep.* 70.9: *Socrates potuit abstinentia finire vitam et inedia potius quam veneno mori; triginta tamen dies in carcere et in expectatione mortis exegit ... ut praeberet se legibus, ut fruendum amicis extremum Socraten daret.* His main assumption in making his classification appears to have been that Socrates accepted death willingly and did nothing to prevent it. Ker (2009) 255–7 notes the Socrates–Cato pairing. See also Griffin (1976) 373–4 on Seneca's treatment of Socrates' death.

4.3 Suicide

choice. As James Ker has shown, *Epistle* 70 unites its scattered examples of *libertas* achieved through death by emphasising 'our inalienable freedom to choose (or to resist) death whenever we wish, and to choose between whatever methods are available'.[155] Anyone who remains steadfast under torture evades the oppressor's grasp just as much as those who take their own lives. The core issue is outmanoeuvring one's aggressor, typically a tyrant or autocrat, and avoiding victimhood.

Further, Seneca's focus on contexts of political oppression highlights his interest in death as a form of autonomy and agency superior even to a ruler's sovereignty. Like the *sapiens*' autarky, with which it is often paired, the self-chosen end to life symbolises for Seneca a power equivalent to or surpassing that of any monarchical figure. While Nero, for instance, is the 'arbiter of life and death' (*vitae necisque ... arbiter, Clem.* 1.1.2) for his subjects, the suicide exercises his own *arbitrium* (e.g. *Ep.* 70.19) in deciding when and how to end his life.[156] The parallel is far from coincidental, and it envisages the suicide's hegemony as equal, momentarily, to the *princeps*'. In fact, it lessens the *princeps*' authority by usurping his role and asserting the individual's fundamental immunity to subjugation. Suicide is another version of Seneca's celebrated 'empire over the self'.

Self-Harm in the Tragedies

Self-inflicted death and harm also claim prominence as assertions of autonomy in the tragedies. We have seen already how Thyestes responds to his predicament with an (ultimately ineffectual) gesture of suicide; Hercules reacts in a similar manner upon learning the true extent of his misfortune. Initially, before realising that he is himself responsible for his family's death, he contemplates revenge as the way to resolve his suffering and restore his honour

---

[155] Ker (2009) 253. Also, Inwood (2005) 312: 'the point of each example [in *Epistle* 77] is that the suicide is thereby preserving his own agency: he *acts* rather than suffers'.
[156] Nor is this solely Seneca's terminology. The phrase *liberum mortis arbitrium* is used to describe suicide at Tac. *Ann.* 11.3.1 and Suet. *Dom.* 11.3. The significance of *arbitrium* lies in indicating not just the element of choice, but the quasi-judicial nature of this choice, as though someone opting to die were assuming the role of a judge.

(*Her.* 1186–91). Once his guilt is made clear, however, he shifts the focus of this act from outside to inside; retaliation becomes self-destruction. Like vengeance, suicide presents Hercules with the opportunity to remedy his losses, both the tangible loss of wife and children, and of abstract qualities such as *fama* (*Her.* 1260). His promise to 'find a way to death' (*mortis inveniam viam*, 1245) signals the agency implicit in this deed via evocation of his earlier, heroic activity. For instance, Amphitryon declares at 276–7 that Hercules will not stay trapped in the underworld forever: 'either he will find a way [out] or he will make one' (*inveniet viam / aut faciet*).[157] When the phrase recurs in the context of disaster, it signals how suicide can reprise Hercules' indomitable faculty for *doing*; the strength and power that enabled the hero to overcome hell's boundaries will enable him now to return, permanently.

Hercules' desire for agency is also apparent in his lurid catalogues of self-harm: he will cremate himself on a huge pyre (1216–17), burn himself along with Thrace's groves and Cithaeron's ridges (1285–7); he will drag down onto himself the whole of Thebes (1287–90), and if that is insufficient, the entire firmament (1293–4). The same colossal heroism as made his labours possible will now be employed for the greatest, most self-defining task of all. That Hercules frames prospective suicide in terms of his heroic past (e.g. *Her.* 1279–82) underscores the agency he perceives it as conferring. If he acted as Juno's instrument in murdering his wife and children, now he aspires to full subjective control of his circumstances. When Amphitryon tries to absolve Hercules of responsibility by pleading, 'Juno launched this arrow, with your hands' (*hoc Iuno telum manibus immisit tuis*, 1297), Hercules refuses consolation in favour of the self-determination offered by suicide: 'now *I* shall use it' (*hoc nunc ego utar*, 1298). He will turn his weapon against himself, ensuring that his instrumentality is matched or exceeded by his capacity for independent action.

Hercules' suicidal inclinations are eventually trumped by an even more solipsistic ambition to preserve his reputation, but other Senecan characters, finding themselves in equally

---

[157] Fitch (1987) *ad Her.* 1245 notes the parallel phrasing.

4.3 Suicide

impossible circumstances, actually follow through with the deed.[158] In the *Troades*, when Astyanax is due to be hurled from Troy's battlements in sacrifice, he takes the initiative and leaps instead (*sponte desiluit sua*, *Tro.* 1101). It is a brief moment, and Seneca does not dwell on matters of agency the way he does with Hercules, but he still manages to suggest it in passing, via a simile comparing the Trojan boy to an immature wild beast, fierce though incapable yet of any real harm (*Tro.* 1093–6). The image revisits in positive terms a simile uttered by the distraught Andromache at the close of Act 3: Astyanax is a tiny calf torn from its mother by a savage lion (*Tro.* 794–8), where the young animal's helplessness and need for parental protection confirm its lack of autonomy. Species is significant, too, for as a *iuvencus* (795), Astyanax embodies a common sacrificial animal, while his later status as a ferocious wild creature removes him from this category. From domestic to untamed, helpless victim to proud aggressor, Astyanax achieves in suicide an autonomy and agency he could not find in life.

The boy's independence is likewise stressed by incessant comparison to Hector, a topic I have explored at length in Chapter 2, where I focus mainly on its obscuring Astyanax's individuality. While this is undeniably the case for most of the tragedy, there are moments when Astyanax's resemblance to his father signifies not just subordination but also a growing capacity for self-determination, which culminates in the sovereign act of suicide. His jumping from the same tower from which he once watched his father's feats in war suggests both the pitiful curtailment of his heroism and its drive to achieve something comparable to Hector's intimidating deeds. If Hector's fighting symbolises the hero's raw ability to perform independent actions and effect changes in the world around him,[159] then Astyanax's self-conferred end grants a similar degree of agency, albeit in terminal form. It is an

---

[158] It is worth noting, at this juncture, my omission of Phaedra from the discussion, mainly because her repeated gestures of suicide have been covered in detail by Hill (2004) 159–75 – although I disagree with many of his findings – and because she is not a particularly good fit for the model of suicide as freedom.

[159] One could quibble that many of the mythological Hector's actions depend upon the whims of gods, but such divine interference is largely absent from Seneca's *Troades*.

achievement matching his father's, and the appropriateness of the setting suggests that Hector is also, in some oblique way, Astyanax's inspiration; suicide claims the same value as martial valour.

Oedipus, too, discovers autonomy in self-harm, although he stops short of complete obliteration. Throughout the play he has decried fate's hold over him, his prophesied parricide and incest, the *praedicta* (*Oed.* 915) that represent his inescapable domestic imbroglio and its prior tellings (*prae/dico*) in earlier literature. As Curtis Perry remarks: 'Seneca's *Oedipus* is about what happens to Oedipus' massively assertive and tyrannical self as he becomes increasingly entangled with various forms of unwelcome contingency or limitation: fate, the family, literary belatedness, the mother as origin and terminus.'[160] If Seneca's Oedipus seems more boastful and autocratic than Sophocles', that is largely a function of his thwarted desire for independence and control. Recollection of his encounter with the Sphinx (*Oed.* 92–102), for instance, is programmatic both in its portrait of Oedipus' self-assured intelligence and more broadly, as an example of his dominance. Oedipus faced an external threat and triumphed over it, and he is moved to recall this when Jocasta accuses him of cowardice, that is, when he feels his power is under siege (*Oed.* 81–6). Further, his recollection can be read as an avowal of literary independence as well, by which I mean that he overcomes the Sphinx qua poet,[161] and thus assumes, implicitly, a certain freedom from the skeins of *carmina* that threaten to entrap him. Of course, this freedom is utterly illusory, as is his autocratic sense of control, but his persistent expression of them throws his actual lack of autonomy into sharp relief. I note in Chapter 3 that Seneca's Oedipus is more a passive object of other people's knowledge than an active possessor of critical insight; the same dynamic applies to all of his actions in the play, which swing between aggressive claims to sovereign power and wretched acknowledgements of constraint. The heavier the constraint, the fiercer Oedipus' claims become, until, in the wake of Jocasta's suicide, he challenges

---

[160] Perry (2015) 411.
[161] Bexley (2016) 357–8.

4.3 Suicide

the knowledge of Apollo himself: 'O lying Phoebus! I have surpassed my wicked fates.' (*O Phoebe mendax, fata superavi impia, Oed.* 1046).[162] There is a feeling of exultation in Oedipus' despair, as though he has overcome his life's impediments and achieved more than was strictly necessary. This is Oedipus in his 'domineering and world-dominating' mode,[163] a man who wants to smash through limitations and outplay even the gods.

In its reference to Apollo, moreover, Oedipus' outburst evokes the shadow of poetic composition and literary precedent, as though Oedipus was also claiming to have outplayed his own prior fictional instantiations. Though speculative, the possibility is worth considering, and on this reading, *Oedipus* 1046 becomes a statement about poetic innovation. Does Oedipus imply that his dual role as matricide and parricide (*Oed.* 1044–5) push him beyond the typical requirements of his *dramatis persona*? Or is Seneca indicating, obliquely, his novel scripting of Jocasta's death, on stage via a sword thrust to her womb?[164] In either case, Oedipus (and Seneca) suggest they have surpassed the decreed (see *fata*) contours of this particular story.

Such hopes and intimations of autonomy find their fullest expression in Oedipus' self-blinding. Although his initial rush into the palace sees him considering only external sources of punishment – someone to stab him (927–8); animals to maul him (929–32); Agave to, presumably, behead him (933) – Oedipus quickly turns his attention to self-inflicted forms of atonement. He insists in Stoic vein that 'death alone frees the innocent from Fortune' (*mors innocentem sola Fortunae eripit*, 934), clearly in reference to himself, despite preceding and ensuing admissions of *scelus*.[165] Having been dogged by fortune throughout his life and over the entire course of his dramatised existence, Seneca's Oedipus seeks in suicide his final – only – means of attaining sovereign control. That he changes tactics and foregoes suicide in

---

[162] Despite the reservations of Boyle (2011) *ad Oed.* 1044–6, I follow Fitch (2004) and Ahl (2008) in inserting a personal pronoun here. Töchterle (1994) *ad Oed.* 1046 assumes 'your' rather than 'my', but the latter option fits the context better.
[163] Perry (2015) 410.
[164] Boyle (2011) *ad Oed.* 1032–6 thinks it likely that Seneca was the first to compose Jocasta's death in this way.
[165] Boyle (2011) *ad Oed.* 933–4.

favour of blinding may seem, initially, to diminish that autonomy, but Seneca continues to emphasise throughout the passage the idea that self-harm constitutes a vital form of self-determination. When, for instance, Oedipus characterises his actions as *poenae* (937; 976) and *supplicia* (944; 947) he effectively assumes the role of judge in deciding on the nature of his case, its specific features and permutations (936–51), and meting out punishment accordingly. This puts Oedipus in a dominant, authoritative position. Significantly, this is the moment when he asserts control over what happens to his own body, whereas for most of his life that body has been subjected to other people's whims and plans, especially in the case of his pierced ankles. The ensuing account of his plucking out his eyes reads like autonomy in technicolour, as the messenger's narrative draws attention not only Oedipus' agency – *he* directs his hands, *he* gouges and rips – but also the agency of his body: the eyes throb (963); they 'hurry to meet their wound' (*vulneri occurrunt suo*, 964); the hands cling (967); the nails tear (968); the torn head vomits blood (979).

Upon completing his self-inflicted brutality, Oedipus is described as *victor* (974), as though the sovereign power invested in his actions amounted to military conquest. When he returns to stage at the beginning of the subsequent Act, his overtly theatrical reference to his visage – 'this face befits Oedipus' (*vultus Oedipodam hic decet*, 1003) – can also be construed as a celebration of the self-determination facilitated in acts of self-harm: Oedipus has created this face with his own hands; this is an act of self-construction, not formation on somebody else's terms or through somebody else's agency.

His authority even acquires a metatheatrical/metapoetic dimension, in the sense that his face doubles as a mask (see discussion in Chapter 3), and that the words *eruentis* (961), *scrutatur* (965) and *evolvit* (967) assimilate his self-blinding to an act of literary interpretation, a search for textual meaning. I propose in Chapter 3 that Oedipus' self-mutilation likens his body to a text and casts him as an object to be deciphered; there, I stress the generally passive role that this consigns him to. While in no way negating the force of this prior argument, here I draw attention to Oedipus' *active* treatment of his own body for the space of the messenger

4.3 Suicide

speech. Throughout the rest of the tragedy, other characters claim the authority to interpret Oedipus' corporeal *signa*, and Seneca invites the audience to do likewise; here, and only here, that authority falls to Oedipus himself. He is the one in charge of unrolling, analysing, and coming to know his features, a capacity that aligns him – momentarily – with the play's audience/readers. Even if Oedipus does not attain the status of a poet or dramaturg, still his literary autonomy is conveyed through his ability to interpret and thus assert control over the material placed before him. As much as Oedipus' self-mutilation configures him as a literary work, it also implies his brief independence from being, merely, the playwright's instrument or the audience's object.

There is, then, a strong sense in which the tragedies' portrayal of suicide and self-harm accentuates characters' quasi-human aspects by presenting them as autonomous beings capable of deciding their own fates. Like the mechanism of revenge, a character's choice and pursuit of death is based on the assumption of a contingent future and on one's individual ability to intervene and alter the course of one's life. Death implies characters' escape not only from others' undue influence, but from the confines of the text itself, a release from authorial control. Yet, as Oedipus' example demonstrates, it can also function as acknowledgement of the limitations imposed by a purely literary existence, by reminding audiences of a character's ultimate instrumentality and of the unavoidable fact that deaths, too, are scripted. However much Seneca's Oedipus interprets his blinding as a declaration of freedom, the event is, nonetheless, an anticipated, much replicated part of his story, so that the autonomy he exercises in this instance, which he seeks so desperately and wins with so much pain, is in the end something subordinate to Seneca and to literary tradition. If Oedipus' face befits him, it is chiefly because that's what his story demands.

As a coda to this section, I consider one last Senecan suicide: Jocasta's, which is noteworthy in both form and presentation. Like Oedipus, Jocasta regards self-inflicted death as punishment for her (unintentional) misdeeds (*poenas, Oed.* 1035, 1040), and although Seneca makes no specific mention of her death as a form of escape or self-determination, still hints of agency and autonomy are present in her choice of weapon, for using a sword associates

Jocasta with masculine activity, both martial and sexual, though the latter connotations prevail here. That the sword belongs to Oedipus only reinforces its sexual symbolism,[166] as does Jocasta's word choice when she declares *rapiatur ensis* ('the sword must be seized' 1034) because *rapio* is commonly used to describe acts of sexual violence and domination. Her decision to pierce her womb, moreover, evokes sexual intercourse recast in the self-reflexive form demanded by suicide.[167] Just as suicide splits the human agent into active subject and passive object, so does Jocasta's death encapsulate both active and passive, masculine and feminine sexual roles.

This attack on her womb also implies agency through its defiance not just of pain and mortality – a standard goal in Senecan suicide – but also of the subjugated female body that must cede independence to children. I remarked earlier in this chapter that Medea's grim desire to scrape embryos from her belly (*Med.* 1012–13) amounts to a reassertion of control over her *corpus* and concomitantly, over the social structures that have trapped her within this maternal function. Similar intimations are present in Jocasta's act, inasmuch as it frees her from the particularly tangled nexus of her own family and prevents any further possibility of incestuous birth. Its symbolism also reflects, once again, the self-reflexive quality of the suicidal deed, for Jocasta's womb is a source of both origins and ends, birth and death, imprisonment and freedom.

It is *just* possible, too, that Jocasta claims poetic/fictional autonomy in the sense that her particular mode of death seems to be the origin of a tradition rather than a reprisal of established and expected motifs. First, the unknown author of the *Octavia* appropriates it and applies it to Agrippina, who demands that the soldier arriving to kill her strike her womb, for its guilt in bearing Nero (386–72). Tacitus follows suit in attributing to his Agrippina much

---

[166] Seneca performs the same trick in the *Phaedra*, first when he has Phaedra express her willingness to die by Hippolytus' sword (*Phaed.* 711–12), and later, when she stabs herself on stage with what is most likely Hippolytus' weapon (*Phaed.* 1197–8). For this latter instance, though, see the caveats in Mayer (2002) 30.

[167] Further, as Boyle (2011) *ad Oed.* 1032–9 notes, the act's reflexivity symbolises Jocasta and Oedipus' incest.

4.3 Suicide

the same sentiment and actions (*Ann.* 14.8.4), possibly via the *Octavia*'s influence.[168] Dio's account of Agrippina's murder (61.13.5) likewise echoes this tradition, albeit in more distant and muted form. The only viable parallel to predate Seneca's Jocasta occurs in the Elder Seneca's *Controversiae* 2.5.7, where the tyrant in a fictional legal scenario threatens to beat a woman's belly, to prevent her from giving birth to a potential tyrannicide.[169] The resemblance is loose, at best, and even if Seneca took some inspiration from it when composing the final Act of his *Oedipus*, still it is the distinct quality of *his* image, not the declamatory one, that proceeds to spawn a tradition. Of course, this argument must remain speculative in the absence of further evidence, but it seems feasible to grant some novelty to Seneca's Jocasta, and in so doing, to liberate her, if only marginally, from the pre-determination that most Senecan *dramatis personae* take for granted as an essential part of their characters. Though she cannot escape her purely fictional ontology, there is in her death the slimmest suggestion of literary as well as personal agency, of the ability to assert one's independence from established motifs and to exert one's power in influencing others.

Conclusion

I have pursued throughout this book the idea that Seneca's *dramatis personae* articulate simultaneously the constructed, textual, and implied human facets of their existence, but autonomy is one instance in which these two facets exhibit an occasional dynamic of competition or tension, as characters' fierce pursuit of independence collides with the inescapable fact of their curtailed fictional being. In revenge and suicide, two of the tragedies' most prevalent themes, characters' assertion of limitless agency

---

[168] Boyle (2008) *ad Oct.* 368–72 tentatively suggests this line of influence, and it seems, from Ferri (1998) that Tacitus draws on this play elsewhere in the *Annales*, though with so much uncertainty over the *Octavia*'s dating and circumstances of composition, it is difficult to be sure.

[169] Boyle (2011) *ad Oed.* 1036–9. Baltussen (2002) situates Seneca's version of Jocasta's death within a broader matricide motif, which he traces back to Euripides *Electra* 1206–13, but even if we accept this background, the details of Seneca's version remain without extant precedent and the case for originality is strong.

is brought up short by the very boundaries of the play's themselves, their enactment, their scripted nature, their engagement with literary traditions, their status as products of Seneca's authorial, authoritative imagination. Metapoetics aside, moreover, revenge and suicide are two actions that likewise affirm an individual's autonomy only to question its ultimate fulfilment, since both represent empty victories for self-determination: the latter by cancelling the agent's existence, the former in its equally self-destructive drive to attain dominion by overriding the social connections via which that dominion is constituted. The same patterns repeat across Seneca's prose, as the *sapiens*' celebrated sovereignty often seems to confer little more than self-satisfied isolation. This is self-determination, certainly, but at the expense of so much that gives the self meaning.

On the other hand, Seneca's tragedies *do* furnish instances of characters' autonomy coinciding with their fictional makeup, as is the case for Medea's magic, Atreus' conscious magnification of his deeds, and Oedipus' active blinding of his passive, textual body. Although typically recognised for their literary connotations, these examples underscore the significance of human autonomy as a theme in Senecan drama, for it is as expressions of independence and control that they acquire much of their power. What makes Medea's and Atreus' revenge so formidable, and so memorable, is less their obviously fictional texture than their engagement with notions of sovereignty, both personal and political, that resonate as loudly in the world outside the tragedies as within them. Hence the need to view these motifs in conjunction with Seneca's prose works, not only for the purpose of better detecting their presence in the dramas, but also, more significantly, for comprehending that the tensions and instabilities exposed by Senecan tragedy are already present, lurking, in Seneca's philosophical precepts. Like the exchange between fictional and quasi-human elements of character, the dialogue between Senecan philosophy and tragedy is precisely that, a dialogue; it goes both ways.

AFTERWORD

Now that we have come to the end, I would like you to turn back, dear reader, to the front cover of this book, or, in the more likely event of your reading it in digital form, to scroll back to the top. Take a close look. The image is of a face carved from the pages of an old volume, a piece of art combining the plastic forms of sculpture and mask with hints of more abstract fictional representation. As sculpture, the work's medium and its content coincide in being fully three-dimensional: this is not a physically flat description in print, or a (slightly less flat) painting, but a material, graspable visage, and the very fact of its materiality draws a particularly close analogy to an actual human face. It is, however, a face with no back; the head stops abruptly at the book's cover. Unlike more traditional sculpted portraits, this is not a bust, it has no neck and shoulders; it is a detached, free-floating face, and this incompleteness evokes, to my mind at least, the theatrical mask. Like a mask, this visage is purely forward-facing, it is the display of a face, the symbol of one, which somewhat – but only somewhat – belies its implied human qualities. Also like a mask, it can take on different expressions when viewed from different angles: smiling from the front; impassive from the side; troubled from above.

Most significant for my purposes, however, is the sculpture's union of recognisably human features with a recognisably textual medium. It is made not just from paper, but from *words* on printed pages. This is a face that can quite literally be read, although to do so would mean having to approach so close to the work that one would lose sight of its form. A few steps back and the opposite occurs: the pages and words grow indistinct, merely instrumental to the image arising from them. Writing morphs into a face and that face dissolves back into writing.

I am sure you will have guessed by now, so I shall state it outright: this sculpture is a metaphor for the qualities of fictional character explored in this book. As a visage emerging from printed text, it encapsulates fictional characters' duality of literary fabrication and implied human being, the recognisably 'human' characteristics that are sometimes undercut, sometimes complemented by the medium that gives them life. The character qua person comes out of the words, is built from the words, but also seems like more than the simple sum of those parts. It is easy for audiences to forget sometimes that the text is there, just as viewers can see the face without necessarily, momentarily, seeing the book. In both instances, though, the text is indispensable.

The sculpture's evocation of a mask is likewise significant for my project, as a reference to the theatrical dimension of Seneca's characters, for whom performance represents both an expansion and a diminution of humanness. On the one hand, the dramatic medium holds out the promise of corporeal reality, subjectivity, and agency, while on the other, it curbs individual autonomy and reduces the body to a spectatorial object. In similar fashion, the sculpture offers to viewers both a face and a symbol, the suggestion of embodiment coupled with the brute fact of its object status. The mask is at once an instrument and a second layer of skin.

The dialogue traced in this book between character in its textual and mimetic modes is by no means restricted to Seneca, but it is something Seneca's work expresses especially powerfully. As a writer of philosophic prose as well as dramatic verse, moreover, as a philosopher chiefly interested in ethics, Seneca is ideally placed for a study that deals with the contours of fictional human beings, their relationship to their literary medium and tradition, and to actual models of human behaviour. Beyond this happy coincidence, though, is Seneca's independent and distinct tendency to blur character's two modes throughout his dramatic work, so that audiences do not have to minimise one in favour of the other, to experience the work only at the intradramatic level and not the extradramatic one, or vice versa. Rather, Seneca's *dramatis personae* tend to draw on both modes simultaneously, to the same ends: coherence is both a moral and an aesthetic trait; vengeance, like acting, is an expression of individual agency; the exemplary replication that confers biological authenticity resembles a process of artistic reproduction, of making copies rather than originals. This intricate layering is a conspicuous aspect of Seneca's style; it is what makes his dramatic creations so potent and makes their impressions last long after we have closed the book, or they have retreated backstage.

BIBLIOGRAPHY

Abrahamsen, L. (1999) 'Roman Marriage Law and the Conflict of Seneca's *Medea*' *QUCC* 62: 107–21.
Adams, J. N. (1982) *The Latin Sexual Vocabulary*. London.
Agamben, G. (1998) *Homo Sacer: Sovereign Power and Bare Life*. Trans. D. Heller-Roazen. Stanford.
Agapitos, P. A. (1998) 'Seneca's *Thyestes* and the Poetics of Multiple Transgression' *Hellenika* 48: 231–53.
Ahl, F. M. (1986) *Seneca: Trojan Women*. Translated and with an Introduction. Ithaca, NY.
  (2008) *Two Faces of Oedipus. Sophocles'* Oedipus Tyrannus *and Seneca's* Oedipus. Translated and with an Introduction. Ithaca, NY.
Albini, U. (1995) 'La Storia di Edipo in Seneca' *RFIC* 123: 428–32.
Allendorf, T. S. (2013) 'The Poetics of Uncertainty in Senecan Drama' *MD* 71: 103–44.
Arcellaschi, A. (1990) *Médée dans le théâtre latin d'Ennius à Sénèque*. Rome.
Arendt, H. (1998) [1958] *The Human Condition*. 2nd ed. Chicago.
Armisen-Marchetti, M. (1989) *Sapientiae facies: étude sur les images de Sénèque*. Paris.
Armstrong, D. (1982) 'Senecan *Soleo*: Hercules Oetaeus 1767' *CQ* 32: 239–40.
Arnott, P. (1962) *Greek Scenic Conventions*. Oxford.
Arnott, W. G. (1972) 'From Aristophanes to Menander' *G&R* 19: 65–80.
Asmis, E. (1990) 'Seneca's "On the Happy Life" and Stoic Individualism' *Apeiron* 23: 219–55.
Austin, J. L. (1962) *How to do Things with Words*. Oxford.
Aygon, J.-P. (2016) *Ut scaena, sic vita: mise en scène et dévoilement dans les oeuvres philosophiques et dramatiques de Sénèque*. Paris.
Baade, E. C. (ed.) (1969) *Seneca's Tragedies*. London.
Baltussen, H. (2002) 'Matricide Revisited: Dramatic and Rhetorical Allusion in Tacitus, Suetonius and Cassius Dio' *Anticthon* 30: 30–40.
Barchiesi, A. (1993) 'Future Reflexive: Two Modes of Allusion in Ovid's *Heroides*' *HSCPh* 95: 333–65.
  (2009) 'Exemplarity: Between Practice and Text' in Y. Maes, J. Papy, and W. Verbaal (eds) *Appropriation and Latin Literature*. Latinitas Perennis vol. 2. Leiden: 41–62.
Baroin, C. (2010) 'Remembering One's Ancestors, Following in their Footsteps, Being Like Them: The Role and Forms of Family Memory in the Building

Bibliography

of Identity' in V. Dasen and T. Späth (eds) *Children, Memory, and Family Identity in Roman Culture*. Oxford: 19–48.

Barrett, W. S. (1964) *Euripides:* Hippolytos. Edited with Introduction and Commentary. Oxford.

Barthes, R. (1972) 'The Face of Garbo' in R. Barthes *Mythologies*. Trans. A Lavers. London: 61–3.

(1974) *S/Z*. Trans. R. Miller. Malden, MA.

Barton, T. (1994) 'The *inventio* of Nero: Suetonius' in J. Elsner and J. Masters (eds) *Reflections of Nero: Culture, History, and Representation*. London: 48–63.

Bartsch, S. (2006) *The Mirror of the Self: Sexuality, Self-Knowledge and the Gaze in the Early Roman Empire*. Chicago.

(2009) 'Senecan Metaphor and Stoic Self-Instruction' in S. Bartsch and D. Wray (eds) *Seneca and the Self*. Cambridge: 188–217.

Bartsch S., and Wray D. (eds) *Seneca and the Self*. Cambridge.

Bassi, K. (2017) '*Mimêsis* and Mortality: Reperformance and the Dead among the Living in *Hecuba* and *Hamlet*' in R. Hunter and A. Uhlig (eds) *Imagining Reperformance in Ancient Culture: Studies in the Traditions of Drama and Lyric*. Cambridge: 138–59.

Battistella, C. (2017) 'The Ambiguous *Virtus* of Seneca's *Medea*' *Maia* 69: 268–80.

Baumbach, S. (2008) *Shakespeare and the Art of Physiognomy*. Penrith, CA.

Beare, W. (1945) 'Plays for Performance and Plays for Recitation: A Roman Contrast' *Hermathena* 65: 8–19.

Bell, S. (2008) 'Introduction: Role Models in the Roman World' in S. Bell (ed.) *Role Models in the Roman World: Identity and Assimilation*. Memoirs of the American Academy at Rome Supplementary Volume 7: 1–39.

Bellardi, G. (1974) 'Gli *exitus illustrium virorum* e il l. XVI degli *Annali* tacitani' *A&R* 19: 129–37.

Belsey, C. (1985) *The Subject of Tragedy: Identity and Difference in Renaissance Drama*. London.

Benton, C. (2002) 'Split Vision: The Politics of the Gaze in Seneca's *Troades*' in D. Fredrick (ed.) *The Roman Gaze: Vision, Power, and the Body*. Baltimore: 31–56.

Berger, A. (1953) *Encyclopedic Dictionary of Roman Law*. Philadelphia.

Bernstein, N. W. (2017) *Seneca:* Hercules. London.

Bettini, M. (1983) 'L'arcobaleno, l'incesto e l'enigma: a proposito dell'*Oedipus* di Seneca' *Dioniso* 54: 137–53.

(1984) 'Lettura divinatoria di un incesto (Seneca *Oed*. 366ss.)' *MD* 12: 145–59.

(1996) 'Guardarsi in faccia a Roma. Le parole dell'apparenza fisica nella cultura Latina' *Parolechiave* 10–11: 175–95.

Bexley, E. M. (2011) 'Show or Tell? Seneca's and Sarah Kane's *Phaedra* Plays' *TIC* 3: 365–93.

Bibliography

(2015) 'What is Dramatic Recitation?' *Mnemosyne* 68: 774–93.
(2016) 'Doubtful Certainties: The Politics of Reading in Seneca's *Oedipus*' in P. Mitsis and I. Ziogas (eds) *Wordplay and Powerplay in Latin Poetry*. Berlin: 355–76.
(2017) 'Double Act: Reperforming History in the *Octavia*' in R. Hunter and A. Uhlig (eds) *Imagining Reperformance in Ancient Culture: Studies in the Traditions of Drama and Lyric*. Cambridge: 160–83.
Bieber, M. (1954) 'Wurden die Tragödien des Seneca in Rom aufgeführt?' *Mitteilungen des Deutschen Archäologischen Instituts, Römische Abteilung* 60–61: 100–6.
Billerbeck, M. (1999) *Seneca Hercules. Einleitung, Text, Übersetzung und Kommentar*. Leiden.
Bishop, J. D. (1966) 'Seneca's *Hercules*: Tragedy from *Modus Vitae*' *C&M* 27: 216–24.
(1972) 'Seneca's *Troades*: Dissolution of a Way of Life' *RhM* 115: 329–37.
(1985) *Seneca's Daggered Stylus: Political Code in the Tragedies*. Königstein.
Blau, H. (1982/3) 'Universals of Performance; or, Amortizing Play' *SubStance* 37–38: 140–61.
Bloomer, W. M. (1992) *Valerius Maximus and the New Nobility*. Chapel Hill.
Bobzien, S. (1998) *Determinism and Freedom in Stoic Philosophy*. Oxford.
Boissier, G. (1861) *Les Tragédies de Sénèque: ont-elles été représentées?* Paris.
Boyle, A. J. (1983) '*Hic Epulis Locus*: The Tragic Worlds of Seneca's *Agamemnon* and *Thyestes*' in A. J. Boyle (ed.) *Seneca Tragicus: Ramus Essays on Senecan Drama*. Berwick: 199–228.
(1985) 'In Nature's Bonds: A Study of Seneca's *Phaedra*' *ANRW* 32.2: 1284–1347.
(1987) *Seneca's Phaedra. Introduction, Text, Translation, and Notes*. Cambridge.
(1994) *Seneca's Troades. Introduction, Text, Translation, and Commentary*. Leeds.
(1997) *Tragic Seneca: An Essay in the Theatrical Tradition*. London/New York.
(2006) *An Introduction to Roman Tragedy*. London/New York.
(2008) *Octavia: Attributed to Seneca. Edited with Introduction, Translation, and Commentary*. Oxford/New York.
(2011) *Seneca: Oedipus. Edited with Introduction, Translation, and Commentary*. Oxford/New York.
(2014) *Seneca: Medea. Edited with Introduction, Translation, and Commentary*. Oxford/New York.
(2017) *Seneca: Thyestes. Edited with Introduction, Translation, and Commentary*. Oxford/New York.
Boys-Stones, G. (2007) 'Physiognomy and Ancient Psychological Theory' in S. Swain (ed.) *Seeing the Face, Seeing the Soul: Polemon's Physiognomy from Classical Antiquity to Medieval Islam*. Oxford: 19–124.
Braden, G. (1970) 'The Rhetoric and Psychology of Power in the Dramas of Seneca' *Arion* 9: 5–41.

Bibliography

(1984) 'Senecan Tragedy and the Renaissance' *Illinois Classical Studies* 9: 277–92.

(1985) *Renaissance Tragedy and the Senecan Tradition: Anger's Privilege*. New Haven/London.

(1990) 'Herakles and Hercules: Survival in Greek and Roman Tragedy (with a Coda on *King Lear*)' in R. Scodel (ed.) *Theatre and Society in the Classical World*. Ann Arbor: 245–64.

Braun, L. (1982) 'Sind Senecas Tragödien Bühnenstücke oder Rezitationsdramen?' *RPL* 5: 43–52.

Braund, S. (2016) *Seneca:* Oedipus. London.

Brennan, T. (2005) *The Stoic Life: Emotions, Duties, and Fate*. Oxford.

Brink, C. O. (1971) *Horace on Poetry II: The Ars Poetica*. Cambridge.

Brower, R. A. (1971) *Hero and Saint: Shakespeare and the Greco-Roman Heroic Tradition*. Oxford.

Brunt, P. A. (1975) 'Stoicism and the Principate' *PBSR* 43: 7–35.

Büchner, K. (1967) *Studien zur römischen Literatur, 6: Resultate römischen Lebens in römischen Schriftwerken*. Wiesbaden.

Burchell, D. (1998) 'Civic Personae: MacIntyre, Cicero and Moral Personality' *History of Political Thought* 19: 101–18.

Burnett, A. (1973) 'Medea and the Tragedy of Revenge' *CP* 68: 1–24.

(1998) *Revenge in Attic and Later Tragedy*. Berkeley.

Burrow, C. (2013) *Shakespeare and Classical Antiquity*. Oxford.

Busch, A. (2007) '*Versane natura est?* Natural and Linguistic Instability in the *Extispicium* and Self-Blinding of Seneca's Oedipus' *CJ* 102: 225–67.

Cairns, D. (ed.) (2005) *Body Language in the Greek and Roman Worlds*. Swansea.

(2011) 'Veiling Grief on the Tragic Stage' in D. Munteanu (ed.) *Emotion, Genre and Gender in Classical Antiquity*. London: 15–33.

Cairns, F. (1989) *Vergil's Augustan Epic*. Cambridge.

Calabrese, E. (2017) *Aspetti dell'identità relazionale nelle tragedie di Seneca*. Bologna.

Calder, W. M. (1976) 'Seneca's *Agamemnon*' *CP* 71: 27–36.

(1983) '*Secreti Loquimur*: an Interpretation of Seneca's *Thyestes*' in A. J. Boyle (ed.) *Seneca Tragicus: Ramus Essays on Senecan Drama*. Berwick: 184–98.

Campbell, C. M. (2019) 'Medea's Sol-Ipsism: Language, Power, and Identity in Seneca's *Medea*' *Ramus* 48: 22–53.

Cancik, H. (1998) 'Persona and Self in Stoic Philosophy' in A. I. Baumgarten, J. Assman, and G. G. Stroumsa (eds) *Self, Soul and Body in Religious Experience*. Leiden: 335–46.

Carlson, M. (2003) *The Haunted Stage: The Theatre as Memory Machine*. Ann Arbor.

Cary, E. (1914) *Dio Cassius: Roman History*. Vols 1–9. Cambridge, MA.

Bibliography

Castagna, E. (1991) 'Storia e storiografia nel pensiero di Seneca' in A. Setaioli (ed.) *Seneca e la cultura*. Naples: 91–117.

Cattin, A. (1956) 'L'âme humaine et la vie future dans les texts lyriques des tragédies de Sénèque' *Latomus* 15: 359–65 and 544–50.

Cave, T. (1988) *Recognitions: A Study in Poetics*. Oxford.

(2008) 'Singing with Tigers: Recognition in *Wilhelm Meister, Daniel Deronda*, and *Nights at the Circus*' in P. F. Kennedy and M. Lawrence (eds) *Recognition: The Poetics of Narrative. Interdisciplinary Studies on Anagnorisis*. New York: 115–34.

Chaplin, J. D. (2000) *Livy's Exemplary History*. Oxford.

Chatman, S. (1978) *Story and Discourse: Narrative Structure in Fiction and Film*. Ithaca, NY.

Christenson, D. (2000) *Plautus: Amphitruo*. Cambridge.

Cixous, H. (1974) 'The Character of "Character"' *New Literary History* 5: 383–402.

Coffey, M., and Mayer, R. (1990) *Seneca: Phaedra*. Cambridge.

Cohen, J. J. (1996) 'Monster Culture (Seven Theses)' in J. J. Cohen (ed.) *Monster Theory: Reading Culture*. Minneapolis: 3–25.

Colakis, M. (1985) 'Life after Death in Seneca's *Troades*' *CW* 78: 149–55.

Connors, C. (1994) 'Famous Last Words: Authorship and Death in the *Satyricon* and Neronian Rome' in J. Elsner and J. Masters (eds) *Reflections of Nero: Culture, History, and Representation*. London: 225–35.

Conroy, C. (2010) *Theatre & the Body*. London.

Corbeill, A. (2004) *Nature Embodied: Gesture in Ancient Rome*. Princeton.

Cornell, T. J. (1986) 'Review of Skutsch, *The Annals of Q. Ennius*' *JRS* 76: 244–50.

(1987) 'Ennius, *Annals* IV: A Reply' *CQ* 37: 514–16.

Costa, C. D. N. (1973) *Seneca: Medea: Edited with an Introduction and Commentary*. Oxford.

Coupland, J., and Gwyn, R. (2003) 'Introduction' in J. Coupland and R. Gwyn (eds) *Discourse, the Body, and Identity*. Basingstoke: 1–16.

Cowan, R. (2011) 'Sinon and the Case of the Hypermetric Oracle' *Phoenix* 65: 361–70.

(2013) 'Haven't I Seen You before Somewhere? Optical Allusions in Republican Tragedy' in G. Harrison and V. Liapis (eds) *Performance in Greek and Roman Theatre*. Leiden: 311–42.

Croisille, J. M. (1964) 'Le Personnage de Clytemnestre dans l'*Agamemnon* de Sénèque' *Latomus* 23: 464–72.

Csapo, E., and Slater, W. (1994) *The Context of Ancient Drama*. Ann Arbor.

Culler, J. (1975) *Structuralist Poetics: Structuralism, Linguistics, and the Study of Literature*. London.

(2011) *Literary Theory: A Very Short Introduction*. 2nd ed. Oxford.

Curley, T. F. (1986) *The Nature of Senecan Drama*. Rome.

Bibliography

Davis, P. J. (1983) '*Vindicat Omnes Natura Sibi*: A Reading of Seneca's *Phaedra*' in A. J. Boyle (ed.) *Seneca Tragicus: Ramus Essays in Senecan Drama*. Berwick: 114–27.

(1989) 'The Chorus in Seneca's *Thyestes*' *CQ* 39: 421–35.

(1991) 'Fate and Human Responsibility in Seneca's *Oedipus*' *Latomus* 50: 150–63.

(1993) *Shifting Song: The Chorus in Seneca's Tragedies*. Hildesheim.

(2003) *Seneca:* Thyestes. London.

(2012) 'Reception of Elegy in Augustan and Post-Augustan Poetry' in B. K. Gold (ed.) *A Companion to Roman Love Elegy*. Malden, MA: 443–58.

DeBrohun, J. B. (2017) 'Tragic *Contaminatio* and Polluted Sacrifice in Seneca's *Oedipus*' *Ramus* 46: 35–57.

Degl'Innocenti Pierini, R. (2014) 'Freedom in Seneca: Some Reflections on the Relationship between Philosophy and Politics, Public and Private Life' in J. Wildberger and M. L. Colish (eds) *Seneca Philosophus*. Berlin: 167–87.

De Lacy, P. H. (1977) 'The Four Stoic Personae' *Illinois Classical Studies* 2: 163–72.

De Temmerman, K. (2014) *Crafting Characters: Heroes and Heroines in the Ancient Greek Novel*. Oxford.

Dillon, J. (1981) *Shakespeare and the Solitary Man*. London.

Dingel, J. (1974) *Seneca und die Dichtung*. Heidelberg.

Docherty, T. (1983) *Reading (Absent) Character: Towards a Theory of Characterization in Fiction*. Oxford.

Dodson-Robinson, E. (2010) 'Rending Others: Ethical *contagio* in Seneca's *Thyestes*' *Museion* 10: 45–68.

(2011) 'Performing the "Unperformable" Extispicy Scene in Seneca's *Oedipus Rex*' *Didaskalia* 8.27: 179–84.

(2019) *Revenge, Agency, and Identity from European Drama to Asian Film*. Leiden.

Dressler, A. 2012. '"You Must Change Your Life": Metaphor and *Exemplum*, Theory and Practice, in Seneca's Prose' *Helios* 39.2: 45–92.

Duckworth, G. E. (1952) *The Nature of Roman Comedy: A Study in Popular Entertainment*. Princeton.

Dufallo, B. (2007) *The Ghosts of the Past: Latin Literature, the Dead, and Rome's Transition to a Principate*. Columbus, OH.

Duff, J. W. (1964) *A Literary History of Rome in the Silver Age: from Tiberius to Hadrian*. New York.

Dupont, F. (1985) *L'acteur-roi*. Paris.

(1995) *Les monstres de Sénèque: Pour une dramaturgie de la tragédie romaine*. Paris.

Dyck, A. (1996) *A Commentary on Cicero,* De Officiis. Ann Arbor.

Dyson, S. L. (1970) 'The Portrait of Seneca in Tacitus' *Arethusa* 3: 71–83.

Eagleton, T. (2003) *Sweet Violence: The Idea of the Tragic*. Malden, MA.

Easterling, P. (1973) 'Presentation of Character in Aeschylus' *G&R* 20: 3–19.

Bibliography

(1977) 'Character in Sophocles' *G&R* 24: 121–9.

(1990) 'Constructing Character in Greek Tragedy' in C. Pelling (ed.) *Characterization and Individuality in Greek Literature.* Oxford: 83–99.

(1993) 'Gods on Stage in Greek tragedy' in J. Dalfen, G. Petersmann, and F. F. Schwarz (eds) *Religio Graeco-Romana: Festschrift für Walter Pötscher.* Grazer Beiträge Suppl. 5. Graz: 77–86.

(1997) 'Form and Performance' in P. Easterling (ed.) *Cambridge Companion to Greek Tragedy.* Cambridge: 151–77.

Eder, J., Jannidis, F., and Schneider, R. (2010) 'Characters in Fictional Worlds: An Introduction' in J. Eder, F. Jannidis, and R. Schneider (eds) *Characters in Fictional Worlds: Understanding Imaginary Beings in Literature, Film, and Other Media.* Berlin: 3–58.

Edmunds, L. (2006) *Oedipus.* London.

Edwards, C. (1993) *The Politics of Immorality in Ancient Rome.* Cambridge.

(1997a) 'Self-Scrutiny and Self-Transformation in Seneca's Letters' *G&R* 44: 23–38.

(1997b) 'Unspeakable Professions: Public Performance and Prostitution in Ancient Rome' in J. P. Hallett and M. B. Skinner (eds) *Roman Sexualities.* Princeton: 66–95.

(2002) 'Acting and Self-Actualisation in Imperial Rome: Some Death Scenes' in P. Easterling and E. Hall (eds) *Greek and Roman Actors: Aspects of an Ancient Profession* Cambridge: 377–94.

(2007) *Death in Ancient Rome.* New Haven/London.

(2009) 'Free Yourself! Slavery, Freedom, and the Self in Seneca's *Letters*' in S. Bartsch and D. Wray (eds) *Seneca and the Self.* Cambridge: 139–59.

(2019) *Seneca: Selected Letters.* Cambridge.

Egermann, F. (1972) [1940] 'Seneca als Dichterphilosoph' in E. Lefèvre (ed.) *Senecas Tragödien.* Darmstadt: 33–57.

Eliot, T. S. (1999a) [1927] 'Seneca in Elizabethan Translation' in T. S. Eliot *Selected Essays.* London: 65–105.

(1999b) [1927] 'Shakespeare and the Stoicism of Seneca' in T. S. Eliot *Selected Essays.* London: 126–40.

Erasmo, M. (2004) *Roman Tragedy: Theatre to Theatricality.* Austin.

(2008) *Reading Death in Ancient Rome.* Columbus.

Evans, E. C. (1950) 'A Stoic Aspect of Senecan Drama: Portraiture' *TAPA* 81: 169–84.

(1969) 'Physiognomics in the Ancient World' *TAPS* 59: 1–101.

Faber, R. A. (2007) 'The Description of the Palace in Seneca's *Thyestes* 641–82 and the Literary Unity of the Play' *Mnemosyne* 60: 427–42.

Fantham, E. (1975) 'Virgil's Dido and Seneca's Tragic Heroines' *G&R* 22: 1–10.

(1982) *Seneca's* Troades. A Literary Introduction with Text, Translation, and Commentary. Princeton.

Bibliography

(1986) 'Andromache's Child in Euripides and Seneca' in M. Cropp, E. Fantham, and S. E. Scully (eds) *Greek Tragedy and its Legacy. Essays presented to D. J. Conacher.* Calgary: 267–80.

Feldherr, A. (1998) *Spectacle and Society in Livy's History.* Berkeley.

Ferri, R. (1998) 'Octavia's Heroines: Tacitus *Annales* 14.63–4 and the *Praetexta Octavia*' *HSCPh* 98: 339–56.

Fitch, J. G. (1979) '*Pectus o nimium ferum*: Act V of Seneca's *Hercules*' *Hermes* 107: 240–8.

(1981) 'Sense-Pauses and Relative Dating in Seneca, Sophocles and Shakespeare' *AJP* 102: 289–307.

(1987) *Seneca's* Hercules. *A Critical Text with Introduction and Commentary.* Ithaca, NY.

(2000) 'Playing Seneca?' in G. M. W. Harrison (ed.) *Seneca in Performance.* Swansea: 1–12.

(2002) *Seneca: Tragedies* Vol. I. Cambridge, MA.

(2004) *Seneca: Tragedies.* Vol. II. Cambridge, MA.

Fitch, J. G., and McElduff, S. (2002) 'Construction of the Self in Senecan Drama' *Mnemosyne* 55.1: 18–40.

Flemming, R. (2005) 'Suicide, Euthanasia and Medicine: Reflections Ancient and Modern' *Economy and Society* 34: 295–321.

Flower, H. I. (1995) '*Fabulae praetextae* in Context: When Were Plays on Contemporary Subjects Performed in Republican Rome?' *CQ* 45: 170–90.

(1996) *Ancestor Masks and Aristocratic Power in Roman Culture.* Oxford.

Forster, E. M. (1927) *Aspects of the Novel.* London.

Fortey, S., and Glucker, J. (1975) 'Actus Tragicus: Seneca on the Stage' *Latomus* 34: 699–715.

Foucault, M. (1986) *The Care of the Self. The History of Sexuality: 3.* Trans. R. Hurley. London.

Fowler, E. (2003) *Literary Character: The Human Figure in Early English Writing.* Ithaca, NY.

Frank, M. (1995) 'The Rhetorical Use of Family Terms in Seneca's *Oedipus* and *Phoenissae*' *Phoenix* 49: 121–30.

Frede, M. (2007) 'A Notion of a Person in Epictetus' in T. Scaltsas and A. S. Mason (eds) *The Philosophy of Epictetus.* Oxford/New York: 153–68.

(2011) *A Free Will: Origins of the Notion in Ancient Thought.* Berkeley.

Frow, J. (1986) 'Spectacle Binding: On Character' *Poetics Today* 7: 227–50.

(2014) *Character and Person.* Oxford.

Frye, N. (1990) [1957] *Anatomy of Criticism.* Princeton.

Fyfe, H. (1983) 'An Analysis of Seneca's *Medea*' in A. J. Boyle (ed.) *Seneca Tragicus: Ramus Essays in Senecan Drama.* Berwick: 77–93.

Galinsky, K. (1972) *The Herakles Theme: The Adaptations of the Hero in Literature from Homer to the Twentieth Century.* Oxford.

Garber, M. (1988) *Shakespeare's Ghost Writers: Literature as Uncanny Causality.* New York.

Bibliography

Gärtner, H. A. (1974) *Cicero und Panaitios: Beobachtungen zu Ciceros* De officiis. Heidelberg.

Garton, C. (1959) 'The Background to Character Portrayal in Seneca' *CP* 54: 1–9.

(1972) *Personal Aspects of the Roman Theatre*. Toronto.

Geiger, J. (1979) 'Munatius Rufus and Thrasea Paetus on Cato the Younger' *Athenaeum* 57: 48–72.

Gelley, A. (ed.) (1995) *Unruly Examples: On the Rhetoric of Exemplarity*. Stanford.

Gibson, R. K. (2007) *Excess and Restraint: Propertius, Horace, and Ovid's* 'Ars Amatoria' BICS Suppl. London.

Gigon, O. (1938) 'Bemerkungen zu Senecas Thyestes' *Philologus* 93: 176–83.

Gill, C. (1987) 'Two Monologues of Self-Division: Euripides, *Medea* 1021–80 and Seneca, *Medea* 893–977' in M. Whitby, M. Whitby, and P. Hardie (eds) *Homo Viator: Classical Essays for John Bramble*. Bristol: 25–37.

(1988) 'Personhood and Personality: The Four-Personae Theory in Cicero *De Officiis* 1' *OSAPh* 6: 169–99.

(1994) 'Peace of Mind and Being Yourself: Panaetius to Plutarch' *ANRW* II.36.7: 4599–640.

(1996) *Personality in Greek Epic, Tragedy and Philosophy: The Self in Dialogue*. Oxford.

(2006) *The Structured Self in Hellenistic and Roman Thought*. Oxford.

(2009) 'Seneca and Selfhood: Integration and Disintegration' in S. Bartsch and D. Wray (eds) *Seneca and the Self*. Cambridge: 65–83.

Gleason, M. W. (1990) 'The Semiotics of Gender. Physiognomy and Self-Fashioning in the Second Century C.E.' in D. E. Halperin, J. J. Winkler, and F. Zeitlin (eds) *Before Sexuality: The Construction of Erotic Experience in the Ancient Greek World*. Princeton: 389–415.

(1995) *Making Men: Sophists and Self-Presentation in Ancient Rome*. Princeton.

Gloyn, E. (2014) 'My Family Tree Goes Back to the Romans: Seneca's Approach to the Family in the *Epistulae Morales*' in J. Wildberger and M. L. Colish (eds) *Seneca Philosophus*. Berlin: 229–68.

(2017) *The Ethics of the Family in Seneca*. Cambridge.

Goar, R. J. (1987) *The Legend of Cato Uticensis from the First Century B.C. to the Fifth Century A.D.* Brussels.

Goffman, E. (1969) *The Presentation of the Self in Everyday Life*. London.

Goldberg, S. M. (1996), 'The Fall and Rise of Roman Tragedy', *TAPA* 126: 265–86.

(2000) 'Going for Baroque: Seneca and the English' in G. M. W. Harrison (ed.) *Seneca in Performance*. Swansea: 209–31.

Goldberg, S. M., and Manuwald, G. (2018) *Fragmentary Republican Latin: Ennius Dramatic Fragments, Minor Works*. Cambridge, MA.

Goldhill, S. (1986) *Reading Greek Tragedy*. Cambridge.

Bibliography

(1990) 'Character and Action, Representation and Reading: Greek Tragedy and its Critics' in C. Pelling (ed.) *Characterization and Individuality in Greek Literature*. Oxford: 100–27.

(1994) 'The Failure of Exemplarity' in I. J. F. De Jong and J. P. Sullivan (eds) *Modern Critical Theory and Classical Literature*. Leiden: 51–73.

Goldman, M. (1985) *Acting and Action in Shakespearean Tragedy*. Princeton.

(2000) *On Drama. Boundaries of Genre, Borders of Self*. Ann Arbor.

Goldschmidt, N. (2013) *Shaggy Crowns: Ennius' Annales and Virgil's Aeneid*. Oxford.

Gould, J. P. (1978) 'Dramatic Character and "Human Intelligibility" in Greek Tragedy' *PCPhS* 24: 43–67.

Gowers, E. (2016) 'Noises Off: The *Thyestes* Theme in Tacitus' *Dialogus*' in S. Frangoulidis, S. J. Harrison, and G. Manuwald (eds) *Roman Drama and its Contexts*. Berlin: 555–71.

Gowing, A. M. (2005) *Empire and Memory: The Representation of the Roman Republic in Imperial Culture*. Cambridge.

Grant, M. D. (1999) 'Plautus and Seneca: Acting in Nero's Rome' *G&R* 46: 27–33.

Graver, M. R. (1998) 'The Manhandling of Maecenas: Senecan Abstractions of Masculinity' *AJPh* 119: 607–32.

(2007) *Stoicism and Emotion*. Chicago.

Gray, P. (2016) 'Shakespeare vs. Seneca: Competing Visions of Human Dignity' in E. Dodson-Robinson (ed.) *Brill's Companion to the Reception of Senecan Tragedy: Scholarly, Theatrical and Literary Receptions*. Leiden: 203–30.

(2018) *Shakespeare and the Fall of the Roman Republic: Selfhood, Stoicism and Civil War*. Edinburgh.

Greenwood, L. H. G. (1928) *The Verrine Orations*. Vol 1. Cambridge, MA.

Greimas, A. J. (1987) *On Meaning: Selected Writings in Semiotic Theory*. Trans. and ed. P. J. Perron and F. H. Collins. Minneapolis.

Griffin, M. (1976) *Seneca: A Philosopher in Politics*. Oxford.

(1986a) 'Philosophy, Cato, and Roman Suicide I' *G&R* 33: 64–77.

(1986b) 'Philosophy, Cato, and Roman Suicide II' *G&R* 33: 192–202.

(2013) *Seneca on Society: A Guide to* de Beneficiis. Oxford.

Grimal, P. (1963) 'L'originalité de Sénèque dans la tragédie de "*Phèdre*"' *REL* 41: 197–314.

Guastella, G. (2001) '*Virgo, Coniunx, Mater*: The Wrath of Seneca's Medea' *CA* 20: 197–220.

Gummere, R. M. (1917) *Seneca Epistles* 3 Vols. Cambridge, MA.

Gunderson, E. (2015) *The Sublime Seneca: Ethics, Literature, Metaphysics*. Cambridge.

(2017) 'Repetition' *Ramus* 46: 118–34.

Habinek, T. N. (1998) *The Politics of Latin Literature*. Princeton.

(2000) 'Seneca's Renown: *Gloria, Claritudo* and the Replication of the Roman Elite' *CA* 19: 264–303.

Bibliography

Hadot, P. (1995) *Philosophy as a Way of Life: Spiritual Exercises from Socrates to Foucault*. A. I. Davidson (ed.). Malden, MA.

Hague, R. (2011) *Autonomy and Identity: The Politics of Who We Are*. London.

Hammond, P. (2009) *The Strangeness of Tragedy*. Oxford.

Hardie, P. (1993) *The Epic Successors of Virgil*. Cambridge.

Harrison, G. M. W. (2000) 'Semper ego auditor tantum? Performance and Physical Setting of Seneca's Plays' in G. M. W. Harrison *Seneca in Performance*. Swansea: 137–49.

(2014a). 'Characters' in G. Damschen and A. Heil (eds) *Brill's Companion to Seneca: Philosopher and Dramatist*. Leiden: 593–613.

(2014b) 'Themes' in G. Damschen and A. Heil (eds) *Brill's Companion to Seneca: Philosopher and Dramatist*. Leiden: 615–38.

Heier, E. (1976) 'The Literary Portrait as a Device of Characterization' *Neophilologus* 60: 321–33.

Heldmann, K. (1974) *Untersuchungen zu den Tragödien Senecas*. Wiesbaden.

Henderson, J. (1983) 'Poetic Technique and Rhetorical Amplification: Seneca *Medea* 579–669' in A. J. Boyle (ed.) *Seneca Tragicus: Ramus Essays in Senecan Drama*. Berwick: 94–113.

(2004) *Morals and Villas in Seneca's Letters: Places to Dwell*. Cambridge.

Henry, D., and Walker, B. (1963) 'Tacitus and Seneca' *G&R* 10: 98–110.

(1965) 'The Futility of Action: A Study of Seneca's *Hercules*' *CP* 60: 11–22.

(1967) 'Loss of Identity: *Medea superest*? A Study of Seneca's *Medea*' *CP* 62: 169–81.

(1983) 'The *Oedipus* of Seneca: An Imperial Tragedy' in A. J. Boyle (ed.) *Seneca Tragicus: Ramus Essays on Senecan Drama*. Berwick: 128–39.

(1985) *The Mask of Power: Seneca's Tragedies and Imperial Rome*. Warminster.

Herington, J. (1966) 'Senecan Tragedy' *Arion* 5: 422–71.

Herrmann, L. (1924) *Le Théatre de Sénèque*. Paris.

Hicks, R. D. (1931) *Diogenes Laertius: Lives of Eminent Philosophers*. Vol 2. Cambridge, MA.

Hijmans, B. L. (1966) 'Drama in Seneca's Stoicism' *TAPA* 97: 237–51.

Hill, T. (2004) Ambitiosa Mors: *Suicide and Self in Roman Thought and Literature*. London.

Hinds, S. E. (1993) 'Medea in Ovid: Scenes from the Life of an Intertextual Heroine' *MD* 30: 9–47.

(1998) *Allusion and Intertext: Dynamics of Appropriation in Roman Poetry*. Cambridge.

(2011) 'Seneca's Ovidian Loci' *SIFC* 9: 5–63.

Hine, H. M. (1981) 'The Structure of Seneca's *Thyestes*' *Papers of the Liverpool Latin Seminar* 3: 259–75.

(2000) *Seneca: Medea. With an Introduction, Text, Translation, and Commentary*. Warminster.

Hochman, B. (1985) *Character in Literature*. Ithaca, NY.

Bibliography

Hölkeskamp, K.-J. (1996) '*Exempla* und *mos maiorum*: Überlegungen zum kollektiven Gedächtnis der Nobilität'. In H.-J. Gehrke and A. Möller (eds) *Vergangenheit und Lebenswelt: Soziale Kommunikation, Traditionsbildung und historisches Bewusstsein*. Tübingen: 301–38.

Hook, B. S. (2000) '"Nothing within Which Passeth Show": Character and *color* in Senecan Tragedy', in G. W. M. Harrison (ed.) *Seneca in Performance*. Swansea: 53–71.

Hughes, K. (2018) 'Stronger than Fiction' *TLS* 31.1.

Hunter, R. (1985) *The New Comedy of Greece and Rome*. Cambridge.

Inwood, B. (1995) 'Politics and Paradox in Seneca's *de Beneficiis*' in A. Laks and M. Schofield (eds) *Justice and Generosity*. Cambridge: 241–65.

― (1997) 'Why Do Fools Fall in Love?' in R. Sorabji (ed.) *Aristotle and After*. BICS Suppl. London: 55–69.

― (2005) *Reading Seneca: Stoic Philosophy at Rome*. Oxford.

Jahn, M. (2001) 'Narrative Voice and Agency in Drama: Aspects of a Narratology of Drama' *NLH* 32: 659–79.

Jakobi, R. (1988) *Der Einfluss Ovids auf den Tragiker Seneca*. Berlin/New York.

Jocelyn, H. D. (1967) *The Tragedies of Ennius: The Fragments*. Edited with an Introduction and Commentary. Cambridge.

Johnson, M. (1992) 'Reflections on Inner Life: Masks and Masked Acting in Ancient Greek Tragedy and Japanese Noh Drama' *Modern Drama* 35: 20–34.

Johnson, W. R. (1987) *Momentary Monsters: Lucan and his Heroes*. Ithaca, NY.

― (1988) '*Medea nunc sum*: The Close of Seneca's Version' in P. Pucci (ed.) *Language and the Tragic Hero: Essays on Greek Tragedy in Honor of Gordon M. Kirkwood*. Atlanta: 85–102.

Jones, J. (1962) *On Aristotle and Greek Tragedy*. London.

Kaster, R. A., and Nussbaum, M. C. (2010) *Seneca: Anger, Mercy, Revenge*. Chicago.

Kennedy, P. F., and Lawrence, M. (eds) (2008) *Recognition: The Poetics of Narrative. Interdisciplinary Studies on Anagnorisis*. New York.

Kennerly, M. (2018) *Editorial Bodies: Perfection and Rejection in Ancient Rhetoric and Poetics*. Columbia, SC.

Ker, J. (2009) *The Deaths of Seneca*. Oxford.

― (2012) 'Seneca in Tacitus' in V. E. Pagán (ed.) *A Companion to Tacitus*. Malden, MA: 305–29.

― (2015) 'Seneca and Augustan Culture' in A. Schiesaro and S. Bartsch (eds) *Cambridge Companion to Seneca*. Cambridge: 109–21.

Kerrigan, J. (1996) *Revenge Tragedy: Aeschylus to Armageddon*. Oxford.

Kiernan, M. (ed.) (1985) *Francis Bacon: The Essayes Or Counsels, Civill and Morall*. Edited with Introduction, Notes, and Commentary. Oxford.

Kirichenko, A. (2013) *Lehrreiche Trugbilder: Senecas Tragödien und die Rhetorik des Sehens*. Heidelberg.

Bibliography

(2017) 'Constructing Oneself in Horace and Seneca' in M. Stöckinger, K. Winter, and A. T. Zanker (eds) *Horace and Seneca: Interactions, Intertexts, Interpretations.* Berlin: 265–86.

Kirk, G. S. (1985) *The* Iliad: *A Commentary. Vol 1: Books 1–4.* Cambridge.

Klein, J. (2015) 'Making Sense of Stoic Indifferents' in B. Inwood (ed.) *Oxford Studies in Ancient Philosophy* 49. Oxford: 227–81.

Knights, L. C. (1979) [1933] 'How Many Children Had Lady Macbeth?' in L. C. Knights (ed.) *'Hamlet' and other Shakespearean Essays.* Cambridge: 270–308.

Knoche, U. (1972) [1941] 'Senecas Atreus. Ein Beispiel' in E. Lefèvre (ed.) *Senecas Tragödien.* Darmstadt: 477–89.

Knox, B. M. W. (1977) 'The *Medea* of Euripides' *YCS* 25: 193–225.

Kohn, T. (2013) *The Dramaturgy of Senecan Tragedy.* Ann Arbor.

Kokolakis, M. M. (1969) *The Dramatic Simile of Life.* Athens.

(1976) Τὸ δρᾶμα τοῦ βίου εἰς τὸν Ἐπίκτητον. Φιλολογικὰ Μελετήματα εἰς τὴν Ἀρχαίαν Ἑλληνικὴν Γραμματείαν. Athens.

Konstan, D. (1983) *Roman Comedy.* Ithaca, NY.

Kozak, L. (2016) *Experiencing Hektor: Character in the* Iliad. London.

Kragelund, P. (2002) 'Historical Drama in Ancient Rome: Republican Flourishing and Imperial Decline?' *SO* 77: 5–51, 88–102.

(2016) *Roman Historical Drama: The* Octavia *in Antiquity and Beyond.* Oxford.

Kraus, C. (2005) 'From *Exempla* to *Exemplar*? Writing History around the Emperor in Imperial Rome' in J. Edmondson (ed.) *Flavius Josephus and Flavian Rome.* Oxford: 181–200.

Labate, M. (1984) *L'arte di farsi amore: Modelli culturali e progetto didascalico nell'elegia ovidiana.* Pisa.

Lacey, D. N. (1978–79) 'Like Father, Like Son: Comic Themes in Plautus' *Bacchides*' *CJ* 74: 132–5.

Langlands, R. (2008) 'Reading for the Moral in Valerius Maximus: The Case of *Severitas*' *CCJ* 54: 160–87.

(2011) 'Roman *Exempla* and Situation Ethics: Valerius Maximus and Cicero *de Officiis*' *JRS* 101: 100–22.

(2015) 'Roman Exemplarity: Mediating between General and Particular' in M. Lowrie and S. Lüdemann (eds) *Exemplarity and Singularity: Thinking through Particulars in Philosophy, Literature, and Law.* London: 68–80.

(2018) *Exemplary Ethics in Ancient Rome.* Cambridge.

Lattimore, R. (2011) [1951] *The Iliad of Homer.* Chicago.

Lavery, G. B. (1980) 'Metaphors of War and Travel in Seneca's Prose Works' *G&R* 27: 147–57.

Lawall, G. (1982) 'Death and Perspective in Seneca's *Troades*' *CJ* 77: 244–52.

(1983) '*Virtus* and *Pietas* in Seneca's *Hercules*' in A. J. Boyle (ed.) *Seneca Tragicus: Ramus Essays in Senecan Drama.* Berwick: 6–26.

Lawall, G., Lawall, S. N., and Kunkel, G. (1982) *The* Phaedra *of Seneca.* Wauconda, IL.

Bibliography

Lefèvre, E. (1972) [1969] '*Quid ratio possit?* Senecas *Phaedra* als stoisches Drama' in E. Lefèvre (ed.) *Senecas Tragödien*. Darmstadt: 343–75.

(ed.) (1972) *Senecas Tragödien*. Darmstadt.

(1981) 'A Cult without God or the Unfreedom of Freedom in Seneca Tragicus' *CJ* 77: 32–6.

(1985) 'Die philosophische Bedeutung der Seneca-Tragödie am Beispiel des *Thyestes*' *ANRW* 2.32.2: 1263–83.

(1997a) 'Die Transformation der griechischen durch die römische Tragödie am Beispiel von Senecas *Medea*' in H. Flashar (ed.) *Tragödie, Idee und Transformation*. Colloquium Rauricum 5. Stuttgart/Leipzig: 65–83.

(1997b) 'Seneca Atreus – die Negation des stoischen Weisen?' in J. Axer and W. Görler (eds) *Scaenica Saravi-Varsoviensia*. Warsaw: 57–74.

Leigh, M. (1997) 'Varius Rufus, Thyestes, and the Appetites of Antony' *PCPhS* 42: 171–97.

Leo, F. (1878) *De Seneca Tragoediis: observationes criticae*. Berlin.

Leppin, H. (1992) *Histrionen: Untersuchungen zur sozialen Stellung von Bühnenkünstlern im Westen des römischen Reiches zur Zeit der Republik und des Principats*. Bonn.

Lesses, G. (1993) 'Austere Friends: The Stoics and Friendship' *Apeiron* 26: 57–75.

Litchfield, H. W. (1914) 'National *Exempla Virtutis* in Roman Literature' *HSCPh* 25: 1–71.

Littlewood, C. A. J. (2004) *Self-Representation and Illusion in Senecan Tragedy*. Oxford.

(2008) 'Gender and Power in Seneca's *Thyestes*' in J. G. Fitch (ed.) *Oxford Readings in Classical Studies: Seneca*. Oxford: 244–63.

Long, A. A. (1968) 'The Stoic Concept of Evil' *PhilosQ* 18: 329–43.

(1996) [1971] 'The Logical Basis of Stoic Ethics' in A. A. Long (ed.) *Stoic Studies*. Cambridge: 134–55.

Lowe, D. (2015) *Monsters and Monstrosity in Augustan Poetry*. Ann Arbor.

Lowrie, M. (2007) 'Making an *Exemplum* of Yourself: Cicero and Augustus' in S. J. Heyworth, P. G. Fowler, and S. J. Harrison (eds) *Classical Constructions. Papers in Memory of Don Fowler, Classicist and Epicurean*. Oxford: 91–112.

Lowrie, M., and S. Lüdemann (eds) (2015) *Exemplarity and Singularity: Thinking through Particulars in Philosophy, Literature, and Law*. London/ New York.

Lucas, F. L. (1922) *Seneca and Elizabethan Tragedy*. Cambridge.

Lyons, J. D. (1989) *Exemplum: The Rhetoric of the Example in Early Modern France and Italy*. Princeton.

MacMullen, R. (1966) *Enemies of the Roman Order: Treason, Unrest, and Alienation in the Empire*. Cambridge, MA.

Mader, G. (2010) 'Atreus *Artifex* (Seneca, *Thyestes* 906–7)' *CQ* 60: 277–80.

Bibliography

(2014) '*Hoc quod volo / me nolle*: Counter-Volition and Identity Management in Senecan tragedy' *Pallas* 95: 125–61.

Maltby, R. (1991) *A Lexicon of Ancient Latin Etymologies*. Leeds.

Manuwald, G. (2001) *Fabulae praetextae. Spuren einer literarischen Gattung der Römer*. Munich.

(2013) 'Medea: Transformations of a Greek Figure in Latin Literature' *G&R* 60: 114–35.

Marshall, C. W. (1999) 'Some Fifth-Century Masking Conventions' *G&R* 46: 188–202.

(2000) 'Location! Location! Location!' in G. W. M. Harrison (ed.) *Seneca in Performance*. Swansea: 27–51.

(2002) 'Chorus, Metatheatre, and Menander *Dyskolos* 427–41' *Scholia* 11: 3–17

(2012) 'Sophocles *Didaskalos*' in K. Ormand (ed.) *Blackwell Companion to Sophocles*. Malden, MA: 187–203.

Marti, B. M. (1945) 'Seneca's Tragedies: A New Interpretation' *TAPA* 76: 216–45.

Marx, F. A. (1937) 'Tacitus und die Literatur der *exitus illustrium virorum*' *Philologus* 92: 83–103.

Mason, H. J. (1984) 'Physiognomy in Apuleius *Metamorphoses* 2.2' *CP* 79: 307–9.

Mastronarde, D. J. (1970) 'Seneca's *Oedipus*: The Drama in the Word' *TAPA* 101: 291–315.

(2002) *Euripides:* Medea. Cambridge.

(2010) *The Art of Euripides: Dramatic Technique and Social Context*. Cambridge.

Mayer, R. G. (1991) 'Roman Historical *Exempla* in Seneca' in P. Grimal (ed.) *Sénèque et la prose latine*. Geneva: 141–76.

(2002) *Seneca:* Phaedra. London.

McAuley, M. (2016) *Reproducing Rome: Motherhood in Virgil, Ovid, Seneca, and Statius*. Oxford.

Meineck, P. (2011) 'The Neuroscience of the Tragic Mask' *Arion* 19: 113–58.

(2018) *Theatrocracy: Greek Drama, Cognition, and the Imperative for Theatre*. London.

Meltzer, G. (1988) 'Dark Wit and Black Humor in Seneca's *Thyestes*' *TAPA* 118: 309–30.

Mendell, C. W. (1968) [1941] *Our Seneca*. New Haven.

Michelon, F. (2015) *La scena dell'inganno finzioni tragiche nel teatro di Seneca*. Turnhout.

Miles, G. (1996) *Shakespeare and the Constant Romans*. Oxford.

Miller, W. I. (2005) *An Eye for an Eye*. Cambridge.

Miola, R. S. (1992) *Shakespeare and Classical Tragedy: The Influence of Seneca*. Oxford.

Bibliography

Misch, G. (1950) *A History of Autobiography in Antiquity*. London.
Misener, G. (1924) 'Iconistic Portraits' *CP* 19: 97–123.
Moore, T. J. (1998) *The Theatre of Plautus: Playing to the Audience*. Austin.
Morelli, A. M. (1995) 'Le preghiere di Fedra. Modelli della seduzione nella "Phaedra" senecana' *MD* 35: 77–89.
Morford, M. (2000) 'Walking Tall: The Final Entrance of Atreus in Seneca's *Thyestes*' *Syllecta Classica* 11: 162–77.
Morgan, T. (2007) *Popular Morality in the Early Roman Empire*. Cambridge.
Most, G. (1992) '*Disiecti membra poetae*: The Rhetoric of Dismemberment in Neronian Poetry' in R. Hexter and D. Selden (eds) *Innovations in Antiquity*. New York: 391–419.
Motto, A. L., and Clark, J. R. (1981) '*Maxima virtus* in Seneca's *Hercules*' *CP* 76: 101–17.
—— (1994) 'The Monster in Seneca's *Hercules* 926–39' *CP* 89: 269–72.
Mowbray, C. (2012) 'Captive Audience? The Aesthetics of *nefas* in Senecan Drama' in I. Sluiter and R. M. Rosen (eds) *Aesthetic Value in Classical Antiquity*. Leiden: 393–420.
Nappa, C. (2018) *Making Men Ridiculous: Juvenal and the Anxieties of the Individual*. Ann Arbor.
Nédoncelle, M. (1948) 'Πρόσωπον et persona dans l'antiquité classique. Essai de bilan linguistique' *Revue des sciences religieuses* 22: 277–99.
Nikolsky, B. (2015) *Misery and Forgiveness in Euripides: Meaning and Structure in the* Hippolytus. Trans. M. Nikolsky. Swansea.
Nussbaum, M. (1994) *The Therapy of Desire: Theory and Practice in Hellenistic Ethics*. Princeton.
—— (2002) 'The Incomplete Feminism of Musonius Rufus, Platonist Stoic and Roman' in M. Nussbaum and J. Sihvola (eds) *The Sleep of Reason: Erotic Experience and Sexual Ethics in Ancient Greece and Rome*. Chicago and London: 283–326.
Oakley, S. P. (1997) *A Commentary on Livy Books VI–X, vol. 1: Introduction and Book VI*. Oxford.
—— (1998) *A Commentary on Livy Books VI–X, vol. 2: Books VII–VIII*. Oxford.
Oliensis, E. (1998) *Horace and the Rhetoric of Authority*. Cambridge.
OKell, E. R. (2005) '*Hercules* and Nero: The didactic purpose of Senecan tragedy' in L. Rawlings and H. Bowden (eds) *Herakles and Hercules: Exploring a Graeco-Roman Divinity*. Swansea: 185–204.
Opeku, F. (1979) 'Physiognomy in Apuleius' in C. Deroux (ed.) *Studies in Latin Literature and Roman History* 1. Brussels: 467–74.
Oshana, M. A. L. (2005) 'Autonomy and Free Agency' in J. S. Taylor (ed.) *Personal Autonomy: New Essays on Personal Autonomy and its Role in Contemporary Moral Philosophy*. Cambridge: 183–204.
O'Sullivan, T. M. (2009) 'Death *ante ora parentum* in Virgil's *Aeneid*' *TAPA* 139: 447–86.

Bibliography

Owen, W. H. (1968) 'Commonplace and Dramatic Symbol in Seneca's Tragedies' *TAPA* 99: 291–313.
  (1970) 'Time and Event in Seneca's *Troades*' *WS* 83: 118–37.
Paratore, E. (1956) 'La Poesia nell'*Oedipus* di Seneca' *GIF* 9: 97–132.
  (1966) 'Il prologo dello *Hercules* di Seneca e *l'Eracle* di Euripide' *Quaderni della RCCM* 9: 1–39.
Perry, C. (2015) 'Seneca and the Modernity of *Hamlet*' *ICS* 40: 407–29.
Pertsinidis, S. (2018) *Theophrastus' Characters: A New Introduction*. London.
Petrides, A. K. (2014) *Menander, New Comedy, and the Visual*. Cambridge.
Petrone, G. (1988) 'Nomen/omen: poetica e funzione dei nomi (Plauto, Seneca, Petronio)' *MD* 20–21: 33–70.
Phelan, J. (1989) *Reading People, Reading Plots: Character, Progression, and the Interpretation of Narrative*. Chicago/London.
Plass, P. (1995) *The Game of Death in Ancient Rome: Arena Sport and Political Suicide*. Madison.
Poe, J. P. (1969) 'An Analysis of Seneca's *Thyestes*' *TAPA* 100: 355–76.
  (1983) 'The Sinful Nature of the Protagonist of Seneca's *Oedipus*' in A. J. Boyle (ed.) *Seneca Tragicus: Ramus Essays on Senecan Drama*. Berwick: 140–58.
  (1996) 'The Supposed Conventional Meanings of Dramatic Masks: A Re-examination of Pollux 4.133–54' *Philologus* 140: 306–28.
Pohlenz, M. (1934) *Antikes Führertum: Cicero De Officiis und das Lebensideal des Panaitios*. Leipzig/Berlin.
  (1965) 'τὸ πρέπον. Ein Beitrag zur Geschichte des Griechischen Geistes' in H. Dörrie (ed.) *Max Pohlenz: Kleine Schriften*. Hildesheim: 100–39.
Porter, J. I. (2017) 'Time for Foucault? Reflections on the Roman Self from Seneca to Augustine' *Foucault Studies* 22: 113–33.
Pöschl, V. (1977) 'Bemerkungen zum *Thyest* des Seneca' in W. Kraus, A. Primmer, and H. Schwabl (eds) *Latinität und alte Kirche. Festschrift für Rudolf Hanslik zum 70. Geburtstag*. Vienna: 224–34.
Pratt, N. T. (1939) *Dramatic Suspense in Seneca and His Greek Precursors*. Princeton.
  (1983) *Seneca's Drama*. Chapel Hill.
Putnam, M. C. J. (1995) *Virgil's Aeneid: Interpretation and Influence*. Chapel Hill/London.
Quint, D. (1993) *Epic and Empire: Politics and Generic Form from Virgil to Milton*. Princeton.
Raby, G. (2000) 'Seneca's *Trojan Women*: Identity and Survival in the Aftermath of War' in G. W. M. Harrison (ed.) *Seneca in Performance*. Swansea: 173–95.
Radice, B. (1969) *Pliny: Letters Books VIII–X, Panegyricus*. Cambridge, MA.
Rayner, A. (2006) *Ghosts: Death's Double and the Phenomena of Theatre*. Minneapolis.

Bibliography

Regenbogen, O. (1927/28) 'Schmerz und Tod in den Tragödien Senecas', *Vorträge der Bibliothek Warburg* 7: 167–218.

Rehm, R. (1988) 'Staging of Suppliant Plays' *GRB* 29: 263–308.

Repath, I. (2007a) 'Anonymus Latinus, Book of Physiognomy' in S. Swain (ed.) *Seeing the Face, Seeing the Soul: Polemon's Physiognomy from Classical Antiquity to Medieval Islam.* Oxford: 549–636.

(2007b) 'The Physiognomy of Adamantius the Sophist' in S. Swain (ed.) *Seeing the Face, Seeing the Soul: Polemon's Physiognomy from Classical Antiquity to Medieval Islam.* Oxford: 487–548.

Reydams-Schils, G. (2005) *The Roman Stoics: Self, Responsibility, and Affection.* Chicago.

Richardson-Hay, C. (2006) *First Lessons: Book 1 of Seneca's* Epistulae Morales *– A Commentary.* Bern.

Rimell, V. (2012) 'The Labour of Empire: Womb and World in Seneca's *Medea*' *SIFC* 105: 211–37.

Rimmon-Kenan, S. (2002) *Narrative Fiction: Contemporary Poetics.* 2nd ed. London.

Ringer, M. (1998) *Electra and the Empty Urn: Metatheatre and Role Playing in Sophocles.* Chapel Hill/London.

Rist, J. M. (1969) *Stoic Philosophy.* Oxford.

Roach, J. (1996) *Cities of the Dead: Circum-Atlantic Performance.* New York.

Robin, D. (1993) 'Film Theory and the Gendered Voice in Seneca' in N. S. Rabinowitz and A. Richlin (eds) *Feminist Theory and the Classics.* New York/London: 102–21.

Rogerson, A. (2017) *Virgil's Ascanius: Imagining the Future in the* Aeneid. Cambridge.

Rohrbacher, D. (2010) 'Physiognomics in Imperial Latin Biography' *CA* 29: 92–116.

Roisman, H. (2000) 'A New Look at Seneca's *Phaedra*' in G. W. M. Harrison (ed.) *Seneca in Performance.* Swansea: 73–86.

Roller, M. B. (2001) *Constructing Autocracy: Aristocrats and Emperors in Julio-Claudian Rome.* Princeton.

(2004) 'Exemplarity in Roman Culture: The Case of Horatius Cocles and Cloelia' *CP* 99: 1–56.

(2015) 'Between Unique and Typical: Senecan *exempla* in a List' in M. Lowrie and S. Lüdemann (eds) *Exemplarity and Singularity: Thinking through Particulars in Philosophy, Literature, and Law.* London/New York: 81–95.

(2018) *Models from the Past in Roman Culture: A World of* Exempla. Cambridge.

Romm, J. (2014) *Dying Every Day: Seneca at the Court of Nero.* New York.

Ronconi, A. (1940) '*Exitus illustrium virorum*' *SIFC* 17: 3–32.

Rose, A. R. (1979–80) 'Seneca's *HF*: A Politico-Didactic Reading' *CJ* 75: 135–42.

Bibliography

(1986–7) 'Power and Powerlessness in Seneca's *Thyestes*' *CJ* 82: 117–28.
Rosenmeyer, T. G. (1989) *Senecan Drama and Stoic Cosmology*. Berkeley/London.
(1993) 'Seneca's *Oedipus* and Performance: The Manto Scene' in R. Scodel (ed.) *Theatre and Society in the Classical World*. Ann Arbor: 235–44.
(2002) '"Metatheatre": An Essay on Overload' *Arion* 10: 87–119.
Ross, D. O. (1975) *Backgrounds to Augustan Poetry: Gallus, Elegy and Rome*. Cambridge.
Ruch, M. (1964) 'La langue de la psychologie amoureuse dans la *Phèdre* de Sénèque' *LEC* 32: 356–63.
Rudd, N. (1989) *Horace* Epistles *Book II and* Epistle to the Pisones *('*Ars Poetica*')*. Cambridge.
Rudich, V. (1997) *Dissidence and Literature under Nero: The Price of Rhetoricization*. London/New York.
Santoro L'Hoir, F. (2006) *Tragedy, Rhetoric, and the Historiography of Tacitus'* Annales. Ann Arbor.
Schetter, W. (1965) 'Sulla Struttura delle Troiane di Seneca' *RFIC* 93: 396–429.
Schiesaro, A. (1997) 'Passions, Reason and Knowledge in Seneca's Tragedies' in S. M. Braund and C. Gill (eds) *The Passions in Roman Thought and Literature*. Cambridge: 89–111.
(2003) *The Passions in Play:* Thyestes *and the Dynamics of Senecan Drama*. Cambridge.
(2009) 'Seneca and the Denial of the Self' in S. Bartsch and D. Wray (eds) *Seneca and the Self*. Cambridge: 221–35.
(2014) 'Seneca's *Agamemnon*: The Entropy of Tragedy' *Pallas* 95: 179–91.
Schlegel, A. W. (1972) [1809] 'Senecas Tragödien' in E. Lefèvre (ed.) *Senecas Tragödien*. Darmstadt: 13–14.
Seeberg, A. (2002–3) 'Tragedy and Archaeology: Forty Years After' *BICS* 46: 43–75.
Segal, C. (1982) '*Nomen Sacrum*: Medea and Other Names in Seneca Tragedy' *Maia* 34: 241–46.
(1986) *Language and Desire in Seneca's* Phaedra. Princeton.
(1988) 'Confusion and Concealment in Euripides' *Hippolytus*: Vision, Hope, and Tragic Knowledge' *Metis* 3: 263–82.
(1992) 'Signs, Magic and Letters in Euripides' *Hippolytus*' in R. Hexter and D. Selden (eds) *Innovations of Antiquity*. New York: 420–56.
(1993) Oedipus Tyrannus*: Tragic Heroism and the Limits of Knowledge*. New York.
Segal, E. (1987) *Roman Laughter: The Comedy of Plautus*. 2nd ed. Oxford.
Seidensticker, B. (1969) *Die Gesprächsverdichtung in den Tragödien Senecas*. Heidelberg.

Bibliography

(1985) '*Maius solito*: Senecas *Thyestes* und die tragoedia rhetorica' *Antike und Abendland* 31: 116–36.

(2008) 'Character and Characterization in Greek Tragedy' in M. Revermann and P. Wilson (eds) *Performance, Iconography, Reception: Studies in Honour of Oliver Taplin*. Oxford: 333–46.

Sennett, R. (1974) *The Fall of Public Man*. New York.

Seo, J. M. (2013) *Exemplary Traits: Reading Characterization in Roman Poetry*. Oxford.

Setaioli, A. (2007) 'Seneca and the Divine: Stoic Tradition and Personal Developments' *IJCT* 13: 333–68.

Shelton, J.-A. (1975) 'Problems of Time in Seneca's *Hercules* and *Thyestes*' *CSCA* 8: 257–69.

(1978) *Seneca's Hercules: Theme, Structure and Style*. Hypomnemata 50. Göttingen.

(2000) 'The Spectacle of Death in Seneca's *Troades*' in G. W. M. Harrison (ed.) *Seneca in Performance*. Swansea: 87–118.

Sissa, G. (2006) 'A Theatrical Poetics: Recognition and the Structural Emotions of Tragedy' *Arion* 14: 35–92.

Skidmore, C. (1996) *Practical Ethics for Roman Gentlemen: The Work of Valerius Maximus*. Exeter.

Skutsch, O. (1987) 'Book VI of Ennius' *Annals*' *CQ* 37: 512–14.

Slaney, H. (2013) 'Seneca's Chorus of One' in J. Billings, F. Budelmann, and F. Macintosh (eds) *Choruses Ancient and Modern*. Oxford: 99–116.

(2016) *The Senecan Aesthetic: A Performance History*. Oxford.

(2019) *Seneca: Medea*. London.

Smith, M. (1995) *Engaging Characters: Fiction, Emotion, and the Cinema*. Oxford.

(2010) '*Engaging Characters*: Further Reflections' in J. Eder, F. Jannidis, and R. Schneider (eds) *Characters in Fictional Worlds*. Berlin: 232–58.

Smith, R. S. (2014) 'Physics I: Body and Soul' in A. Heil and G. Damschen (eds) *Brill's Companion to Seneca: Philosopher and Dramatist*. Leiden: 343–61.

Solimano, G. (1991) *La prepotenza dell' occhio: riflessioni sull'opera di Seneca*. Genoa.

Staley, G. (1981) 'Seneca's *Thyestes*: *quantum mali habeat ira*' *GB* 10: 233–46.

(2010) *Seneca and the Idea of Tragedy*. Oxford.

(2014) 'Making Oedipus Roman' *Pallas* 95: 111–24.

Star, C. (2006) 'Commanding Constantia in Senecan Tragedy' *TAPA* 136: 207–44.

(2012) *The Empire of the Self: Self-Command and Political Speech in Seneca and Petronius*. Baltimore.

States, B. O. (1985a) 'The Anatomy of Dramatic Character' *Theatre Journal* 37: 86–101.

(1985b) *Great Reckonings in Little Rooms: On the Phenomenology of Theatre*. Berkeley.

Bibliography

(1992) *Hamlet and the Concept of Character*. Baltimore.

Steele, R. B. (1922) 'Some Roman Elements in the Tragedies of Seneca' *AJPh* 43: 1–31.

Stevens, J. (2018) 'Senecan Meta-Stoicality: in the Cognitive Grasp of Atreus' *CQ* 68: 573–90.

Stöckinger, M., Winter, K., and Zanker, A. T. (eds) (2017) *Horace and Seneca: Interactions, Intertexts, Interpretations*. Berlin.

Storm, W. (2014) '*Troas*' in G. Damschen and A. Heil (eds) *Brill's Companion to Seneca: Philosopher and Dramatist*. Leiden: 435–47.

(2016) *Dramaturgy and Dramatic Character: A Long View*. Cambridge.

Struck, P. T. (2004) *Birth of the Symbol: Ancient Readers at the Limits of Their Texts*. Princeton.

Sutton, D. F. (1986) *Seneca on the Stage*. Leiden.

Svenbro, J. (1984) 'La découpe du poème. Notes sur les origins sacrificielles de la poétique grecque' *Poétique* 58: 215–32.

Swain, S. (ed.) (2007) *Seeing the Face, Seeing the Soul: Polemon's Physiognomy from Classical Antiquity to Medieval Islam*. Oxford.

(2007) 'Appendix: The Physiognomy Attributed to Aristotle' in S. Swain (ed.) *Seeing the Face, Seeing the Soul: Polemon's Physiognomy from Classical Antiquity to Medieval Islam*. Oxford: 637–62.

Tadic-Gilloteaux, N. (1963) 'Sénèque face au suicide' *L'antiquité classique* 32: 541–51.

Taplin, O. (1977) *The Stagecraft of Aeschylus*. Oxford.

Tarrant, R. J. (1976) *Seneca, Agamemnon*. Cambridge.

(1978) 'Senecan Drama and its Antecedents' *HSCPh* 82: 213–63.

(1985) *Seneca's Thyestes*. Edited with an Introduction and Commentary. Atlanta.

(2006) 'Seeing Seneca Whole?' in K. Volk and G. Williams (eds) *Seeing Seneca Whole: Perspectives on Philosophy, Poetry and Politics*. Leiden: 1–17.

(2012) *Virgil. Aeneid Book XII*. Cambridge.

Thalmann, W. G. (1988) 'Thersites: Comedy, Scapegoats and Heroic Ideology in the *Iliad*' *TAPA* 118: 1–28.

Thévanaz, P. (1944) 'L'interiorité chez Sénèque' in *Mélanges offerts à M. Max Niedermann* Recueil de travaux 22, Université de Neuchâtel: 189–94.

Tietze Larson, V. (1989) 'Seneca's Epic Theatre' in C. Deroux (ed.) *Studies in Latin Literature and Roman History V*. Brussels: 279–304.

(1994) *The Role of Description in Senecan Tragedy*. Frankfurt am Main.

Töchterle, K. (1994) *Lucius Annaeus Seneca Oedipus Kommentar mit Einleitung, Text und Übersetzung*. Heidelberg.

Todorov, T. (1966) (ed.) *Théorie de la literature: texts des formalists russes*. Paris.

Traina, A. (1974) *Lo Stile 'Drammatico' del Filosofo Seneca*. Bologna.

(1979) 'Due Note A Seneca Tragico' *Maia* 31: 273–6.

Bibliography

(1981) 'Seneca *Thyest*. 713 S. *Mactet Sibi* o *Sibi Dubitat*? Un Recupero Esegetico' *Maia* 33: 151–3

Trilling, L. (1973) *Sincerity and Authenticity*. Cambridge, MA.

Trinacty, C. (2007) 'Seneca's *Heroides*: Elegy in Seneca's *Medea*' *CJ* 103: 63–78.

(2014) *Senecan Tragedy and the Reception of Augustan Poetry*. Oxford/New York.

(2016) '*Imago res mortua est*: Senecan Intertextuality' in E. Dodson-Robinson (ed.) *Brill Companion to the Reception of Senecan Tragedy: Scholarly, Literary and Theatrical Receptions*. Leiden: 11–33.

(2017) 'Retrospective Reading in Senecan Tragedy' *Ramus* 46: 175–96.

(2018) '*Nulla res est quae non eius quo nascitur notas reddat* (*Nat.* 3.21.2): Intertext to Intratext in Senecan Prose and Poetry' in S. Harrison, S. Frangoulidis, and T. Papanghelis (eds) *Intratextuality and Latin Literature*. Berlin: 309–24.

Turner, B. S. (2012) 'Introduction: The Turn of the Body' in B. S. Turner (ed.) *Routledge Handbook of Body Studies*. Abingdon: 1–17.

Turner, V. (1982) *From Ritual to Theatre: The Human Seriousness of Play*. New York.

Turpin, W. (2008) 'Tacitus, Stoic *Exempla*, and the *Praecipuum Munus Annalium*' *CA* 27: 359–404.

Tytler, G. (1982) *Physiognomy in the European Novel: Faces and Fortunes*. Princeton.

Uden, J. (2010) *The Invisible Satirist: Juvenal and Second-Century Rome*. Oxford.

Van Der Blom, H. (2010) *Cicero's Role Models: The Political Strategy of a Newcomer*. Oxford.

Vermeule, B. (2010) *Why Do We Care about Literary Characters?* Baltimore.

Veyne, P. (2003) *Seneca: The Life of a Stoic*. Trans. D. Sullivan. New York and London.

Viansino, G. (1993) *Lucio Anneo Seneca. Teatro. Testo critico, traduzione e commento*. Milan.

Vogt, K. (2009) 'Sons of the Earth: Are the Stoics Metaphysical Brutes?' *Phronesis* 54: 136–54.

Volk, K. (2000) 'Putting Andromacha on Stage: A Performer's Perspective' in G. W. M. Harrison (ed.) *Seneca in Performance*. Swansea: 197–208.

Volk, K., and G. Williams (eds) *Seeing Seneca Whole: Perspectives on Philosophy, Poetry and Politics*. Leiden

Von Glinski, M. L. (2017) 'All the World's Offstage: Metaphysical and Metafictional Aspects in Seneca's *Hercules*' *CQ* 67: 210–27.

Waldenfels, B. (2015) 'For Example' in M. Lowrie and S. Lüdemann (eds) *Exemplarity and Singularity: Thinking through Particulars in Philosophy, Literature, and Law*. London/New York: 36–45.

Walsh, L. (2012) 'The Metamorphosis of Seneca's *Medea*' *Ramus* 41: 71–93.

Warmington, E. H. (1988) *Remains of Old Latin*. Vol. 1. Cambridge, MA.

Bibliography

Webster, T. B. L. (1956) *Greek Theatre Production*. London.
Weiler, I. (1996) 'Physiognomische Überlegungen zu *mens sana in corpore sano*' in C. Klodt (ed.) *Satura Lanx: Festschift Werner A. Krenkel zum 70. Geburtstag*. Hildesheim: 153–68.
Weisenheimer, J. (1979) 'Theory of Character: *Emma*' *Poetics Today* 1: 185–211.
West, D. (1974) 'The Death of Hector and Turnus' *G&R* 21: 21–31.
Westphal, J. (2016) *The Mind–Body Problem*. Cambridge, MA.
Wilamowitz-Moellendorff, U. von. (1919) *Griechische Tragödie*. 4 vols, Berlin.
Wilcox, A. (2006) 'Exemplary Grief: Gender and Virtue in Seneca's Consolations to Women' *Helios* 33: 73–100.
(2008) 'Nature's Monster: Caligula as *Exemplum* in Seneca's *Dialogues*' in R. Rosen and I. Sluiter (eds) *Kakos: Badness and Anti-value in Classical Antiquity*. Leiden: 451–75.
Wiles, D. (1991) *The Masks of Menander: Sign and Meaning in Greek and Roman Performance*. Cambridge.
Willcock, M. (1964) 'Mythological Paradeigmata in the *Iliad*' *CQ* 14: 141–54.
Williams, G. (2003) *Seneca: de Otio, de Brevitate Vitae*. Cambridge.
Williams, G. D. (2012) *The Cosmic Viewpoint: A Study in Seneca's Natural Questions*. Oxford/New York.
Williams, R. (2014) [1976] *Keywords: A Vocabulary of Culture and Society*. London.
Wilshire, B. (1977) 'Role Playing and Identity: The Limits of the Theatrical Metaphor' *Cultural Hermeneutics* 4: 199–207.
(1982) *Role Playing and Identity: The Limits of Theatre as Metaphor*. Bloomington.
Wilson, E. (2007) *The Death of Socrates*. London.
(2010) *Seneca: Six Tragedies*. Oxford.
Wilson, M. (1983) 'The Tragic Mode of Seneca's *Troades*' in A. J. Boyle (ed.) *Seneca Tragicus: Ramus Essays on Senecan Drama*. Berwick: 27–60.
(1997) 'The Subjugation of Grief in Seneca's *Epistles*' in S. Braund and C. Gill (eds) *The Passions in Roman Thought and Literature*. Cambridge: 48–67.
Winterbottom, M. (1976) Review of Costa, Seneca *Medea*, *CR* 26: 39–40.
Wirszubski, C. (1968) *Libertas as a Political Idea at Rome during the Late Republic and Early Principate*. Cambridge.
Woloch, A. (2003) *The One vs. The Many: Minor Characters and the Space of the Protagonist in the Novel*. Princeton.
Worman, N. (2002) *The Cast of Character: Style in Greek Literature*. Austin.
Worthen, W. B. (1984) *The Idea of the Actor: Drama and the Ethics of Performance*. Princeton.
Wyles, R. (2013) 'Heracles' Costume from Euripides' *Heracles* to Pantomime Performance' in G. W. M. Harrison and V. Liapis (eds) *Performance in Greek and Roman Theatre*. Leiden: 181–98.

Bibliography

Zamir, T. (2014) *Acts: Theater, Philosophy and the Performing Self.* Ann Arbor.

Zanker, P. (1990) *The Power of Images in the Age of Augustus.* Trans. A. Shapiro. Ann Arbor.

Zanobi, A. (2008) 'The Influence of Pantomime on Seneca's Tragedies' in E. Hall and R. Wyles (eds) *New Directions in Ancient Pantomime.* Oxford: 227–57.

(2014) *Seneca's Tragedies and the Aesthetics of Pantomime.* London.

Zeitlin, F. (2012) 'A Study in Form: Recognition Scenes in the Three Electra Plays' *Lexis* 30: 361–78.

Zimmerman, B. (1990) 'Seneca und der Pantomimus' in G. Vogt-Spira (ed.) *Strukturen der Mündlichkeit in der römischen Literatur.* Tübingen: 161–7.

Zintzen, C. (1972) [1971] '*Alte virtus animosa cadit:* Gedanken zur Darstellung des Tragischen in Senecas *Hercules*' in E. Lefèvre (ed.) *Senecas Tragödien.* Darmstadt: 49–209.

Zissos, A. (2009) 'Shades of Virgil: Seneca's *Troades*' *MD* 61: 191–210.

Zwierlein, O. (1966) *Die Rezitationsdramen Senecas.* Meisenheim am Glan.

(1978) 'Die Tragik in den Medea-Dramen' *Literaturwissenschaftliches Jahrbuch* 19: 27–63.

(1983) 'Der Schluss der Tragödie "Atreus" des Accius' *Hermes* 111:121–5.

(1986a) *L. Annaei Senecae Tragoediae.* Oxford.

(1986b) *Kritischer Kommentar zu den Tragödien Senecas.* Stuttgart.

INDEX OF PASSAGES DISCUSSED

Accius
Atreus
  fr. 198–201 Ribbeck *TRF*², 322
Anonymus Latinus
Physiognomia
  11, 201
Aristotle
Poetics
  1542a, 27, 61
pseudo-Aristotle
Physiognomica
  805b5–9, 197
  813a10, 196
  813b35–814a1, 197

Cassius Dio
  44.12, 105–6, 109
Cicero
ad Familiares
  9.14.6, 174
de Divinatione
  1.34, 255
de Legibus
  1.26, 209–10
de Officiis
  1.69–70, 267–8
  1.97–8, 73–6
  1.107–15, 37–8
  1.111, 84
  1.113–14, 40–2, 92
  1.122–4, 71–2
in Verrem
  2.1.32, 105
  2.5.116, 174

Diogenes Laertius
  7.122, 267
  7.173, 199–200

Epictetus
Discourses
  4.6.26, 71
Euripides
Heracles
  340, 155
  631–2, 155–6
  798–800, 155
  1264–5, 155
  1401, 155
  1424, 155–6
Hippolytus
  273, 205
  279, 205
  280, 205–6
  416–18, 206
Melanippe
  fr. 498 Kannicht, 286

Homer
Iliad
  1.1, 125
  1.205, 127
  1.226–8, 126
  1.287–8, 126–7
  1.165–7, 127
  2.212, 242
  2.213, 241
  2.214, 241
  2.216–19, 241–2
Horace
Ars Poetica
  92, 42
  105–6, 42
  119–27, 86–7
  123–4, 68
  312–16, 77–8
Sermones

Index of Passages Discussed

1.4.12, 102–3
1.4.62, 231

Livy
  praef. 1.10, 102–3
  5.18.5, 111
  6.6.9, 173–4

Martial
  Epigrams
    10.4.2, 257

Nepos
  Agesilaus
    1.4, 57

Ovid
  Heroides
    6.151, 36
  Tristia
    4.5.31–2, 104

Plautus
  Amphitruo
    501, 95–6
    889, 315
  Captivi
    923, 59
  Menaechmi
    1124, 94
  Rudens
    1175, 94
Pliny, the Younger
  Panegyricus
    13.3–5, 171–3
Plutarch
  Caesar
    58.5, 160–1
Polemon
  Physiognomy
    B4, 197
    B21, 201

Quintilian
  Institutio Oratoria
    5.11.6, 167
    7.1.14, 57–9
    9.2.64, 255
    11.3.73, 68

Sophocles
  Electra
    1225, 94
Seneca, the Elder
  Suasoriae
    3.7, 29
Seneca, the Younger
  Agamemnon
    128, 202, 239
    237–8, 239
  Consolatio ad Polybium
    8.4, 85
  de Beneficiis
    2.17.2, 72
    6.12.1, 188
    7.6.2, 268
  de Brevitate Vitae
    2.1, 275–6
    2.3, 276
    2.4, 276
    4.3, 277–8
  de Clementia
    1.1.2, 337
    1.1.6, 173
  de Constantia Sapientis
    6.3, 84
    8.2, 282–3
  de Ira
    1.1.3–5, 188–91
    1.1.5, 209
    1.3.4, 225
    1.8.6, 88
    2.9.1, 286–7
    2.9.4, 286–7
    2.10.6, 36
    2.17.1, 70
    2.35.3, 225
    2.35.3–36.2, 188–9
    3.15.4, 331
  de Providentia
    2.9, 52
    2.10, 51–3
    2.10–11, 332–3
    6.6, 281–2
  de Tranquilitate
    14.3, 270
    14.8, 270
    16.1, 110–11
  de Vita Beata

Index of Passages Discussed

Seneca, the Younger (cont.)
    3.3, 50
    Epistles
        1.1, 277
        5.7, 290
        6.7, 280
        9.8–9, 279–80
        9.18–19, 270–2, 290
        14.4–10, 278
        20.1, 276
        20.2, 84
        20.5, 90–1
        26.10, 334
        31.1, 35
        31.9, 96, 281
        35.4, 85
        37.4, 268
        41.8, 50
        48.11, 281
        51.9, 334
        52.12, 200–1, 232–3
        53.11, 281
        62.1, 276
        66.4, 187
        66.45, 85
        70.6–7, 336
        70.19–23, 335
        73.12–14, 282
        75.18, 276
        77.14–15, 335–6
        80.7, 70
        89.1, 231
        92.3, 96
        92.29, 281, 288
        108.13, 268–9
        113.31, 273–4
        114.23–4, 268, 273
        120.8, 110–11
        120.22, 34–8, 53, 87, 93
    Hercules
        39–40, 167
        42, 163
        50, 168
        60–1, 169
        62, 168
        84–5, 160–1, 176
        116, 162, 176
        226, 167
        276–7, 338

        337–9, 178–9
        398, 163
        433, 163
        440–1, 156
        595–6, 169
        603–4, 168
        650–1, 167
        761, 157
        907–8, 157
        924–5, 157
        931–2, 175
        932–3, 175
        935, 175
        936–7, 175
        938–9, 175
        955–7, 174
        965–8, 159–60
        987–9, 177
        1001–2, 177–8
        1017–18, 159
        1101, 32
        1150–4, 170–1
        1202–4, 158
        1239, 164–5
        1245, 338
        1246–8, 153–4
        1279–80, 164
        1282, 164
        1297–8, 338
        1301, 164
        1306–17, 161–3
    Medea
        1–2, 57
        8–9, 35
        22, 57
        25–6, 39
        32–4, 47
        40, 39
        43, 220
        44–5, 39–40, 46
        47–8, 39–40
        49–50, 40
        52–5, 44–5
        55, 39
        123–4, 48–9
        129–30, 44
        132, 32
        134–5, 33
        140–1, 44

Index of Passages Discussed

159–67, 289–92
166, 35
171, 36, 296
197, 43
218–19, 46
246, 43
266, 306
272–3, 43
382–96, 189–91
394, 198
397–8, 45
446, 202
447, 46
447–9, 33–4
451, 43
452–3, 33
459, 43
482, 43
487–8, 57
489, 43
516–17, 35
520, 290
523–4, 35
525, 44
540–1, 290
561–2, 46
566–7, 35, 295–6
669, 299
681, 305
684–5, 305
689, 305
699–700, 305
734, 306
754, 305
760, 305
767, 305
769, 305
910, 35, 41–2, 301
914, 53, 306–7
933–4, 35
935, 295
939, 49
946–7, 32
950–1, 46
976, 53
979, 306
982–6, 58–9
993–4, 55
1012–13, 39, 297

1016, 53
1021–2, 28–33, 55, 294
1024, 59
1025, 47

Oedipus
54, 257
82–6, 244–5
92, 255
100, 255
101, 256
212, 248, 256
216, 246–7
235, 247
233–8, 258–9
297, 254
318, 248
331, 245–6
341, 243
343, 244
348–50, 243–4
352, 245–6
372, 254
509–10, 250
640–1, 247, 256–7
702, 249
811, 245–6
819, 246
820–1, 246, 253–4
840, 250
841–2, 250
915, 340
921–4, 250–1
934, 341
949–51, 251–2
960, 253
961, 254
965, 254
977, 251–2
978, 244
1003, 20, 252–3, 342
1009–10, 248
1034, 344
1046, 341
1051, 249

Phaedra
92, 31–2
101, 204
102–3, 203
113–4, 100–1

377

Index of Passages Discussed

Seneca, the Younger (cont.)
  122, 207
  147, 209
  151, 206
  153, 206, 209
  157–8, 206
  159, 206
  218, 203
  280, 203
  282, 204, 209
  362, 204
  362–73, 183–4, 191–3, 201
  371–2, 211
  377–8, 204
  381–2, 214
  438–9, 284–5
  451–3, 284
  453, 221
  481, 284
  490, 285
  492, 285
  501, 285
  502–3, 226
  522–5, 207–8
  578–9, 286
  597, 206
  641–3, 203
  646–7, 222
  654–60, 222–4
  690–3, 208
  721, 216
  731–2, 213
  734, 214, 216–17
  743–4, 224
  761, 224
  773, 224
  778–80, 209
  823, 225, 227
  825, 213
  826–8, 213–14
  860, 210
  886–7, 209, 216–17
  891–2, 217–18
  896, 303
  898–901, 218–19, 303–4
  915–22, 220–2
  918, 209
  933, 209
  1107, 233
  1110, 225
  1168–9, 228
  1170–3, 225
  1173, 228
  1194, 211
  1249, 230–1, 234–5
  1250, 234
  1256–8, 231
  1257, 230
  1260, 231–3
  1264, 230
  1265, 225, 230
  1267, 234
  1270, 204
Thyestes
  56–7, 323
  59, 95–6
  176, 310–11
  176–80, 67–71
  195–6, 324
  212, 90
  218, 288
  237, 91
  240, 316
  242–3, 100–1
  252–3, 312–15
  253–4, 310–11, 321–3
  255, 323
  256, 312–15
  259, 324
  267–8, 323
  271, 75–6
  274, 324
  303, 91
  327, 316
  330–2, 202
  390, 269
  401, 93
  403, 93
  420, 90
  422, 90
  429–30, 90
  466–7, 92
  476–82, 89
  504–5, 67, 79
  505–7, 63
  507, 67
  508–11, 78–80, 82
  512–14, 79

Index of Passages Discussed

517, 63
521–6, 63–4
527–8, 80, 82
540, 90
545, 81, 83
696–7, 84
703–4, 84–7
713, 83
782–3, 92
885, 83, 96, 288
889–90, 312–15
890–1, 311
895, 312–15
899–900, 312–15
901–2, 64
903, 321
903–7, 64–5
911, 83
911–12, 319
913, 315
923–4, 91
937, 91
942–3, 65–6
950, 90
970, 65–6
971–2, 319–20
973, 312–15
976–8, 81, 94–5
979, 311
980, 312–15
982–3, 81
985–6, 90
997–8, 94–5
998, 82
1001, 92
1004–5, 94–5
1005–6, 61–3, 66, 83, 95, 97
1021–3, 82
1023, 94–5
1041–7, 330–1
1050–1, 92–3, 136
1050–3, 324–5
1067–8, 92
1096, 80
1096–9, 316–18
1109–10, 317

Troades

5–6, 141
215–28, 119–21
217, 121
232, 121
236–7, 119
238–43, 119–21, 136
249, 32
250–3, 125–6
263–4, 124–5
302, 126
303, 126–7
305, 127
308–10, 127
309, 121
310–13, 122
325–6, 122–3
360, 32
369, 128
415, 135–6
464–8, 129–31, 134–5, 139, 142
470–4, , 131–2, 138
491, 135–6
501–2, 135
504–5, 134
528, 128
551, 128, 132
554, 128
559, 129
597, 129
603, 135–6
605, 129
646–7, 129
647–8, 130–1
681, 135
689, 135
690–1, 136
715–17, 139
718–20, 139
730, 140
761, 138
784–5, 141–2
788–9, 134
805–6, 121–2, 136
1087, 140
1098–100, 141
1101, 339
1113, 142
1116–7, 136
1117, 136–7, 142
1125, 140–1
1129, 140

379

Index of Passages Discussed

pseudo-Seneca
  Hercules Oetaeus
    705, 202
Suetonius
  Augustus
    31.5, 109–10
  Nero
    21.3, 68

Tacitus
  Annals
    15.60–4, 147–8
    15.62.1–2, 145–7
    15.63.2–3, 151
    16.19, 150
    16.34–5, 149–50
    16.34.2, 151
Terence
  Adelphoe
    415, 110
  Hecyra
    818–19, 59

Vergil
  Aeneid
    2.540–3, 123
    2.547–9, 123–4
    3.489–90, 134–5
    4.2, 204
    4.66–7, 204
    12.435–40, 115–17, 125

GENERAL INDEX

Accius, 62, 75, 113–14, 322
acting
  and agency, 308–9
  and deception, 37, 53–4, 81–2, 211–16
  and family models, 111–14, 128, 139,
    142–3, *See also* 'exemplarity'
  and selfhood, 18, 25–6, 38, 40–1,
    69–70, 73–5
  and the body, 181, 193–4, 212–13, 260–1
Adamantius, 195, 201
adultery, 79, 95, 207, 213, 307, 310, 316
Aeneas, 115–17, 133–5
Agamemnon
  in *Thyestes*, 95, 316–17
  in *Troades*, 117–28
agency. *See also* 'acting'
  and Greimas' *actant*, 303–4
  and implied humanness, 10–17, 233–4,
    263–5, 290–331, 337–45
  and revenge, 292–329
  and suicide, 329–45
Agrippina, 344–5
Amphitryon, 153–71, 176–7
Andromache, 118, 121, 128–42
anger
  in *de Ira*, 188–91, 225
  of Atreus, 68–9, 88
  of Hippolytus, 286–7
  of Medea, 189–91
Apollo, 340–1
Aristotle, 23
  on tragic recognition scenes, 27, 61
Arria, wife of Thrasea Paetus
  and exemplarity, 151
Ascanius, 115–16, 133–5
Astyages
  in *de Ira*, 331
Astyanax
  and death, 133–8
  and suicide, 338–40

  as actor, 138–44
  as copy of Hector, 128–44
Atreus
  and *constantia*, 83–8
  and deception, 78–83
  and *decorum*, 70–8, 84, 87–8
  and fullness/satisfaction, 312–15
  and masculinity, 309–12, 314–15
  and metatheatre, 66–9, 320–1
  and paternity, 95–6, 316–17, 319–20
  and prior literary models, 62–3, 75–6,
    321–4
  and recognition, 60–3, 94–7
  and self-coherence, 78–83
  and the *maius* motif, 321–5
  and the Stoic *sapiens*, 83–8, 287–9
  as actor, 66–70
  as avenger, 307–29
  as dramaturg/playwright, 63–6, 320–1
  linguistic prowess of, 78–82, 319
Attalus
  teacher of Seneca, 268–9
audience
  and actors, 308–9
  and bodily signals, 181–2, 192–3,
    212–16, 219, 221, 245–7
  and dramatic irony, 80–1
  and dramaturgy, 210
  and *Hercules*, 165–9
  and metapoetics, 29–31
  and metatheatre, 62–6, 140–1
  and *Oedipus*, 20–1, 245–7, 249–54,
    258–60, 342–3
  and *Phaedra*, 192–5, 210, 213–16
  and sympathetic engagement, 2–3, 14,
    193, 251, 304, 328
  and *Thyestes*, 62–70, 80–1
  and *Troades*, 139–44
  authorising function of, 55–6
  external, 33, 139–41, 252–3

381

General Index

audience (cont.)
  internal, 33, 139–41, 252–3
  reception of theatrical performance, 18–19
Augustus, 109–10, 173, 277–8
autarkeia, 265
  and Atreus, 96–7, 287–9
  and Hippolytus, 284–7
  and Medea, 60, 289–99
  and suicide, 331–7
  and the Senecan *sapiens*, 265–83
autonomy. *See also* 'agency', '*autarkeia*'
  and fictional beings, 1–2, 263–5, 299–302, 304–9, 340–3
  and identity formation, 263, 292–9, 309–20
  and individual supremacy, 265–74
  and literary belatedness, 321–4
  and self-harm, 337–45
  and self-mastery, 265–74, 284–7
  and Seneca's views on suicide, 329–37
  and Senecan isolationism, 274–92
  and stage performance, 308–9
  and the body, 227–8, 297, 311, 341–2
  and the Senecan *sapiens*, 265–83
  and tyranny, 265–74, 287–8, 318–20
avenger, the
  as instrument, 307–8, 322–3, 328–9
  complicity with the audience, 302–3
  similarity to actor, 308–9
  similarity to director/author, 300, 304–7, 320–1

Barthes, Roland, 12, 222
behaviour
  and acting, 70
  and beauty, 224–6
  and deception, 212
  and *decorum*, 35–42, 49–51, 70–8
  and Homer's Thersites, 241–2
  and intertextuality, 28–31, 127–8, 147–50
  and physiognomy, 195–201
  and Senecan *constantia*, 83–8
  continuity of, 23–4, 31–5, 61–2, 78–83, 163–5
  exemplary patterns of, 102–7, 122–5, 144–6
  inconsistency of, 89–93
body, the. *See also* 'acting', 'physiognomy'
  and 'character portraits', 235–42
  and anger, 188–90
  and interiority, 188–9, 191–5, 201–10
  and Stoic materialism, 186–90, 225–6, 228–9
  and Stoic virtue, 224–7
  and Vergil's Dido, 204–5
  as index of identity, 181–262
  of Astyanax, 129–31, 136–7
  of Hippolytus, 224–35
  of Oedipus, 243–9, 254–60
  of Phaedra, 183–4, 191–5, 202–17
  of Thyestes, 64–5, 92–3, 311–12, 324–5, 330–1
  physiognomic and pathagnomic interpretations of, 195–202
  similarity to a text, 190, 201, 230–3, 245–7, 254–60
Brutus
  Lucius Junius, 105–8, 109, 113–14
  Marcus Junius, 105–8, 109, 113–14
Brutus, the
  of Accius, 113–14

caesar
  as title, 132
Caesar, Julius, 105, 109, 113, 332–3
  in Lucan, 144
  in Plutarch, 160
Calchas, 32, 128
Caligula, 270, 288, 292, 336
Canus, Julius, 270, 272, 292, 336
Cato the Younger, 51–3, 55–6, 99–100, 110–11, 147–51, 332–3, 336
character, fictional
  and contingency, 1, 114, 263, 297–8, 300–2, 328, 343
  and formalism, 4, 11
  and metatheatre, 28–31, 35–6, 42, 62–9, 128, 138–44, 163, 169–71, 211–15, 221–3, 252–4, 257–60, 304–7, 320–2, 341–3
  and structuralism/poststructuralism, 9–14
  as textual construct, 27–31, 33–6, 42, 45, 62–9, 75–6, 86–7, 114–17, 124–8, 138–44, 163, 165–71, 219–23, 229–33, 243–7, 252–60, 295–6, 297–8, 304–7, 320–8, 344–5
  human qualities of, 3, 16–17, 27–8, 31–56, 61–2, 69–88, 115–16, 118–38,

General Index

153–65, 191–5, 202–19, 221–9, 233–7, 240–2, 247–52, 263–5, 283–320, 324–31, 337–45
humanist theories of, 4, 13, 15
in the novel, 17, 235–40
in the twentieth century, 9–15
theoretical approaches to, 9–16
chorus
  in Euripides' *Heracles*, 155
  in Euripides' *Hippolytus*, 205–6
  in *Phaedra*, 213–15, 224–5, 227
  in Senecan tragedy, 7
  in *Thyestes*, 93, 269
Chrysippus, 187
Cicero
  and *autarkeia*, 267–8
  and exemplarity, 104–5
  and *persona* theory, 37–8, 40–1, 49–50, 71–7, 83–4
  and self-*aemulatio*, 173–4
  on physical appearance, 209–10
  on poetry and divination, 255
Cixous, Hélène, 10
Cleanthes, 187, 199–200
Clytemnestra
  in Seneca's *Agamemnon*, 239–40
comoedia palliata, 59, 94–6, 314–15
consciousness, 1–2, 22, 181, 192, 205, 209, 237, 302
constantia, 34–6, 40–3, 51–6, 82, 84–8, 91
costumes, 64, 66, 169–71, 211–12, 215, 219–20, 321
cover image
  significance of, 347–8
Creon
  in *Medea*, 43–4, 298–9
  in *Oedipus*, 248–9, 258–60

deception. *See also* 'acting'
  and physiognomy, 201–2
  in *Medea*, 53–4
  in *Phaedra*, 207–19
  in *Thyestes*, 78–82
Decii Mures, 103–5
decorum
  and Atreus, 70–2, 75–8, 84, 87–8
  and Cato the Younger, 52–3
  and Hippolytus, 284–5
  and Medea, 40–2

and Stoic ethics, 49–51, 71–2
  in Cicero, 40–1, 72–5
  in Horace, 77, 86–7
deification
  and Atreus, 83, 96–7, 288–9
  and the *sapiens*, 96–7, 288–9
Demetrius Poliorcetes, 270–2, 292
description
  and 'character portraits', 235–42
  and 'running commentaries', 184
  and enactment, 219
  in *Hercules*, 166–7
  in *Phaedra*, 183–4
  in Senecan tragedy, 183–6, 189–91
Dido, 204–5
dismemberment, 227–8, 230–1
dramaturgy
  in *Hercules*, 165–6
  in *Phaedra*, 210
dubius
  motif in *Oedipus*, 244–5, 247–9

effeminacy, 199–200
Eliot, T. S., 2, 8
embodiment, 18–19, 109–14, 128–31, 181–2, 223–4, 261
emotions. *See also* 'face'
  and aesthetic appropriateness, 42, 86–7
  and Hercules, 153–9, 161–5
  and Oedipus, 250–1
  and pathognomy, 197–8
  and performance, 212
  and Stoic materialism, 187–92, 200–2
  and the body, 181, 183–4, 187–92
  and the theatrical mask, 194
  and Thyestes, 65
  and typology, 240
Epictetus, 71–2
eulogy
  and the Roman funeral, 112–13
  in *Troades*, 120–1
Euripides
  Heracles, 154–6
  Hippolytus, 184, 205–6, 217
  Hippolytus Kalyptomenos, 216–17
  Medea, 28–30, 35, 59, 298
  Melanippe, 285–6
exemplarity

383

General Index

exemplarity (cont.)
  and biology, 100–2, 104–5, 107–8, 111, 112–14, 116–17, 123–8, 134–5, 138, 154–6, 159
  and family models, 99–101, 103–7, 111–13, 115–39, 141–4, 146–7, 150–1, 159–60
  and metapoetics, 114–17
  and mimesis, 99–103, 107–14, 131, 137, 142–4, 159
  and statuary/sculptures, 108–11
  and the Roman funeral, 112–13, 120–1
  and theatrical performance, 128, 138–44
  self-reflexive forms of, 160–5, 171–9
extispicy
  in *Oedipus*, 243–6, 254–7

fabula praetexta, 113–14
face, the. *See also* 'mask'
  and anger, 188–90
  and disposition, 194, 197–8, 200, 209–10, 220
  and physiognomy, 197–8, 238
  and Stoic materialism, 186–90, 225–6
  and Stoic pathognomy, 197–8
  as index of emotion, 202, 239–40
  of Astyanax, 129–31, 134–5
  of Clytemnestra, 239–40
  of Euripides' Phaedra, 205–6
  of Heathcliff, 238
  of Hippolytus, 219–26, 228
  of Oedipus, 20–1, 243–4, 246–7, 249–54, 341–3
  of Phaedra, 183–4, 192–3, 214–17
  of the Minotaur, 208
  of Thyestes, 64–5
family, the. *See also* 'exemplarity', 'recognition scenes'
  and Atreus, 309–12
  and Hippolytus, 285–6
  and paternity, 95–6, 309–12
  and reunion, 56–60, 94–6, 319
  as source of emulation, 99–144, 150–1, 159–60
  in Euripides' *Heracles*, 154–6
  in *Hercules*, 153–60, 178–9
father–son relationships, 104–5, 111, 115–16, 118–38, 141–2, 153–60, 177–8, 222–3, 339–40

formalism
  and theories of fictional character, 11–12
freedom
  in Senecan Stoicism, 264–83
  overlap between political and personal, 267–74, 276–8, 332–3
  positive ('freedom to') versus negative ('freedom from'), 274, 285
  revenge as source of, 293, 307–9, 313–14, 318, 326
  suicide as source of, 329–37
friendship
  in Senecan Stoicism, 278–80

genealogy
  and Astyanax's relationship to Hector, 128–33
  and Atreus' revenge, 321–3
  and exemplarity, 103–11, 128–33, 150–1
  and poetic imitation, 114–17, 125–8, 321–2
gesture, 18–19, 63–4, 66, 138–9, 142, 181, 184, 188, 190, 193, 201, 209, 211–12, 215–17, 232, 261
Greimas, Algirdas, 11, 303–4

habit
  and dispositional traits, 197–8
  and identity, 23
  and literary repetition, 30–4
  and *soleo*, 31–3
Hamlet, 300–2
Harpagus
  in *de Ira*, 331
Heathcliff, 236–8
Hector
  as role model for Astyanax, 128–39, 141–4, 339–40
  in the *Aeneid*, 115–16
  ransom of, 122–3
Hercules
  and family relationships, 153–60
  and Stoicism, 161–2
  and suicide, 337–8
  as fictional character, 163, 165–71
  in *Troades*, 139–40
  madness of, 170–1, 174–6
  self-reflexive exemplarity of, 160–5
  similarity to Lycus, 176–9
Hippolytus

384

General Index

and anger, 225–6, 285–7
and *autarkeia*, 284–7
and autonomy, 227–8, 284–7
and Stoic ethics, 225–7, 284–7
and women, 285–6
as fictional construct, 220–3, 229–33
beauty of, 222–6, 228–9
body of, 224–35
face of, 219–24
implied human qualities of, 221–4, 233–5
in Euripides, 216–17
sword of, 217–19
violence against Phaedra, 213
Homer, 116, 126–8, 241–2
Horace, 42, 68, 77–8, 86–7, 102, 231

identity
and acts of recognition, 24–35, 47–8, 54–63, 66, 69, 83, 93–7
and behavioural imitation, 99–152, 159–60
and corporeality, 129–31, 181–254, 260–2
and fragmented subjectivity, 9–10
and freedom/self-determination, 227–8, 263–346
and habitual conduct, 23, 31–4, 42–8, 162–5
and metapoetics, 27–8, 33–6, 45, 125–8, 131, 133–5, 165–9, 220–1, 230–3, 238, 255–60, 263–4, 295–6, 300–1, 304–7, 320–4, 326–9, 341–3
and metatheatre, 28–31, 62–9, 138–44, 163, 169–71, 220–3, 252–4
and self-knowledge, 91–3
and Stoic *constantia*, 34–43, 48–54, 82, 84–8, 165
and Stoic *decorum*, 40–2, 71–8
and Stoic *persona* theory, 37–8, 49–51, 70–5
and theatrical performance, 17–19, 25–31, 37, 69–70, 75, 111–14, 128, 138–43, 193–4, 211–13, 223–4, 308–9
as selfsameness, 23
in context of family relationships, 56–60, 94–7, 99–160, 293–5, 309–12, 316–18
Iliad, the
and the *Aeneid*, 116, 123–4
and Thersites, 241–2

and *Troades*, 125–8
imago / imagines, 110–13, 144–8
individuality
and 'character portraits', 237
and twentieth-century literary theory, 9–11
and corporeal integrity, 278
and interiority, 194–5, 237, 300–1
and self-conferred morality, 49–50, 73–5
of Seneca's characters, 8
versus normativity, 6, 37–8, 55, 71–2, 240
versus the collective, 95, 99–180
interiority
as motif in *Phaedra*, 202–10
psychological, 181–2, 187–9, 191–5, 203–10, 240, 251, 302–3
intertextuality. *See also* 'metatheatre'
and exemplarity, 114–17, 126–8, 133–5, 148–50
and Tacitean death scenes, 148–50
in *Medea*, 28–31, 36, 45
in Senecan scholarship, 4
in *Thyestes*, 75–6, 320–8
isolation
and Atreus, 94–7, 317–18
and Hercules, 156–65
and Hippolytus, 284–7
and Medea, 56–60
and self-*aemulatio*, 171–9
and the Senecan *sapiens*, 267, 274–83

Jane Eyre, 3
Jason, 28–30, 32–4, 43–8, 54–60, 290, 293–5, 298–9
Jocasta, 243–5, 248
suicide of, 340–1, 343–5
Juno, 165–9, 175–6, 338
Jupiter
and the *sapiens*, 282–3
in *Hercules*, 153–60
in Plautus' *Amphitruo*, 95–6, 314–15

Knights, Lionel, 15

Lavater, Johann Caspar, 235–7
legitimacy. *See also* 'family'
and acts of recognition, 56–60, 95–6
of Atreus' sons, 95–6, 316–17

385

General Index

literary portraiture, 235–42
Livy, 102–3, 111, 173
Lucilius
  in Seneca's *Epistles*, 34–6, 84, 87–8
Lycus, 156–9, 176–9

maius
  motif in *Thyestes*, 321–5
Manto, 243, 245, 248, 254
masculinity
  in *Thyestes*, 309–12, 315–16
mask, the
  and cover image, 347–8
  and *imagines*, 110–12, 146
  and metatheatre, 20–1, 68, 220–3, 252–4
  and physiognomy, 221–2
  similarity to face, 181, 194, 219–24, 347–8
Medea
  and *autarkeia*, 60, 289–99
  and *decorum*, 40–2
  and isolation, 56–60
  and metatheatre, 28–31, 36, 42, 52–4, 55–6, 304–7
  and recognition, 28–35, 47–8, 54–60
  and revenge, 291–9
  and self-coherence, 31–56
  and self-division, 48–9
  and self-naming, 35–7
  and Stoic 'indifferents', 290
  and the Stoic *sapiens*, 37–42, 48–54, 289–92
  as author/playwright, 304–7
messenger speeches, 185, 259–60
metatheatre
  in *Hercules*, 163, 169–71
  in *Medea*, 28–31, 36, 42, 52–4, 55–6, 304–7
  in *Oedipus*, 21, 252–4, 259–60, 342–3
  in *Phaedra*, 213, 219–24, 234–5
  in *Thyestes*, 62–9, 320–1
  in *Troades*, 138–44
Minotaur, the, 207–8

names
  significance of in fiction, 12
  significance of in Roman exemplarity, 103–6, 151
  significance of in Senecan prose, 51–2

significance of in Senecan tragedy, 35–7, 68–9, 129, 153–4, 163, 244, 246–7, 250, 252–3, 295–6
Nero, 68, 152, 173, 337
nota/notus
  and Hippolytus, 231–3
  motif in *Oedipus*, 245–7, 250, 253–4
novel, the, 17–18, 235–40
Nurse, the
  as descriptive narrator, 183–5, 189–93
  in *Agamemnon*, 239
  in *Medea*, 189–91
  in *Phaedra*, 183–4, 191–3, 213–14, 216, 284–5

Oedipus
  and self-harm, 340–3
  and the *dubius* motif, 244–5, 247–9
  face of, 20–1, 243–4, 246–7, 249–54, 341–3
  resemblance to a text, 254–60
Ovid, 28–30, 76, 104, 323, 330

paternity
  and exemplarity, 104
  and Oedipus, 245
  in recognition scenes, 232
  in *Thyestes*, 95–6, 309–12, 316–17, 319–20
Paulina, wife of Seneca
  and exemplarity, 151
person schema, 16–17
persona
  in Stoic ethics, 6, 34–5, 37–42, 50–2, 71–8, 84–6
Petronius 'Arbiter', 149–51
Phaedra
  and deception, 208–19
  and Euripides' Phaedra, 205–6
  and interiority, 191–5, 203–9
  and veiling, 215–17
  and Vergil's Dido, 204–5
  experience of love, 203–6, 214–15, 222
  face of, 183–4, 192–3, 213–17
Philomela, 75–6, 310, 323–4
physiognomy
  and Cleanthes, 199–200
  and Homer's Thersites, 241–2
  and Polemon, 195–7, 199
  and revelation, 201–2

General Index

and Stoic materialism, 195–202
and the Latin *Physiognomia*, 201
and the pseudo-Aristotelian
    Physiognomica, 196–7
in Seneca, 200–2, 239–40
in the eighteenth/nineteenth-century
    novel, 235–40
versus pathognomy, 196–8
Pliny the Younger, 171–3
Priam, 121–4, 139–40
Procne, 75–6, 310, 323–4
Propp, Vladimir, 11–12
psychologising
    in literary theories of character, 13
psychology
    and interiority, 181–2, 189, 191–5,
        204–5, 208–10, 240, 251
    and material realities, 186–9, 261
    and the body, 187–9
    in the eighteenth/nineteenth-century
        novel, 235–7
    of characters in the novel, 12
    of Seneca's characters, 8, 181–2, 191–5,
        204–5, 208–10, 234, 247–8, 251
Pyrrhus
    and *soleo*, 32
    citing the *Iliad*, 126–7
    in the *Aeneid*, 123–4
    in *Troades*, 118–28, 143–4
Pythia, the, 256–9

recognition scenes. *See also* 'identity'
    and family ties, 26–7, 56–60, 94–6,
        231–2
    and metatheatre, 28–31, 62–9
    and reunion, 56–60, 94–7
    and revelation, 27, 34–5, 47–8, 54–6,
        61, 233
    Aristotle's definition of, 27, 61
repetition
    and Atreus, 322
    and exemplarity, 102–4
    and structure of *Troades*, 117–18
    and the dynamics of revenge, 325–6
    as motif in *Medea*, 32–4, 42–8
    of events in *Hercules*, 168–9
revenge
    and Atreus, 307–29
    and focalisation, 302–3

and intertextuality, 325–6
and Medea, 291–9
and oppression/powerlessness, 307,
    309–20
and recompense/equilibrium, 292–4,
    307–8, 324–5
and Theseus, 303–4
and undoing the past, 58, 296, 316–17
as 'satisfaction', 312–14
as source of autonomy, 292–329
Rezitationsdrama, 166, 185, 190

sapiens, the
    and contingency, 274–83
    and divinity, 280–3
    and immovability, 84–6
    and invulnerability, 282–3
    and self-sufficiency, 264–83
    as monarch, 267–9
    isolation of, 267, 274–83
    versus the tyrant, 269–74
satis
    motif in *Thyestes*, 312–15
Schlegel, August Wilhelm von, 7
Scipio Aemilianus, 105
Scipio Africanus, 105
self-*aemulatio*, 160–5, 171–9
Seneca
    and physiognomy, 197–8, 200–2
    and reflexive language, 276–8
    and slaves/slavery, 334–6
    and writing for stage performance, 19–20
    as *exemplum*, 144–9
    death scene in Tacitus, 145–7
    on public life, 275–8
Shakespearean scholarship, 15, 49
Socrates
    death of, 147–51
Sophocles, 26, 47, 76, 94, 232, 251,
    259, 340
sovereignty, individual
    and revenge, 293, 326
    and self-harm, 340–2
    and suicide in Seneca, 332–4, 337
    in Senecan tragedy, 264–5, 296–7, 318,
        320, 323, 340–2
    of the Senecan *sapiens*, 264–5, 272,
        274–7, 279–80
    of the tyrant / ruler, 272, 337

General Index

spectatorship, 55–6, 63–6, 139–42
Sphinx, the
  in *Oedipus*, 255–6, 340
statues, 108–11, 132
Stilbo, 270–2, 279, 285, 290, 292
Stoicism
  and 'indifferents', 266, 272, 278–9, 289–90, 332, 334
  and Atreus, 83–8, 288–9
  and *constantia*, 34–5, 48–50, 83–6
  and *decorum*, 40–2, 70–8, 83–4, 284
  and emotions / passions, 48–9, 88, 187–92, 197–8
  and freedom, 265–92, 329–37, See also 'autarkeia', 'autonomy'
  and friendship, 278–80
  and Hercules, 162
  and Hippolytus, 224–9, 284–7
  and isolation, 266–92
  and kingship, 267–9
  and materialism, 186–90, 194, 200, 210–12, 260–1
  and Medea, 48–54, 289–92
  and *persona* theory, 6, 37–8, 40–2, 52–3
  and physiognomy, 195–202
  and scholarship on Senecan tragedy, 4–5, 49, 93, 162
  and self-fashioning, 36
  and Seneca's suicide, 147–8
  and Senecan ideas of suicide, 332–7, 341
  and *sympatheia*, 248
  and the Cynics, 267
  and the Senecan retreat from public life, 275–8
  and theatrical analogies, 37, 41–2, 50–1, 73–5
  and Thyestes, 93, 269
  and *virtus*, 162, 225, 280–1, 289–90
structuralism
  and theories of fictional character, 9–14, 303–4
suicide. See also 'freedom'
  affinities with revenge, 329–30, 337–8
  and Astyanax, 339–40
  and exemplarity, 145–52
  and Hercules, 337–8
  and Jocasta, 343–5
  and Thyestes, 330–1

  in *de Ira*, 331
  in the *Epistles*, 334–6
  of Seneca, 145–9

Tacitus
  death scenes in the *Annals*, 145–52
Tereus, 75–6, 310, 323–4
Thersites
  and 'character portraits', 241–2
Theseus
  as physiognomic interpreter, 215–21
  in Euripides' *Heracles*, 155–6
  in Euripides' *Hippolytus*, 205
  in *Hercules*, 157
  in *Phaedra*, 209–10, 215–23, 229–35, 303–4
  reassembles Hippolytus, 229–35
Thrasea Paetus
  suicide of, 149–52
Thyestes
  and metatheatre, 62–6
  and pregnancy, 310–12
  and suicide, 330–1
  as actor, 63–6
  changeability of, 89–93
Tiresias
  in *Oedipus*, 243–5, 254, 257–9
Tomashevsky, Boris, 11
Trajan, 171–3
tyrants/tyranny, 70–2, 147–8, 175–8, 265–74, 287–8, 309–10, 317–20, 332, 335–7

Ulysses
  in *Troades*, 117–18, 132, 139–41

veil
  of Phaedra, 209, 215–17
Vergil, 115–17, 123–4, 133–5, 204–5
virtus, 161–3, 166, 175–9, 225, 280–1, 283, 289–90, 332, 336
voice, the
  in physiognomy, 201
  of Medea, 305–6

Wuthering Heights, 236–9

Zeno, 187, 199

388